Economics for the Common Good

ECONOMICS FOR
THE COMMON GOOD

JEAN TIROLE

TRANSLATED BY STEVEN RENDALL

PRINCETON UNIVERSITY PRESS
PRINCETON AND OXFORD

Published by Princeton University Press,
41 William Street, Princeton, New Jersey 08540

In the United Kingdom: Princeton University Press,
6 Oxford Street, Woodstock, Oxfordshire OX20 1TR

Originally published in 2016 under the title *Économie du bien commun* © Presses Universitaires de France

press.princeton.edu

Jacket design by Chris Ferrante

ISBN 978-0-691-17516-4

Library of Congress Control Number: 2017945101

British Library Cataloging-in-Publication Data is available

This book has been composed in Adobe Garamond Pro
by T&T Productions Ltd, London

Printed on acid-free paper ∞

Printed in the United States of America

10 9 8 7 6 5 4 3 2 1

CONTENTS

ACKNOWLEDGMENTS

I am very grateful to the entire Princeton University Press team for its superb work during the process leading to the publication of this book. Bilingual Sarah Caro, its publisher for Social Sciences for Europe, supervised the translation process with talent, good humor, and patience. Peter Dougherty, its director, has been enthusiastic about the book since day 1 and has brought precious advice; I was delighted to work with him once again. The translation team was composed of Steven Rendall, who had the hard task of translating a long book in a short time, and of Professor Diane Coyle and Tim Phillips, who did a great job at making sure that the economics was sound and adapted to an international audience. The reader will, I think, take notice of the resulting high quality of the translation. Finally, let me thank Jon Wainwright from T&T Productions Ltd and Julie Shawvan for their careful work typesetting and indexing the book.

The French version had benefited from helpful comments from Philippe Aghion, Roland Bénabou, Olivier Blanchard, Christophe Bisière, Paul Champsaur, Frédéric Cherbonnier, Mathias Dewatripont, Augustin Landier, Alain Quinet, Patrick Rey, Paul Seabright, Nathalie Tirole, Philippe Trainar, and Étienne Wasmer, who of course cannot be held responsible for any errors and omissions.

Like any book, *Economics for the Common Good* heavily borrows from the author's intellectual environment, primarily Toulouse School of Economics (TSE) and the Institute for Advanced Study in Toulouse (IAST). This exciting environment is a tribute to its founder Jean-Jacques Laffont, the epitome of the economist serving the common good. I also have much benefited from MIT's extraordinary economics department, from which I graduated, where I taught and which I still regularly visit; and from insights from many colleagues in various great research environments. The intellectual influence of my coauthors is also omnipresent in the book. I have been very fortunate to interact with and benefit from the talent and generosity of such wonderful teachers, colleagues, and students.

Finally, I thank all those who have encouraged me to write this book. While I have long taken part in policymaking, conversing with private and public decision-makers, as yet I had never engaged with the wider public. After receiving the Nobel Prize I was regularly asked by people I met in the street or as I gave talks to explain to a broader audience the nature of economic research and what it contributes to our well-being. They inquired about whether economists are useful, whether economics is a science, whether the key challenges we face can be solved. They made me aware of my responsibility to get out of my laboratory, describe my daily activity, and explain the logic and insights of economics—not to act as a commentator on each and every topic, but simply to share with the public my passion for the discipline and to explain how scientific knowledge can guide economic policies and help us understand the world we (will) live in.

INTRODUCTION
Whatever Happened to the Common Good?

Since the resounding failure of the planned economies – the fall of the Berlin Wall and China's economic transformation – the market economy has become the dominant, not to say exclusive, model for our societies. Even in the "free world," the market and its new economic actors have become more influential, at the expense of political power. Privatizations, globalization, a greater emphasis on competition, and the systematic use of auctions to award public contracts have all restricted the power of elected officials. What remains of public decision making has increasingly come to rely on independent regulatory bodies, central banks, and the legal system, none of which is subject to direct political control.

Even so, the market economy has achieved only a partial victory, because it has won neither hearts nor minds. For many, the pursuit of the common good, the guiding principle behind significant public intervention, has been sacrificed on the altar of this new economic order. Around the world, the supremacy of the market is regarded with widespread distrust, sometimes accepted only with an outrage laced with fatalism. A fragmented opposition laments the triumph of economics over human values, a world with neither pity nor compassion and prey to private interests. These critics warn us of the disintegration of the social contract and the loss of human dignity, the decline of politics and public service, and the environmental unsustainability of the present economic model. A popular slogan that strikes a chord internationally reminds us that "the world is not for sale." These issues resonate with particular force in our current circumstances, which are marked by the financial crisis, increased unemployment and inequality, the ineptitude of our leaders in coping with climate change, the undermining of the European project, geopolitical instability and the migrant crisis resulting from it, and the rise of populism around the world.

Have we lost sight of the common good? If so, how might economics help us get back on track in pursuing it?

Defining the common good – our collective aspiration for society – requires, to some extent, a value judgment. The judgment each of us makes might reflect our individual preferences, the information available to us, and our position in society. Even if we were to agree on the basic desirability of certain objectives, we might still differ over the relative importance of equity, purchasing power, the environment, or work versus private life – not to mention more personal dimensions such as moral values, religion, or spirituality, where people's opinions differ profoundly.

It is possible, however, to eliminate some of the arbitrariness inherent in defining the common good. The following thought experiment is a good way to approach the question. Suppose you have not yet been born, and therefore do not know what place you will have in society, what your genes or who your family will be, or even what social, ethnic, religious, or national environment you will be born into. Now ask yourself, "In what society would I like to live, knowing that I might be either a man or a woman, endowed with good or bad health, from a rich or a poor family, well- or ill-educated, atheistic or religious, a person who could grow up in a big city or the middle of the countryside, or one who could seek fulfillment in work or adopt an alternative lifestyle?" This kind of questioning requires us to abstract ourselves from our attributes and our position in society, to place ourselves "behind the veil of ignorance." It emerged from an intellectual tradition that began in seventeenth-century England with Thomas Hobbes and John Locke, was pursued in continental Europe in the eighteenth century by Immanuel Kant and Jean-Jacques Rousseau (who proposed the idea of a social contract), and was more recently revived in the United States by philosopher John Rawls, in his *Theory of Justice* (1971), and by economist John Harsanyi, who explored how we might compare the well-being of different individuals (1955).[1]

To narrow your choices (and to rule out fanciful answers) I will reformulate the question: "In what social system would you like to live?" The key question here is not what type of ideal society you would like to live in – for example, one in which citizens, workers, business leaders, political officials, and nations spontaneously put the common interest ahead of their personal interests. Even though human beings are not constantly seeking their own material interest, they often give precedence to their self-interest over the common good, and the failure to consider personal incentives and entirely foreseeable behaviors has led in the past to totalitarian and impoverishing forms of social organization (a failure exemplified by the Soviet myth of the "new man"[2]).

This book therefore takes as its point of departure the following principle: whether they are politicians, CEOs, or employees, whether they are out of work, independent contractors, high officials, farmers, or researchers – whatever their place in society – people react to the incentives facing them. These material or social incentives, combined with their personal preferences, define their behavior; and this behavior may or may not be in the general interest. The quest for the common good therefore involves constructing institutions to reconcile, as far as possible, the interests of the individual with the general interest. From this perspective, the market economy is not an end in itself. At most, it is an instrument – and an imperfect one at that – when we consider how to align the common interest and the private interests of individuals, social groups, and nations.

Although it is difficult to put ourselves behind the veil of ignorance, insofar as we are conditioned by the place we already occupy in society, this thought experiment will help lead us toward potential grounds for agreement. Perhaps I create pollution or consume too much water, not because I take pleasure in doing so, but because it serves my economic interest. I can produce more vegetables, or I can cut costs by installing less insulation, or I can save money by buying a car with a dirtier engine. Other people suffer from my actions, and they disapprove of them. But, if we think about the organization of society, we can agree on whether my behavior is desirable from the point of view of someone who does not know whether he or she will be its beneficiary or its victim – in other words, whether the cost of being the victim outweighs the gain of being the beneficiary. The individual interest and the common interest diverge as soon as my free will clashes with your interests, but they converge in part behind the veil of ignorance.

Another benefit of reasoning from behind the veil of ignorance is that rights acquire a rationale that transcends sloganeering. The right to health care provides insurance against the misfortune of having bad genes. Equality of opportunity in education aims to insure us against disparities arising from the situation in which we are born and grow up. Human rights and freedoms protect us against arbitrary government. From this perspective, rights are no longer abstract concepts that society can grant or deny us at will. In practice, rights can be granted at differing levels, or they can conflict (for example, one person's freedom stops where that of others begins); this perspective also makes rights more operational.

The quest for the common good takes as its starting point our well-being behind the veil of ignorance. It does not prejudge solutions and has no criteria other than the collective interest. It allows the private use of goods for the well-being of individuals, but not their abuse at the expense of others.[3] Take for the example the idea of the commons, the goods that, behind the veil of ignorance, must for reasons of equity belong to everyone: water, air, biodiversity, cultural heritage, the planet, or the beauty of a landscape. These goods belong to everyone, but are ultimately consumed by individuals. They can be enjoyed by all of us to the extent that my consumption does not infringe on yours (this is also true of knowledge, public street lighting, or national defense).[4] In contrast, if the good is available in limited quantities, or if the community chooses to restrict it, as some have in the case of carbon emissions, for example, then its use has to be privatized in some way. Setting prices for public goods like water, carbon, or bandwidth privatizes their use by granting some economic agents exclusive access as long as they pay for it. Yet it is precisely the quest for the common good that motivates this privatization: the aim is to keep water from being wasted, to make individuals responsible for the harm they cause by carbon emissions, or to allocate a scarce resource – bandwidth – to those operators who will make good use of it.

These examples anticipate the answer to the second question posed above – how economics might contribute to the quest for the common good. Economics, like other human and social sciences, does not seek to usurp society's role in defining the common good. But it can contribute in two ways. First, it can focus discussion of the objectives embodied in the concept of the common good by distinguishing ends from means. Far too often, as we will see, these means or instruments – whether an institution (such as the market), a "right" to something, or an economic policy – acquire a life of their own and lose sight of their true purpose. They can even end up working against the notion of the common good that justified them in the first place. Second, and more important, once a definition of the common good has been agreed upon, economics can help develop tools that contribute to achieving it.

Economics is not in the service of private property and individual interest, nor does it serve those who would like to use the state to impose their own values or to ensure that their own interests prevail. It does not justify economies based entirely on the market nor economies wholly under state control. Economics works toward the common good; its goal is to make the world a better place. To that end, its task is to identify the institutions and policies that will promote the common good. In its pursuit of the well-being of the community, it incorporates both individual and collective dimensions. It analyzes situations in which individual interest is compatible with the quest for collective well-being, as well as those in which, by contrast, individual interest hinders that quest.

ITINERARY

Our journey through the economics of the common good will be demanding but, I hope, rewarding. This book is not a course of lectures or a series of precooked answers. Instead, it is a tool for questioning, like research. It conveys my personal view of what economic science is, the way it is constructed, and what it involves. This is a vision of research based on the interaction between theory and practice, and on a society recognizing both the virtues of the market and also the need to regulate it. You may find yourself disagreeing with some, or indeed most, of my conclusions, but I hope that even in that case you will find food for thought here. I am counting on your desire to gain a better understanding of the world around us, and on your curiosity to peer through the looking glass.

My other ambition for *Economics for the Common Good* is to share my passion for a discipline: economics. Until I took my first course in the subject at the age of twenty-one or twenty-two, my only contact with economics had been through the media. I was trying to understand society. I liked the rigor of mathematics and physics, and I was deeply interested in the human and social sciences, in philosophy, history, and psychology. I was immediately captivated by economics because it combines a quantitative approach with the study of individual and collective behavior. I later appreciated that economics opened a window onto the everyday world that I understood poorly, and that it offered two opportunities: to tackle problems that were intellectually demanding and fascinating, and to contribute to decision making in both public and private spheres. Economics not only documents and analyzes individual and collective behavior; it also aspires to recommend better public policy.

This book is organized around five major themes. The first is *the relationship between society and economics* as a discipline and a paradigm. The second is devoted to *the economist's work*, ranging from his or her daily life as a researcher to the potential relevance of that research to society. *The institutions of state and market* forms the third theme, which situates these institutions in their economic context. The fourth theme reflects on four of *the great macroeconomic challenges* at the heart of our current preoccupations: climate change, labor market challenges, the euro, and finance. The fifth theme deals with a set of microeconomic questions that are less prominent in public debate, but which are nonetheless crucial to our everyday life and the future of our society. Grouped under the heading of *the industrial challenge*, these questions include competition policy and industrial policy, new economic models, social challenges presented by the digital revolution, innovation, and the regulation of public utilities.

THE RELATIONSHIP BETWEEN SOCIETY AND ECONOMICS

The first two parts of this book concern the role of the discipline of economics in our society: the position of the economist, the everyday work of a researcher in economics, economics' relation to other social sciences, and the question of the moral foundations of the market.

I hesitated to include these chapters, as I feared that they might contribute to the contemporary trend to turn economists into media personalities. I feared this might distract the reader's attention from the real focus of this book: economics itself. I finally decided to take the risk. My discussions in high schools, universities, and elsewhere have reinforced my awareness of the questions the discipline raises. The questions people pose are always the same: What does an economist actually do? Is economics a (real) science? If economics is based on "methodological individualism," in which collective phenomena result from, but also shape, individual behavior, what issues does this raise? Is it right to presume a form of rational behavior, and if so, what form does it take? Are markets moral? As they were unable to predict the 2008 financial crisis, are economists even useful?

Economics is simultaneously demanding and accessible. It is demanding because, as we will see in chapter 1, our intuition frequently plays tricks on us. We are all vulnerable to, and yield to, certain heuristics and beliefs. When we think about an economic problem, the first answer that occurs to us is not always the correct one. Our reasoning often does not transcend appearances, the beliefs we hold, or our emotions. Economics is a lens that shapes our view of the world and allows us to peer through the looking glass. The good news is that if we take care to avoid these pitfalls economics becomes accessible. Understanding it does not require a superior education or an above-average IQ. Intellectual curiosity and a map of the natural traps that our intuition, emotions, and beliefs lay for us are enough to understand economics. In each of the following chapters, I will offer concrete examples to illustrate theory and enhance understanding.

Echoing the vague malaise mentioned above, many books inquire into the morality of the market and emphasize the need to establish a clear boundary between commercial and noncommercial domains. Chapter 2 shows that some of the moral criticisms of the market are simply reformulations of the concept of "market failure," which therefore demand public action but do not raise specifically ethical problems. Other criticisms are more profound. We will try to understand why we are disturbed by market transactions involving, for instance, the sale of human organs, surrogate motherhood, or sex. I will stress the point that, although our feelings of indignation may alert us to aberrant individual behavior or the need to organize society differently, these feelings are a poor guide for economic action. In the past, indignation has often led to the assertion of individual preferences to the detriment of others' freedom – and indignation all too often dispenses with the need for further reflection. Finally, chapter 2 analyzes concerns about the increase in inequality and the loss of social cohesion in market economies.

THE ECONOMIST'S PROFESSION

The second part of the book deals with the economist's profession. It begins in chapter 3 with the engagement of economists in civil society. As a discipline, economics has a special place among the human and social sciences. More than any other, it challenges, fascinates, and disturbs us. The role of economists is not to make decisions, but to identify the recurring patterns structuring our economies, and to convey economic science's current state of knowledge. In doing so, they face two contradictory criticisms. To some people, economists are ineffective. To others, on the contrary, they are influential, and often make arguments used to justify policies that do not serve the common good. I will concentrate on the second criticism, leaving the book as a whole to reply to the first.

It is entirely legitimate to question the role of the economist in society. Economic researchers, like their counterparts in other scientific disciplines, are usually financed at least in part by the state. They influence economic policy, either directly through their participation in civic life or indirectly through their research and teaching. They are fallible, like all scientists, but they should be accountable. As absorbing as academic economists might find their intellectual life, collectively their research must also be useful to society.

The researcher's involvement in civic life takes many forms: inter- action with the public and private sectors, or participation in public debate, in the media, or in politics. Each of these interactions, if well structured, is useful to society – but each also contains the seeds of self-destruction. Chapter 3 reviews what might compromise research and its transmission, taking economics as an illustration although the same lessons apply to academic research more broadly. This section offers some personal reflections on the way in which institutions can limit the risk that money, friendships, and the desire for recognition or celebrity might alter the researcher's behavior inside and outside the laboratory.

Chapter 4 describes the daily life of an economic researcher. I explain why the "dismal science" (as Thomas Carlyle called econom- ics in 1849, in a tract proposing the reestablishment of slavery[5]) is, on the contrary, fascinating, and why a school or university student wondering what to do with his or her future might want to consider becoming an economist.

I discuss the complementarity of theory and empirical investi- gation and the back-and-forth exchange between them; the role of mathematics; how we validate knowledge; the things about which economists agree and disagree; and economists' styles of cognitive reasoning. Finally, I offer an intuitive description of two theoretical advances, game theory and information theory, which have revolu- tionized our understanding of economic institutions over the past forty years.

Anthropologists, economists, historians, legal scholars, philoso- phers, political scientists, psychologists, and sociologists all take an interest in the same individuals, the same groups, and the same socie- ties. Chapter 5 places economics within the humanities and social sci- ences, of which it was part until the end of the nineteenth century. In the twentieth century, economics developed independently through the fiction of *homo economicus*: the hypothesis that decision makers (consumers, politicians, and enterprises, for example) are rational, in the straightforward sense that they act in their own best interest

– most often understood as their *economic* interest – given the information they have available (although economics also emphasizes that this information may be partial or manipulated). In reality we are all biased in our thinking and our decision making, and we all have goals beyond our material self-interest, which is not something we pursue systematically. For the past twenty years, research in economics has increasingly incorporated contributions from other social and human sciences to improve its understanding of the behavior of individuals and groups, political decision making, and the ways in which laws are fashioned. Chapter 5 shows how we enrich the description of our economic behavior if we allow for phenomena such as procrastination, errors in belief formation, and the influence of context. The chapter then returns to morality and its fragility, discussing the connection between intrinsic and extrinsic motivation and the influence of social norms on our behavior.

INSTITUTIONS

The following chapters examine two of the main actors in economic life: the state and the firm. In chapter 6, I make the case for a new concept of the state, on the basis of the common good. Our choice of society is not between the state and the market, as partisans of state intervention and those of laissez-faire policies would have us believe. The state and the market are complementary, not mutually exclusive. The market needs regulation; the state needs competition and incentives.

The state no longer provides as much employment through public sector jobs as in the past, nor does it produce as many goods and services through public enterprises. It has transformed itself primarily into a regulator. I show that the state's new role is to establish ground rules, to intervene when markets fail, to ensure healthy competition, to regulate monopolies, to supervise the financial system, to create true equality of opportunity, and to redistribute resources through taxation. Chapter 6 also analyzes the role and relevance of independent authorities and the primacy of politics. It insists on the need to reform the state (because the condition of public finances in many countries now threatens the survival of existing social systems) and proposes some avenues for reform.

Chapter 7 deals with the firm. It opens with an enigma: Why is a particular form of management – capitalist management – so prevalent all over the world? This kind of management grants decision-making power to shareholders or, if debts are not repaid, to creditors. Yet a firm has many other stakeholders: employees, subcontractors, customers, local authorities, the country or countries in which it operates, and those who live nearby. Hence, there are many potential forms of organization in which stakeholders might share power in diverse configurations and arrangements. We also tend to forget that other ways of managing firms (such as the self-managed or cooperative firm) are possible in a world of free enterprise. Analyzing how viable these alternatives would be leads me to a discussion of the strengths and weaknesses of alternative forms of corporate governance. I analyze ideas of corporate social responsibility and socially responsible investment. What do these concepts mean? Are they incompatible with a market economy, or are they on the contrary a natural product of it?

A WINDOW ON OUR WORLD

The chapters dealing with a selection of key economic challenges (chapters 8 to 17) require much less of a road map, as their themes are so familiar. This part of the book is a journey through subjects that affect our everyday life, but over which we exercise no individual control: global warming, labor market challenges, the European Union, finance, competition and industrial policy, our relation to the digital world, innovation, and sectoral regulation. In each case, I analyze the role of public and private actors, and reflect on the institutions that might contribute to the convergence of individual and general interest – in short, to the common good.

My message is optimistic. I explain why the ills from which our societies suffer are not inevitable (there are solutions to unemployment, to global warming, and to the decay of the European Union). I also explain how we can meet the industrial challenge, and what we can do to ensure that goods and services benefit the public as a whole, rather than simply increase the incomes of a firm's shareholders or employees. I show how we can regulate finance, monopolies, markets, and the state itself, without either derailing the economic engine or denying the state's role in the organization of society.

The choice of subjects is necessarily selective. I give priority to those on which I have published studies in academic journals. I have not addressed themes on which other economists could comment with far more expertise than I, or (as with globalization or inequality) discussed them only where they were necessary to complete the chapter's treatment.

THE COMMON THREAD

Although this book is organized around themes that are familiar to everyone, the common thread is a concept with which many readers will probably be unfamiliar – information theory, one of the major advances in economics over the past forty years. This theory is based on an obvious fact: decisions made by economic actors (households, firms, the state) are constrained by limited information. We see the consequences of these informational limits everywhere. They make it difficult for citizens to understand and evaluate the policies of their governments, or for the state to regulate banks and powerful firms, to protect the environment, or to manage innovation. Lack of information also contributes to the difficulty investors have in controlling the way their money is used by the firms that they finance; to the way those firms are structured; to our interpersonal relations; and even to our relationship with ourselves, when for example we construct an identity or believe what we want to believe.

As I show, the need for public policies that reflect the information available has crucial implications for the design of employment policy, environmental protection, industrial policy, and sectoral and banking regulation. In the private sector, asymmetries of information underlie institutions of governance and modes of financing. The problem of limited (or "asymmetric") information is everywhere: at the heart of our institutional structures and of our political choices – and at the heart of the economics of the common good.

A guide to reading this book: It is possible to read the seventeen chapters independently. If you have limited time or specific interests, you can therefore concentrate on your preferred subjects. It is, however, advisable to read chapter 11 (on finance) before reading chapter 12 (on the 2008 crisis).

PART I

ECONOMICS AND SOCIETY

ONE
Do You Like Economics?

IF YOU ARE NOT an economist by training or profession you might be intrigued by economics (otherwise you wouldn't be reading this book), but you do not necessarily like it. You probably find economic discourse abstruse, even counterintuitive. In this chapter I would like to explain why that is, describe a few cognitive biases that sometimes play tricks on us when we think about economic questions, and propose some ways of spreading an understanding of economics more widely.

Economics concerns all of us in our everyday lives; it is not just for experts. Once we look beyond appearances, and identify and overcome the initial obstacles, it is also accessible and fascinating.

WHAT PREVENTS OUR UNDERSTANDING ECONOMICS

Psychologists and philosophers have long examined the factors that shape our beliefs. Numerous cognitive biases work to our advantage (which no doubt explains why they exist) but they also occasionally mislead us. We will encounter these biases throughout this book, and see how they affect our understanding of economic phenomena and our view of society. In short, what we see – or want to see – and reality are different.

WE BELIEVE WHAT WE WANT TO BELIEVE, AND WE SEE WHAT WE WANT TO SEE

We often believe what we want to believe, rather than what the evidence points to. Thinkers as diverse as Plato, Adam Smith, and the great nineteenth-century American psychologist William James have all pointed out that the way we form and revise our beliefs serves to confirm the image we want to have, both of ourselves and of the world around us. When these beliefs are aggregated, they determine a country's economic, social, scientific, and geopolitical policies.

Not only are we subject to cognitive biases, we also frequently seek out things that reinforce them. We interpret facts through the prism of our beliefs; we read the newspapers and seek the company of people who will confirm us in those beliefs; and thus we stick obstinately to these beliefs, whether or not they are correct. When Dan Kahan, a professor of law at Yale University, confronted Americans who voted Democrat with scientific proof of the anthropogenic factor (the influence of human beings on global warming), he observed that they were more convinced than ever of the necessity of taking action against climate change. When Republicans were confronted with the same data, many of them were confirmed in their skepticism.[1] Even more astonishing, this was not a matter of education or intelligence: statistically, the refusal to face up to the evidence was at least as firmly anchored in Republicans who had advanced degrees as it was in less well-educated Republicans. No one is immune to this phenomenon.

The desire to reassure ourselves about our future also plays an important role in our understanding of economic (and more generally, scientific) phenomena. We do not want to hear that the battle against global warming will be expensive. Hence the popularity in political debate of the idea of "green growth." The name suggests that in environmental matters we can have our cake and eat it too. But if it is really so easy, why hasn't it already been implemented?

We like to think that accidents and illnesses only afflict others, not ourselves or those close to us. This can lead to harmful behavior, such as driving carelessly or not looking after our health (though this is not entirely negative since worrying less improves our quality of life). In the same way, we do not want to believe the possibility that an explosion of public debt might endanger the survival of our social safety net – or at least we want to believe that someone else will foot the bill.

We all dream of a world in which the law would not have to encourage or constrain people to behave virtuously, a world in which companies would voluntarily stop polluting and avoiding their taxes, in which people would drive carefully even without police officers around. That is why movie directors (and not only of Hollywood movies) invent endings that meet our expectations. These happy endings confirm our belief that we live in a fair world where virtue wins out over vice (what the sociologist Melvin Lerner called "belief in a just world"[2]).

When populist parties on both the right and the left promote the vision of an economy free of difficult choices, anything that questions this sugarcoated fairytale is perceived at best as scaremongering, at worst as lies put about by global warming fanatics, austerity ideologues, or other enemies of humanity. The insistence on reality rather than fairytale is one reason why economics is often called "the dismal science."

What We See and What We Don't See

First Impressions and Heuristics

The teaching of economics is usually based on the theory of rational choice. To describe the behavior of an individual, economists start by describing his or her objectives. Whether the individual is selfish or altruistic, seeking profit or social recognition, or has some other ambition, in every case he or she is assumed to act as far as possible in his or her own interest. This hypothesis is sometimes applied too strongly, and not only because an individual does not always have the necessary information to make a good choice. As the victim of cognitive biases, this agent is also likely to make a mistake when evaluating the best way to attain an objective. Humans are subject to many biases in reasoning or perception. These biases do not invalidate the theory that rationality defines the choices that individuals ought to make to act in their best interest (*normative* choices), but they explain why we don't necessarily make those choices.

We will make use of the notion of heuristics, as described by Daniel Kahneman,[3] a psychologist who won the Nobel prize in economics in 2002. Heuristics are rules of thumb for thinking, shortcuts to an answer to a question. They are often very useful because they allow us to make decisions quickly (if we are face-to-face with a tiger, we don't have time to calculate the optimal response), but heuristics can also mislead. They channel emotion, which can be a reliable guide but can also be very ill-advised.

For example, we are more likely to remember situations in which our activity has been interrupted. Thinking "the telephone always rings when I'm in the shower" is clearly a trick played by our memories. The call that interrupted the shower remains imprinted on our memories, unlike the calls that did not. Similarly, we are afraid of airplane crashes and terrorist attacks because they are covered at length in newspapers; we forget that car accidents and "ordinary" murders kill many more people than these fortunately rare events. Since September 11, 2001, there have been 200,000 homicides in the United States, of which only 50 were carried out by (American) Islamic terrorists.[4] This does not, however, prevent terrorist acts from being etched on our psyche.

The main contribution of Kahneman and Tversky's work has been to show that these and other heuristics often mislead us. They give many examples, but one is particularly striking: medical students at Harvard made significant errors[5] when calculating the probability that a patient had cancer given certain symptoms. These were the brightest American students, yet their shortcuts in reasoning were not corrected, not even by their brilliant intellects and stellar education.[6]

In economic matters too, first impressions can mislead us. We look at the direct effect of an economic policy, which is easy to understand, and we stop there. Most of the time we are not aware of the indirect effects. We do not understand the problem in its entirety. Yet secondary or indirect effects can easily make a well-intentioned policy toxic.

Throughout this book we will encounter many examples of this phenomenon, but let us start with a deliberately provocative example.[7] I have chosen this example because it allows us to see immediately the kind of cognitive bias that leads to poor public policy decisions. Let's suppose an NGO confiscates ivory from traffickers who kill endangered elephants for their tusks. The NGO has to choose between destroying the ivory or selling it discreetly on the market. The immediate reaction of most readers would be that the latter choice is reprehensible. My spontaneous reaction would be the same. But let us examine this example more closely.

The NGO would receive revenue from selling the ivory, which it could use to provide more resources to detect and investigate, or to provide additional vehicles to limit the traffic in ivory. Selling the ivory might also have the immediate effect of lowering its price. The price would be a little lower if not much was sold, and a lot lower if a lot of ivory was put on the market.[8] Traffickers are economically rational actors: they consider how much money they can make from their activity and consider the risks they take (in this case, prison or meeting armed police). If the price of ivory falls, it would therefore discourage some of them from killing elephants. Given this, would the NGO's sale of ivory be immoral? Possibly. A conspicuous sale by an organization with a respectable reputation might legitimize the trade for potential buyers who would otherwise feel guilty about their desire to purchase ivory – hence my emphasis on a "discreet sale" in this scenario. But at the very least, we ought to think twice before we condemn the choice of selling the ivory, especially since doing so would not prevent the government from exercising its sovereign authority to prosecute poachers or retailers of ivory or rhinoceros horn, or from communicating to the public the importance of protecting endangered animals in the hope of changing the accepted social norms.

This hypothetical scenario helps explain why the 1997 Kyoto Protocol failed. The Protocol promised to be a major step in the battle against global warming. Because of carryover effects (known in environmental economics jargon as "the leakage problem"), whereby polluting activities tend to migrate to countries with more lenient regulations, the battle against greenhouse gases in a single region may have little or no effect on worldwide pollution. Suppose, for example, that the United States reduces its consumption of fossil fuels (oil, gas, and coal). On its own, this effort would be laudable. Experts agree that it would require similar major efforts by every country to limit the global rise in temperature to the 1.5 to 2 degrees centigrade that is considered to be a bearable level of global warming. The problem is that when one country saves a ton of coal or a barrel of oil, the price of coal and oil falls, which encourages greater consumption elsewhere in the world.

Similarly, if a virtuous country forces its resident industries to pay to emit greenhouse gas, these industries are likely to move to another country where the absence of carbon taxation would make it cheaper to produce. This would partly or entirely cancel out the reduction in greenhouse gas emissions in the virtuous country, and there would be only a weak effect on the environment. Any serious solution to the problem can only be global. In economic matters, the road to hell is paved with good intentions.

The Bias toward the Identifiable Victim

Our empathy is naturally directed toward people who are geographically, ethnically, and culturally close to us. Our natural inclination, which has evolutionary origins,[9] is to feel more compassion for people in economic distress from our own community than for children dying of hunger far away, even if we recognize intellectually that the starving children are in more urgent need of help. More generally, we feel greater empathy when we identify with victims; and to do so it helps if we can recognize them. Psychologists have identified our tendency to attach more importance to people whose faces we know than to other, anonymous people.[10]

This bias toward the identifiable victim, no matter how instinctive it is, affects public policies. In the words of the quotation often attributed to Joseph Stalin: "The death of one man is a tragedy. The death of a million men is a statistic." Thus, a deeply distressing photo of Aylan Kurdi, a three-year-old Syrian child found dead in 2015 on a Turkish beach, forced us to pay attention to a situation it would have been more comfortable to ignore. It had much more impact on Europeans' awareness of refugees than the statistics about the thousands of migrants who had already drowned in the Mediterranean. The photo of Aylan had a similar impact on European attitudes toward migration as the 1972 photo of Kim Phúc, a Vietnamese girl burned by napalm running naked down a street, had on opinions about the Vietnam War. A single identifiable victim may affect many more minds than millions of anonymous victims. In the same way, an advertising campaign against drunk driving has a more powerful effect when it shows a passenger flying through a windshield than when it announces the annual number of victims (a statistic that provides, however, far more information about the consequences of drunk driving).

The bias toward the identifiable victim also leads astray the employment policies practiced in Southern European countries, in which some permanent jobs are strongly protected while other jobs are insecure. In many countries with this kind of strong employment protection, the media focuses on the battles to save jobs fought by employees with permanent contracts; their tragedy is made more acute because they live in a country where they have little chance of finding another similarly secure job. These victims have a face. Yet the media reports ignore the much larger group of people who alternate between short-term jobs and spells of unemployment. They have no faces, they are only statistics. As we will see in chapter 9, they are the victims of institutions – some of them set up to protect the first set of employees on permanent contracts – that cause firms to prefer to hire employees on fixed-term contracts rather than create stable jobs. While we worry about dismissals of protected workers, we forget the people who are excluded from the labor market in the first place, even though these groups are two sides of the same coin.

A Tale of Two Professions

The contrast between economics and medicine is striking: in contrast to its low opinion of "the dismal science," the public regards medicine – rightly – as a profession devoted to people's well-being (we call it "the caring profession"). Yet economics takes a similar approach to that of medicine. The economist, like the oncologist, makes a diagnosis on the basis of the best available (though necessarily imperfect) knowledge, and then either proposes the most suitable treatment on that basis or recommends no treatment at all, if none seems necessary.

These diverging perceptions of medicine and economics are easy to explain. In medicine, the victims of secondary effects are for the most part the same people who are being treated (epidemiology is an exception – think for example of the consequences of the spreading resistance to antibiotics, or of the loss of herd immunity when vaccination levels decline). A doctor has only to remain faithful to the Hippocratic Oath and recommend what is in the best interest of the patient. In economics, the victims of secondary effects are rarely the same people who received the original treatment, as the example of the labor market shows very clearly. An economist is obliged to think about invisible victims as well, and so the public sometimes accuses that economist of being indifferent to the sufferings of the visible victims.

THE MARKET AND OTHER WAYS OF MANAGING SCARCITY

Air, water from a stream, or a beautiful landscape can be enjoyed by one person without others being prevented from benefiting as well. But for most goods, one person's consumption means that others cannot consume it too. An essential question in organizing societies is how to manage the scarcity of goods and services that we all want to consume or possess, in rivalry with other people's demands: the apartment we rent or buy, the bread we buy at the bakery, or the rare earths needed to make metal alloys, or dyes, or green technologies. Although society can diminish scarcity by producing goods more efficiently, either by innovation or by commerce, it must also manage people's consumption of goods from one day to the next. Societies vary widely in how well they do this.

Historically, scarcity has been managed in many ways: queues when there are shortages of vital goods such as food or gasoline; drawing lots for green cards, concert tickets, or organ transplants; distributing goods administratively to priority groups; fixing prices below the level that would balance demand and supply. Scarcity is also managed by corruption, favoritism, violence, wars, and, finally, by the market. The market, then, is only one of many ways to manage scarcity. Though the market prevails today and allocates resources between firms (B2B), between firms and individuals (B2C, as in e-commerce), and between individuals (C2C, on platforms such as eBay), it hasn't always been so.

The alternatives, though, all imply prices set below the market clearing level that would match demand and supply. Buyers in these cases search for a "windfall" (economists call this "economic rent") created by this excessively low price. Suppose that buyers are all prepared to pay one thousand dollars for a good available in limited quantities, and that there are more buyers than available goods. The market price is the one that balances supply and demand. At more than one thousand dollars, no one buys; at less than one thousand dollars, there is excess demand. The market price is therefore one thousand dollars.

Now suppose the state sets the price of the good at four hundred dollars and prohibits its sale at a higher price. There are more interested buyers than there are goods available. Buyers would each be prepared to spend six hundred dollars more than the set price to get the good. If they have an opportunity to spend other kinds of resources to get their hands on this scarce good, they will take it. Take the example of the queue, a method used systematically in the Soviet Union (and still used today to allocate seats at some sporting events or concerts). Consumers may arrive several hours early and wait in line, sometimes in the cold,[11] to obtain the scarce commodity. Lower the price further, and the queue will form even earlier. This loss of utility means that, in addition to the other perverse effects of a price that is too low (to which we will return later), the so-called "beneficiaries" of the low-price policy are actually not benefiting at all. The market is not working through prices, but through the use of another "currency": time. This leads to a considerable loss of social well-being. In the example given above, the equivalent of six hundred dollars per purchase has disappeared: the (public or private) owner of the resource has lost six hundred dollars per sale, and yet the buyers have gained nothing – their financial advantage has evaporated because they had to spend time in a queue.

Some methods of allocating goods, such as corruption, favoritism, violence, and war, are profoundly unjust. But they are also inefficient for society as a whole, once we take into account the costs paid or imposed by the actors in their ambition to get their hands on goods without paying the market price for them. There is no need for us to dwell on the inadequacy of these methods of allocating goods.

As long as they are not tainted by favoritism or corruption, waiting in line, drawing lots, and the administrative distribution of rationed goods are fairer solutions. But they cause three kinds of problems. The first has already been mentioned: a price that is too low leads to waste through the search for an advantage (for instance, by standing in a queue). Second, the quantity of the good in the example was fixed, but in general it is not. Clearly, if the price of the good was one thousand dollars, sellers would produce more of it than they would if it was four hundred dollars. In the long run, setting a price too low leads to a shortage. That is what we see when rents are capped: the stock of quality housing gradually diminishes, creating scarcity and ultimately penalizing the potential beneficiaries. Finally, some mechanisms lead to a bad allocation of something in fixed supply. For example, drawing lots to allocate seats at a sporting event will not necessarily give the seats to those who have the greatest desire to be there (unless there is a secondary market to resell the tickets); or, to return to the waiting-in-line example, a mechanism may allocate the good to those who are available on a particular day, or to those who least feel the cold, rather than to those who have the greatest desire to consume the good in question.

A poor allocation of resources arises when they do not necessarily go to those who value them most. If they are distributed administratively, essential goods may fall into the hands of people who already have them or who would prefer other products. That is why it would never occur to anyone to allocate housing in an arbitrary way. The housing unit given to you would probably not be the one you desired in terms of location, square footage, or other characteristics – unless it could then be traded without restriction for one you did want. But that brings us back to the market.

The assignment of scarce radio spectrum is another relevant example here. Bandwidth is a resource that belongs to the community, but unlike air, the quantity of airwaves available to consume is limited. There is a high demand for bandwidth from telecommunications and media companies, so there is a problem of how best to allocate it to them. In the United States, a 1934 law ordered the agency regulating telecommunications (the Federal Communications

Commission or FCC) to allocate spectrum frequencies "in the public interest." In the past, the FCC often held public hearings at which the candidates competing for licenses had to present their cases, at the end of which licenses were granted to the candidate that seemed make the best case. These hearings consumed time and resources; moreover, we don't really know whether the FCC made good choices, because competence in this process is not the same thing as good strategic planning or good management. The FCC also sometimes used lotteries to grant licenses.

When using either a hearing or a lottery, the United States government granted private agents a public resource free of charge (in many countries, valuable taxi licenses have been similarly granted free of charge). Furthermore, there was no guarantee that the person or firm receiving this privilege would be capable of making the best use of it. For that reason, selling licenses on a secondary market was authorized, or at least tolerated. When it is possible to transfer a license, the allocative benefits of the market reappear. But the giveaway remains: the benefit derived from scarcity goes into the pockets of private individuals, rather than to the community to which it belongs.

So for the past twenty years, the United States (like most countries now) has used auctions to assign spectrum licenses. Experience shows that auctions are an efficient way to make sure that the licenses are assigned to the companies who will make the most of them,[12] while at the same time recouping the value of the scarce resource for the community. For example, auctions of bandwidth in the United States have earned about sixty billion dollars for the US Treasury since 1994. This is money that would otherwise have gone, without any justification, to private actors. Economists' role in designing these auctions has helped to increase greatly the financial benefit they brought to the state.[13]

What We Want to Do and What We Can Do

You might now be asking what the connection is between this discussion of the mechanisms of managing scarcity and the cognitive biases discussed earlier. When the state decides to set the price of a scarce good at four hundred dollars rather than its market price of one thousand dollars, it has the laudable intention of making this good accessible to more people. But it does not consider the indirect effects: in the short run, that means waiting in line or some other form of inefficiency; in the longer run, it means a depletion of property supply due to a price that is set too low.

When the state tries to allocate bandwidth free of charge to those it judges able to make the best use of it, it often confuses what it would *like to do* with what it *can do*, forgetting that it does not have all the information needed to make the right decision. Information is at the heart of the issue, and the mechanism of the market reveals it. The state does not know which firms have the best ideas or the lowest development costs for a particular slice of the radio spectrum, but bandwidth auctions reveal which firms are prepared to pay the most for it.[14] Generally speaking, the state hardly ever has the information it needs to make allocation decisions by itself. That does not mean the state has no room to maneuver, but it has to accept its limits. We shall see later in the book how *hubris* – in this case, a government's excessive confidence in its ability to make complex choices in the realm of economic policy – can lead to harmful environmental and labor-market outcomes especially if combined with the desire to retain oversight and thereby the power to distribute favors. Citizens may worry about a world in which a faceless market makes the decisions: they want real people to look out for them. But citizens should also recognize that public officials are not superheroes. Voters are entitled to expect officials to implement what is feasible and useful, but should not label them as incompetent or corrupt when they fail to work miracles.

The Rise of Populism around the World

Throughout the world, populist parties on both the right and left are gaining ground. "Populism" is hard to define because it takes many forms, but one common thread is the exacerbated eagerness to exploit the ignorance and prejudice of voters. Fanning widespread hostility to immigrants, distrust of free trade, and xenophobia plays on people's fears. Rising populism clearly has specific causes in different countries, but anxieties about technological change and employment, the financial crisis, the slowdown in economic growth, rising debt, and increasing inequality seem to be universal factors. On a purely economic level, the contempt that populist programs have for elementary economic mechanisms, and even for simple public accounting, is striking.

Economists – and academics in general – have to ask themselves how much influence they have. Take the example of the vote in the UK referendum in favor of leaving the European Union ("Brexit") on June 23, 2016. We cannot measure the impact on the electorate of the nearly unanimous message from British and international economists (as well as reputable organizations such as the Institute for Fiscal Studies, the IMF, the OECD, and the Bank of England) that the United Kingdom had nothing to gain economically, and possibly a great deal to lose, by leaving the European Union.[15] To be sure, the election seems to have been determined by other concerns – immigration in particular – that were also easy for populists to misrepresent. The British electorate did not seem engaged by what it believed (or wanted to believe) was an esoteric debate among economic experts who were popularly regarded as unable to agree among themselves. The same might be said of the high degree of consensus amongst economists against President Trump's proposed economic policies during the US election campaign.[16]

HOW TO MAKE ECONOMICS BETTER UNDERSTOOD

Economics is like any culture, for instance music, literature, or sports. We like it more the better we understand it. So how can we make economic culture more accessible?

Economists as Conveyers of Knowledge

First of all, economists themselves could play a more active role in sharing their knowledge.

Researchers respond, like anyone else, to the incentives they face. Academic careers are universally judged on the basis of the research academics publish and the students they train, but only rarely on public outreach or impact. What's more, staying safely in the ivory tower is much more comfortable for academics, because, as we shall see in chapter 3, switching from academic debate to communicating with the public is not as simple as it seems.

The most creative researchers often do not engage in public debate. Unless they have exceptional energy, it is difficult for them to combine their mission to create knowledge and impart it to their students with communicating ideas to the public. No one would have expected Adam Smith to make predictions, produce reports, speak on television, write a blog, and compose popular economics books. Each of these new demands that society makes are legitimate, but they sometimes open a gap between those who create knowledge and those who convey it.

Even economists exercising their mission as strictly defined are not exempt from criticism. They need to make greater efforts to construct a pragmatic and intuitive education, relying not only on their tried-and-tested conceptual frameworks, simplified for pedagogical purposes, but also on empirical observation. Teaching obsolete economic ideas or less-than-rigorous debates between earlier economists – or, conversely, promoting an exaggeratedly mathematical approach – does not meet the needs of secondary school and university students. The overwhelming majority of students will not become professional economists, and very few will be researchers in economics. They need a pragmatic initiation into the subject that is both intuitive and rigorous.

Everybody's Responsibility

Our personal economic understanding, like our scientific or geopolitical understanding, guides the choices made by our governments. The conventional wisdom agrees with Joseph de Maistre that "every nation gets the government it deserves." That may be true – even if, as the philosopher André Comte-Sponville observed, it is better to constructively help public officials than to constantly criticize them.[17]

What I do know is that we get the economic policies we deserve, and as long as a lack of economic understanding prevails among the general public, making good policy choices will take a lot of political courage. Politicians hesitate to adopt unpopular policies because they fear an electoral backlash, so if the public had a better understanding of economic mechanisms, this would be a public good. We want others to make the intellectual investment required to encourage political decision makers to make more rational collective choices, but we are often not prepared to make that intellectual investment ourselves. We lack intellectual curiosity, and so behave like "free riders" who leave others to put in the effort to understand economic mechanisms rather than bothering to do so ourselves.[18]

In his book *The Age of Diminished Expectations: U.S. Economic Policy in the 1990s* (MIT Press, 1997), Paul Krugman, a Nobel laureate and one of the few economists who has succeeded in making difficult economic concepts accessible, describes the situation like this:

> There are three kinds of writing in economics: Greek-letter, up-and-down, and airport.
>
> Greek-letter writing – formal, theoretical, mathematical – is how professors communicate. Like any academic field, economics has its fair share of hacks and phonies, who use complicated language to hide the banality of their ideas; it also contains profound thinkers, who use the specialized language of the discipline as an efficient way to express deep insights. For anyone without graduate training in economics, however, even the best Greek-letter writing is completely impenetrable. (A reviewer for the *Village Voice* had the misfortune to encounter some of my own Greek-letter work; he found "equations, charts, and graphs of stunning obscurity ... a language that makes medieval scholasticism seem accessible, even joyous.")
>
> Up-and-down economics is what one encounters on the business pages of newspapers, or for that matter on TV. It is preoccupied with the latest news and the latest numbers, hence its name. "According to the latest statistics, housing starts are up, indicating unexpected strength in the economy. Bond prices fell on the news ..." This kind of economics has a reputation for being stupefyingly boring, a reputation that is almost entirely justified. There is an art to doing it well – there is a Zen of everything, even short-run

economic forecasting. But it is unfortunate that most people think that up-and-down economics is what economists do.

Finally, airport economics is the language of economics bestsellers. These books are most prominently displayed at airport bookstores, where the delayed business traveler is likely to buy them. Most of these books predict disaster: a new great depression, the evisceration of our economy by Japanese multinationals, the collapse of our money. A minority have the opposite view, a boundless optimism: new technology or supply-side economics is about to lead us into an era of unprecedented economic progress. Whether pessimistic or optimistic, airport economics is usually fun, rarely well-informed, and never serious.

We must all take responsibility for our limited understanding of economic phenomena, our desire to believe what we want to believe, our relative intellectual laziness, and our cognitive biases. We all have the ability to understand economics, but as I have already shown, errors in reasoning cannot necessarily be explained away by IQ or educational level.

Let's admit it: it's easier to watch a film or devour a good thriller than to launch into a book on economics (this is not a criticism, by the way: I myself read too little about climate science, biotechnology, medicine, and other scientific fields that influence public policy design). When we muster the resolve to do so, we expect the economics book to be easy to understand, exemplified in an extreme form by the simplistic theses of what Paul Krugman calls "airport economics" books. In every area of academic study, going beyond appearances requires more effort, less certainty, and more determination in the quest for understanding. But that is the price we have to pay if we are to get the policies we deserve.

TWO
The Moral Limits of the Market

In the kingdom of ends, everything has either a price, or a dignity. What has a price can be replaced with something else, as its *equivalent*, whereas what is elevated above any price, and hence allows of no equivalent, has a dignity.

Immanuel Kant[1]

If you pay a child a dollar to read a book, as some schools have tried, you not only create an expectation that reading makes you money, you also run the risk of depriving the child forever of the value of it. Markets are not innocent.

Michael Sandel[2]

PEOPLE'S BELIEF IN THE MERITS of free enterprise and the market economy varies widely around the world.[3] In 2005, 61 percent of our planet's inhabitants thought the market economy was the best system as a basis for the future. But while 65 percent of Germans, 71 percent of Americans, and 74 percent of Chinese said so, only 43 percent of Russians, 42 percent of Argentinians, and 36 percent of the French trusted the market. These beliefs affect the economic choices each country makes.

When there is enough competition, the market drives down the prices firms charge and increases household purchasing power. It creates incentives to reduce production costs through innovation and trade. Perhaps less obviously, it protects ordinary people from the lobbying and favoritism that are so much a part of more centralized systems for allocating resources. (Such abuses contributed both to the French Revolution, which abolished privileges in 1789 and guilds in

1791, and to the implosion of the centrally planned economies in the late 20th century.) For all these reasons, competitive markets play a central part in economic life.

As I intend to show in this book, however, departures from laissez-faire economics are often needed to capture the benefits of the market. Indeed, economists have devoted much of their research to identifying both the failures of the market and ways those failures might be corrected through public policy: competition law, regulation by sectoral and prudential authorities, taxes on environmental externalities, fees intended to reduce traffic congestion, monetary policy and financial stabilization, mechanisms for providing "merit goods"[4] such as education and health care, wealth redistribution, and so on. While they recognize its drawbacks, the overwhelming majority of economists are, for the reasons given above, in favor of the market. But they see it simply as an instrument, never as an end in itself.

Specialists in other disciplines (such as philosophers, psychologists, sociologists, legal scholars, or political scientists), a large part of civil society, and most religions have a different view of the market. While they recognize its virtues, they often accuse economists of not sufficiently considering the ethical issues it raises, and of not acknowledging the need to establish a clear boundary between the commercial and the noncommercial.

A sign of this difference in perception is the worldwide success of the book *What Money Can't Buy: The Moral Limits of Markets*, by Michael Sandel, a professor of philosophy at Harvard.[5] Sandel argues that a range of goods and services, such as the adoption of children, surrogacy, sexuality, drugs, military service, voting rights, pollution, and organ transplantation (to cite only a few) must not be trivialized by the market; that it should not be possible to buy friendship, admission to major universities, or the Nobel Prize; that genes and living tissues should not be able to be patented.[6]

More generally, society is uneasy about the market, an uneasiness reflected in the familiar slogan "the world is not for sale." This chapter analyzes these reservations concerning the market, the distinction between commercial and sacred domains, the role of emotion and outrage in our social choices, and the threat to social cohesion and to equality that the market may represent. The goal is to embark on a scientific investigation of the foundations of our morality, rather than to provide solutions – which I often don't have – to very complex problems. Reflecting scientifically on these issues challenges our preconceptions (including my own), but this intellectual digression seems essential if we are going to examine the way we create public policy, even if, in the end, our analysis confirms the beliefs we began with.

It is necessary in the first place because the things we consider to be morally sound change over time, even in economic matters. Life insurance and interest paid on savings used to be perceived as immoral; more recently, the solutions to the problems of unemployment or climate change that many economists advocate – solutions that imply people be made accountable for the consequences of their actions[7] – are still sometimes considered immoral, even though public opinion has changed a little over the last thirty years.

Second, this digression is necessary because morality can have a highly personal dimension. When the flame of indignation burns brightly, people use moral arguments to impose their own value judgments and reduce the freedom of others. Thus, until recently in many societies, sex acts between persons of the same sex or of different races have been considered immoral by the majority of citizens. The best response to such claims of moral superiority is not necessarily another moral claim – pitting my morality against yours leads to confrontation, making problems impossible to resolve. The better response may instead be to reason, beginning with simple questions, such as: Who is the victim? What is the basis of your belief? Can anything other than your own indignation justify infringing the freedom of others? Do not misunderstand me: indignation is often a useful indicator of dysfunction in society or the inappropriate nature of some kinds of behavior. My argument is simply that we cannot stop there. We need to understand the source of those beliefs.

This chapter shows, first of all, why the regulation or prohibition of a market can be a response to a problem of information (because the monetization of a good can destroy its value by altering its meaning), or an externality (a cost imposed by an exchange on a third party), or an "internality" (the behavior of an individual that conflicts with his own interest). In all three cases, regulation or prohibition of the market is a response to a straightforward market failure. When this is the case, invoking ethics adds little to either the analysis or the conclusion. Most importantly, it would fail to tell us which markets should be regulated or prohibited, or how to devise solutions better aligned with our ethical objectives.

Next I tackle subjects about which we all have ethical reservations: payment for organ transplants, surrogate motherhood, prostitution, and so on. The point here is not to challenge the regulations and prohibitions that already exist, but to examine the basis for them. For one thing, reasoning helps us understand why we make the policies we do. Furthermore, some reflection could improve them. To illustrate the point, I shall describe the way economists have succeeded in saving lives by encouraging organ donation without raising major ethical objections.

The last two parts of the chapter focus on other reservations about the market – the charges that it weakens social ties and creates inequality – with an emphasis on the way economics can help alleviate these problems. One of the leitmotifs here is that public policy must be guided by the need to achieve specific objectives, rather than by posturing and hype, which sometimes work against the intended effects of a policy or waste public money.

THE MORAL LIMITS OF THE MARKET OR MARKET FAILURE?

To concentrate on the real questions, let us first deal with some of the criticisms of markets that simply reflect an ignorance of economists' work – even when that work is now a standard part of economics, like the economics of information and the economics of externalities.[8] They also display an ignorance of the multidisciplinary studies undertaken over the last twenty years, both theoretical and experimental (in the field, in the laboratory, or in neuroeconomics), that have dealt with subjects as diverse as morality and ethics, social norms, identity, trust, and the crowding out of intrinsic motivation by extrinsic incentives. A series of examples can illustrate the confusion between market failures and the moral limits of the market.

INFORMATION

The idea that friendship, admission to a university, or a scientific prize can be bought contravenes elementary theories of the asymmetries of information: these "goods" would lose all value if they could be bought. We would no longer be able to tell whether a friendship was real, whether admission to a university was a sign of talent, or whether the prize was deserved. In these circumstances, a university diploma would be a sign of wealth, not of ability, so it would not impress a prospective employer. From this point of view, the fact that some American universities, particularly in the Ivy League, ever admit students simply because their parents made a donation to the university is particularly shocking.[9] Clearly, most donations to universities are not motivated by such considerations, and the phenomenon is not common enough to call into question the average quality of students. But that is precisely the point: some very wealthy parents are prepared to spend enormous amounts of money to "buy" admission to a university where their children will blend in with the majority of brilliant students and later benefit from having a diploma from a highly respected institution.

EXTERNALITIES AND INTERNALITIES

In a different realm, a market for adopting babies in which the "sellers" (the biological parents or adoption agencies) and the "buyers" (adoptive parents) exchanged children for hard cash would neglect a third party very much involved in the transaction: the children themselves. Another example of an externality created by the market is the trade in "blood diamonds" that feeds a civil war. Obviously, authorizing diamond trafficking by armed factions inflicts serious harm on the civilian population. As for pollution, experience shows that the recommendations made by economists – to tax emissions or to grant negotiable emission permits – have significantly reduced the ecological cost of environmental policies, and in that way have helped improve the environment. Some people find the idea that a firm could buy the right to pollute immoral, but their underlying argument is weak. Today, firms that emit carbon only pay a ridiculously small sum compared to the stakes involved: Is that really more moral than a carbon tax or permit? Ultimately, we have to reduce pollution. Since we cannot eliminate it entirely, we have to make sure that those firms that can most cost effectively reduce their pollution output will do so. That is exactly what putting a price on carbon emissions ensures.

The question of drugs raises the problem of self-control (in addition to the problems of violence and public health connected with hard drugs). The absence of self-control leads to addiction, the primary victims being the addicts themselves. This is not a question of morality, but rather of protecting citizens against others (externalities) and even more so against themselves (internalities).

Considerations of externality and internality can, of course, coincide, as in the case of doping in sports. The regulation of doping is justified both by an internality (the athletes sacrifice their long-term health in the desire for recognition, glory, or money) and by an externality (the athlete who engages in doping both gains a competitive edge and damages the reputation of the sport, and so has a negative effect on other athletes).

One more example. A country where voting rights were traded at the market price would be unlikely to adopt policies to which we would subscribe behind the "veil of ignorance."[10] The wealthiest households could buy voting rights and then pass laws favorable to themselves. This reasoning has been used to limit individual contributions to electoral campaigns or to finance them in part with public monies. Directly purchasing votes would be more harmful than contributing money to an electoral campaign that "buys" votes indirectly by augmenting a particular candidate's ability to be visible by the electorate; so a fortiori an open market for votes is undesirable.

As these examples show, the range of market failures is relatively wide, and economists have always highlighted them.

The Counterproductive Effects of Incentives

Economics emphasizes the need for individual and collective objectives to be aligned. It is a matter of putting individuals in step with society, in particular by using incentives that discourage harmful behavior (like pollution) or encourage virtuous behavior. Other social sciences to some extent dispute this principle; in their view, extrinsic motivations (incentives) can crowd out intrinsic motivations, making incentives ultimately counterproductive. In the passage quoted at the beginning of this chapter, Michael Sandel pins the blame on the market, but more generally it is incentives that he opposes: a policy to reward children for reading could be promoted just as easily by the government or by an aid organization; the market simply creates a specific system of incentives.

Sandel deploys in his argument a criticism psychologists had previously made of the economic premise that increasing a good's price increases its supply. Although this premise has been empirically verified in very many areas of economic life, it is not always correct; the challenge for social scientists is to identify precisely the situations in which extrinsic incentives crowd out intrinsic motivation. Paying a child to read a book or to pass an examination can push them to read or to revise thoroughly, but the short-term benefit can also be nullified by what happens later – for example, if the child has less desire to learn when the reward is no longer available. Policies relying on incentives in this case may turn out to be counterproductive.

In another domain, we know that paying blood donors does not necessarily increase the amount of blood given. Although some people react positively to the incentive, others lose their motivation. As we shall see in chapter 5, our desire to look good, to project an attractive image either to ourselves or to others, can give rise to some counterproductive effects from incentives. This is even more likely if the behavior is public (especially in the presence of people we want to impress) and memorable. The possibility of a financial reward for doing something that is otherwise for the good of society, like giving blood, makes us worry that our contribution might be interpreted as a sign of greed rather than of generosity, and that consequently the signal of virtue we send to others or to ourselves might be diluted.

Contrary to the basic economic principle, a financial reward can thus impede the behavior that we wish to encourage. Several empirical studies have supported this conclusion.

THE NONCOMMERCIAL AND THE SACRED

The examples above all follow from standard economics, but we all have other reservations of an ethical or moral character about specific markets or types of incentives. Examples include organ donations, surrogate mothers, stem cell research, prostitution, or paying to avoid military conscription. Why?

Life Has No Price

In the quotation at the beginning of this chapter, Kant draws a clear line between what has a price and what has dignity. Our negative attitude toward the market in some cases may also be related to our refusal to compare money with other goals. For example, financial considerations conflict with our belief in the sacredness of human life. We all know that life has no price. The taboos on life and death – part of the "incommensurable" things so important to sociologist Émile Durkheim – have consequences. So being explicit about the economic tradeoffs involved in health care and personal lifestyles (the allocation of budgets for hospitals or medical research, or the choices we make about safety) gives rise to fierce controversies. But the refusal to compare the therapeutic effects and the number of lives saved by these unexamined choices causes more deaths. Isn't it absurd to spend a large sum on saving one life when, for the same amount of money, dozens of others could be saved?[11] Yet the financial nature and apparent cynicism of such considerations shock people, who refuse to engage with them.

Philosophers have long reflected on our reluctance to confront these utilitarian calculations.[12] One of the most famous philosophical dilemmas of this type is the trolley problem: Would we be prepared to push someone under a tram to derail it, if that meant that five people further down the line would be saved? Or, to put the dilemma another way, would a surgeon be prepared to kill someone in good health to save five people who will die if they do not receive an immediate organ transplant? Or what would we do if asked to choose between saving our own child from drowning and saving five others, if saving all of them would be impossible? These hypothetical choices make many people uncomfortable, and they argue that they would not sacrifice one life to save five others. Yet behind the veil of ignorance, we are five times more likely to be among the beneficiaries of such choices than to be the victims.

Are these purely hypothetical questions? Not at all. There are many examples in the real world. Governments are confronted with this dilemma when hostages are taken: Should they pay the ransom to avoid sacrificing one life and so expose their citizens to more hostage attacks in the future? Note that here we reencounter the identifiable victim problem discussed earlier. A person taken hostage today has a face, but future hostages – the victims of paying the ransom – do not. The dice are loaded. That is why governments must adopt a general policy and not make decisions on a case-by-case basis.

Consider another example that might become a problem in the near future. In a few years, driverless cars will appear on our roads. This will be a good thing. Accidents could be reduced by 90 percent. Our streets and roads will be much safer. But our societies will have to make some morally sensitive choices.[13] Suppose that I am driving my car alone, and I find myself in a rare situation in which I cannot avoid an accident. My choice is limited to two options: sacrificing myself by steering into the ditch, or killing five pedestrians who are on the road. Today the driver makes this kind of decision in a fraction of a second. Tomorrow, it will be an algorithm installed in the car, programmed in advance to react dispassionately to the situation. In the future, the algorithm will make the decision one way or the other. Would I prefer a car that would sacrifice its driver, or one that would run down five pedestrians? Intuitively, I would perceive the first car as more "moral," but which would I choose for myself? "Behind the veil of ignorance" my chance of being one of the pedestrians is five times greater than my chance of being the driver of the car, so I would pick the car that would create fewer victims. But things would be very different if I was choosing a car in real life. I would have to decide whether I am prepared to make this kind of ethical choice explicitly. In experiments, however, many people who are faced with this question refuse to allow the choice to be dictated by the state. There is a clash between our abstract ethical position (which here differs from our position in relation to the trolley problem) and our self-interest as a driver.

In general, we are ill at ease making choices related to life and death. To take a case less extreme than the ones just considered, Yale professors Judith Chevalier and Fiona Scott Morton[14] have shown that the US funeral market, which we might think, a priori, would be very competitive, enjoys almost monopolistic profit margins because of our reluctance to talk about money when someone close to us dies. Nonetheless, we should examine the origin of these taboos, ask whether they are socially justified, and evaluate their effect on public policies. De facto, we all implicitly attribute a value to life, whether the lives of patients when hospitals have to make hard choices about what equipment they buy, or our children's lives when we are choosing a car, or a vacation. But we do not want to admit that we make these choices, which we find unbearable. Are these taboos caused by the fear of loss of dignity if we make such choices explicit?[15] Or are they provoked by the fear that society might start down a slippery slope?

Organ Markets

We can pursue this question by examining a debate that has aroused many passionate reactions on both sides: payment for organ transplants. Gary Becker, a professor at the University of Chicago who famously advocated using the prism of economics to study social behavior (for example, drug taking or how families behave), noted that the prohibition on the sale of, say, a kidney, limited the number of suitable donors (essentially to family and close friends) and so condemned thousands of people to die every year in the United States alone. Becker concluded that the question was complex, and that considering the thousands who die due to the shortage of donors, people opposed to markets for organs should not claim moral superiority.

Despite the force of Becker's argument, most of us continue to disapprove of paying people for their organs. But, given the stakes involved, should we not ask why? A first, uncontroversial argument is the fear that donors might not be sufficiently well informed about the consequences of their actions. Losing a kidney can have long-term consequences for the donor that are not trivial. The process leading to the transplant would need to be strictly supervised, and the donor would need adequate information about the consequences of his or her action. This is nothing new: information protocols are already mandatory when an organ is donated to a close friend or relative. A second argument is the possibility that if you could earn money by donating, some people attracted by the short-term financial benefit (whether for themselves or to help their family, especially if they are poor) might later regret their choice. Here we are considering an internality and the concomitant protection of individuals from themselves.

A third line of discussion is that the willingness of some people to swap a kidney for a few hundred dollars reveals inequalities we would rather ignore.[16] It is, de facto, the least well-off, and in particular the desperately poor, who would be most willing to sell their kidneys. A variant of the same argument is the repugnance we feel about transplant tourism.[17] Obviously, trying to hide from reality by prohibiting organ exchanges is no way to solve the problem of poverty. But this third argument reinforces the second, because poverty creates an urgent need for resources, and may lead individuals to make choices that are harmful to them. Trafficking in human organs exists. The point is that we need to take steps to control it, and to find solutions to the problem that causes it – namely, the despair of those waiting for donors. Hence, we should facilitate and encourage the donation of organs at the time of death, and promote innovative solutions (such as the kidney exchanges), which I discuss below.

Finally, a fourth line of argument is the possibility that donors do not really consent, and are forced to sell their kidneys by Mafia-like organizations. This argument is valid, of course, but it is not specifically about the sale of organs: Mafia-style organizations can force an individual to hand over savings, or can transform someone into a virtual slave by regularly skimming off part of their income, quite apart from the sale of organs. The most we can say is that the existence of a market for human organs increases the opportunities for extortion.

Sometimes other considerations, often implicit, are at the root of our disapproval. Consider, for example, the spectacle of violent sports such as mixed martial arts (which is banned in France) or boxing. Perhaps our sense of well-being depends on not living in a violent society, to the extent that even the sight of spectators taking pleasure in such violence may cause us distress. It is not merely a matter of protecting the combatants against themselves (giving priority to the long-term consequences for their health or the immediate physical risks they face, rather than the money they earn), but also of protecting ourselves against being disturbed by the collective enjoyment of such events. Public executions of condemned criminals were forbidden in France between 1939 and 1981 (when capital punishment was abolished) for exactly this kind of reason.[18]

Another shocking example is that of catapulting Little People. Many people first became aware of the practice through films like *Lord of the Rings* and *The Wolf of Wall Street*. There was in some countries a bizarre custom of paying Little People – who fully consented – to participate in competitions in which others tried to throw them as far as possible onto a mattress (the Little Person wore a helmet, and other safety precautions were taken). In France, the *Conseil d'Etat* (which performs some of the functions of a supreme court) had to rule on this topic as late as 1995. In 1991, the commune of Morsang-sur-Orge in the department of Essonne prohibited one of these contests, due to take place in a nightclub. The Little Person concerned embarked on a legal battle to preserve his right to practice his occupation: the Versailles administrative tribunal ruled in his favor, but the *Conseil d'Etat* decided that respect for human dignity was integral to public order. In North America, there have been bans on this so-called dwarf tossing (it was made illegal in Florida in 1989, for example), but there is still an occasional debate between the majority, who view it as a degrading practice, and a handful of Little People who argue that bans restrict their freedom to work. Most of us would have no interest in such a spectacle anyway, but why do we feel repugnance when faced with what is, according to its defenders, just a mutually consensual exchange? One answer – offered by an association for Little People – is the external effect on other Little People and their collective image. This would lead to a general loss of dignity, not only for the person who agreed to play the game.[19]

The example of prostitution combines, to some extent, all the lines of argument we have already encountered: internalities, the desire not to face up to inequalities (incidentally the policies adopted in such matters sometimes only mask or shift the problem), externalities (such as the damage done to the image of women in general), and the violence and non-consensual exploitation practiced by pimps.

Let us return for a moment to organ transplants. To address the shortage of organs for transplantation, Alvin Roth (who won the Nobel Prize in 2012)[20] and his coauthors invented a new approach designed to increase the number of transplants without involving payment. Their approach was subsequently put into practice. Normally, donations between living people are limited to close relatives or partners. The donor and the receiver might, however, not be compatible (particularly if their blood types are different), which greatly limits the number of possibilities. Roth had the following idea: In the simplest version of the mechanism, A wants to give a kidney to B, and C wants to do the same for D; unfortunately, A and B are incompatible, and so are C and D. Rather than giving up any hope of transplantation, there can be two successful transplants if A and D are compatible, and so are B and C. The four individuals involved are paired off by a centralized exchange mechanism. Four operating rooms are used simultaneously: A gives his kidney to D, and C does the same for B. In the United States, there are exchanges involving many more people when one of the kidneys comes from a deceased person.[21] In France, paired organ exchanges were authorized on an experimental basis under the bioethics law passed in 2011.

Exchange does not necessarily involve money. Economics studies more generally the matching of supply and demand. Economists can promote the common good by constructing better methods of allocation, as has been shown by the creation of paired kidney exchanges and more broadly by the work of researchers on what is now called "market design."

INDIGNATION, A POOR GUIDE TO MORAL JUDGMENT

In addition to these examples of moral dilemmas, taboos change over time and space. As I noted at the beginning of this chapter, this is illustrated by the change in society's attitudes to life insurance and paying interest on loans, two practices that used to be widely condemned as immoral. In the field of economics, negotiable rights to pollute aroused wide distaste twenty years ago, and became more commonplace only when people understood that they advanced the environmental cause. We may be concerned about the extension of the market economy to the so-called noncommercial sector, but economic policies do not map onto an arbitrary dichotomy between commercial and noncommercial domains – or, to return to Kant, between what has to do with the market and what has to do with superior considerations. Moral postures cannot neatly divide up policies.

We feel indignant when confronted, for example, with injustice or behavior that shows little respect for human life. Feeling indignant is often a sign of something wrong with individual behavior or public policies. For all that, indignation can also be a bad counselor. It can lead to the assertion of individual preferences to the detriment of other people's freedom, and it sometimes leads to a lack of thorough reflection.

As Jonathan Haidt, a professor of psychology at New York University, has noted, common morality applies not only to externalities, but also when we condemn behavior that has no identifiable victim.[22] Recall that less than fifty years ago, many people disapproved of sexual relations between people of the same sex, or (for instance in the United States in the not-too-distant past) between people of different races, or involving an unmarried woman (but not an unmarried man). Who were the victims of this behavior that was deemed to be repugnant? Without clearly identifying externalities, the assertion of some people's preferences can quickly override the freedom of others.

So feelings of revulsion are an unreliable source of ethical inspiration. They can provide us with a way forward, or indicate that something is not right in society or in our own behavior, but that is all. It is essential to question these strong moral feelings and ensure we reflect on them in developing public policy. We must better understand the foundations of morality and our fears about the commercialization of certain domains. That is what the academic community seeks to do.

THE MARKET, A THREAT TO SOCIAL COHESION?

Another category of objections to market economics is inspired by a vague unease associated with the loss of social cohesion. Clearly, there are many other contributors to this unease: urbanization, for example, or the replacement of direct by online communication (even though social networks, Skype, and e-mails make it possible to maintain much more frequent contact with family and friends far away). Nonetheless, social cohesion can be weakened by phenomena connected with the market, such as globalization or increased mobility.[23] We now trade with China rather than the neighboring town. We often live far from our relatives and our roots. The political popularity of slogans like "Buy French" or "Buy American" taps into this unease – rather than, as one might hope, a reasoned judgment of the relative merits or needs of French and American workers, compared with those of Chinese or Indian workers.

The market makes relationships anonymous, but that is, in part, its purpose: it is supposed to free people from the economic power others can exercise. In other words, the market limits any one person's or business's power to dictate the terms of trade – for example by preventing powerful firms from imposing high prices and mediocre quality on captive consumers. As those who lament the weakening of social cohesion often note, the market can make possible an ephemeral, anonymous trade – the antithesis of a gift economy. Yet even in modern economies, the notions of reputation and repeated relationships play a crucial role in aspects of trade that are not easy to specify in a contract and therefore depend on the mutual goodwill of the parties. So it is not surprising that the giants of the Internet, from Uber to eBay or Booking.com, have created systems for recording and sharing experiences among users.

But this weakening of social bonds by the market also has its virtues. A gift economy can create dependency. Sociologist Pierre

Bourdieu saw in it a relationship of superiority between the giver and the receiver in which "violence is masked by an appearance of generosity without calculation."[24] More generally, while social bonds have many virtues, they can also be suffocating and restrictive (think about a villager who eats bad bread all his life because he doesn't want to antagonize the local baker). In contrast, the market allows us to extend our sphere of interactions, but only if we build trust. Commerce in fourteenth-century Florence was built on unprecedented trust among merchants. Eighteenth-century writers such as Voltaire and Hume emphasized the necessity of behaving in a civil manner in a trade economy.[25] Montesquieu spoke of "gentle commerce" (*doux commerce*); in his view, the market teaches us to interact with foreigners and to get to know them. The American economist Sam Bowles, a post-Marxist, a former associate of Martin Luther King, and one of the pioneers who broadened economics to other disciplines of the human and social sciences, adopts a similar position in his works, for example in a newspaper column with the evocative title "The Civilizing Effect of Market Economics."[26]

Those who express concern about the impact of the market on social cohesion often conflate three very different issues.

First concern: *The market reinforces the selfishness of its actors, which makes them less capable of forging effective bonds with others.* After all, wasn't it Adam Smith who said famously:

> It is not from the benevolence of the butcher, the brewer, or the baker, that we expect our dinner, but from regard to their own interest. We address ourselves, not to their humanity but to their self-love.

Self-interest seems to be at the heart of the market economy, even if, as Daron Acemoglu[27] (one of our most brilliant contemporary economists) points out, echoing Adam Smith himself, that what matters is not necessarily what motivates the result, but the result itself:

> A deep and important contribution of the discipline of economics is the insight that greed is neither good nor bad in the abstract. When

channeled into profit-maximizing, competitive and innovative behavior under the auspices of sound laws and regulations, greed can act as the engine of innovation and economic growth. But when unchecked by the appropriate institutions and regulations, it will degenerate into rent-seeking, corruption and crime.

Second concern: *The market encourages citizens to distance themselves from traditional institutions, such as their villages and extended families, which weakens their ties to the society that surrounds them.*

Third concern: *The market, as we have already seen, allows citizens to envisage certain transactions that would otherwise be unthinkable – for instance selling their organs or their sexual services – which puts aspects of their private life on the same level as everyday commercial transactions.*

In his book *The Company of Strangers: A Natural History of Economic Life*, my colleague Paul Scabright, director of the Institute for Advanced Studies in Toulouse (IAST), analyzes these three concerns about the influence of the market economy.[28] He notes that, far from relying only on its participants' self-interest, the market also demands from them a significant capacity to establish trust – and nothing is more corrosive of trust than pure selfishness. Seabright shows how, since prehistory, it has been the social aspect of human nature that has allowed us to broaden the sphere of our economic and social exchanges. To be sure, this does not transform us into purely altruistic creatures. The market involves both competition *and* collaboration, and the balance between the two is always delicate.

It is also true that, by allowing us to choose our trading partners, the market makes it easier to break some traditional ties. This is, though, a transformation of inherited ties into chosen ties, not simply a deterioration of social cohesion. In the long run, relationships are probably less durable in a market economy, but neither the durability nor the inheritability of social bonds are virtues in themselves. Who would really regret the disappearance of the strongest social bonds that have ever existed: those between a slave and his master, between a wife and her all-powerful husband, between a worker and a monopsonistic employer, or – to return to a lighter example – the bond between our villager and his not-very-talented baker?[29]

As for the commercialization of some transactions that had previously belonged to the realm of the sacred, Seabright emphasizes how the concept of the realm of the sacred has fluctuated over time and in different cultures. A rejection of explicit commercialization, he says, can coexist with an implicit commercialization: people who are scandalized by the very idea of prostitution or of paying someone to keep them company can nonetheless stay with a spouse whom they no longer love out of a desire for financial security, or out of fear of being alone. There are no easy conclusions in this area, and this observation is not an argument in favor of legalizing the market no matter what, nor in favor of a particular form of regulation (which differs greatly between countries).

Returning to an observation I have already made about inequality, the conclusion I would prefer to draw is that the market is sometimes made a scapegoat for our own hypocrisy. Even when it neither strengthens nor weakens our social bonds, the market becomes a mirror to our souls that reflects realities of our societies, facets of our aspirations, and preferences that we would rather conceal – from ourselves as well as others. We can break the mirror by doing away with the market, but to do so only suspends judgment on our personal and collective values.

INEQUALITY

An analysis of the relationship between the market and morality would not be complete without at least a brief discussion of inequality. The market economy has no reason, a priori, to generate a structure of revenues and wealth that conforms to society's wishes. That is why a redistributive system of taxation has been established in all countries.

Insofar as the market has often been perceived as the cause of increased inequality[30] over the past thirty years, we might speculate that distrust of the market in some countries is a reaction to that increase. Yet this does not seem to be the case. For example, in 2007, the 1 percent of French people who earned the highest salaries earned half as much (in proportion to the country's total income) as their counterparts in the United States. Similarly, post-tax inequality[31] is significantly lower in France than in the United States. Yet twice as many Americans as French people believe in the virtues of the market. Moreover, there is no reason to think that attitudes toward the market depend on the level of inequality; as the Scandinavians demonstrate, a country can adhere fully to the market economy and still use taxation to reduce inequality.

Modern economic science has done a great deal of research on the measurement and understanding of inequality. A whole book could be devoted to the question. Here I would like to simply offer a few remarks concerning what economics can and cannot contribute to the debate on inequality.

Economic Analysis of Inequality

Let us begin with what economists feel most comfortable with when analyzing inequality: documenting it, understanding it, and suggesting effective policies (meaning specifically policies that do not waste public funds) to obtain a given level of redistribution.

Measuring Inequality

The many statistical studies carried out over the past two decades have given us a more precise view of inequality. In particular, the relative increase in the wealth of the top 1 percent has been studied in great detail by economists, notably by Thomas Piketty and his co-authors in their analysis of wealth inequality.[32] The increase in the share of income captured by the top 1 percent has also attracted a great deal of attention. For example, average income in the United States increased 17.9 percent between 1993 and 2012; that of the top 1 percent rose 86.1 percent; while that of the other 99 percent rose only 6.6 percent. The share of income received by the top 1 percent increased from 10 percent in 1982 to 22.5 percent in 2012.[33] Economists have also studied inequality in general along the income ladder, not just the very top and bottom.[34]

Economists have, moreover, devoted much effort to studying the phenomenon of polarization that began in the United States about forty years ago, and which now occurs in most countries. This polarization consists of a significant increase in the earnings of highly skilled workers, and stagnation in the earnings of workers who have few skills; at the same time, the number of workers in occupations that are neither high or low skilled has decreased.[35] Finally, economists have analyzed the decrease in inequality between nations and the reduction of global poverty (a significant decrease mainly due to the dynamism of the increasingly market-oriented Chinese and Indian economies, although their levels of poverty are still much too high).

All these studies measuring inequality are indispensable, because they provide a snapshot of the present situation and highlight the extent of the problem.

Understanding Inequality

The growth of inequality has multiple causes, and the causes depend on the type of inequality we are talking about, income or wealth, as well as on the groups being compared (for instance, the 1 percent vs. the rest).

The increase in the earnings of top earners has been explained in several ways.[36] The first factor is technological change favoring highly skilled workers in information technology, biotech and medicine, banking and other industries.[37] Second, a group of economists[38] has recently shown that economic activity has been reallocated in part to "superstar firms" with high markups on their products. High markups benefit capital and mechanically decrease the share of production that goes to labor.[39] The digital economy's "winner takes all" characteristic has made the founders, investors and employees of Amazon, Apple, Facebook, Google, Microsoft and other successful firms rich; more generally, the firms' ability to raise price, i.e. market power (proxied by how concentrated the industry is), has increased across much of the private sector. The authors also show that industries with larger increases in concentration exhibit a larger decline in labor's share.

Globalization has enabled successful enterprises to rapidly export their model throughout the world.[40] Conversely, in unprotected sectors (subject to international competition), it also puts employees in countries with low salaries in competition with employees in developed countries, offering the former an opportunity to emerge from poverty, but at the same time putting downward pressure on the latter's wages. This has been particularly the case since 1990, when developing and emerging countries abandoned their import substitution policies and converted to the market economy; the cost of container transportation meanwhile fell dramatically. Both factors lifted hundreds of millions of people out of poverty.[41] It is not widely appreciated that the liberalization of trade greatly increases inequality among equally skilled individuals within a given country; this occurs because trade liberalization, while benefitting efficient enterprises (which can export), weakens less efficient ones (faced with competition from imports).[42]

Globalization has also increased competition for talent. Entrepreneurs can choose where to locate their startups, and the best researchers, doctors, artists, and managers are increasingly moving to the locations where they are offered the best conditions. We can deplore it, but it's a fact in our internationalized world. Competition for talent certainly liberates the talented, but it can go too far – as my colleague Roland Bénabou (of Princeton University) and I have recently shown in an article on the culture of bonuses.[43] Firms offer very high, variable remuneration to attract or retain the most talented employees. These rewards are often overly determined by short-term performance. This pushes the beneficiaries, especially the least scrupulous among them, to neglect the long term, or even to engage in unethical behavior.

When an entrepreneur, a researcher, a company, or an asset is lost to another country, the home nation suffers a loss – such as the loss of the jobs that would have been created by the person or the company concerned, the loss of tax revenues, the loss of the transmission of skills and knowledge, and so on. The question is how to measure the phenomenon. At the heart of the problem is a lack of reliable data; the consequent poor quality of empirical studies allows preconceived ideas to take hold on all sides.[44]

It is easy to see the stumbling blocks in the way of researchers who seek to help structure this debate by establishing the facts. Delayed reactions (people don't leave immediately in reaction to a policy they consider unfavorable; the effects are seen over time) complicate econometric assessments. So does the "nonstationary" character of the phenomenon (there are time trends – for instance, the younger generations have a more international mindset and are therefore more likely to leave for another country than their elders were). In addition, we are interested not only in the number of departures, but also in who is departing. Among entrepreneurs, researchers, and the liberal professions, the most talented are also the most likely to move abroad. For example, in the research sector, the number of European researchers who move to the US is small, but the loss occurs disproportionately among the most creative people, who are in great demand.[45] Similarly, losing the new Steve Jobs or the new Bill Gates would be disproportionately expensive in terms of job creation, tax revenues, and the environment of innovation.[46]

Globalization and technology, both of which favor the most highly skilled individuals, are not the only reasons for the top 1 percent's increasing wealth.[47] Some people have pointed the finger at earnings in the finance industry, especially in the US and the UK.

One idea on which economists agree, whatever their attitude toward redistribution, is that not all inequality is the same. Wealth acquired by creating value for society is not equivalent to wealth that comes from economic rents. For example, a very important factor in the increasing inequality of wealth in many countries has been the increase in real estate prices.[48] But the owner of a building, unlike the inventor of a new treatment for cancer, does not create value for society. In the same way, to take an example used by Philippe Aghion in his inaugural lecture at the Collège de France, the Mexican billionaire Carlos Slim – who built his fortune by protecting his businesses from competition and is now one of the richest people in the world – compares unfavorably with peers like Steve Jobs and Bill Gates, who built their careers on innovation. Aghion's conclusion is that we have to redesign fiscal systems so they distinguish clearly between the creation of value and the enjoyment of economic rents, even if, in practice, this distinction is not always easy to make.[49]

Suggesting Solutions and Evaluating Them

Economists can also explain how wealth might be redistributed efficiently, or whether a given policy of redistribution has achieved its objective. Virtually all economists are in favor of simplifying the fiscal system. In many countries (including France), the fiscal complexity and the piling up of taxes and tax loopholes makes taxation completely incomprehensible – but each successive government postpones the tax revolution. Sometimes partial (and often short-lived) reorganization is undertaken, but while each change, taken in isolation, is well-intentioned and wins legislative approval without difficulty, the reformers never consider the coherence of the measures. The same problems constantly recur: the sequence of small benefits granted to the poorest, each individually justifiable, eventually combine to generate threshold effects, setting a "poverty trap" that is very damaging to society.[50]

As in other areas, the evaluation of income redistribution schemes leaves much to be desired.[51] Whether out of ignorance or as a reflex, public discourse seems sometimes to give more importance to the presence of various "markers" of a redistributive policy than to its actual ability to achieve basic objectives. Many supposedly egalitarian policies either disadvantage the intended beneficiaries or bring only minor benefits to them, all while being very expensive for taxpayers, thus threatening in the long run the social welfare system we want to sustain. Chapter 9, on unemployment, shows in detail how policies that are supposed to benefit wage earners – like protecting jobs by making dismissals a matter for the courts, or increasing the minimum wage rather than redistributing more through the tax system – often backfire against their intended beneficiaries, or at least against the most vulnerable.

Here are a few examples, taken from other domains.

In housing, seeking to protect renters who are in arrears appears to be a generous and humane policy. But arrears lead landlords to select renters more carefully, excluding those who are on fixed-term employment contracts and young people (unless their parents can provide guarantees) from the private rental market. Similarly, although it is entirely legitimate to protect renters against abusive rent increases during the term of a lease, a policy of controlling rent increases between lease agreements always produces a rental market in which housing is in short supply and of poor quality. The economic impact of this will fall primarily on those who are struggling the most. Once again, housing policies that appear to be progressive can easily backfire against the individuals most in need of help.

Housing subsidies or benefits in many countries are meant to be an important redistributive tool, but these subsidies have contributed to rent inflation: the supply of housing for rent has not increased in line with demand because the number of tall buildings is limited by regulation in the large cities – the very places where they are most needed. This is good news for landlords, whose earnings are rising thanks to the subsidies, but they are, of course, not the group that the policy is intended to help. Housing subsidies, a powerful tool that is meant to be redistributive, help their intended beneficiaries only moderately, and require high public spending that could be better used for other things.

Another paradoxical example: the French education system claims to have egalitarian goals (through a uniform curriculum, for example), but it creates great inequalities to the detriment of the most disadvantaged and in favor of the better informed and those whose parents live in well-off neighborhoods. State schools in Britain and the US similarly reflect the wealth or poverty of their neighborhoods. Another paradoxical aspect of the supposed egalitarianism of the French educational system is the rejection of selective admission to university. This policy leads to selection by flunking out at the end of the first or second year, with the unfortunate result that the least prepared students not only do not receive diplomas, but are also discouraged or even stigmatized, having wasted one, two, or even three years. This mess has little effect on the elites, whose children are rarely affected by this phenomenon. On the whole, the French educational system is a vast insider-trading crime.

The lesson to be drawn from these examples, along with many others, is that to determine whether a public policy is redistributive or not, it is not enough to know the socioeconomic condition of the groups it targets. We also have to consider all of its potential consequences.

Finally, at a macroeconomic level, the need to control public finances is too often seen as a brake on redistributive policies. Yet by challenging the need for careful monitoring of public expenditure, vocal critics of cautious fiscal policies threaten the sustainability of that very same welfare system; a large decrease in spending on health care and education, and a decline in retirement pensions, which would be bound to result from a fiscal crisis, would represent a de facto rupture of the compact between the state and its citizens and would particularly affect the neediest people.

The Limits of Economics

A Just World?

When we understand the extent of inequality and have analyzed the effects of redistributive policies, we can begin to make choices about the kind of society we want. On this an economist has little to say, except as an ordinary citizen.

In a coherent fiscal system, there is bound to be a trade-off between a little more redistribution and a little less purchasing power or growth (if not, the fiscal system would be badly constructed and in need of improvement). It is, however, difficult to make the right choice when faced with the need to compromise. For one thing, the choice depends on attitudes toward redistribution, a personal value judgment. For another, we do not have all the information we need about the trade-off between redistribution and growth.

This brings me back briefly to the connection between the causes of inequality and the desirability of redistribution. Intuitively, it would be good to know whether someone's income comes down to influential connections or chance – in which case the beneficiary has done nothing to deserve it and the redistribution ought to be total (a tax rate of 100 percent). Many people share this point of view. Even the most conservative American Republicans, who are opposed to many redistributive policies, think disabled people are not responsible for their condition and society should help them. But if, on the contrary, income is the result of an effort or an investment, there is a convincing argument for a tax rate that leaves room for incentives.

The problem is that we have only a vague idea of what generates financial success: Is it effort or circumstances? On this question, economists, sociologists, and psychologists have discovered an astonishing phenomenon: 29 percent of Americans believe that poor people are caught in a poverty trap, and 30 percent believe that success is due to chance and not to effort or education; for Europeans, the figures are 60 percent and 54 percent, respectively.[52] Similarly, 60 percent of Americans (including a large proportion of the poor) and only 26 percent of Europeans answered "yes" to the question: Are poor people poor because they are lazy or lack determination?

These are incompatible views of the world. Many more Americans believe in a just world in which people get what they deserve, and they tend to overestimate social mobility in their country. Are they wrong? Perhaps. But so too are the French, who are probably too pessimistic, even if they can justify their skepticism about the role of merit by pointing to numerous unfair institutions: tax loopholes, closed professions, an educational system that favors the well-off, poor integration of groups descended from immigrants, public decisions made under pressure from interest groups rather than analysis of the common good, or the excessive role played by personal contacts in obtaining internships or permanent jobs (although the work of the sociologist Mark Granovetter shows the same factors with regard to internships are at work in the United States).[53] The truth is that we have little empirical knowledge about the connection between merit and success in most countries, and that is precisely the heart of the problem: in the absence of information, anyone can believe what they want.

But that is not the whole story. However unfounded people's beliefs might be, they are nonetheless consistent with the fiscal and social systems of the countries they live in. Roland Bénabou and I have pointed out that these beliefs about what determines income and wealth, which clearly affect the choices made about taxation and social protection (and which are logically more progressive in Europe, given the difference in beliefs), are in part endogenous.[54] In a country with a weak welfare system, it is better to think that success is heavily dependent on personal effort, and that only hard work can ensure a decent future; the opposite is true in a system with a strong welfare system. Beliefs about the relationship between merit and success have other consequences. For example, the belief in a just world has, as its corollary, a greater stigmatization of the poor and those who depend on social welfare. It can lead to overestimating mobility (which seems to be the case in the United States), but it favors growth and does a better job of connecting merit to net income, which can have beneficial economic effects (though not for the poor), even if the belief in a just world proves to be specious.

Inequality among Whom?

It is also difficult to define the boundaries within which we judge inequality. To appreciate the problem, think about the example of the liberalization of trade, which may have increased inequality in wealthy economies, but has also made it possible for large groups of people in emerging countries to escape from poverty. Or think about our reaction to migrants (even if we do not always realize that immigration flows can bring many benefits to the host country – at least if the labor market does not exclude the newcomers). The question of who is most deserving of attention is an ethical one, regarding which the economist will have a point of view but no specific knowledge to contribute.

Whether well founded or not, ethical judgment strongly determines redistribution policies and economic policies in general. The works of Alberto Alesina, Rez Baqir, and William Easterly have shown that redistribution by providing public goods at the local level is far more successful when the population groups concerned are homogeneous, whether ethnically or religiously.[55] Even if we are personally shocked by communitarian preferences (or national or other forms of narrowly conceived preference regarding redistribution), they are nonetheless realities that confront us when devising public policies.

Just as the way individuals evaluate inequality depends on where they live, the intergenerational horizon may also vary a great deal: How much consideration do we give to our children's and our grandchildren's generations and those that follow? Our societies do not show much generosity toward future generations, despite all the talk of sustainable policies. To be sure, it is likely that technological progress will make future generations wealthier than we are, as well as better protected against disease and old age. But we are bequeathing a very uncertain future to them. Young people in many countries are faced with unemployment (in France, for example, their unemployment rate was 5 percent in 1968; now it is 25 percent) or less attractive jobs (in 1982, 50 percent of newly created jobs offered permanent contracts; only about 10 percent do so today). Taking France again as an illustration, there are many other problems for the young: a housing shortage in desirable areas (implying vigorous competition for flats among potential tenants, many young people living with their parents, and the difficulty of buying a home), schooling that is inadequate and not always suited to the labor market, a halt in social mobility, higher education that is increasingly expensive for families, unfinanced retirement plans, high public debt, global warming, and inequality. Obviously, we cannot claim generosity to future generations, since policies are, in reality, largely guided by the well-being of the generations that are old enough to vote.

Nonfinancial Dimensions of Inequality

Finally, although inequality is usually measured in financial terms (income or wealth), it takes on many other dimensions, such as integration into society. Access to health care is another. Health care inequality is well known, but it is less well understood that this inequity has recently grown greatly. A recent study[56] shows that in the United States, if the income of a man born in 1920[57] was in the top 10 percent, his life expectancy was 6 years longer than if he was in the bottom 10 percent; for women, the difference was 4.7 years. For a man and a woman born in 1950, the difference rose to 14 and 13 years, respectively. Life expectancy between these two cohorts increased by only 3 percent for the most destitute, but by 28 percent for those with high incomes. Researchers are now trying to pinpoint the causes of this disparity, which is crucial for devising the best public policy response. They must begin with the problem of causality: Does poverty generate bad health or is it the other way around, with bad health increasing the risk of poverty? Do the best-off people have a healthier way of life? (The authors of the study suggest as much: in the United

States, smoking, for example, has become a class phenomenon, much more prevalent among the poor.) Do they have access to better health care? All these factors are undoubtedly involved to some extent, but clearly identifying the causes will make it possible to direct public policy toward the areas in which it will have the greatest impact.

Dignity is particularly important. Most people naturally want to feel useful to society rather than a burden on it. In their legitimate demand for respect with regard to their condition, disabled people want more than just money: they also want work.

Ethical questions also arise when it comes to redistributive policies in the labor market – for example, the choice between a higher minimum wage or a minimum income for those of working age. By increasing the minimum wage beyond that of most other countries, France opted to increase the income of the lowest-paid employees by raising their salaries rather than redistributing through the income tax system. This contributed to unemployment among those whose skills placed them around, or below, the minimum wage. These unemployed workers lose their human capital (making them harder to employ in the future), part of their social fabric, and their dignity.

Here then is another debate about morality and the market – one that will prove unavoidable as the automation of the economy progresses, as this will have consequences for virtually all kinds of work. The impact in terms of jobs and social cohesion will be brutal, and I do not believe we are prepared for it.

PART II

THE ECONOMIST'S PROFESSION

THREE

The Economist in Civil Society

> The age of chivalry is gone. That of sophists, economists, and calcu-
> lators has succeeded and the glory of Europe is extinguished forever.
>
> Edmund Burke[1]

THE DISCIPLINE OF ECONOMICS provokes, fascinates, and disturbs.
Sometimes economists become superstars, equally envied and deni-
grated. Relegated to the status of sophists[2] and calculators[3] more than
two centuries ago by Edmund Burke, one of the founding fathers of
British conservatism, economists have always been regarded with a
certain suspicion. They are accused of all thinking the same thing.
But what use would economists be if they could not reach a consensus
about anything?

Economists are simultaneously flattered by, and ill at ease with, the
attention paid to their discipline. They either take refuge in abstrac-
tion or rush to make policy recommendations; they remain in their
ivory tower or set themselves up as dispensers of advice; they work in
obscurity or seek the media spotlight.

What use are economists? Do they all think the same thing? What
exactly do they do? What influence do they have over how society
evolves? These questions deserve an entire book but, failing that, their
importance means we should at least sketch some answers here. The
task is complicated because I am an actor in this debate. This means
that I risk falling into one of two pitfalls that academics face, whatever their field. One is to yield to conformism, complacency, and
corporate defensiveness; the other is to try to present oneself as a free
spirit, independent of one's own community while having built a reputation based on work rooted in the dominant consensus. I have tried

to avoid these pitfalls, but it will be up to the reader to judge whether I have succeeded. By describing an academic economist's everyday life (a life largely unknown to the general public), I would also like to explain the complex links between an economist's research and the uses to which it can be put.

THE ECONOMIST AS PUBLIC INTELLECTUAL

THE ACADEMIC PROFESSION

Whatever his or her discipline, the academic researcher has the good fortune to belong to a profession in which intrinsic motivation is central. The great majority of my colleagues are passionate about their work – "crazy about research," as Jean-Jacques Laffont, the founder of the Toulouse School of Economics, used to say. The same goes for research groups in every academic discipline. The academic community is an attractive working environment, more so than many others.

A distinctive feature of research is its long-term horizon, celebrated by the academic community. With this long horizon comes not only doubt, the equivalent of writer's block, but also moments of genuine intellectual excitement. Henri Poincaré, the great French scientist, described the unparalleled pleasure of discovery: "Thought is only a lightning bolt in the middle of a long night, but this lightning bolt is everything." The researcher's profession is without question a privileged one, offering great freedom and, furthermore, intense moments when confusion suddenly gives way to simplicity and clarity. Then the researcher has, like every teacher, the pleasure of sharing this knowledge.

Of course, intrinsic motivation is not the only driver. Academics are no different from every other profession: they react to their environment and to the incentives they face. They organize and carry out their activity on the basis of both their inner motivation and their desire for recognition from their peers and by society, for promotion, or power, or an ambition to make money.

All researchers care about being recognized by their peers; usually they also want to have the best students, minimize their administrative duties, and increase their quality of life. But the closer an academic discipline comes to concrete applications, as in the case of economics, computer science, biology, medicine, or climatology, the more the extrinsic motivations are likely to multiply: remuneration from private and public sectors, relationships outside academia, the quest for media attention, or a desire for political influence.

The motivations are varied and complex, but in the end they are not what matters. A researcher can develop a theory out of pride, greed, or rivalry with a coworker, but what really counts is that it advances science and is validated through an open process of review.

THE ACADEMIC AND SOCIETY

New Challenges

The implicit contract between the citizen-taxpayer and the researcher that has been in force for the past fifty years is now with increasing frequency being challenged. Researchers, who in the past have sometimes adopted a detached, even irreverent attitude, increasingly need to justify their work collectively to those who fund the system. We are living through a period in which the general public distrusts academic expertise as soon as it affects real-world topics such as economics, medicine, the theory of evolution, climate science, or biology. Public mistrust is buttressed by the scientific community's errors, such as the failure to remove harmful drugs from the market, or scientific fraud connected with nonexistent or falsified data – which affects numerous fields ranging from political science to biology. Economists, as for them, have been blamed for their failure to predict the 2008 financial crisis (in chapter 12, I shall return to this crisis and to the question of the responsibility economists bear).

Confronted with these criticisms, one possible reaction would be to retreat back into the heart of the academic world. This "ivory tower" approach, however, cannot be justified by the academic community en masse. Nations need independent experts to participate in public life, to contribute to debates in decision-making bodies, and in the media. But this is a collective responsibility since some researchers have no appetite for this kind of engagement, lack the ability to intervene effectively, and prefer to work on methodological questions and to specialize in basic research (even though the boundary between basic and applied research is often quite permeable). These academics are an indispensable part of the process of research, but they often feel less at ease than some of their colleagues in talking about its applications.

Academics and the Private Sector

The relationship between universities and industry is often controversial. For detractors, interactions with industry are (at best) a risky activity or (at worst) a kind of corruption of thought, even a pact with the devil. Defenders of the relationship argue that these interactions encourage new lines of research, make it possible to fill gaps in research funding, and more generally improve the competitiveness of the academic environment. Other interactions academics have with the world outside the university provoke a similar debate.

These interactions with the real world, however, are probably one of the best ways for academics to understand the problems facing the economy and society, and to develop and fund relevant, original topics of research that those who stay cloistered in their ivory towers could never imagine. The work of Albert Fert is one example among many. He won the 2007 Nobel Prize in physics for discovering giant magnetoresistance (GMR) while collaborating with Thomson-CSF (now Thales) on the production of adjacent ferromagnetic layers, which are used in making playback heads for computer hard disks. Other recent Nobel Prizes in physics illustrate the same point: Charles Khao, winner for fiber optics in 2009, performed his research in several IT/telecom companies before finally joining academia; one of the 2014 awardees (for the blue light-emitting diode [LED]), Shuji Nakamura, made his discoveries while at Nichia Corporation.[4]

The same may hold for economics as well, as I can testify; several of the studies cited by the Swedish Royal Academy of Sciences in its 2014 report for the economics prize proceeded from new questions that arose in the context of sponsored research contracted by my academic institution with public and private organizations. The economics community can be overly focused on areas of "intensive research"

– the kind that refines existing knowledge – while neglecting fundamental topics staring practitioners in the face, because researchers have not done enough extensive or broad-ranging research of the kind that is needed to explore new scientific territories.

Cautions about the dangers of these different interactions are important, yet they have significant economic value and also a value to society, which is why they are tolerated. Today's ideas, patents, and startups are tomorrow's public policies, tax revenues, and jobs.

The Academic Economist and Public Affairs

The duty of an academic is to advance knowledge. In many cases (mathematics, particle physics, the origins of the universe) perhaps we should not be too preoccupied with the application of knowledge, but only with finding the truth – applications will come later, often in unexpected ways. Research driven only by the thirst for knowledge, no matter how abstract it may be, is indispensable – even in the disciplines that are naturally closest to real-world applications. But academics must also collectively aim to make the world a better place; consequently, they cannot refuse, as a matter of principle, to take some interest in public affairs. Economists, for example, should help to improve sectoral, financial, banking, and environmental regulations, as well as competition law; to improve our monetary and fiscal policies; to reflect on how Europe is organized; to understand how to overcome poverty in developing countries; to make education and health care policies more effective and fair; to foresee the development of (and provide remedies for) inequality; and so on. They should also take part in government hearings, interact with the administration, and sit on technical commissions.

Researchers have an obligation to society to take positions on questions on which they have acquired professional competence. For researchers in economics, as in all other disciplines, this is risky. Some fields have been well explored, others less so. Knowledge changes, and what we think is correct today could be reevaluated tomorrow.

Finally, even if there is a professional consensus, it is never total. Ultimately, a researcher in economics can, at most, say that, *given the current state of our knowledge*, one option is better than another. This word of caution applies to all the proposals I make in this book, but it is not the sole prerogative of economists: A climatologist may indicate areas of uncertainty regarding the extent and causes of global warming, but can also usefully present likely scenarios given the current state of our knowledge. A professor of medicine can likewise give an opinion on the best way to treat a type of cancer or degenerative disease. Thus academics must maintain a delicate balance between necessary humility and the determination to convince their interlocutors of both the usefulness of the knowledge they have acquired and its limits. This is not always easy, because others will find certainties easier to believe.

THE PITFALLS OF INVOLVEMENT IN SOCIETY

Academics who become involved in public and business life are driven by the intrinsic motivation at the heart of their profession: the advancement and communication of knowledge. But they also respond to extrinsic motives: additional remuneration, or recognition by a wider audience. These extrinsic motives are not a problem as long as they do not change behavior within and outside academia – but they do present a danger.

ADDITIONAL REMUNERATION

The first temptation is financial. This is something of a taboo subject, including in countries (like France) where academic pay is much lower than in some leading scientific countries like the US, the UK, or Switzerland. It is customary to assert that academics do not choose to do research for financial reasons. It is true that many of them could have chosen a better-paid profession, but opted for a career as a researcher because it appealed to them – but that does not mean that they do not care about their salaries, or that they should have to sacrifice whatever interests them intellectually to earn more. In practice, although some researchers resign themselves to a university salary, the great majority of those with international reputations supplement their incomes in various ways, depending on their domain of research and their own preferences. These may include giving additional occasional or regular courses; holding permanent positions in foreign universities; founding start-ups; registering patents; consulting for private enterprises and public organizations; taking partnerships in auditing or consulting firms; writing textbooks or books aimed at the general reader; having a private medical or legal practice; appearing as a witness in an antitrust suit or before regulatory authorities; holding directorships; receiving speaker fees for keynote talks at conferences; and so on.

Some people condemn the tolerance that universities have for these practices. For the reasons I have given (and not just because I take on some work outside my everyday university role) I do not agree. These activities usually have social utility. Furthermore, in countries where academic salaries are low, tolerance is the price the country has to pay to keep many of its best researchers, who – unlike previous generations – are entirely internationalized and completely mobile.

But it would be equally irresponsible to ignore the two dangers of these extracurricular activities. First of all, they may reduce the time spent on the primary goals of research and teaching. This distraction does not seem to me to be a serious problem, as long as the researchers face independent evaluations of their academic contribution. Researchers who neglect their research and teaching in favor of external activities should not be treated on the same terms – salary, teaching load, and more generally, working conditions – as their colleagues who remain faithful to their core mission. Similarly, the evaluation of teachers by students has always seemed fundamental to me, despite its well-known shortcomings (good evaluations sometimes reward crowd pleasers, while good professors whose opinions are not very popular or who give tough grades get bad evaluations). Unfortunately, those who oppose academics undertaking external activities also often reject the principle of independent evaluation.

In my view, the greater danger lies in the "corruption" of academic activity or the "capture" of researchers by their personal stake in other activities. In particular, academics may be tempted to change the way they talk about things to indulge the firms or administrations who are paying them or providing their research budgets. I shall return to this subject later.

The Temptation of the Media

Academics can also be tempted by the media, for good (knowledge transfer) and bad (attention seeking) reasons. Seeing one's name or face in the newspaper or on television flatters the ego. At the same time, in a democracy it is important for experts to communicate with the public so that access to expertise is not confined to a small elite. Many academics regularly appear in the media. Whether this is to satisfy their egos or to serve the common good, once again the result is more important than the motivation.

The media is not, however, a natural habitat for an academic. The distinctive characteristic of academics, their DNA, is *doubt*. Their research is sustained by their uncertainty. The propensity for putting forward arguments and counterarguments – as academics systematically do in specialized articles, in a seminar, or in a lecture hall – is not easily tolerated by decision makers, who have to form an opinion rapidly. "Give me a one-handed economist. All my economists say, 'on the one hand ... on the other hand,'" President Harry Truman is supposed to have said in exasperation. But above all, academic reasoning is ill adapted to the format of television or radio debates. Slogans, sound bites, and clichés are easier to put across than a complex argument concerning the multiple effects of a policy; even weak arguments are difficult to refute without engaging in a long explanation. Being effective often means acting like a politician: you offer a simple – or even simplistic – message, and stick to it. Do not misunderstand me: academics should not try to hide behind scientific uncertainty and doubt. As far as possible, they must reach a judgment. To do that, they have to overcome their natural instincts, put things in perspective, and convince themselves that, in these circumstances, some things are more probable than others: "In the present state of our knowledge, my best judgment leads me to recommend ..." They have to act like a doctor deciding which treatment is best, even in the face of scientific uncertainty.

But that presents another hitch: since scientific knowledge is constantly evolving, it is natural to change one's mind. Yet intellectuals participating in public debates often stick to their past positions to avoid appearing to flip-flop. To be sure, this intellectual determination to stick to a position also occurs within academia, but an academic's research is constantly being questioned in seminars and conferences around the world, and the need to publish in journals with anonymous peer review (I shall return to this) opens conclusions to challenge.

Moreover, although remarks made in the media are widely repeated in tweets and blogs, colleagues rarely comment on their scientific merit and mostly engage in casual water cooler remarks about their colleague's celebrity. As with their external consulting activities, unfortunately academics sometimes advance arguments in the media that they would never dare to defend – or would rapidly correct – if they made them in a seminar or a specialized journal.

Finally, appearing in the media exposes an academic to questions on subjects on which he or she is not an expert, even if they fall broadly within that academic's field. (The propensity to offer comment outside one's own area of expertise is sometimes called "Nobel Prize Syndrome"!) It is not easy to say, "I won't give you an answer because I have nothing to say about that." So one has to strike a difficult balance: Should we go ahead and answer even if we are not specialists on the subject, but simply have some knowledge picked up from conversations with trustworthy academic colleagues or wider reading? Or if we can simply rely on common sense?

THE CALL OF POLITICS

For Plato, philosophers – caring little about the organization of the *res publica* and not considered useful by ordinary mortals – were free, in contrast to politicians, who were constantly absorbed by public life. In this spirit, neither the UK nor the United States has a strong tradition of intellectuals engaged in public life.[5] By contrast, there is a longstanding tradition in France celebrating the politically engaged intellectual, "*l'intellectuel engagé*."[6] I will not reproach all academics and intellectuals who take political positions; many do so out of conviction. And many do it well. Moreover, researchers may find neglected lines of research to pursue as a direct result of this engagement. But my view – and this is strictly a personal opinion – is that we should have three reservations about the notion of the politically engaged intellectual.

First, the academic with a political message is quickly pigeonholed ("left-wing," "right-wing," "Keynesian," "neo-classical," "liberal," "anti-liberal") and the labels will be used to either support or discredit what he or she says, as if the role of a researcher, in any discipline, was not to create knowledge, disregarding preconceived ideas and labels.

The audience all too often forgets the substance of the argument, instead judging the conclusion on the basis of their own political convictions. They will welcome the argument favorably or unfavorably depending on whether the academic seems to be on their side or not. In these circumstances, an academic's participation in public debate loses much of its social utility. It is already difficult enough to avoid being drawn into politics. For example, when a question is about a technical subject on which the government and the opposition disagree, the academic's every response will be quickly interpreted as a political position. This can inadvertently drown out the message and prevent it from contributing to an enlightened debate.

Second, by becoming politically engaged, intellectuals risk losing their freedom of thought. An extreme but particularly striking example is the way many left-wing intellectuals and artists remained blind to, and then in denial of, obvious totalitarianism – particularly in the Soviet, Maoist, and Cuban experiments. It was not that these intellectuals endorsed the privation of freedoms, the genocides, the economic and environmental chaos, or the repression of cultural innovation – on the contrary, the products of totalitarianism represented everything they hated – but their political commitment had deprived them of critical thinking. Of course, we can also find many intellectuals who did not succumb to the sirens of "progress," such as Albert Camus and Raymond Aron in France, George Orwell in the UK, and many well-known economists, but the moral equivocation of the intelligentsia in this tragic historical episode is nonetheless striking. Few intellectuals today would adopt such extreme positions, but the lesson stands: political engagement involves the risk of sticking to an untenable position so as not to disappoint one's allies or a public audience.

Third, as in the case of the media, the relationship between the scientific and the political is uncomfortable, even though many politicians show some intellectual curiosity. Academics' and politicians' time horizons differ, as do the constraints they face. The researcher's role is to analyze the world as it is and to propose new ideas, freely, without the constraint of having to produce an immediate result. Politics necessarily lives in the present, always under the pressure of the next election. However, these very different time pressures, in response to very different demands, cannot justify a visceral mistrust of the political class.[7] Academics can help politicians make decisions by providing them with tools for reflection, but cannot take their place.

The Trap of Labels

Returning to the way we label researchers, economists, like any other researchers, have to go where theories and facts take them, without any intellectual constraints. In private, of course, they are ordinary citizens, forging their own opinions and perhaps making political commitments. But as soon as personal leanings (such as attachment to a political cause or a school of economic thought) become public, they may suggest that the researcher has sacrificed academic integrity for a personal agenda, whether it involves the media, politics, ideology, or money.

More insidiously, these labels cause economics to run the risk of being perceived as a science with no consensus on key questions, meaning economists' views can be safely ignored. This overlooks the fact that, although their personal opinions may be different, leading economists agree on many subjects – at the very least on what must *not* be done, even if they do not agree on what should. This is just as well. If there were no majority opinion, financing research in economics would be hard to justify, despite the colossal importance of economic policies. However, research and professional debate concern questions economists understand less well – this is what is distinctive about research – and that are therefore likely to inspire only limited consensus. And it goes without saying that professional consensus can, and should, develop as the discipline advances.

A FEW SAFEGUARDS FOR AN ESSENTIAL RELATIONSHIP

There is no perfect way to regulate the interactions between researchers and society outside the academic milieu, but a few practices can clarify researchers' relationship to society without diminishing its potential synergies.

INDIVIDUAL BEHAVIOR

As in any profession, the personal ethics of academics will affect their behavior. Two basic rules might be:

1. debate ideas, never persons (no ad hominem arguments);
2. never say anything you are not prepared to defend before your peers in a seminar or at a conference.

An ethical charter also helps remind researchers of certain basic principles concerning the transparency of their data and the methodology they should follow, along with the duty to divulge potential conflicts of interest. It is obviously difficult to give a precise statement of conflicts of interest because, as we have seen, they are so multifarious and context dependent. Similarly, it is not easy to define a researcher's duty when the research is used by third parties who ignore the careful caveats in the work: Where does the academic's responsibility stop in a case like this? In the end, ethical principles, whether they are stated in a formal code of conduct or simply personal rules, are always fragile, because they have to be observed in spirit, not just the necessarily imperfect letter. Nonetheless, these ethical principles play an essential role, and the profession should defend them vigorously.

INSTITUTIONAL PARTNERSHIPS

The partnerships formed between a group of researchers (in a laboratory or a university) and any private or public organization also have to obey certain rules. The challenge for these research institutions is to preserve complete freedom for their researchers – even at the risk that the external partner will not renew its funding – while at the same time responding to the legitimate demand that research financed in this way must have some bearing on the funders' interests. The world's greatest universities all face this challenge and have responded to it in a way that is mostly satisfactory, offering their researchers extraordinary intellectual freedom. This too is a complicated question, and there are several possible models.

Here I will limit myself to sketching a few ideas, rather than claiming to cover the subject definitively or pretending that these safeguards apply to all academic environments. There are at least six foundations of intellectual independence: agreement regarding the objective of the contract and its terms and conditions; a long-term perspective; a diversity of partnerships; the right to publish freely; validation of the research by the best international journals; and independent governance.

Being clear about these principles before signing a research contract helps select appropriate partners – those who accept the conditions are, by definition, prepared to play by the rules. A long-term arrangement that accommodates the speed at which research can be done encourages independence, which is a guarantee of credibility: over the medium and long run, authors of reports seeking to support special interests are often discredited. Having a number of contracts with different partners is also a guarantee of independence, because it makes it easier to resist any pressure to take a particular position. If you are dependent on just a few, it is harder to resist this type of pressure.

The need for researchers' right to publish freely is obvious. What's more, it is important to insist that the work will be validated by the best international professional journals, a process perhaps unfamiliar to nonacademics. "Peer-reviewed" professional journals allow others in the field to evaluate the work: An article submitted to a journal is sent to several specialists for review. These referees write an evaluation for the editor of the journal, who sends their (anonymized) reports to the author along with a decision regarding publication. Anonymity is crucial: if the author knew the identity of the referees, the referees might pull their punches.

In the great majority of academic fields, professional journals are ranked by their quality.[8] In economics, for example, the five "generalist" journals most widely read by the academic community[9] are the most selective in choosing which articles to publish (the acceptance rate for articles ranges from 5 to 10 percent); the articles they publish are also the ones most often cited. Then come the best specialized (or "field") journals, and so on. They all use referees from around the world.

For one thing, validation by international professional journals reminds researchers of an important goal in partnering with private or public organizations: the pursuit of pioneering research on new problems. Furthermore, whereas financial considerations, media appeal, politics, or simply friendship may lead academics to advance arguments they would never dare defend – or would immediately retract – if they were among academics, the requirement to publish in the best professional journals is a test: if the theory or the collection and processing of data is biased in favor of the organization financing the research, the journal's reviewers may spot it. The obligation to publish acts as a form of long-term intellectual discipline.

Finally, it is important to create an external supervisory authority in some form to intervene if the reputation of the institution is in danger of being tarnished by short-term considerations. This should consist of an independent board of directors or trustees (an institution's academics cannot sit in verdict on themselves) and entirely external scientific councils and advisory committees playing a complementary role to that of the peer review process, evaluating the institution's academic integrity and reporting to the board of directors.

FROM THEORY TO ECONOMIC POLICY

I would like to conclude this chapter with a few remarks (which are personal and no doubt a little idiosyncratic) concerning the way ideas help to inform public policy.

Keynes described economists' influence this way: "Practical men, who believe themselves to be quite exempt from any intellectual influences, are usually the slaves of some defunct economist."[10] This grim view is not entirely out of step with reality. Whatever area of economics they pursue, there are two ways in which researchers can influence debate on economic policy and the choices made by businesses (there is no single good model, and we all act in accordance with our own temperament). The first is by getting involved themselves. Some, overflowing with energy, succeed in doing so, but it is rare that a researcher can continue to do extensive research and be very active in public debate at the same time.

The second way is indirect: economists employed by international organizations, government ministries, or businesses, read the work of academics and put it to use. Sometimes this work is a technical research article published in a professional journal; sometimes it is a version written for the general public.

The technical nature of microeconomic debates over competition policy, the prudential regulation of banks, or the regulation of network industries (telephone, railroad, electricity, or postal service) need not be an obstacle to economic decisions being based on this research. In fact, decision-making power in these areas has often been entrusted to independent authorities (a competition authority, central bank, or sectorial regulator, for example). These authorities are much less politically constrained than ministers in their choices, and they can more easily incorporate technical and economic knowledge into their decisions. The journey from idea to action has accelerated since Keynes made his observation.

FOUR

The Everyday Life of a Researcher

The world of economic research is not well known to the public. What could academic economists possibly do with their time when they are not teaching students? How does the creation of knowledge in economics happen? How is economic research evaluated? Research in economics has been much criticized in recent years. Some of these criticisms are justified and others are not, but all have raised important questions: Is economics a science? Is it too abstract, too theoretical, too mathematical? Do economists have a distinct way of seeing the world compared to other social sciences? Is the discipline too dominated by orthodoxy and by the English-speaking world?

This chapter and the following one try to answer these questions. I begin by describing what researchers do on a typical day, the process of modeling, and empirical validation in economics. Next, I describe the strengths and weaknesses of the process of evaluating research. Then I examine economists' cognitive characteristics: Are they different from specialists in other disciplines? Are they "foxes" or "hedgehogs," to adopt the distinction introduced by philosopher Isaiah Berlin (foxes know many things, hedgehogs know one big thing)? I discuss the use of mathematics. Finally, I describe two tools that have revolutionized the discipline over the past forty years: game theory and information theory. I end with a discussion of the importance of methodological innovations.

THE INTERPLAY BETWEEN THEORY AND EMPIRICAL EVIDENCE

As with most academic disciplines, research in economics requires a combination of theory and empirical evidence. Theory provides the conceptual framework. It is also the key to understanding the data. Without a theory – that is, without a system of interpretation – data is no more than some interesting observations, implying no conclusions for economic policy. Conversely, a theory is enriched by empirical evidence that may invalidate its hypotheses or conclusions, and thus can improve or overturn it.

Like all academics, economists learn by groping their way forward by trial and error. They adhere to the method of the philosopher Karl Popper, who argued that all sciences are founded on (imperfect) observations of the world, and that the scientific method consists in deducing general laws from these observations, corroborated by further testing. This process of constantly shuttling back and forth between theory and empirical evidence never produces certainty, but it gradually increases our understanding of the phenomena under study.

At the time of Adam Smith, economic theory was descriptive, but it has been gradually mathematicized. Historically, theory has played a very important role in the development of the discipline of economics. To mention only a few names that will be familiar to readers, Kenneth Arrow, Milton Friedman, Paul Krugman, Paul Samuelson, Amartya Sen, Robert Solow, and Joseph Stiglitz have built their careers on their theoretical insights, as have (at least in part) many economists who became well known to the public as central bankers (e.g., Ben Bernanke, Stanley Fischer, Mervyn King, Raghuram Rajan, and Janet Yellen), as Treasury secretary (e.g., Larry Summers), as chief economists of multilateral organizations (e.g., Olivier Blanchard, who was an influential economic counsellor and director of the Research Department at the International Monetary Fund from 2008 through 2015), or as heads of the Council of Economic Advisors. Let us note that the great majority of the names I've just mentioned are macroeconomists (who analyze the behavior of the economy in the aggregate rather than individual markets or organizations). Media attention has tended to focus on only a few areas of the discipline, despite the fact that microeconomists have had no less of an influence on policy, for example competition policy and regulation, through their academic writings, in their capacity of chief antitrust enforcer or chief economist in agencies,[1] or as government advisers on various policy issues (such as Sir Nick Stern on climate change).

For several decades, empirical data has rightly played an increasingly important role in economics. There are many reasons for this: the improvement of the statistical techniques applied to econometrics, the development of techniques such as randomized controlled trials like those used in medicine, and a systematic use of experiments in the laboratory and in the field. These approaches were at one time quite rare, but they are now used widely in top universities. Finally, new technology has made possible the rapid and widespread dissemination of databases, helped analyze data using efficient and inexpensive software programs, and provided greater computing power. Today, Big Data is enriching the empiricist's toolbox.

Many nonspecialists view economics as essentially a theoretical science, and do not appreciate how far this is from the truth. Although theory continues to play a crucial role in the development of public policies, from competition law to monetary policy and financial regulation, policy takes data into account much more than it used to; in truth, a large part of current research is empirical. As early as the 1990s, most of the articles published in the *American Economic Review*, one of the five most influential journals in the profession, were already empirical or applied.[2] That is unquestionably still the case today. Most of the rising stars at prestigious American universities have turned to applied work, though without abandoning theory.[3]

At heart, modeling in economics is rather like modeling in engineering. Economists start with a real-world problem, whether it is well recognized or a new question posed by a public or private decision maker. They then identify the substantive core of the problem in order to focus on the essentials. The theoretical model is said to be ad hoc: it is never an exact representation of the truth, but a simplification, and its conclusions can never explain reality as a whole. There is always a trade-off between a theoretical model describing behavior in a detailed and realistic way, and the much greater difficulty of analyzing such a model in more general terms.

An analogy with some familiar concepts from physics might be useful at this point. The Newtonian theory of gravitation and the theory of ideal gases are founded on hypotheses that we now know to be false.[4] These theories have, however, proved to be important in two ways: first, later theories (such as the theory of relativity) would probably never have been formulated without them. The simplicity of the theories made them easier to understand and so made it possible to move on to the next stage. Second, Newton's laws and the theory of ideal gases have been excellent approximations in many environments (low velocities in the case of Newton's laws, and low pressures in the case of the theory of ideal gases), and thus have direct applications. In most sciences, especially the social sciences, approximations have proved to be much less precise than those derived from these examples from physics, but their usefulness is undeniable.

I do not pretend to compare the precision of predictions in the social and human sciences with those of Newtonian theory. In some ways, the human and social sciences are more complex than either the natural or life sciences. Some people argue that the social sciences are too complex to be modeled at all. Human beings are governed by many motivations, some of them dependent on their environment. They make mistakes, and their emotions influence them to behave in ways that others would consider irrational. The social sciences are at the heart of the organization of our society, however, and so we must try to make progress in them. Fortunately for researchers in the social sciences (whose work would otherwise be hard to justify), patterns of individual and collective behavior can be observed.

An Example

Without going into the details of the analysis to follow in chapter 8, we can take global warming as an example. Climatologists observe that we have only a small "carbon budget," that is, the volume of greenhouse gases (GHG) that we can still emit before we reach the maximum threshold of a 1.5 or 2.0 degree Celsius increase in global surface temperature. Economists rely on this consensus among climatologists, and take it as their point of departure. Their challenge is to describe the policies that will allow us, at a reasonable cost, to remain below this threshold. To do this they have to model the behavior of the agents emitting GHGs: businesses, government agencies, and households. To make a start, they assume – and this is a hypothesis – that these will all make a rational choice: if the cost of avoiding pollution is higher than the cost they are made to pay for emitting pollutants, they will choose to pollute, otherwise they will abate; in other words, they will act in their material self-interest.

The next step in modeling behavior is a normative analysis of regulation. Economists ask what arrangement might produce the result the regulator would favor. Once again, we adopt a simple, even simplistic, hypothesis to get a sense of what is going on. The assumed aim is to limit the cost of implementing the environmental policy. Otherwise the policy would decrease the purchasing power of consumers, make businesses less competitive, and reduce employment – and would also increase the fervor and persuasiveness of lobbyists who oppose this type of environmental policy.

If regulators knew enough about each business, they could adopt an "administrative" approach and simply order the firm to cease polluting every time the cost of not polluting dropped below a specific level. If this approach were adopted, this level would have to be set to keep the global temperature increase below the maximum threshold. However, regulators are unlikely to have enough information to take this approach. In this case, the economic analysis shows that it is better for society to trust the firm to make the decision, making it responsible for its pollution by requiring it either to pay a carbon tax or to purchase negotiable emission permits.[5] This analysis goes back to the work of the British economist Arthur Cecil Pigou, first published in 1920; it leads to straightforward economic policy recommendations that have greatly contributed to the success of environmental policy in the past thirty years.

But, of course, this is only an initial approximation. The actors do not behave exactly as we have described. They do not always have the information to allow them to make good economic decisions (for example, about the level of the carbon tax that a polluting business will have to pay twenty years from now). They may also not always maximize their economic profits. The actors might have a genuine environmental conscience, or they might want to behave virtuously in the eyes of their neighbors or colleagues. A company may wish to behave in a more socially responsible way.[6]

A deeper analysis thus involves consideration of economic agents' social preferences and the imperfect nature of their information. Then numerous other relevant factors, such as the credibility of the state's commitment, the uncertainty of the science of climatology, innovation, negotiations between states, geopolitics, and so on come into play. Enriching the analysis also involves testing the underlying hypotheses. For example, the recommendation that an economic instrument like a carbon tax or negotiable emission rights should be used rather than the case-by-case administrative approach is based on the hypothesis that regulators lack enough information (or else that a case-by-case approach might lead unscrupulous regulators to grant special privileges to their friends or to powerful pressure groups). Although this seems justified anecdotally, it is also only a hypothesis. We can either study it directly or verify it indirectly by studying its consequences. Economists have conducted empirical studies showing that, depending on the type of pollutant, the use of an administrative approach increases the cost of an ecological policy by between 50 and 200 percent. This confirms our intuition that regulators have incomplete information about the best ways to reduce pollution.

THEORETICAL FORMULATION

To get back to the general issue of economic modeling, a lot of the difficulty of the exercise lies in defining its scope. Since it is not feasible to take everything into consideration, we have to distinguish between what is important and what is merely anecdotal (and can therefore be safely ignored). Researchers' experience and their discussions with practitioners prove very useful at this stage, even if – once the problem has been better understood and, if possible, explored empirically – it is ultimately necessary to return to the initial assumptions. Any model will therefore be at best a metaphor for (and at worst a caricature of) reality.

The economist's construction of a model, whether it is a model of the internal organization of a firm, competition in a market, or a macroeconomic mechanism, needs a description of the decision makers' goals as well as hypotheses about their behavior. For example, we can assume, as a first approximation, that capitalist enterprises seek to maximize their profits to satisfy their shareholders; this calculation is, of course, intertemporal.[7] It is often in the long-term interest of the firm to sacrifice short-term gains – for example, by respecting the interests of employees, suppliers, or customers and by spending on equipment or maintenance – in order to reap profits in the long term. If necessary, we can refine our simplistic hypothesis of profit maximization with an enormous body of knowledge about the governance of businesses and the effects of the incentives offered to CEOs and boards of directors. In this way, we can understand and incorporate behavior that is distinct from the analytical framework of maximization of profit – for example the emphasis that business leaders may in reality put on short-term profits to the detriment of long-term profits.

So far as behavior is concerned, remember that our initial assumption was that decision makers act in a rational manner – i.e., in their best interests as assumed – given the limited information available to them. Once again, we can refine this basic analysis thanks to recent research into behavior that exhibits limited or bounded rationality. Finally, we need to model the way in which multiple actors, for example competitors in a market, interact. For this, game theory is useful (I shall return to this).

This pared-down, even simplistic, model allows us on the one hand to predict what will happen in a market or the economy as a whole and, on the other hand, to formulate recommendations for private or public decision makers – in other words, for economic policy making. More than other social sciences, economics claims to be normative; it aspires to "change the world." Analyzing individual and collective behavior and finding certain patterns in it is important; but the ultimate goal is economic policy.

Thus, economics compares the costs and benefits of alternative policies. It could stop at selecting the solution that gives society the greatest net benefit (the benefits less the costs). This would be the right approach if it might be possible to compensate through transfers those who would lose out from the policy. In the absence of such transfers, the analysis is more complex, because public decision makers must then weigh the well-being of different actors, deciding which ones they want to prioritize.

Although they are pared down and simplistic, these models can nevertheless be quite complicated to analyze. Criticism is easy, but the art of modeling is difficult – and criticism of a model is not very useful if there is no viable alternative. Consequently, although debates in seminar rooms and lecture halls may be lively, although reviews by anonymous referees in international professional journals are often unsparing, and although the academic community agrees that questioning theories is essential, criticism is only truly useful if it is constructive.

The economist's approach is that of "methodological individualism," according to which collective phenomena are the result of individual behavior and in their turn affect individuals' behavior. Methodological individualism is fully compatible with (and perhaps even indispensable to) the comprehension and subtle analysis of group phenomena. Economic agents react to incentives, some of which derive from the social groups to which they belong: they are influenced by social norms; they yield to conformism and fashions, construct multiple identities, behave gregariously, are influenced by the individuals with whom they are directly or indirectly connected in social networks, and tend to think like just other members of their communities.[8]

Empirical Tests

Once a theory has been formulated and its implications understood, we need to test the robustness of the results against the initial hypotheses and, as far as possible, test the model's hypotheses and predictions. We can imagine two kinds of tests (three, if we include the "common sense test"). If past data are available in large quantities and are of sufficient quality, we can subject the model's predictions to econometric tests. Econometrics is the application of statistics to economics and more generally to the social sciences; it determines the degree of confidence we can have in the relationship between several variables.

But maybe the data are insufficient or the world has changed so much that past data are not a reliable guide to the present. For example, when governments decided in the 1990s to put radio spectrum frequencies up for auction (rather than allotting them free of charge, as they had often done in the past), they had to proceed in two stages.

From a theoretical point of view, they had to decide how best to sell the spectrum over several geographical zones, knowing that telecom companies might be more interested in one segment of spectrum if they also had contiguous segments. Furthermore, once the government had decided on an auction, they had to determine whether the businesses really understood the mechanism for the sale – and also whether the economists designing the auction had overlooked details that could become important when it was implemented. (Had they, for example, accounted for the possibility that buyers might try to manipulate the auction mechanism?) For these reasons, both economists and governments conducted experiments to check the theory before putting the radio spectrum up for sale. The auctions have since brought in a great deal of money for public treasuries (sixty billion dollars in the United States alone since 1994).

There are two alternatives to standard econometrics: experiments in the field and experiments in the laboratory. In a field experiment, a sample of individuals may be, for example, subjected to a "treatment" in an environment distinct from that of a "control" sample, to analyze differences in behavior and consequences as a result. Experimentation using random sampling[9] is a well-trodden procedure in physics, the social sciences, marketing, and medicine (in the latter case, for clinical trials of drugs and vaccines). Let us recall, for instance, that in 1882, Pasteur had randomly divided a group of fifty sheep into two subgroups – one vaccinated, the other not – and had them all injected with anthrax to test a vaccine.

Sometimes the sample is naturally divided into two parts; then we speak of a "natural experiment" – for example, two identical twins who have been separated at birth and brought up in different families. A social scientist can then try to distinguish innate characteristics from those acquired from the social environment. Another example is when a person's fate is determined not by their choices, which depend on individual characteristics or circumstances, but by a lottery (for example, admitting pupils to school or assigning conscripts to their units).[10]

Economists have developed and deployed a methodology for "randomized control trials" (RCTs), using control and treatment groups to study, for instance, the impact of new electricity tariffs, new forms of health insurance, or support for the unemployed. This approach has come to play a particularly important role in development economics.[11] A famous example of this approach is the *Progresa* program, which was set up in Mexico in 1997 to fight poverty. It gives money to mothers on the condition that they allow medical supervision of their family, that their children attend school regularly, and that they promise to devote part of the family's budget to food. This program was evaluated using an RCT.

Similarly, the situation captured in a theoretical model can be recreated in the laboratory by having subjects (students, lay persons, professionals) act it out and observing what happens. This method of laboratory experimentation won a Nobel Prize in 2002 for psychologist Daniel Kahneman and economist Vernon Smith. A famous experiment conducted by Vernon Smith analyzed markets such as those for government bonds or commodities. It divided the participants into two equal categories: sellers (with one unit to sell) and buyers (who could buy one unit). Actors who did not exchange anything received nothing except the initial sum they were paid for taking part in the experiment. Gains other participants could make from exchange above this initial sum were set by the experimenter (and also varied from group to group – they were determined by drawing lots). For example, a buyer might gain $10 - p$, where p was the price he paid and 10 represented his willingness to pay (that is, the maximum he was prepared to pay to go ahead with the transaction). Similarly, a seller might be allocated a cost of 4, so that he would emerge from the experiment with a gain of $p - 4$ if he sold at the price p. The theoretical outcome is a price p^* such that the number of sellers with costs lower than p^* is equal to the number of buyers willing to pay more than p^*. The market is then said to be in equilibrium. But what happens when the sellers and buyers know only their own valuations (cost or willingness to pay) and have to make offers to buy and sell? The details make some difference, but the classic result obtained by Vernon Smith was that prices and quantities exchanged do indeed converge toward the theoretical competitive equilibrium when there are enough buyers and sellers.[12] Finally, many lab experiments seek to measure the effectiveness of public policies or business strategies, while others seek to test whether real-world behaviors conform to those that are predicted by economic theory: For example, do the bidders really understand what strategy they should adopt in different auction mechanisms?[13]

Laboratory experiments – which are also randomized – can more easily be replicated and allow us greater control over the agents' environment than an experiment conducted in the field. They are like the tests engineers conduct in wind tunnels. The drawback is that the environment is more artificial than in a field experiment.

Experiments conducted both in laboratories and in the field are not just used in economics and psychology, but also in other human and social sciences, notably political science, where they are helping to improve the understanding of executive decision making.

Is Economics a Science?

The field of economics is scientific in the following sense.[14] Its hypotheses are explicit, meaning they are open to criticism, and its conclusions and their scope follow from logical reasoning, the application of the deductive method. These conclusions can then be tested using the tools of statistics. On the other hand, economics is not an exact science, as its predictions are far from having the precision of, for example, those of celestial mechanics. Like seismologists studying earthquakes or physicians worrying about the possibility of a patient having a heart attack, economists who try to predict a banking or exchange-rate crisis are more comfortable identifying factors that might lead to this event than they are trying to specify the date it will happen – or even whether it will happen at all. I will return on several occasions to the question of prediction, but it is useful to emphasize here that there are two obstacles to predictability. The first is common to most of science: a lack of data or a partial comprehension of the phenomenon. For example, economists can have only partial knowledge of a bank's true balance sheet or of the banking regulator's competence and true objectives; they can understand that mutual exposures among banks and other financial institutions may give rise to a domino effect and a systemic crisis following the failure of one of them without really grasping the complex dynamics that would propagate such a crisis.

The second obstacle to predictability is specific to the social and human sciences. In certain circumstances, even if they have all the relevant information and understand the situation perfectly, economists can still find prediction difficult. The fact that my choices will depend on your choices creates "strategic uncertainty" – that is, a difficulty in predicting how each will behave – for an observer. This is the world of "self-fulfilling prophecies" and "multiple equilibria," of which there will be more examples later in this book,[15] and which can produce a run on a bank or an attack on a currency. For now, we should note that a recurrent theme in economic policy is that citizens may wish to coordinate their choices and form pressure groups to influence political decision making. If I, acting alone, were to decide to build my house near an airport, that would not be enough to prevent a future expansion of the airport, so I would have no interest in building there. If, on the other hand, many people built homes near the airport, a powerful lobby would be able to prevent its expansion, and so I now would have an incentive to build my house there. Predicting collective behavior thus requires us to understand how people will find ways to coordinate.

THE MICROCOSM OF ACADEMIC ECONOMICS

The Validation and Challenging of Knowledge

As in all scientific disciplines, research is a process of cocreation through debates with colleagues, at seminars and conferences, and in publications. These debates are intense. Indeed, the essence of research is to focus on the phenomena that are not well understood, and about which divergences of opinion are likely to be sharpest. The dominant trends in research change according to how solid the theories are and whether there is evidence to support them. Thus, behavioral economics was a relatively unknown field twenty-five or thirty years ago. Some research centers, such as those at Cal Tech or Carnegie Mellon, made a smart bet on this neglected area, and since then behavioral economics has become part of the mainstream. The great universities have experimental laboratories in this discipline and researchers who devote themselves to it.

Macroeconomics offers another example of the debate and evolution of knowledge in economics.[16] Until the mid-1970s, this field was completely dominated by Keynesian theory. Was this a sign that economics was monolithic? No, because in some American universities, mainly in the Midwest, a movement emerged to challenge it.[17] A minority questioned both the empirical scope of existing theories and their very foundations. For example, according to Keynesian theory, an increase in government spending financed by printing new money raises the demand for labor and reduces unemployment. Firms must compete for workers by raising nominal wages. Higher wage costs are passed through to consumers in the form of higher prices, i.e., inflation. This inverse relationship between the rates of unemployment and of inflation within an economy is called the Phillips curve. The stimulus and the concomitant surprise surge in inflation thus lowers real salaries and raises employment in an economy with unemployment and rigidity in nominal salaries (that is, salaries not indexed to the cost of living); it also gives borrowers a shot in the arm by diminishing their real-terms indebtedness, as their debt is usually expressed in nominal terms. It is not hard to appreciate, however, that the systematic creation of inflation would not fool consumers, creditors, or employees for long. They would adapt: either savers would hold fewer assets that are not indexed to inflation, or else they would ask for much higher rates of interest. Similarly, employees would demand that their salaries be indexed to inflation (this was, in reality, a tough nut to crack for many governments around the world). Nor in the 1970s did the facts seem to justify Keynesian theory, because of stagflation (the combination of sluggish growth and high inflation).[18]

Relatedly, an old-style Keynesian would assume that expectations were entirely adaptive or "backward looking": economic agents would extrapolate the trends observed in the past, but their expectations were not "forward looking." But consider the case of a financial bubble, that is, an asset that is overvalued with respect to its fundamental value.[19] Someone choosing to buy an overvalued asset will do so only if they intend to resell it, and think they can get the timing right. Therefore they must ask themselves whether other agents will remain invested in this asset in the future and for how long. Similarly, asset managers who have to choose the maturity (what is called the *duration*) of a bond portfolio, or who have to decide whether to hedge against fluctuations in interest rates, have to anticipate the way in which the central bank will react to the state of the economy. Or again, a company that decides to invest abroad or repatriate its revenues has to consider the factors that will cause exchange rates to evolve in the short and long run. The absence of a role for forward-looking expectations in Keynesian theory was paradoxical because Keynes himself evoked the "animal spirits" that he argued reflected optimistic expectations liable to destabilize the economy.

Economists challenging the Keynesian consensus refined the models, making them more dynamic, and also developed time series econometrics, statistical tools tailored to macroeconomic data. These economists became dominant in their turn. But their models also had their limits: many of these "neo-Keynesian" macroeconomic models suffered from the quasi-absence of a financial system (a remarkable omission, as macroeconomics had always emphasized the mechanism of monetary transmission by the banking and financial system) and paid little attention to financial bubbles or to the problems of a shortage of liquidity in the economy.

Today, whether they are Keynesians or not, macroeconomists are working to improve their models by trying to synthesize the points of view of the different schools, so as to improve our understanding of macroeconomic management.

THE EVALUATION OF RESEARCH

How research is evaluated can determine the allocation of funds among researchers, laboratories, or universities, can indicate whether a research group is functioning well or not, and can help students make choices. How should we evaluate the quality of research in economics and other scientific disciplines? There are, put simply, two approaches to this problem. One approach, roughly, is based on statistics, the other on peer review.

The general public knows about the statistical approach through the Academic Ranking of World Universities (ARWU), better known as the Shanghai Ranking. Every year, universities all over the world feverishly wait to see how the team at Jiao Tong University has rated them. But is this classification an appropriate way to rank universities globally? The Shanghai Ranking has its defects. For example, in measuring productivity, it does not properly take into account the quality of the scientific journals in which scholarly articles are published. In addition, the ranking favors universities that have a Nobel laureate or Fields Medal winner among their alumni; but what do these dignitaries contribute to a university if they are not present on its campus or no longer do research and advise students?

What, then, are the criteria and the types of analyses that a good measure ought to include? First of all, there must be rankings for each discipline, which is the level most relevant for students choosing a university, or for university presidents seeking to steer their institutions. The Shanghai Ranking breaks down its ranking by discipline to some extent, but not enough. On the other hand, students who have not yet chosen a subject need a ranking at the university level so they can compare alternative institutions. Thus, we need worldwide rankings by both discipline and by university.

Measuring the productivity of researchers is a complex task. One way to measure a researcher's academic productivity is by number of publications. But publications are not all equal; publication in a mediocre journal is not equivalent to publication in *Nature* or *Science*. To reflect the differing quality of academic journals, the best approach is to weight the number of publications by the quality of the journals (itself measured either by the journal's influence or impact factor – this is calculated by an algorithm based on citations, similar to the one Google uses for search results – or by committees of experts). The best rankings also give less credit to a researcher whose published article was written in collaboration with many others. But the limitations of this exercise are clear. The journal is a sign of quality, but articles of greatly differing importance may appear in the same journal.

Furthermore, the number of published articles, even when weighted by the quality of the journal, is anyway only an approximate measure of the significance of the research. Gérard Debreu, an American of French origin who won the Nobel Prize in 1983, was not very "productive," but the articles he produced every three to five years were very influential.

The second approach to measuring research productivity counts citations, and may also weight the citations according to the importance of the source (once again, measured by citations of the person doing the citing – a problem that mathematicians will recognize as being a fixed-point problem). By this measure, Maurice Allais, the last great non–English speaking economist writing in his native language and the first French winner of the Nobel Prize in economics (1987), would not have looked so good. More importantly, some fields are more often cited than others, and citations in themselves are not a measure of quality: controversial or media-friendly subjects are more often cited than others. To take an extreme case, Holocaust-denying historians will be frequently commented upon and therefore often cited, but that does not mean that they are great scholars! Surveys of the literature on a subject, and books synthesizing research done by other scholars – though very useful because they allow a nonspecialist to quickly gain familiarity – are naturally often cited, but usually do not represent notable advances in knowledge. Finally, citations appear only after some delay. This can disadvantage young researchers.

So rankings have many defects on which I shall not dwell further. And yet, even though I am one of the harshest critics of these rankings, I would vigorously defend their use. Is that a paradox? Not really: in a country like the United States, where the governance of universities and funding agencies is entirely focused on excellence, the use of these objective measures remains limited (though it is has increased). In contrast, the measures are an indispensable tool for identifying centers of excellence in many European countries. For instance, unlike its principal competitors in research and innovation, France does not have the culture of academic evaluation that could expose the significant differences in creativity between

French research groups or between those groups and the best institutions globally. Therefore it is often difficult for students and decision makers to identify the most innovative and internationally high-profile French research institutions. Rankings are important when there is a shortage of other relevant information.

This leads me to peer evaluation and the good governance of academic research. Well-managed funding agencies distribute research budgets on a competitive basis through independent panels composed of the best experts. The European Research Council (ERC) does this in Europe, for example, and in the United States it is the National Science Foundation and the National Institutes of Health. But to do so, they must persuade the best people, who are always much in demand elsewhere, to undertake the evaluation. To be truly effective, this approach requires a procedure that is not too time consuming, plus a guarantee that decisions made by the peer reviewers will be implemented by the funding agency.

Peer evaluation is also crucial in the process of appointing professors. In the countries on the research frontier, professors are increasingly often recruited in the following way: First, the department discusses potential recruits, both internal and external, whether the academics concerned have applied or not. The department professors have (in principle) read the candidates' key articles. A vigorous (and confidential) debate about the candidates' relative merits ensues. And then – this is the essential point – the administration acts as a "quality champion." Appointments to every permanent (i.e., tenured) position are subjected to more than a dozen comparative evaluations by experts outside the university, which are analyzed by the university's president, provost, or relevant dean. External referees are asked to compare the quality of the preferred candidate with a list of researchers working elsewhere in the same area. This allows the president, provost, or dean, who may not be specialists in the discipline, to find out more. Thus the idea is to reduce the asymmetry of information between the university's administration and the department, and thus to check the quality of the recruits the department has proposed. Other countries, especially those not at the research frontier, would do well to adopt similarly rigorous academic governance.

Weaknesses and Abuses of Academic Evaluation

The process by which peers read and assess one another's articles is at the heart of academic evaluation. Academic articles are submitted to the editors of a journal. Other scholars review them anonymously to decide if they are suitable for publication. On the basis of the reviewers' reports, as well as their own conclusions, the journal editors decide whether to accept the article (usually after some requests for improvements) or to reject it. Careful evaluation of articles is essential if the research community is to function properly, and for the accumulation of scientific knowledge: researchers cannot possibly read the thousands of articles that are written in their field or even subfield each year, let alone go through them in any great detail. Academic journals have the task of verifying the quality of an article's data and the integrity of its statistical analysis, the logical coherence and interest of its theory, and the extent to which the article contributes something new to the field.

We should not, however, be naive or take an overly utopian view of this process. The system has its weaknesses. One is the herd behavior of researchers, which means that one subject may hog the attention of the scientific community while equally important subjects are neglected. Another is the bias toward publishing work with "impact." Thus an empirical study carefully replicating an already published result has less chance of attracting the attention of the academic community, and therefore the interest of a journal editor, than the initial experiment, especially if it produced a surprising result. Another issue is the lack of replication of some empirical results – when other researchers cannot reproduce the conclusions of earlier studies, even well-known ones, when they try.[20] Sometimes reviewers simply "free ride." Although they are supposed to spend time evaluating other people's research and thus contributing to the common good, they may fail to reflect in sufficient depth on the quality, originality, and relevance of the contribution.

Finally, of course, in all academic fields there are inevitably cases of straightforward fraud. Usually these involve fabricated data or, exceptionally, hacking the website of an academic journal to change the referees' reports. Sometimes in the case of journals that make the mistake of asking the author to suggest reviewers, it involves false e-mail addresses directing requests for reviews to a friend, rather than to the intended reviewer!

In my opinion, the only solution to these problems is to be aware of them and try to limit them as much as possible. Recently there has been increased transparency in some respects, requiring that data be made public and possible conflicts of interest be stated. It is tempting to say that, like democracy, the system of peer review is the worst system except for all the others. Internal evaluation, one of these alternative systems, tends to be captured by the institutions' corporate interest, and so external evaluation and peer review have become the cornerstones of academic assessment.

A Relative Consensus and American Domination of Economics

A common criticism of economics concerns the relatively high degree of consensus among economists, something that tends to astonish other social scientists. There are, of course, different sensibilities – to take only one example, economics at MIT is traditionally more liberal and Keynesian than it is at the University of Chicago, whose economics department is more conservative and monetarist. There is, nevertheless, a consensus about the way research should be conducted. As Paul Samuelson, the figurehead of MIT economics, explained, there wasn't a hair's breadth of difference between him and his counterpart at Chicago, Milton Friedman, concerning what constituted good research. They both agreed that a quantitative approach was essential (formal theories and empirical tests of these theories), agreed on the importance of analyzing causality, and emphasized the normative aspect of economics as a discipline whose purpose is to serve decision making.

This methodological consensus does not mean, of course, that all economic research is incremental, mechanically plowing the furrows already marked out by the profession. On the contrary, as Robert Solow – another MIT figurehead – emphasized, researchers most often make a name for themselves by challenging current beliefs and plowing new furrows.[21] Now economics draws on several new fields of analysis: price rigidity, incentive problems, imperfect competition, incorrect expectations, behavioral biases, and so on. To repeat, there are fierce debates in seminar rooms, journals, and conferences, and so much the better: the head-on clash of ideas and criticisms between peers allows everyone to move forward.

It is essential that different approaches enrich each other, which requires mobility. Nothing is worse than a school of thought in which disciples limit themselves to interpreting the works of their "masters." An Anglo-Saxon custom that is very useful in this regard is the ban on endogamy: upon gaining their PhD, students have to get a job at a different university (they can return later). As well as promoting better relations between professors (who no longer fight to place "their" students in their own departments), the ban forces the students to learn new ideas and approaches, and their home departments to appoint new lecturers who are cast in a different mold.

Another criticism leveled at economics is the dominance of American departments in the subject. Without going into details, the ten top economics departments are roughly all American, as are, moreover, a great many of the top one hundred universities in the field. I regret this. But for non-Americans, rather than being indignant, it is better to roll up their sleeves. To cite Robert Solow once again, it is not surprising that the United States ranks first: it trains an enormous number of students in the discipline. The strong competition between universities to attract the best professors and students creates an excellent research environment, and above all, the academic system rewards merit rather than hierarchy.

The Impact of Teaching Economics on Individual Behavior

Economists have carried out experiments in the laboratory and in the field to study the behavior of their students. Faced with choices involving a trade-off between their own well-being and that of others, students taking courses in economics tend to behave more selfishly than other students.[22] For example, when they register, students at the University of Zurich are offered an opportunity to give seven Swiss francs to finance student loans, and five Swiss francs to help foreigners studying at the university. Only 61.8 percent of students in economics and business contribute to at least one of these funds, as opposed to 68.7 percent students in other disciplines.[23] Other experiments confirm this conclusion. An important question is whether this is due to self-selection (students are more likely to major in economics or business if they are more selfish) or to indoctrination (students become selfish as a result of studying economics). If the former, studying economics is harmless (you can carry on reading this book, it's not contagious); if the latter, economics could be "performative," that is, exposure to economics could shape our worldview and lead us to view the world through a distorting lens.

Unfortunately, our understanding of this question is incomplete. The Zurich study also examines the evolution of generosity during students' university careers, and concludes that there is no evidence of indoctrination (at least as far as economics students are concerned). This means self-selection appears to be the sole explanatory factor. Some studies support this conclusion, while others disagree. For example, law students at Yale are initially assigned randomly to certain courses.[24] Those who are assigned to courses overlapping with economics (law of civil liability, for instance) and who are taught by professors with training in economics behave in the short run more selfishly than those assigned to less economics-oriented courses (such as constitutional law) and exposed to professors trained in the humanities. Since assignment is random, this cannot be due to self-selection.

The possibility that training in economics might change a person's state of mind must be taken seriously. But to assess its consequences, we would have to understand the channel through which this change in mentality might occur. One hypothesis (at this stage it is only a hypothesis) is based on the fragility of altruism. As we will see in some detail in the following chapter, altruism is greatly reduced when we are able to justify acting selfishly with an excuse, however feeble.[25] During their training, economics students study, for example, competitive strategies in a market (suggesting that the world is pitiless);

they learn that self-interested behavior can give rise to social harmony in the allocation of resources[26] (suggesting that it is reasonable to be selfish); they read empirical studies drawing attention to behavior that is dysfunctional for society when incentives are inappropriate (suggesting that we cannot always trust economic or political agents). All these influences create narratives that, however valid empirically, provide (weak) excuses for less ethical behavior.

Even if this hypothesis turns out to be correct, the students' later professional lives or personal relationships may provide alternative narratives with a different but equally strong impact. The experiments above only speak to the immediate impact of studying economics; we do not have much information about whether economists working for the state, the private sector, or universities are worse or better citizens than other people in terms of their donations or their behaviors regarding public goods, pollution, or voting. Whatever the answer to this question, we would also like to know whether the difference between economists and noneconomists, if any, is due to self-selection or to indoctrination. In other words, beyond understanding the short-run effects of a training in economics, the long-term impact of studying the subject is the key research question.

ECONOMISTS: FOXES OR HEDGEHOGS?

The British philosopher Isaiah Berlin begins his little book *The Hedgehog and the Fox* by quoting a fragment attributed to the Greek poet Archilochus: "The fox knows many things, but the hedgehog knows one big thing."[27]

Forty years ago, almost all economists were hedgehogs. In short (perhaps slightly unfairly), we could say that they knew the model of competitive markets, the most intellectually complete paradigm in the discipline, like the back of their hands. They were, of course, aware of the limits of this model, and they were pursuing other possibilities, but without having an adequate intellectual framework for doing so. A kind of theory of ideal gases for economics, the competitive model was applied to a wide range of situations: the volatility of markets, finance, or international trade, for instance.

THE COMPETITIVE MARKET PARADIGM

In this paradigm, buyers and sellers are small relative to the markets in which they trade, and therefore cannot make prices rise by limiting supply or make them fall by reducing demand: their individual impact on market prices is negligible. They are also assumed to have perfect knowledge of products' price and quality, and behave rationally according to their own free choice. Buyers maximize their gains from trade and sellers maximize their profits. Without necessarily being able to predict the future with precision, agents have rational expectations about every future event.

This model was used to explain how supply and demand are balanced across markets, which makes it possible to study the phenomenon of "general equilibrium." For example, a change in supply in one market may affect other markets through two channels. On the one hand, products might be complementary (if I book a flight to a city, I may also rent a car or book a hotel room there) or could be substituted for one another (I may substitute a high-speed train trip for a flight). On the other hand, it operates through income effects (a change in prices in this market affects how much of the product a buyer consumes, and also the income available to spend on other products, even if those other products have no direct relation to the market affected – so, for example, if the cost of renting their apartment goes up, people buy fewer of the other goods they usually consume).

General equilibrium was an important stage in the development of economic theory, but one that has two intrinsic limitations. First, its implications for economic policy are not obvious: the absence of friction (because there is always competition, symmetric information, and rational behavior) would mean that these markets are efficient, so the only public policy to consider would be the implementation of income taxes. If that were the case, most ministries, independent authorities, and local government would be useless! Second, and relatedly, this model describes almost none of the situations I discuss in this book.

Since then, economic theory has been greatly refined. It has learned how to analyze imperfect competition in a market that has a small number of sellers or buyers, and so how to deduce rules for regulating competition. It can incorporate asymmetries of information about prices and the quality of goods (or even a lack of knowledge concerning possible trading partners) in order to predict market failures and suggest remedies for them. It has learned how to account for observed deviations from rational decision making. It can now analyze the implications of the separation within a firm between property rights (belonging to investors) and real control (often in the hands of the managers, whose interests may differ from those of the investors). The introduction of these "frictions" into the old model is hard work, but it has borne fruit. The models have become less parsimonious (meaning they take into account more considerations), but they allow the study of new questions essential for public policy and business strategy.

Even in the world of foxes that prevails today, some economists tend to be more foxlike, and others more hedgehoglike. Hedgehogs are guided throughout their lives by a single idea, and often try to convince their protégés to take the same path. They take an admirable risk in defending a paradigm that they have judged to be important, even all encompassing. Foxes, on the other hand, regard universal theories with suspicion and are often engaged in a variety of approaches. They move from one line of research to another when they think they have arrived at a point of diminishing returns in the first.

Neither of the two styles is superior to the other. Science needs hedgehogs, who keep pushing an idea, even when unpopular, and keep digging in a certain direction when other researchers reckon such intensive research has reached strongly decreasing returns; science also needs foxes, who bring together disparate pieces of knowledge and open new areas of research. Moreover, experience seems to show that the world of research rewards both.[28]

In public debates, is it better to be a fox or a hedgehog economist? We know little about this subject, but the work of Philip Tetlock, a psychologist at the University of Pennsylvania, on experts in political science is fascinating.[29] Tetlock offers two answers to this question. The first concerns the reception of ideas in public debate. Hedgehogs irritate only the people who disagree with them, while foxes annoy everyone – by deploying various ideas, they spare no one's sensitivities.

The foxes, taking more parameters into account, often undermine their own recommendations. This tries the patience of their audience, who wants certainties. So foxes do not get invited into the television studios (in fact, pushing hard on a fox can produce a long list of recommendations; foxes sometimes have to force themselves to pick just one). The media prefers hedgehogs.

Secondly, Tetlock studied the predictions of 284 experts in political science for almost twenty years. In total, he asked them to make twenty-eight thousand predictions: for instance, regarding the fall of the Soviet Union, the probability that a nation-state would disintegrate, the war in Iraq, and the decline of powerful political parties. Based on fourteen criteria, he divided these experts into foxes and hedgehogs.[30] Tetlock also classified experts according to their political opinions. This dimension was not entirely independent of their cognitive style. Somewhat unsurprisingly, foxes were less likely than hedgehogs to be at the extremes of the political spectrum. But their exact politics had little effect on their error rate. For example, in the 1980s, experts on the left were blinded by a low opinion of Reagan's intellect, while those on the right were obsessed by the Soviet threat. The richest lessons concern cognitive style. Foxes produce far better predictions. They are more aware of the probability (not negligible) that they are wrong. Conversely, Tetlock selects Marx and libertarians[31] as examples of hedgehogs who stick to a simple worldview and whose grand predictions never materialize. It is not easy to draw definitive conclusions from this innovative research, even though it is based on a large sample. We will need other studies in different domains of expertise.

THE ROLE OF MATHEMATICS

Among the social sciences and humanities, economics is the one that makes the most use of mathematics – more than political science, law (including the subfield of law and economics), even evolutionary biology, and certainly much more than sociology, psychology, anthropology, or history. For this reason, critics often accuse economics of being too formalized and abstract.

The mathematization of economics is relatively recent, even though mathematical economists of the nineteenth century (such as Antoine-Augustin Cournot, Jules Dupuit, and Joseph Bertrand in France, Léon Walras and Vilfredo Pareto in Lausanne, Johann Heinrich von Thünen in Germany, Francis Edgeworth at Oxford, and William Stanley Jevons at University College London) did not hesitate to formalize their work. Economics was gradually mathematicized during the twentieth century, a trend that accelerated in the 1940s and 1950s. The works of the great economists of that period, such as Kenneth Arrow, Gérard Debreu and Paul Samuelson, were to economics as the works of Bourbaki[32] were to mathematics. In formalizing economic thought, they organized it. Even more importantly, they formalized and validated (or invalidated) the logic of the insights, innovative but imprecise, of the great classical economists from Adam Smith to Alfred Marshall and John Maynard Keynes. The mathematization of economics was an essential foundation on which later studies could build; but the subject had to keep progressing.

The Need for Mathematics

As in the physical or engineering sciences, mathematics has contributed to economics on two levels: theoretical modeling, and empirical verification. The need to use econometrics (statistics applied to economics) to analyze data is not particularly controversial, as identifying causal effects is a prerequisite for decision making. Correlation and causality are two different things. As the French comedian Coluche joked, "When you're sick, above all you should avoid going to the hospital: the probability of dying in a hospital bed is ten times greater than in your own bed at home" – which is clearly complete nonsense, even if you count the chances of getting an infection in the hospital. There is a correlation, but not a causal relationship, between hospitals and death (otherwise we would have to do away with hospitals). Or consider a diagram showing that hotel occupancy increases with hotel prices; hopefully few would conclude from this observation that raising prices will attract more customers (except perhaps for some upscale hotels, which may allow the client to display his wealth and status); understanding this covariation between price and occupancy requires one to bring in a piece of theory: that hotel managers lower prices when demand (and therefore occupancy) is low. Only an empirical strategy based on econometrics will allow us to identify a causal impact and thus to make recommendations about economic decisions.

Mathematical models used to represent the essence of a problem may be more controversial. As I have explained, every model is a simplified – sometimes outrageously simplified – representation of reality, even if subsequent research makes it possible to enrich it and to fill in the gaps. As Robert Solow put it in the first lines of a famous article on growth (which won him the Nobel Prize):

> All theory depends on assumptions which are not quite true. That is what makes it theory. The art of successful theorizing is to make the inevitable simplifying assumptions in such a way that the final results are not very sensitive. A "crucial" assumption is one on which the conclusions do depend sensitively, and it is important that crucial assumptions be reasonably realistic. When the results of a theory seem to flow specifically from a special crucial assumption, then if the assumption is dubious, the results are suspect.

Despite its defects, I regard modeling as indispensable for several reasons. First of all, models are a language and thereby facilitate communication among economists. As in any other field of research, economists benefit from using commonly known paradigms that researchers can refer to without having to enter into long explanations about what is assumed and delivered. While completely arcane to noneconomists, phrases like "vector auto regressions (VAR)," "the Arrow-Debreu model of perfect competition," or "Akerlof's lemons model" immediately brings a ready reference point to the discussion for an economics audience.

Second, modeling forces researchers to state their assumptions clearly. Explicit assumptions can be criticized and subjected to common-sense tests. A realism filter must be applied to critical assumptions, those that actually drive results.[33] The same holds true for the logic of the argument. Taken together, modeling can contribute to transparency. As Dani Rodrik, an economist at Harvard, notes in his recent book, there is no need for the endless debates about what Samuelson or Arrow had in mind, unlike for earlier authors such as Keynes, Marx, or Schumpeter.[34]

Third, using mathematics also forces economists to check the logic of their arguments, since intuition can sometimes be deceptive. Dani Rodrik puts it very well:

> We need the math to make sure that we think straight – to ensure that our conclusions follow from our premises and that we haven't left loose ends hanging in our argument. In other words, we use math not because we're smart, but because we aren't smart enough. We are just smart enough to recognize that we are not smart enough. And this recognition, I tell our students, will set them apart from a lot of people out there with very strong opinions about what to do about poverty and underdevelopment.

Fourth, writing and solving a model makes researchers think about other ideas. (If the hypotheses lead to conclusions that prove to be false, are they inappropriate, or is something missing in the model?)

Fifth, models guide empirical research. For sure, "model-free analysis" can be useful. The identification of correlations may still be useful for prediction. Indeed, Big Data (which so far has focused on the identification of such correlations) does wonders when it comes to a search engine's ability to predict what I am searching for, or an Internet-based company's ability to recommend books or movies I might enjoy. Supervised machine learning of the kind used today – for instance in clinical medicine, the analysis of political bias in texts, criminal justice, or the measurement of consumer churn – takes as inputs "training" data sets by which it makes predictions on new data.[35] But without a model to test, data reveal little that is useful for economic policy. The model is what makes it possible to analyze well-being and therefore economic policy.

Finally, theoretical models are the main game in town when there is a shortage of data. This happens with new technologies, for which data have not yet accumulated (think about a competition authority's decision as to whether to allow the acquisition of an Internet start-up by an incumbent firm or the formation of a patent pool – see Chapter 16); when contemplating abrupt institutional changes (as was the case in the 1990s for both the deregulation of network industries – see Chapter 17 – and the transition of Soviet economies toward a market economy); or when adjusting regulations to institutional or product innovations (think of the prudential treatment of new financial instruments). Empirical analysis meets its limitations when entering a "new world": the impact of climate change on migration, the effects of the disintegration of the European Union, or the consequences of a large OECD country's default on its sovereign debt are not easily extrapolated from previous events.

On a related point, data may exist, but if they are "local" they will not be very informative when it comes to assessing the consequences of a potential new policy that changes the economic environment significantly. Macroeconomists were dumbfounded by the end of the Great Moderation (the observed reduction in the volatility of business cycle fluctuations starting in the mid-1980s, attributed to stabilization policies) and by the skewedness of the distribution of financial returns in the 2008 financial crisis when the assumption of normally distributed returns had previously done a good job. In microeconomics, an accurate, but local measurement of demand may provide misleading estimates of what would happen if a contemplated merger moved prices far away from their current values.[36]

The Cost of Mathematization

Nonetheless, mathematization has its costs. First, it is sometimes difficult, and initial attempts to study a topic are often rough and ready. Patience is required, even though economists are often expected to make instant economic policy recommendations. Forty years ago, we had little idea how to model expectations, interactions between firms, or asymmetric information, so whole areas of economics were then difficult to formalize.

Secondly, economists are sometimes inclined to look for something "under the lamp post" – a phrase used to describe looking for an object where the light happens to be, rather than in the dark corner where it is more likely to have been lost. For example, macroeconomists have for a long time referred to a "representative agent" (in other words, they assumed that all consumers were identical), simply because that made the model easier to analyze. Nowadays, they increasingly abandon this assumption because consumers differ in many ways (tastes, wealth, income, access to loans, sociodemographic variables, and so on). Greater precision, though, comes at the price of increased complexity. The more hypotheses are refined, and the greater the complexity of the description of economic agents, the greater the need for mathematics to ensure that the reasoning is complete.

Thirdly, the teaching of economics is often too abstract, a tendency that the use of mathematics sometimes accentuates. Mathematics itself, however, is not to blame, because teachers are free to choose how to teach. The teaching material must be compatible with the knowledge emerging from research, but it can be communicated in a different way. English-language textbooks for undergraduates usually do not make extensive use of mathematics, but the easy way for a teacher to convey research is to use its existing form rather than to make it more accessible.

Finally, the research community in economics is often reproached for being too concerned with aesthetics. Mathematics is said to have become less an instrument than a goal, because using it to construct elegant and coherent models is seen as a signal of scientific quality. No doubt this flaw exists, but we also must remember that, as in other scientific disciplines, articles that are clever but superficial may enjoy their heyday, but they are later forgotten – unless they represent a true methodological advance that makes applied research possible.

GAME THEORY AND INFORMATION THEORY

Game theory and information theory have revolutionized all areas of economics, where they are widely used – just as they are in evolutionary biology, political science, law, and occasionally in sociology, psychology, and history.

GAME THEORY

Modern microeconomics is based on game theory, which represents and predicts the strategies of agents who have their own goals and are interdependent, and information theory, which models their strategic use of private information.

Game theory allows us to conceptualize the strategic choices made by agents when they have different interests. Thus, game theory does not only apply to economics, but also politics, law, sociology, and even (as we shall see later) psychology. It was initially developed by mathematicians: in France by Émile Borel in 1921; in the United States by John von Neumann, in a paper published in 1928 and a book written with Oskar Morgenstern, published in 1944; and by John Nash,[37] in a paper published in 1950. More recent developments in game theory have been motivated by applications in the social sciences, and the great majority of these developments have been due to economists, although biologists and mathematicians have also contributed.

From Individual Behavior to Collective Behavior

The social and human sciences suggest the importance of our expectations of what others will do, either concurrently or in reaction to one's own actions. These expectations are rational if the agent understands the incentives of other agents and anticipates their strategy, at least "on average," and accordingly acts to the best of his interests. Strategies are then said to be in equilibrium (in 1950, John Nash developed the general theory of this equilibrium, referred to as a "Nash equilibrium"). Understanding the likely behavior of others may result from either reasoning (agents imagine what they would do if they were in the other person's shoes) or, if the game is familiar, from past experience.

A person who does not leave a wallet on the café table or a bicycle unsupervised on the street, or who does not step onto a pedestrian crossing without looking (in a country where drivers do not stop for pedestrians) is solving elementary problems in game theory, in as much as he or she correctly anticipates how others are likely to behave.

The example of the pedestrian crossing also illustrates that multiple equilibria are possible: drivers who do not slow down as they approach pay no cost (other than psychological) as a result of their behavior, as long as there is no pedestrian crossing the street (or intending to cross) as the car approaches. Conversely, drivers who anticipate that pedestrians will cross will slow down as they approach, while pedestrians will be able to cross if they expect civilized behavior from drivers.

Like Monsieur Jourdain (in Moliere's *Le Bourgeois Gentilhomme*), surprised to find he has been speaking in prose, we are all experts in game theory without knowing it, because every day we participate in hundreds or thousands of "games": we are involved in situations in which we need to anticipate the way others will behave, which encompasses their reaction to the way we act. Of course, we are far more expert in some games that we play repeatedly throughout our lives (for example, those associated with personal and social relations) than in others that we play only now and then. Thus, few people will instantly hit on the right strategy at an auction where each person has private information concerning the actual value of the object up for sale, such as a mining license or shares in a firm going public. Most people, unlike professionals, tend to bid too optimistically, because they fail to put themselves in the place of other potential buyers and to understand that the latter will bid lower if they have negative information about the asset. This phenomenon is called the "winner's curse," because people tend to make a winning bid precisely when the object has little value.

How people behave often depends on what others do. If other car drivers or subway users leave for work at 8 a.m., it may be to my advantage to leave at 6 a.m., even if that is really too early from my point of view. In equilibrium, flows stabilize so that each person makes the best trade-off between their ideal schedule and the congestion they will suffer on their commute. In making such choices, agents seek to differentiate their behavior from that of others. On other occasions, agents have a problem with coordination. They would like to choose to behave the same way as others. For example, if most of my fellow citizens did not pay their parking tickets, there would be (unfortunately) strong pressure for an amnesty for such offenders, which would reduce my incentive to pay my parking tickets too. As in the pedestrian-driver game, there may be multiple equilibria, so that two otherwise identical societies may adopt different behavioral patterns.

"Predicting on average" reflects the fact that an equilibrium is sometimes based on a "mixed strategy": in soccer, a good goalkeeper must avoid getting a reputation for diving more to the left than to the right, or for remaining in the middle when facing a penalty kick; and the same goes for the player who is taking the kick. Studies of professional players (amateurs are more predictable) clearly show that their behavior is unpredictable: a good goalkeeper, for instance, has the same probability of preventing a goal (about 25 percent) from each of the three options.[38]

It may also be impossible to predict other people's actions perfectly because we don't know everything about them. At best we can make a conditional prediction: "In their place, in these circumstances, I would do this." For example, in the auction mentioned earlier, we can predict a high bid if the other person receives good news about the value of the object put up for auction (and a low bid if the news is bad).

To illustrate the power and limits of game theory, let's consider a situation called "the prisoner's dilemma," a strategic framework that enables the description and analysis of many conflicts. Its name refers to the following situation: two prisoners are correctly suspected of having committed a crime together, but a confession is required. They are put in separate cells and asked to confess their crime. If one confesses, he or she will be punished more leniently, but if both confess, both are punished. Collectively, they are better off if neither of them confesses but, individually, they each have an incentive to confess. The equilibrium is that both confess.

This simple situation is shown in Figure 4.1, which involves two players: Player 1 (in bold) and Player 2. Each player has a choice between two actions: cooperating with the other player or deviating from the agreement by behaving opportunistically. Cooperating is denoted by C, and deviating by D. In the table, Player 1's scores are shown first in bold, then Player 2's. For example, if Player 1 cooperates and Player 2 deviates, Player 1 scores zero and Player 2 scores 20 points. Each player knows all the information shown in the table, but

		Player 2	
		C	D
Player 1	C	**15**, 15	**0**, 20
Player 1	D	**20**, 0	**5**, 5

Figure 4.1. The prisoner's dilemma.

has to make his decision without knowing what decision the other has made. Collectively the two players are better off cooperating (i.e., both choosing *C*) since they score 15 each, for a total of 30, a higher total than would be obtained in any of the three other possible outcomes of the game (which is 20 if their choices differ, 10 if both deviate). But individually, they have an interest in opportunistic behavior. The equilibrium of the game is that each person deviates and receives only 5 points. To see this, note that Player 2 always gets more points by deviating, no matter what Player 1 does: if Player 1 chooses to cooperate, Player 2 gets 20 points by deviating, but only 15 from cooperating; if Player 1 chooses to deviate, Player 2 scores 5 points by deviating and zero by cooperating. Exactly the same incentives apply to Player 1.

Thus, this game is particularly easy to analyze because it has a "dominant strategy." That is, to make a decision, a player does not actually need to anticipate what the other one will do: whether the other prisoner chooses *C* or *D*, each player is better off choosing strategy *D*.

From this we can conclude that, faced with this situation, every rational individual should choose the opportunistic strategy. However, in practice, under laboratory conditions,[39] not all players deviate: 15 to 20 percent of players choose to cooperate. Chapter 5 returns to this phenomenon, which will lead us to question not game theory, but the assumption that economic agents behave selfishly.

Despite its simplicity, the prisoner's dilemma game allows us to represent very important strategic situations. For example, before the

OPEC oil cartel was established, each petroleum-exporting country had an interest in increasing its production (strategy D) rather than decreasing its production and cooperating with other countries to limit supply (strategy C). The introduction of quotas (and sanctions if quotas were exceeded) permitted OPEC to increase its members' revenues by forcing them to play C. In a situation of this kind, we can understand why the players (individuals, enterprises, or states) might have an interest in creating a cartel, cemented by an agreement and the threat of reprisals for deviant behavior on the part of any of the participants.

This game has also inspired competition authorities to introduce a form of plea bargaining to fight the formation of cartels. This "leniency program," which has long been in effect in the United States, has recently been introduced in Europe, where it is bearing fruit. The system guarantees quasi-immunity for any firm revealing to the competition authorities the existence of a cartel of which it is a member; the authorities then punish the other firms. The program destabilizes the cartel by recreating the prisoner's dilemma neutralized by the internal cartel agreement.

The battle against global warming studied in chapter 8 is another example of the application of the prisoner's dilemma. Individually, each country has an interest in not reducing its greenhouse gas emissions, but the collective consequences of this selfish attitude are disastrous. Garrett Hardin describes this "tragedy of commons" in an article published in 1968 in the journal *Science*. It explains the failure of the Kyoto and Copenhagen agreements on climate change. To avoid this tragedy we would need an agreement that would force all countries to choose strategy C. In practice, they all choose strategy D.

The Dynamics of Interactions

The theory of dynamic games is based on the idea that an agent's current decisions have an impact on the future actions of other agents, so every agent needs to understand how his or her decisions will influence the future strategies of others. For example, a state working on a new law or regulation must expect consumers and enterprises to react to the new institutional context by changing their behavior; to that end, the state must imagine itself in their place and anticipate what they will do. This kind of equilibrium is called, in the (not particularly appropriate) jargon of economics, "perfect equilibrium." In a perfect equilibrium, each agent is aware of the effects of their actions on the future behaviors of other agents and acts accordingly.

An agent's behavior often reveals information that they alone possess. For example, investors who buy shares in a company reveal that their information, or their knowledge of the situation, makes them optimistic about the value of the company; revealing this information tends to drive up the price of shares in the company, thereby reducing the buyers' profits. Consequently, stock investors try to make large purchases discreetly by dividing up their buy orders or using intermediaries. Another example is when a friend or a supplier behaves in an opportunistic way and betrays the trust placed in him or her. This act reveals information concerning the character of the person in question, who will therefore think twice before endangering his or her reputation. These situations are studied by using the concept of perfect Bayesian equilibrium, which combines perfect equilibrium with rational information processing in the sense of Bayes's theorem. Which brings me to information theory.

Information Theory

The second unifying framework of modern economics is information theory, which is also known as incentive theory, contract theory, signaling theory, or principal-agent theory, depending on the use to which it is put. This theory concerns the strategic role of the private information that decision makers possess. A good understanding of human or economic relations needs to acknowledge that agents do not all have the same information, and will use their private information to achieve their goals.

Information theory was developed by Kenneth Arrow (who won the Nobel Prize in 1972), George Akerlof, Michael Spence, and Joseph Stiglitz (who shared a Nobel Prize in 2001), James Mirrlees and William Vickrey (Nobel Prize, 1996), Leonid Hurwicz, Eric Maskin, and

Roger Myerson (who shared a Nobel Prize in 2007), Bengt Holm-ström (who won the 2016 Nobel Prize jointly with Oliver Hart, who investigated the consequences of contracts that are incomplete), Jean-Jacques Laffont, and Paul Milgrom, among others.

Information theory is constructed on two basic concepts. The term *moral hazard* refers to the fact that someone's behavior may not be observable by the counterparty who will be affected by it (this counterparty is the "principal"), or by a court of law that has to enforce the terms of a contract in the event of a suit. Take for example a share-cropping contract between a "principal" (the landowner) and an "agent" (the farmer). The farmer might not pay enough attention to his choice of crop or when best to sow his seeds, or he might not devote enough effort to ensuring an abundant, high-quality harvest: in this case, we say that there may be a "moral hazard" on the part of the farmer. A bad harvest might be either the result of some exogenous shock to supply, such as the weather, or might be the result of the farmer's (the "agent's") lack of effort, reflecting the incentives he faces.

Given that the principal cannot observe the effort made by the agent (or prove to a court that this effort is insufficient), and knowing that the result depends not only on the farmer's effort but also on events outside his control, who should bear the risk inherent in the activity, the principal or the agent? Sharecropping is a rural lease in which the landowner, the lessor, entrusts the cultivation of a parcel of land to a farmer in exchange for part of the harvest. A sharecropping arrangement in which the farmer hands over half the harvest to the landowner assigns less responsibility and offers less incentive for effort than a standard farm tenancy in which the farmer pays a fixed sum (a rent) to the landowner and receives all the proceeds of his labor above this amount. A tenancy of this kind, which makes the farmer bear all the risk, including climatic or other hazards over which he has no control, proves to be costly if he is risk-averse and wants a predictable income.[40] If, on the other hand, a risky income does not scare the farmer, then this kind of lease is optimal, because the farmer will then be fully responsible for his work and will consequently choose how much effort he wants to put in. If all or part of the risk were borne by the landowner, the farmer would not try as hard. The arrangement that offers the least incentive for the farmer to work hard is one in which he receives a fixed salary and therefore does not benefit at all from putting in more effort.

Adverse selection refers to the possibility that the agent has private information when the contract between the two parties is signed. To stay with the example of sharecropping, only the farmer knows how much time he will put into cultivating the land, his skill as a farmer, and his desire to work. Conversely, the landowner can have private information about how fertile the land is. Adverse selection affects contracts because people will be suspicious about their counterparties. To illustrate this idea, suppose the landowner knows how fertile his land is, but the farmer does not. Even if the farmer does not care about risks to his income (and so a tenancy agreement in which he pays a fixed sum and receives all the remaining profit would be, a priori, optimal), he will be suspicious if the landlord proposes a lease of this kind: he will think that the landowner knows the land is not very productive and is just trying to reduce his own risk. So the farmer might prefer a sharecropping agreement with the landowner as a demonstration that the land is actually productive.

It is immediately obvious that this framework for analyzing institutions in terms of moral hazard and adverse selection is also applicable to the regulation of network industries and banks (the regulator has imperfect information regarding a company's technology and its effort to reduce its costs, or the exact risk involved in a bank's portfolio), to the governance and financing of firms (shareholders, creditors, and other stakeholders are imperfectly informed about the management's choices or their consequences), to the sociology of organizations (divisions or work groups strategically retain information for their own purposes), and so on.

The developments in information theory during the last three decades have allowed the definition of principles essential for understanding the mechanisms of negotiation and supervision. These principles mean that a few simple rules should govern the drawing up and execution of any contract. For example, the party that draws up the contract must accept the idea that if the other party has some private information, he will have to make concessions to induce the counterparty to reveal it.

A formal contract is based on quantifiable elements that are observable and verifiable, an idea that plays an important part in our analyses of employment policies and of the fight against global warming in chapters 8 and 9. The contract then has to be founded on a set of credible rewards and punishments. It also needs to be flexible enough to reflect changing information, notably because things will inevitably occur that could not be predicted at the time the contract was signed. Thus, methods for renegotiating or even breaking the contract must be provided, notably exit options and rules for calculating indemnities. Finally, in the absence of such formal incentive mechanisms, trade must rely on a more informal relationship between the two parties, in which the repetition of poor performance by one makes the other suspicious and leads to a loss of confidence and cooperation.

These examples are only a brief introduction to information theory, but they clearly show how agents have incentives to use their informational advantage to take advantage of others, and how institutions must account for the presence of asymmetric information.

AN ECONOMIST AT WORK: METHODOLOGICAL CONTRIBUTIONS

In many academic disciplines, upstream, fundamental research develops new techniques and ideas, which can then be employed in downstream, more applied research. That is the case in economics. Many studies do not have a specific application, nor do they try to solve a particular economic problem. Rather, they focus on methodology enabling other theoretical work to model specific phenomena, or they provide a conceptual framework for empirical studies.

For example, econometricians adapt statistics or construct their own techniques in order to allow applied economists to measure economic phenomena with greater precision, and to attribute causality (does a variable influence another variable or is it simply correlated with it?). This is a sine qua non when applying empirical analysis to public policy. Similarly, theorists may work on frameworks that have no direct application. The following remarks are both abstract and self-indulgent (because they describe the subject of my own research, for which I ask reader's pardon). Their main purpose is to help the reader grasp the diversity of the work done more generally by researchers in economics. I hope they will also make readers realize how much even theoretical research depends on teamwork. I could not have done this work without the close collaboration of the people I mention, as well as that of many others.

My studies on *pure game theory* have dealt with dynamic games, that is, conflict situations that take place over time and in which the players (the agents) react to choices made by other players. The first step was defining (with Eric Maskin, my PhD supervisor at MIT, now a professor at Harvard) the notion of a "Markov perfect equilibrium." According to this concept, for any game developing over time we can identify unambiguously a summary of the past (called a "state variable") conditioning future strategies. This summary, which synthesizes every instant of the game up to that point, captures everything the players need to know about the impact of future strategies on the players' future gains. For example, in an oligopolistic market, the current level of productive capacities can, if the mode and the timing of the acquisition of these capacities are not relevant, sum up the industry's past. This notion is useful in what is called structural industrial economics, now the dominant approach in empirical industrial economics: the notion of a Markov perfect equilibrium is now routinely used in econometrics to analyze and measure the dynamic behavior of firms in competition with one another.

With Drew Fudenberg, now a professor at MIT (and like me one of Eric Maskin's first students), I refined the notion of "perfect Bayesian equilibrium."[41] This concept combines the notion of a Bayesian equilibrium, which makes it possible to study games involving asymmetric information, with the notion of perfect equilibrium, which describes equilibria in a dynamic context. Again with Drew Fudenberg, I defined a methodology for studying games involving preemption (or more generally, games in which the agents' strategy consists in choosing the moment to act) in continuous time.

My work on the pure theory of contracts has consisted in extending the analytical framework in four directions:

Dynamics. A contractual relation is often repeated. In addition, it can be renegotiated while it is being executed. My studies on this subject written with Jean-Jacques Laffont, Oliver Hart, and Drew Fudenberg (as well as earlier works written with Roger Guesnerie and Xavier Freixas) have developed a dynamic and evolving view of contracts. For instance, in the context of adverse selection (in which the agent has information that the principal does not have), the agent's performance reveals information about his or her characteristics or those of his or her environment (the difficulty of his or her task, talent, or taste for hard work) and so influences future contracts. To return to the farming example, the landowner who observes an abundant harvest can infer that the land is fertile or that the farmer is efficient. The landowner will then tend to offer more onerous contracts in the future; for example, the landowner will demand a higher price for a farming lease or will set more ambitious goals for the harvest. If the farmer anticipates this "ratchet effect," he in turn will be encouraged to reduce his effort (or to hide part of his harvest!).

Hierarchies. Contracts often involve more than two parties (a principal and an agent). For example, in a sharecropping lease in which the landowner and the farmer each receive half the harvest, the landowner may delegate the measuring/supervision of the harvest to an intermediary. In fact, we see intermediaries like this everywhere in the economy: financial intermediaries (banks, investment funds, venture capitalists), company foremen and directors, regulators, and so on. When there are more than two agents, collusion between a subset of these agents and other agents in the organization is possible. My research consists in connecting this danger of collusion in "cliques" (to use a sociological term) with the structure of information (its distribution within the organization), and in studying the consequences of the threat of collusion for the design of organizations. Intuitively, collusion is easier to achieve in groups endowed with the same information; "clusters of information" therefore give rise to cliques that threaten organizational efficiency.

The "informed principal" theory. These studies (written in collaboration with Eric Maskin) have provided conceptual tools for modeling the choice of contract offered to an agent by a principal who has information the agent does not have. For example, an entrepreneur (the principal) who is raising funds on the financial markets by selling shares for assets may either have a real need of cash to finance a good project, or be seeking to sell before bad news concerning the company (or the assets) becomes public. The quantity issued, as well as its mode (stocks or bonds) will be interpreted by investors (the agents) as signals.

The internal organization of business enterprises and the state. With Mathias Dewatripont (of the Université libre de Bruxelles), I have analyzed ways of structuring organizations to create a greater sense of responsibility within them; thus we showed how an adversarial procedure that has advocates (rather than more neutral representatives) on each side can help a judge, or more generally a neutral decision maker, to obtain more information, and can do so even when these advocates keep silent about information unfavorable to their cause. We have also examined the missions that can be assigned to government officials and agencies, and showed when specific, clear missions can be superior to a more all-encompassing approach ("grasp all, lose all").

This chapter has sought to present the principal characteristics of research in economics: the back and forth between theory and experience and between methodological research and applied research, how research is evaluated, the character of academic debate and the evolving consensus as understanding advances, and finally the role of mathematics and new conceptual tools. As in any science, the advancement of knowledge in economics goes hand in hand with a specialization of the researchers that sometimes amounts to fragmentation, because it is becoming increasingly difficult to master the different approaches, domains, and available tools. Interdisciplinary research, however, remains an important source of progress in economics, as well as between the social sciences and humanities, which are the subject of the following chapter.

FIVE
Economics on the Move

In the twentieth century, economics, which had previously been completely integrated into the social and human sciences, created a new identity for itself – but at the price of becoming disconnected from the other disciplines.

The science of economics developed the fiction of *homo economicus*, that is, the simplifying hypothesis that decision makers are rational, meaning that they act in their own best interests given the information at their disposal (although economics emphasizes that this information may be partial or manipulated). Economic policy recommendations are consequently based on the idea of externalities, or market failures, which result in a difference between individual rationality and collective rationality such that what is good for an individual economic agent is not necessarily good for society as a whole.

Recently, through research on behavioral patterns and neuroeconomics, economists have turned back to psychology. The motive for this revival is the need to gain a better understanding of behavior. In fact, the construct of *homo economicus* (and its counterpart, *homo politicus*) has been controversial, as it is evident that we do not always behave as rationally as this hypothesis predicts. We all suffer from flawed thinking and decision making. More generally, over the past twenty years, economics has moved closer to the other social sciences, taking on board many of their insights. To be mildly provocative, I would even argue that anthropology, law, economics, history, philosophy, psychology, political science, and sociology are really one discipline, because their subjects of study are the same: the same people, groups, and organizations.

These forays by economists into the other human and social sciences are not evidence of voracious imperialism. Other disciplines have their own characteristics. They are often (though not always) less quantitative and less inclined toward formal theoretical analysis and the statistical processing of data. Perhaps a more significant difference is that researchers in other areas of the human and social sciences do not all adhere to the principle of methodological individualism cherished by economists,[1] according to which the incentives and behavior of individuals must be the starting point for understanding the behavior of the groups to which they belong. In my view, it is essential that all the disciplines in the human and social sciences are open to, and nourish, one another. Economists have much to learn from other disciplines, and in turn their work can open new lines of research into individual behavior and social phenomena.[2]

Whole books could be written about how the discipline of economics now operates far beyond its traditional boundaries. The purpose of this chapter will be simply to provide a few examples of this, and for this purpose I have chosen mainly themes close to my own research interests. I hope the reader will pardon this self-indulgent choice. My research covers only a small part of this expanded domain, but I hope to give the reader an idea of how much research economists currently do outside their classical territory.

AN AGENT WHO IS NOT ALWAYS RATIONAL: *HOMO PSYCHOLOGICUS*

For a long time, *homo economicus* has been represented as a decision maker who is aware of his own interests and pursues them in a rational way. He might lack information, in which case his decisions might not be as good as those he would make if he had full knowledge of the facts. He could also choose not to be completely informed, or to not think things through in detail, because to do so costs time and, potentially, money.[3] But he pursues his own interests perfectly, whatever they were.

CONTRARY TO OUR PERSONAL SELF-INTEREST

Now let us give, by way of contrast, a few examples that do not correspond to the *homo economicus* model, possibly leading to dysfunctional behavior.[4]

We Procrastinate

The first example results from a simple lack of will. Too strong a preference for the present leads to procrastination, to putting off disagreeable tasks, to not committing enough to the future, to behaving impulsively. Many studies have been devoted to this short-termism, the early Greek philosophers discussed it, and Adam Smith addressed it in his book *The Theory of Moral Sentiments* (1759). But for almost the entire twentieth century, the subject disappeared from economists' field of research. This has changed now.

Economists are interested in the phenomenon of procrastination because it has important consequences for economic policy. We often act against our own interests: left to ourselves, we tend not to save enough for our retirement, to abuse alcohol and drugs, to become addicted to gambling, to buy too quickly from door-to-door salesmen just to get rid of them, to eat too much fat and sugar, to continue to smoke when we would like to stop, to watch television when we really wanted to work or to spend time with other people. In short, what we do today is not always consistent with what we might have wished we would do.

We can think about our short-term behavior in terms of a conflict of goals between our different, successive "selves" (or "temporal incarnations"). We would like to stop smoking, but our present self wants to smoke one last pack of cigarettes, and leaves the disagreeable task of stopping to tomorrow's self. Of course, tomorrow's self also won't have the self-discipline to stop. We always put too much weight on immediate pleasures and costs, and thereby sacrifice our long-term interests.

Policy makers face the dilemma of whether to respect the choices made by individuals (the present selves who make the decisions) or to act paternalistically (which can be interpreted as defending the individual's longer-term interests). There are good reasons to be wary of paternalism generally, because it can be used to justify all kinds of state intrusion into personal choices. But it is easy to see why a government might want to correct the bias of procrastination. That is what they do when they heavily subsidize retirement saving through a funded pension scheme, or guarantee a minimum retirement pension through a pay-as-you-go system, as in France and some other European countries. The government is also acting paternalistically when it levies high taxes on tobacco; or prohibits or regulates the market for drugs or gambling; or insists on a "cooling-off period" to allow consumers time to change their minds about certain purchases made by their present selves (for example, in the case of door-to-door selling).

Neuroscientists are also very interested in this phenomenon. Researchers have studied, for example, what happens in the brain when individuals are faced with intertemporal choices (decisions made today about the future). Volunteers are asked whether they would prefer to receive ten dollars immediately or fifteen dollars in six months – an extremely high interest rate, well in excess of normal interest rates on our savings. When they choose the immediate ten dollars, their limbic system is activated. The limbic system, which plays an important role in emotion, is an ancient part of the brain, well developed in all animals. When the option of fifteen dollars in six months is chosen, the prefrontal cortex, much more developed in humans, is activated.[5] There may be a tension between the drive for instant gratification and our long-term interests, aspects handled by different parts of the brain.

We Make Mistakes in Forming Our Beliefs

Most of our decisions have uncertain effects. This makes it important not to have too distorted a view of the respective probabilities of possible consequences of our actions. We are sometimes very poor statisticians, though. For example, a classic mistake is to think that nature will make sure that the actual outcomes will quickly match the theoretical probability of those outcomes. (Those who have learned statistics know that this in fact requires a very large number of draws, in order to be able to apply the "law of large numbers.") We all know that flipping coins will give an equal chance of heads or tails; if we flip a coin a great many times, the proportion of tails will be close to 50 percent.[6] Yet many of us make the mistake of believing that, when heads comes up three times in a row, the probability that next time it will be tails is greater than the probability that it will be heads.[7] However, the coin has no memory; it will fall either way with a probability of 50 percent. This bias is also found when professionals carry out repetitive tasks: judges ruling on requests for asylum, loan officers in a bank granting credit, or baseball umpires calling strikes, all tend to make decisions that "compensate" for their recent decisions. In other words, a decision one way is more likely if the preceding decision went in the opposite direction.[8]

Another widespread flaw is the difficulty we have in correctly adjusting our beliefs to take account of new information. High school and university statistics lessons teach Bayes's theorem, a formula describing the correct way to update probabilities in the light of new information. In standard micro- and macroeconomic models, agents are assumed to review their beliefs rationally (that is, in line with Bayes's theorem) as soon as they have new information. But in the real world this is often not the case. This is true for even the best-educated. As I noted in chapter 1, Kahneman and Tversky showed that medical students at Harvard, an elite group, made elementary statistical errors in calculating the probability of an illness on the basis of symptoms alone, demonstrating that statistical computation is not intuitive.[9] Another famous experiment by the same authors involved asking, "Is it more probable that more than 60 percent of the births on a given day would be boys in a small or in a large hospital?"[10] Most people reply that the probability must be the same, no matter what the size of the hospital. However, the probability that more than 60 percent of newborns are male is higher when the hospital is smaller. Intuitively, in a hospital that had one birth per day, the probability of this being a boy would be (about) 50 percent; with two births per day, the probability that more than 60 percent of the births would be boys is the probability that both the births would both be boys, or 25 percent.

With a large number of births, the probability that more than 60 percent of newborns are boys becomes almost zero: the number of boys born in a large hospital will be close to 50 percent, and thus lower than 60 percent.

We Feel Empathy

We don't always act in our own material interest, for example the self-interest that would maximize the money in our bank account or more generally our command over goods or amenities. We give to charities. We help strangers when we know we will never see them again. In both cases, we expect nothing in return.

Adding empathy to the description of an economic agent's goals poses no problem for classical economic theory, as it simply requires redefining self-interest: if I internalize part of your well-being, it becomes, de facto, mine. However, pro-social behavior – that is, behavior in which the individual does not put his own interests above those of everyone else – is much subtler than that, as we will see. Simply adding a dose of empathy to *homo economicus* only slightly improves this paradigm's power to explain how individuals really behave.

And Then Also ...

There are other deviations from pure rationality studied in experimental economics: excessive optimism, a strong aversion to losses, the sometimes useful but often counterproductive role of our emotions in decision making, selective memory, and our own manipulation of our beliefs.

PRO-SOCIAL BEHAVIOR

Let us turn to pro-social behavior, that is, behavior in which individuals do not give priority to their own material interests, but internalize the well-being of others in a disinterested way. This behavior contributes greatly to the quality of social life. Of course, some of our cooperative behavior only appears to be pro-social. In a repeated relationship we have an interest in behaving well, even from the narrow perspective of our self-interest. The person with whom we are interacting, or the social group to which we belong, will behave differently toward us depending on whether we cooperate or pursue our own short-term interest.

But as we have noted, in a narrow economic model, no one gives to charities, invests in socially responsible mutual funds, buys fair trade products, or works for NGOs at salaries far below the average. Nor do we find any economic agent who votes, because voting cannot be explained by self-interest: the probability that your vote is pivotal, and could change the election result, is almost zero, except in very small groups. Even in the famously close American presidential election in 2000, when the Florida outcome determined the winner, the difference was a few hundred votes. One single vote would have changed nothing. Voting solely to increase the chances that one's preferred candidate is elected would never be worth the quarter of an hour it takes to do it, in the narrow rational choice approach. This means we are either deluding ourselves by thinking that our vote will in reality advance our preferred cause, or we are not voting to satisfy our economic or ideological interest, but rather because we think it is a duty to do so; we want to look good to others and to ourselves. [11]

More generally, individuals sometimes make decisions that do not correspond to their strict material interests, and altruism is one of the reasons we might use to explain why they do so. But altruism alone is a much too simplistic explanation, as we are about to see.

ALTRUISM AND SELF-IMAGE

The internalization of others' well-being allows us to explain the existence of charitable donations, but it doesn't explain everything. To understand why, it is useful to refer to a well-known game in the social sciences, the "Dictator Game" (see Figure 5.1).

In conditions of anonymity, [12] an individual (an active player, called the Dictator) is asked to choose on the computer between action A, which guarantees the Dictator gets six dollars and gives one dollar to

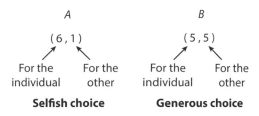

Figure 5.1. The Dictator Game.

the other participant in the experiment (a passive player unknown to the Dictator); and action *B*, which gives five dollars to each of them. We can describe action *A* as selfish and action *B* as generous. Rational behavior, in the classic sense, implies the active player will choose *A*, which maximizes the Dictator's revenue. In practice, however, about three-quarters of the players asked to choose pick *B*.[13] The sacrifice associated with generosity is small enough that most players choose it. But can we say that this is because they have simply internalized the other player's well-being?

In fact, generosity is a very complex phenomenon with three motivating factors: intrinsic motivation (we are spontaneously and naturally generous), extrinsic motivation (we are moved by external incentives such as tax deductions to be generous), and the desire to look good (to project a good image to others and to ourselves).

It turns out that our self-image plays an important role in the Dictator Game, where the Dictator is dealing only with him- or herself. (Anonymity is total. Even the experimenter doesn't know who the player is. Hence, concerns about social image play no role in most laboratory experiments.) More broadly, social image and social prestige are also essential motivations, indicated by the fact that only 1 percent of the donations made to museums or universities are anonymous. The same point is illustrated in Figure 5.2, which shows that when there are categories of donations (for example, a "Silver Donor" gives between $500 and $999, and a "Gold Donor" gives more than $1,000) we see more donations in amounts that allow the donor to just squeak into the next category up, rather than a uniform distribution of amounts donated.

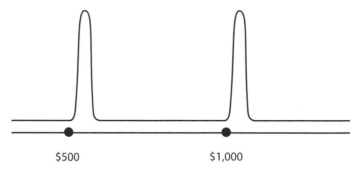

Figure 5.2. Grouping phenomena (donations by category).

An interesting study of the same phenomenon focused on the introduction of voting by mail in several Swiss cantons.[14] According to traditional economics, a priori the introduction of voting by mail would be expected to increase participation in elections, because the cost of voting (at least for those who prefer to vote by mail rather than going to the polling station) decreases. However, the experience showed that participation did not increase – and in some cantons, especially rural ones, it even decreased after voting by mail was introduced. The reason is that in villages where the electors know each other, and therefore social pressure is intense, people go to the polling station partly to show they are good citizens. As soon as there is a reasonable excuse for not going to the polling station, the loss of social prestige connected with not voting is no longer obvious, as no one can be sure you did not vote. This study demonstrates, once again, the complexity of social behavior and its motivations.

Reciprocal Altruism

Humans have an important characteristic distinguishing them from other species: cooperation among large groups of individuals who are not closely genetically linked. (Bee hives and ant colonies have strong genetic links among themselves, while cooperation within other species such as other primates occurs in small groups.) As I noted earlier, we need to distinguish between cooperation motivated by self-interest, based on a repeated relationship with another individual or group, and cooperation based on social preferences, as in the Dictator Game.

Another famous game involving social preferences is the Ultimatum Game. Player 1 is given the task of dividing a total of ten dollars between him- or herself and Player 2. So far, it resembles the Dictator Game. As in the Dictator Game, the ultimatum game guarantees the players' anonymity: they do not know with whom they are playing, to rule out cooperation inspired by material self-interest. The Ultimatum Game differs from the Dictator Game because the outcome depends on Player 2's goodwill: if Player 2 rejects the allocation proposed by Player 1, neither receives anything. In practice, an offer to split the ten dollars equally is always accepted, whereas when Player 1 offers Player 2 nothing, or just one or two dollars (leaving ten, nine, or eight dollars for Player 1) this is often rejected by Player 2. This happens even though Player 2 would be better off accepting one or two dollars rather than getting nothing. Anticipating this situation, Player 1 often rationally proposes distributions that are less extreme, or even equal.[15] We are frequently moved by reciprocal altruism: we tend to be nice to people who treat us well, and conversely take revenge on people whose behavior to us, or people close to us, we find objectionable – even if this vengeance is costly for us.

Reciprocity seems to be universal. Research undertaken in fifteen microsocieties (such as the Hadza in Tanzania or the Tsimanes in Bolivia) found behaviors in the Ultimatum Game that are similar to those reported above. Interestingly, societies that involve a high level of exchange (and thus do not have a way of life centered on the family) seem to be more cooperative in these experiments.[16]

THE FRAGILITY OF ALTRUISM AND HONESTY

The Power of Excuses and Moral Wriggle Room

To understand the difficulties in trying to produce a coherent picture of altruism, let's return to the Dictator Game, modifying it in the way illustrated in Figure 5.3.

There are two "states of nature." In the first state, the rewards are the same as before, choice *A* being the selfish action and choice *B*

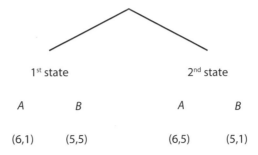

Figure 5.3. The moral wriggle room game.

the generous action. If the Dictator chooses *A*, the Dictator gets six dollars and the other player gets one dollar, whereas if the Dictator chooses *B*, both players receive five dollars. In the second state of nature, *A* is better than *B* for both players. In this second state of nature, it is therefore optimal for the Dictator to choose action *A*, from both his own individual and the collective points of view.

So far so simple, except that at the beginning of the experiment the Dictator does not know which state of nature prevails. Both states are equally likely. The experimenter asks if the Dictator would like to know which it is (it will cost nothing to find out). A rational player should say yes. In particular, an altruist will want to know whether to choose *B* (in the first state of nature) or *A* (in the second state of nature, in which both players will do best with *A*). But experiments reveal that most Dictators do not want to make an informed choice; most prefer not to know the state of nature and choose *A*, the selfish act, hiding behind the "excuse" that there is a state of nature in which this choice would not penalize the other player. In other words, they prefer not to know that they may be in the first state, which would force them to choose between selfishness and altruism. This is the behavior of the pedestrian who crosses the road to avoid meeting a beggar to whom he or she will feel "obliged" to give. [17]

A laboratory experiment conducted by Armin Falk (of the University of Bonn) and Nora Szech (of the University of Karlsruhe) and published in *Science* shows that sharing responsibility may erode moral values.[18] This erosion applies to markets, but it is just as power-ful as soon as a decision involves a single other person, enabling a sem-blance of shared responsibility. In all organizations, the existence of excuses ("I was asked to do it," "Someone else would do it if I didn't," "I didn't know," "Everybody does it") makes individuals less resistant to unethical behavior. An important goal of research is to understand better how institutions, from markets to administered organizations, affect our values and behavior.

Contextual Effects

Let's consider another variant of the Dictator Game (Figure 5.4) in which the experimenter adds a third option, C, which is even more selfish than option A. Normally, one would expect a subject who altruistically chooses B when the choice is between only A and B (as in Figure 5.1) to choose B again when the more selfish option C is on the table. In other words, the introduction of option C should not affect the frequency of the generous choice B;[19] and in particular it should not affect the choice between A and B for those who would not choose C whatever happened. In practice, however, the addition of C significantly diminishes the frequency with which B is chosen, and makes the choice of A proportionately much more probable than B.[20] Alternatives may be relevant, even if they are not chosen!

There are several possible interpretations of the importance of context here. For instance, it may be that option C provides the Dictator with a narrative ("I wasn't really being selfish") by making option A seem less selfish than when the choice was only between A and B. Option A becomes a compromise. Or perhaps the player interprets the introduction of option C as a signal of a norm, indi-cating that the experimenter does not necessarily expect him or her

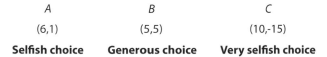

A	B	C
(6,1)	(5,5)	(10,-15)
Selfish choice	**Generous choice**	**Very selfish choice**

Figure 5.4. The importance of context.

to be generous. Either way, this experiment and others show the importance of the context in which decisions are made – an irrelevant alternative (to the extent that we would not choose it in any case) can affect our choice.

More generally, context can influence choices when individuals interpret the way in which choices are presented (and not solely the options themselves) as relevant. This idea has been applied in many ways. For example, a company or a state that offers its employees or citizens a default option for a retirement savings strategy is implicitly asserting that this choice is suitable for most people, even if other choices might be better for some people in some situations. There is an extensive literature on this guidance of decisions, described as "libertarian paternalism," [21] (or "nudging"). The oxymoron "libertarian paternalism" expresses the idea well: the individual has complete freedom to make the best choice, if he knows what it is; but his choice is guided when he lacks important information or remains undecided.

The Role of Memory

Many other experiments show that our pro-social behavior is fragile and complex, and that memory plays an important role. Consider a game created by psychologists in which players can cheat without being unmasked. For example, a volunteer participant in the experiment receives a random allotment of between one dollar and ten dollars (a figure shown on his computer screen), with a probability of 1/10 for each amount. The experimenter does not know this figure. The volunteer declares the figure, and receives the amount he declares. He can therefore cheat and declare seven dollars (and receive seven dollars) even though he is only entitled to five. How can cheating be spotted under such conditions? By the frequency of the declarations. [22] If the subjects are honest and the sample is sufficiently large, approximately 10 percent of the sample should declare one dollar, 10 percent two dollars, and so on. So, if high figures are declared more frequently than they should be, that indicates cheating (probably not in a uniform way though: we know from other experiments that some people never cheat, whereas others do cheat, but to varying degrees). But the experiment is not over.

In a second phase, the game is played again, but only after the experimenters have read out the Ten Commandments or the university's honor code to the participants.[23] The participants cheat much less in this second experiment than they did in the first. This is another experiment that undermines the traditional concept of a wholly rational *homo economicus*, just as it disproves any other equally simplistic theory of behavior. Reading the Ten Commandments or the university's honor code makes one's cheating harder to ignore, and thus more difficult to repress in one's memory.

When We Are Punished for Our Good Deeds …

To illustrate the full complexity of generosity, we should mention the experiments on ostracism conducted by Benoît Monin and his coauthors.[24] These experiments confirm that we like generous people … unless they are *too* generous. We do not much care for people who give us lessons in morality, even indirectly. Individuals perceived as too generous end up being ostracized by others. The problem is that people who are too virtuous provide a comparison point[25] that does no favors to our own image. Rather than endure this permanent reminder of our selfishness, we prefer to cold-shoulder those who make it too obvious.

MANIPULATING OUR OWN BELIEFS

Game theory and information theory have found an unexpected but natural home in psychology. For centuries (even millennia), psychologists and philosophers have emphasized the way people manipulate their beliefs: individuals usually seek to repress, forget, or reinterpret information that is unfavorable to them.[26] Economists have recently been exploring these themes regarding individuals' "self-manipulation" of their beliefs. For example, Roland Bénabou (Princeton University) and I have described the self-manipulation of beliefs as the equilibrium of a game between the different selves of the same individual – a game in which the individual may try to "forget" (repress) information that might damage his self-confidence.[27] The individual manipulates his beliefs, and at the same time may be aware that he has a selective memory.

To understand self-manipulation, we must first understand the "demand" for self-manipulation: Why would an individual want to lie to himself? After all, classical decision theory shows that having better information allows us to make better decisions, in full knowledge of the facts. To repress information is to lie to oneself and thus degrade the quality of information and, consequently, one's decision making as well. We can identify three reasons why individuals may try to lie to themselves:

1. The fear of a lack of willpower and of the concomitant procrastination that might occur in the future (more self-confidence enables one to counteract, at least in part, this lack of willpower, by giving oneself the energy to act).

2. The fact that we feel pain and pleasure before the actual experience – our projecting into the future gives rise to "anticipatory utility or disutility." We enjoy vacations and other pleasant events well before they occur. Conversely, the very prospect of a surgical intervention makes us unhappy. The existence of anticipatory (dis)utility explains why we often forget possible negative outcomes such as accident or death, with both functional and dysfunctional consequences: this lack of concern makes for a happier life while at the same time leading to inefficiencies in decision making – for example, not having a medical test or not wearing a seatbelt in one's car.

3. The "consumption" of beliefs people have about themselves (we care about our self-image; we want to believe that we are intelligent, attractive, generous, and so on).

On the "supply" side of self-manipulation, self-deception may operate through:

1. The manipulation of memory (through strategies of encoding, repression, or rehearsal)
2. The refusal to hear, process, or pay attention to certain kinds of information
3. The choice of actions that signal particular character traits.

Plato insisted that manipulating one's own beliefs is bad for individuals. On the other hand, many psychologists (William James, Martin Seligman, and others) have emphasized that people need to see themselves in a positive light in order to motivate themselves both to engage in activities and to further their own well-being. When motivated by the fear of a future lack of willpower, this self-deception can be shown to be beneficial for individuals with a serious self-control problem, but not otherwise. Since then, we and other researchers have studied other themes connected with the manipulation of beliefs, ranging from the analysis of personal resolutions, rules of life, identity, and religious precepts to the impact of collective beliefs on political choices.[28]

HOMO SOCIALIS

TRUST

Trust is at the heart of economic and social life. True, it is not always necessary. The invention of money, for instance, has simplified the mechanics of exchange. So long as we can verify the quality of a good, we can buy it from a stranger in exchange for money. If we cannot verify the quality of the good before purchase, we can often count on the mechanism of reputation: we return to a merchant with whom we were satisfied, or go to a merchant a friend has found satisfactory; the merchant understands this mechanism and will make an effort to build up and retain a loyal clientele.

In analyzing behavior, researchers are interested in the trust we place in others. In economic terms, it is simple to formalize this concept. It is treated as a problem of imperfect information about the reliability and preferences of others. Over time, all agents revise their beliefs about the people with whom they interact. By being around others and interacting with them, we learn about them and can evaluate better their reliability and the trust we can place in them.

We can thus learn whether people are trustworthy if we repeatedly interact with them, but we have less information about how to behave in a one-off interaction with a stranger; for instance, when we buy a souvenir whose quality we cannot evaluate at a tourist attraction, or when we decide to trust a neighbor or a babysitter we do not know well to take care of our children, or when we begin a personal relationship. We can form an opinion very rapidly about someone based on certain signals, but these opinions are very imperfect, a fact that has even served as the basis for TV game shows based on trust.[29]

We now know that our hormones influence us in this situation. The economists Ernst Fehr (Zurich), Michael Kosfeld (Frankfurt), and their coauthors[30] injected volunteers with the hormone oxytocin[31] as part of an experimental "trust game." This game for two players, Player 1 and Player 2, can be described as follows:

- Player 1 receives money from the experimenter, perhaps ten dollars, and chooses a sum between zero and ten dollars to give to Player 2. Player 1 keeps the rest.
- Player 2 then receives, also from the experimenter, three times the amount of the figure given by Player 1; for example, Player 2 receives fifteen dollars if Player 1 has given half the initial ten.
- Player 2 freely decides to give a sum back to Player 1. There is no obligation as to the amount. Player 2 is then in the position of a Dictator and can decide not to give anything, hence the importance of Player 1's confidence in the reciprocity of Player 2.

Once again, the players are anonymous. Each player is behind a computer and does not know (and will never know) the identity of the player with whom he or she has been paired.

The ideal for both players (if they could agree in advance) is for Player 1 to give all ten dollars to Player 2. This would leave Player 1 with nothing, but would maximize the size of the pie to be shared (3 x $10 = $30). But the structure of the game means they cannot agree to a strategy in advance. The way the thirty dollars is shared is therefore totally at the discretion of Player 2. Giving all ten dollars to

Player 2 would thus require Player 1 to have an enormous amount of confidence in Player 2's reciprocity.

Player 2's "rational" behavior (that is, the choice that maximizes revenue) obviously consists in keeping everything. For Player 1, anticipating that Player 2 will give nothing back, it consists in not giving anything. These "rational" choices minimize the size of the pie (which remains equal to the initial ten dollars kept by Player 1). In practice, things go differently in experiments. A nonnegligible number of individuals in the position of Player 2 feel obliged to reciprocate when Player 1 has trusted them. Rationally anticipating this behavior, Player 1 gives some money, hoping that Player 2 will behave reciprocally.

The interesting point noted by Ernst Fehr, Michael Kosfeld, and their coauthors is that the injection of oxytocin makes it possible to increase the feeling of trust in the other player, and thus increase, on average, how much Player 1 gives. This is not very reassuring, because it is easy to imagine commercial applications for altering behavior in this way.

With or without oxytocin, the trust game just described reproduces in the laboratory the mechanism of reciprocity, one of the most powerful social mechanisms. As I have said, we feel an obligation to those who have shown generosity toward us, and we may seek to take revenge on people who are rude to us – even at a personal cost. This principle is commonly used in marketing, where free samples and gifts try to play on the principle that "who gives, receives."

Reciprocity in economics inspired the hypothesis that an employer can increase profits by offering a higher salary to prospective employees than is needed to attract them (i.e., the market rate for the job) because they will be grateful for the generosity and will work harder. This seems to be true.[32] However, the effect may be temporary, as is shown by an experiment conducted on a tea plantation in India.[33] The base salary of the pickers was increased by 30 percent, while their variable remuneration (which depended on the quantity of tea they picked) was reduced. Overall they would earn more, no matter how much tea the pickers harvested (but the least productive pickers had the highest relative pay raise).[34] Contrary to the predictions of the classic economic model, the productivity of the pickers (who now had weaker incentives to work because their remuneration depended less on the quantity picked) significantly increased in comparison to the control group. At the end of four months, however, *homo economicus* was back: the conventional economic prediction that weaker incentives would reduce effort was more or less verified.

STEREOTYPES

Sociologists rightly emphasize the importance of not observing individuals out of context, that is, without taking into account their social environment. Individuals are part of social groups, and these groups affect how they will behave. The group defines the individual's identity and the image that he or she wants to project to others and to him- or herself. Individuals serve as models or examples: seeing people close to us, people we trust and with whom we identify, behaving in a certain way affects our behavior. Here I would like to discuss another kind of influence exercised by the group: the influence that operates through the way others view the group.

Countries and ethnic or religious groups are perceived as "honest," "industrious," "corrupt," "aggressive," or "concerned about the environment," in the same way that firms get a good or a bad reputation depending on the quality of their products.[35] Such stereotypes and collective reputations affect the trust placed in members of a group when they interact with people outside the group.

In a way, the group's reputation (whatever it is at a particular moment in time) is no more than the result of the past behavior of the individuals who compose it. Suppose that individual behavior is observed only imperfectly; in fact, if individual behavior was observed perfectly, individuals would be judged entirely on this behavior, and collective reputation would play no role at all. Conversely, if they were never observed, individuals would make little effort to behave responsibly, because the collective reputation is a public good for the group. Defending the collective reputation entails an entirely private cost but a benefit that is shared by the whole community. This is why there is a tendency toward free-riding. Taxi drivers who charge undue supplements or winemakers who adulterate their wine do great harm to other members of their profession. It is thus possible to reconcile methodological individualism (the taxi driver will pursue his own interest, which may not coincide with that of the group) and holism (according to which the behavior of individuals cannot be understood without considering the properties of the whole of which they are parts).

Individual behavior and collective behavior are, to some extent, complementary. An individual has weak incentives to behave well if his community has a bad reputation, because he will not be trusted by others anyway and therefore will have fewer opportunities to interact with – and less incentive to develop a good reputation among – those outside his community. In turn, this rational behavior by the individual reinforces others' prejudices regarding the group and contributes to its negative stereotype. Two groups that are, a priori, identical may have very different stereotypes. It is possible to show, moreover, that collective reputations are subject to hysterisis;[36] in particular, a country, a profession, or an enterprise can suffer from prejudices for a very long time before being able to correct its reputation. Thus it is better to avoid a bad collective reputation at all costs, because it can become self-fulfilling and may very well persist.

HOMO INCITATUS: THE COUNTERPRODUCTIVE EFFECTS OF REWARDS

The Limits of Incentives in Mainstream Economics

In chapter 2, we saw that economists are often criticized for emphasizing the role of incentives, i.e., for envisioning a world in which an agent's behavior is guided only by carrot and stick. There is some truth in this view, insofar as understanding the role of incentives is the bread and butter of the discipline of economics, but it also ignores the evolution of economics over the past thirty years.

First, economists have argued that incentives "work better" – that is, create behavior more in accord with the objectives of the organization or the society – in some circumstances than in others, when the effects of incentives can be limited or even counterproductive. The corresponding theories and empirical results are entirely in line with our personal experiences. Here are a few examples.

Suppose that the economic agent has several tasks to complete. For example, a teacher (in a school or university) has, on the one hand, to pass on to the student the knowledge necessary to move on to the next class, pass an exam, or get a job. On the other hand, taking a longer-term perspective, the students must be trained to think for themselves. If the teacher is paid based on the success of pupils in their exams, the teacher will focus on exam technique, to the detriment of the students' long-term development, which is much more difficult to measure and thus more difficult to reward. That does not mean that we have to give up on the idea of providing incentives for teachers; in certain environments, they may be beneficial. Esther Duflo, Rema Hanna and Steve Ryan have shown, through an experiment conducted in India, that teachers react positively to financial incentives and supervision, with the result that students are absent less often and perform better.[37] But we must be very careful not to distort the educational process by introducing incentives that are not well thought out and tested.

The problem of "multitasking" is found in many domains.[38] This book provides some examples: some agents in finance, facing incentives based on short-term performance, behaved in ways that were harmful over the long term, leading to the crisis of 2008 (chapter 12). A regulated company that is generously rewarded for reducing costs will tend to sacrifice maintenance, increasing the risk of accidents. Therefore, strong incentives to reduce costs must be accompanied by increased supervision of maintenance by the regulator (chapter 17).

Numerous other drawbacks of strong incentives have been pointed out in economic research. These kinds of incentives are not appropriate when the individual contribution of an agent within a team is difficult to identify, or more generally when the agent's performance depends on factors that cannot be measured, and over which the agent has no control. In such circumstances the agent would end up being rewarded simply for being lucky enough to have good teammates. Conversely, the agent might be unjustly punished for the bad luck of having poor teammates. Another limitation of strong incentives arises in a hierarchy. Such incentives increase the benefits of manipulating information and thereby encourage collusion in internal cliques. For example, a foreman may collude with workers to misreport performance or the difficulty of their task, or top executives may capture the board of directors to the detriment of shareholder interests. Finally, strong incentives may not be needed: if the relation between principal and agent is repeated, a relation of trust may helpfully replace formal incentives and actually improve on them to the extent that it is flexible, i.e., contingent on fine information.

The Crowding Out of Intrinsic Motivation

Another kind of criticism is that extrinsic incentives can kill intrinsic motivation. Consequently, an increase in extrinsic incentives may be counterproductive and result in less participation or less effort. This question is crucial for public policy. For example, should people be paid for giving blood, as is the case in some countries? Should we count on the goodwill of individuals or put a policeman on duty? To protect the environment, is it better to subsidize the purchase of hybrid cars or the purchase of green boilers in the home instead?

To study pro-social behavior, Roland Bénabou and I started with the assumption that individuals differ both in terms of their intrinsic motivation to participate in providing a public good and in their desire for individual gain. Individuals are moved by three factors: an intrinsic motivation to contribute to the public good, an extrinsic motivation in the form of a financial reward (r in Figure 5.5) for behaving well – or, equivalently, in the form of a penalty equal to r for bad behavior – and attention given to the image of themselves that they project. Starting from a statistical distribution of agents' characteristics of intrinsic motivation and financial motivation, we determined the way in which behavior changes (on average) according to the extrinsic incentive given to individuals (see Figure 5.5, which shows on the vertical axis the total quantity of the public good provided by the agents, and on the horizontal axis the payment given to those who contribute).

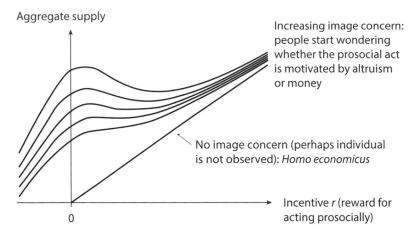

Figure 5.5. Intrinsic motivation and extrinsic motivation. Supply of public good in relation to a monetary incentive *r*; the different curves correspond to different levels of the individual's attachment to the image of himself that he projects (a higher curve corresponds to a greater importance accorded by the individual to his image). When the image becomes sufficiently important for the individual, an interval appears in which an increase in the reward has a counter-productive effect.

Using this model, we can look into questions such as: Should we pay someone for giving blood? For *homo economicus*, it is clear that a reward will encourage him to increase his donations; this is shown in Figure 5.5 by the lower curve, for which a higher reward increases "donations" of blood. But if the individual is preoccupied with his image, the results are what an economist would have to describe as curious.

In a famous book published in 1970, Richard Titmuss explained that we should not pay blood donors because it would destroy their motivation to behave in a pro-social way.[39] Considering the contribution of different types of motivation helps us understand this argument. On the graph in Figure 5.5, we can see that if the donor puts enough weight on his image, there comes a point at which the total quantity of blood donated diminishes as the financial reward increases. This is because, if they are paid, then donors who give their blood in part to project an image of themselves as generous fear that others will suspect that they are in it only for the money. Thus, the presence of image concerns can break the positive relationship (generally assumed in microeconomics) between remuneration and effort or results.

Thus, extrinsic incentives can squeeze out intrinsic incentives. Beyond the possible crowding-out effects of incentives, which probably feature less frequently in the contracting and trading situations most often studied by economists than in social contexts, the theory predicts that financial incentives will promote pro-social behavior less often when the people being paid are observed by peers who might doubt their motivations. When that happens, the image the beneficiaries project if they respond to financial incentives may suffer. These considerations are very useful for public policy. If we return to the question asked earlier – Is it better to subsidize the purchase of a hybrid car or the purchase of a green boiler? – the answer is clearly that it is better to subsidize the heating system, because it is not usually seen by other people, so financial incentives will be more powerful in this case. A car is visible to everyone, and thus the weight of social approval will also be taken into account by the buyer.

This theory has been tested in the laboratory and in the field. In particular, a team of two economists and the psychologist Dan Ariely[40] have shown that individuals contribute more to a good cause if others can see them doing it (confirming the hypothesis that people are motivated by the image of themselves that they project), and that financial incentives are very powerful when the contribution is not observed. But the team also showed that monetary incentives have little effect when the contribution is observed. This confirms the theory that people worry that if they are paid, their contribution will be interpreted as a sign of greed rather than generosity, and thus send the "wrong" signal to others.[41]

The idea that norms emerge from the social signals conveyed by behavior can also be tested in the field. Recent studies have measured the impact of extrinsic incentives on social norms and individuals' behavior in areas as varied as tax evasion in Britain,[42] which ethnic group Chinese parents of mixed origin (one parent being Han and the other belonging to a minority) claim their children to belong to,[43] and the desertion of British soldiers during the First World War.[44]

In the example of blood donations, we saw that the contribution to the public good may decrease if donors are paid, because their generosity may then be interpreted as greed. A different channel for the crowding out of intrinsic motivation by extrinsic incentives arises when the payment might reveal information held by the "principal" (the individual who sets the reward) about the task, or about his trust in the person doing it. This idea once again overlaps with the work of psychologists, for whom a reward can have two effects: the classic incentive effect (it encourages us to make a greater effort) and the effect connected with what this reward reveals about the agent's competence or the difficulty of the task. For example, paying your child to get good grades in school can, over the long run, have a perverse effect, because children risk losing their intrinsic motivation to study and may become motivated solely by the money. The theoretical explanation is different from that for blood donations:[45] children may interpret the promise of a reward as a signal of the task's lack of intrinsic interest, or of a lack of confidence in their ability or their motivation to do the work, all of which reduce their intrinsic motivation. This theory predicts that the reward will have a short-term positive effect, but will also have an addictive effect over a longer term. If the reward is subsequently removed, the child's motivation will be less than it would have been if no reward had ever been offered.

More generally, we need to pay attention to what others infer from our choices. In a company, we know that supervising the effort made by subordinate employees too closely can send a signal that they are not trusted, and can destroy their self-confidence and personal motivation. Supervision can also undermine the norm of reciprocal altruism analyzed earlier in this chapter. A classic experiment based on a variant of the trust game shows that the desire of Player 1 (who must decide whether to trust the reciprocity of the other player or not) to ensure that the other player returns at least part of the sum given him can be counterproductive: you can't simultaneously trust another person and show that you don't trust him![46]

HOMO JURIDICUS: LAW AND SOCIAL NORMS

Economists often see the law chiefly as a set of incentives: the prospect of a fine or prison term dissuades us from driving too fast, stealing, or committing other crimes. Psychologists and sociologists do not entirely share this view. They think it may often be more effective to use persuasion and social sanctions to induce pro-social behavior.

For one thing, the state cannot establish formal incentives everywhere. For many minor misdemeanors, such as dropping litter or disturbing the peace, the police and the courts cannot be used because the cost would be too high. Furthermore, it is impossible to define precisely what is expected of us: It is natural to give directions to a stranger, but where do our obligations to help stop? At some point, society has to decide for itself, and so social norms have an important role to play both in defining what is expected of us and in creating social incentives to behave better than we otherwise would.

A second line of departure is the emphasis on "expressive law." Legal scholars, while recognizing the importance of the law in shaping incentives, stress that a law or regulation also expresses social values. Thus, according to legal scholars, in matters of public policy one cannot count exclusively on sanctions and financial incentives to obtain pro-social behavior from economic agents.

The sociologist Robert Cialdini of Arizona State University has defined two types of norms.[47] The descriptive norm reveals to individuals how their peers or their community behave. For example, they can be shown their peers' average consumption of electricity, how much other people recycle or give to charities. The prescriptive norm is the one endorsed by their peers or their community. Clearly some of our choices are dictated by considering the judgment of our peers and by their behavior. In an experiment focusing on prescriptive norms, conducted at Princeton in reaction to the overconsumption of alcohol on campus, the experimenters showed that, in reality, most students did not necessarily drink too much because they wanted to. Rather they did it because they thought (wrongly) that other students found it "cool." This type of intervention in the creation of social norms thus seeks to provide information to economic agents about what others do (the consumption of alcohol or electricity, for example) or what people find acceptable.

But according to Cialdini, as in economic theory,[48] we need to take care about the messages we choose. A government that asked its citizens to pay their taxes by arguing that "many of your fellow citizens avoid paying taxes, so because we are not collecting enough revenue, your payment is particularly valuable for society" would probably not be very successful in boosting tax collection. Messages more likely to encourage pro-social behavior must be chosen. For example, information must be given when it is likely to produce pro-social behavior: "x percent of your fellow citizens recycle," where x is a surprisingly high percentage, if true. It is better to highlight the positive virtues of our fellow citizens.

Laws are equally expressions of social values and thus send messages concerning the cost of individual behavior, general morality, or social values. Clearly some public policies are dictated by these considerations. Consider, for example, the punishments imposed for crimes: the classic economic analysis might recommend alternative punishments (financial or public service) that are more effective socially and that cost less than sending someone to prison. Yet some citizens would consider this too economic an approach, normalizing behavior they consider to be unacceptable.

Similarly, the debate about capital punishment is essentially based on the idea that capital punishment reflects on the society that imposes it. For most legislators in the majority of developed countries, this is an image which is violent and disrespectful of human dignity; but, by contrast, for the majority of the legislators in the United States, capital punishment is a clear signal that society does not tolerate some types of behavior. The cost-benefit approach (which would frame capital punishment in the following terms: Does capital punishment deter people from committing crimes, and at what cost to society?) plays a minor role in the debate. In short, the debate on capital punishment generally does not take place in the context of classic cost-benefit analysis, but rather in the context of the values of the society. This is an area that lies outside traditional economics. This example also allows us to understand why modern societies, seeking to signal their values, outlaw cruel and unusual punishment, even in cases where the person involved consents to the punishment in full knowledge of what he is doing. Thus, a majority of citizens might say that substituting a flogging for a prison term, even with the full consent of the criminal, would be wrong, despite the fact that it would be cheaper for society.

Finally, the use of incentives can signal our fellow citizens' lack of enthusiasm for the public good, and so damage the norms of civil behavior and be counterproductive. To the extent that we all want to retain the illusion that the society in which we live is virtuous, this also sheds light on the widespread resistance to what economists have to say, because economists are often the bearers of bad empirical news concerning how virtuous people are.

MORE UNEXPECTED LINES OF INQUIRY

Finally, I would like to say a few words about two fields that one does not normally associate with economics, but which are rapidly expanding: evolutionary economics and the economics of religion.

Homo darwinus

One of the most significant advances in the last two decades of economic research is that we can begin to reconcile the economic view of humans with Darwin's vision of us as the result of natural selection. There are many examples of cross-pollination between economics and evolutionary biology. For example, social preferences, which are crucial for an economist (as this chapter has shown) can also be examined from the point of view of evolution.[49]

Biologists have also contributed to game theory. For instance, we owe the first model of the "war of attrition" (which describes the collective irrationality of situations such as a war or a strike in which each party suffers but clings to the hope that the adversary will surrender first) to the biologist Maynard Smith (1974). This idea was subsequently refined by economists.

The theory of signaling is a third area of interest shared by biologists and economists. The general idea of this theory is that wasting resources can be beneficial for an individual, an animal, a plant, or even a state, if doing so can convince others to adopt conciliatory behavior. Animals use a whole series of signals that are expensive or even dysfunctional (such as the peacock's plumes) to seduce partners or to deter predators. Similarly, humans sometimes take risks to impress their rivals or a person they want to attract, or a company might sell at a loss in the attempt to convince its rivals that its costs are low or that its financial basis is solid, thereby encouraging them to quit the market. Shortly after the appearance of a famous article on signaling by the economist Michael Spence,[50] the biologist Amotz Zahavi published research on the same theme.[51] These articles take up and formalize the works of sociologist Thorstein Veblen (*The Theory of the Leisure Class,* 1899) and French sociological approaches to social differentiation (Jean Baudrillard, *The Consumer Society: Myths and Structu*res, 1970; Pierre Bourdieu, *Distinction: A Social Critique of the Judgment of Taste,* 1979). Ideas about signaling have their origin in Darwin's *The Descent of Man* (1871), published long before economists or sociologists took an interest in them.

Overall, the boundaries between economics and the natural sciences are no more watertight than those between economics and other human and social sciences.

Homo religiosus

In view of the importance of religion in the organization of political and economic life in most countries, the economist cannot, as a scientist, ignore it. To avoid any misunderstanding, it must be emphasized that the economist's role is not to evaluate religious belief itself, but to focus on those aspects of religion upon which economics may usefully shed light. The "economics of religions" reappeared in the discipline about twenty or thirty years ago, but it was an old area of investigation.[52] Adam Smith was interested in the financing of the clergy.[53] His theory, demonstrating an awareness of the problem of moral hazard, was that if they were financed directly by believers (rather than by the state or the religious hierarchy), the clergy would serve believers and religion better.

Max Weber's *The Protestant Ethic and the Spirit of Capitalism* defined the theme of the socioeconomic impact of religion. Weber's thesis was that the Protestant Reformation had a major impact on the rise of capitalism, generating a vast amount of debate in the human and social sciences. Today, econometric studies allow us to examine the facts in greater detail. Weber noted that Protestants earned more than Catholics in those regions where they lived side by side, and that in addition wealthy families and territorial collectivities embraced Protestantism more rapidly. The research also sheds light on causalities. For instance, Maristella Botticini (Bocconi University in Milan) and Zvi Eckstein (University of Tel Aviv) have challenged the traditional explanation of Jewish economic success. The traditional view was that, having been driven out of certain professions, Jews took refuge in banking, craftsmanship, and commerce, which transformed them into an urban, educated community.[54] According to Botticini and Eckstein, this transformation happened before they were excluded from other professions. They argue that because Judaism required the reading of the Torah and promoted literacy in Talmudic academies, the Jewish community's human capital increased and prepared it for the financial and juridical aspects that were later to prove more useful than traditional skills, such as knowing how to plant wheat.

In the same spirit, Mohamed Saleh has studied the Islamization of Egypt in the centuries following the Muslim conquest in AD 640.[55] He documents conversions to Islam and the development of the relative incomes of Copts and Muslims. The Coptic community, which initially constituted almost the entire population of Egypt, became much smaller than the Muslim community, but was educated and wealthy. Mohamed Saleh has an economic explanation. As in many similar countries, non-Muslims had to pay a poll tax but Muslims did not. Less wealthy and less religious Copts converted to Islam, making the remaining Coptic community on average more pious and wealthy. This selection effect lasted for many centuries.

Of course, economists have also studied competition between religions – here again, not over religious ideas, about which they have no specific expertise, but in economic dimensions. It is well known that religions offer benefits to attract believers. Sometimes they even fulfill the function of the "welfare state" (which may be one of the factors explaining the alliance between religious groups and the fiscally conservative right wing).[56] For example, some Muslim organizations provide insurance, education, and local public goods. Religious groups even sometimes act as "two-sided markets"[57] by helping their members select a potential marriage partner.[58] Finally, economists investigate the connections between religion and science.[59]

Taken together, these examples constitute, of course, no more than a brief and selective introduction to a vast disciplinary field that is steadily evolving. We are witnessing a gradual reunification of the social sciences. This reunification will be slow, but it is inevitable – in fact, as I said in the introduction to this chapter, anthropologists, economists, historians, legal scholars, philosophers, political scientists, psychologists, and sociologists are interested in the same individuals, the same groups, and the same societies. The convergence that existed until the end of the nineteenth century must be reestablished. This will require these scientific communities to be open to the techniques and ideas of the other disciplines.

PART III

AN INSTITUTIONAL FRAMEWORK
FOR THE ECONOMY

SIX
Toward a Modern State

"I don't want to live in the world you describe."
—Anonymous panel comment at the presentation of Laffont's report

Paris, December 1999: Jean-Jacques Laffont, the best-known French economist of his generation, presented his report[1] on the pathway to a modern state to the Council of Economic Analysis. It had been two years since Prime Minister Lionel Jospin created this advisory Council, an iconoclastic act in a country where economists are regarded with great suspicion. The response? Laffont's balanced report was deemed heretical by the audience of senior officials, academics, and politicians. There was a general outcry, along with a series of speeches congratulating Laffont on his "remarkable report," all the better to explain that he had understood nothing—or, worse still, that he was likely to corrupt French youth.

What did this report say? That politicians and officials respond to the incentives they face—just like CEOs, employees, the unemployed, intellectuals, or … economists—and that the way government is organized should take this reality into account. Despite having an original and profound mind, Jean-Jacques Laffont did not in this regard show a great deal of creativity. The possibility that the state can be captured by special interests at the expense of the collective interest, and that in a democratic system the desire to be elected or reelected may take priority over any other concern, has been at the foundation of all political thought, from Montesquieu to the Founding Fathers of the American constitution, including all the great constitutionalists, and even Karl Marx.

Laffont was deeply concerned with the public interest.[2] He was not accusing government officials. He understood that many politicians begin their careers as idealists, eager to make the world a better place. He also knew that condemning politicians is dangerous for democracies, and should be left to populist parties and demagogues. But he triggered a wave of protests simply by suggesting that France's leaders might, like everyone else, act in their own interest. Challenging the benevolence of the state touched a raw nerve for those commenting on his report that day.

Most of us throughout the world live in a market economy, with a greater or lesser degree of state intervention. We may like, tolerate, or hate this way of organizing society, but we don't constantly ask ourselves whether other systems might be possible. Following the almost total economic, cultural, social, and environmental failure of planned economies, in regards to the market we observe or experience a kind of fatalism, for some spiced with indignation. The French feel particularly disoriented, as they are perhaps more distrustful than any other nationality of the market and competition.

Some of those who want change envision a vague alternative in which the market would no longer be central to society; others, on the contrary, favor a minimalist state that would make laws and dispense justice, maintain order and conduct national defense, the minimum functions necessary to enforce contracts and property rights necessary for free enterprise. Neither of these two approaches help deliver the common good. In this chapter we will try to understand why this is, and will explore a different concept of the state that could reestablish faith in the system that governs our lives.

Reflecting on the role of the state requires identifying both the problems the market poses for the proper functioning of our society, and the limits of state intervention. We will therefore step back a bit and examine the logic behind the way our society has been constructed. Next, we will show that the market and the state are complementary—not substitutes for one another, as the public debate often implies. Then we will discuss the primacy of politics, and its loss of influence. Finally, we will take up the sensitive subject of how to reform the state. While reasonable people can disagree on the desirable size of the state - more taxes, redistribution and public goods or less of these - all would rightly object to a bloated public sector providing a mediocre-quality public service; and yet reforms to improve public sector performance are often fraught with difficulty, which raises the issue of how to go about implementing such reforms.

THE MARKET HAS MANY DEFECTS
THAT MUST BE CORRECTED

Supporters of the market emphasize its efficiency and integrity. By efficiency, they mean the way free competition forces businesses to innovate and offer consumers goods and services at reasonable prices. This improves households' buying power, which is particularly important for the middle classes and for those with low incomes.

Market integrity is more abstract, but no less important. Just as political and cultural freedom protects the minority against oppression by the majority, freedom of enterprise and commerce protects citizens against interest groups who wish to use the political system to obtain privileges at the expense of the rest of us.

A comparison of standards of living in planned and market economies at the time of the fall of the Berlin Wall in 1989 (or of South Korea's living standard today, more than ten times higher than North Korea's) leaves little doubt as to the benefits of economic freedom. But we know the market is not perfect, and this book deals with numerous "market failures." To think about these failures, we can ask a simple question: How might a mutually agreed upon exchange between a seller and a buyer pose a problem for society? This exchange must assuredly benefit both parties if they decide to engage in it. So why interfere?

Market failures can be divided into six categories:

1. *The exchange can affect third parties, who are, by definition, not consenting.* For instance, businesses can pollute their environment when they manufacture the product they are selling to consumers. An energy company producing electricity in a coal-fired plant emits greenhouse gases such as carbon dioxide, and pollutants (sulfur

dioxide, nitrogen oxide) that generate acid rain. There is no market mechanism for protecting those who passively suffer this harm. As a result, society has to cope with air polluted with fine particulates, sulfur dioxide, and greenhouse gases, and water tables, rivers, and seas contaminated by fertilizers and chemical spills. Thus, the market needs to be complemented by an environmental policy or, in another domain, a nuclear safety authority.

2. *The exchange may not take place with full knowledge and consent.* For a trade to be carefully considered and consenting, the buyer must be properly informed. But the buyer may not know how dangerous a drug or another product might be, or may not be enough of an expert to avoid being cheated. That is why we need a consumer protection authority regulating business and punishing fraud. It may also be that the exchange has taken place under duress (for instance, a threat of physical violence) or that it involves the assets of a person who is not competent to manage them, which is clearly problematic.

3. *Buyers can become victims of their own actions.* People may lack self-control and act impulsively.[3] Since the dawn of time (for economists, that is, since Adam Smith), philosophers, psychologists, and economists have emphasized the possibility that people may have an excessive preference for the present for their own sake. They may put too little weight on their own future when they consume something now. This is the justification for taxing cigarettes or fatty or sugary goods, limiting access to drugs, or requiring a cooling-off period for certain purchases of durable goods or financial services in order to protect consumers against themselves (or similarly against door-to-door salesmen to whom people might give in just to get rid of them). It is also the argument invoked in many countries to force or encourage individuals to contribute to retirement pensions (in countries with funded pension schemes) or even to use payroll taxes levied on active workers to pay for the pensions of those who have already retired (for countries with pay-as-you-go pensions). The underlying idea is that people are preoccupied by their immediate well-being and don't think or care enough about their long-term future. The shortcomings of the paternalistic argument are clear (the state cannot infantilize us and decide too often what is good for us!), but the individual's understanding that he or she may lack

willpower is a potential benchmark for determining when the state can substitute itself for personal judgment.

4. *Implementing the exchange may exceed the individual's capacities.* When you put your money in the bank, contract terms specify the conditions under which you can withdraw your deposit (anytime in the case of sight deposits). Similarly, your insurance policy stipulates that you can receive a benefit in the event of an accident or fire, and your investment in a life insurance policy or investment account gives you the right to an income (guaranteed or not). But there is the risk that on the day that you want to withdraw your deposit or receive your insurance payout, the bank or the insurance company may have declared bankruptcy, leaving you paying out of pocket. Of course, in theory you could continuously monitor a financial institution's on- and off-balance sheet activities in order to detect an impending failure and withdraw your savings or cancel your insurance policy in time, but there are obvious limits to how well you could do this. It takes time to find the information, and technical expertise to draw conclusions from it. In practice, in every country a banking supervisor and an insurance regulator spare you this effort.

5. *Businesses can have market power*—that is, an ability to make consumers pay prices far above costs, or to get away with mediocre products. This is especially the case when markets are monopolized, for example when there are substantial returns to scale. Market power is the rationale for competition law and sectoral regulation, and most countries have a number of bodies regulating it. Thus, in the UK the Competition and Markets Authority enforces both consumer protection and competition laws, and there are other regulatory bodies for communications, railroads, and energy. In the United States, the Federal Trade Commission, the Department of Justice, and sectoral regulators such as the Federal Communications Commission or the Federal Energy Regulatory Commission have similar responsibilities.

6. *Finally, although the market improves efficiency, there is no reason it will deliver equity.* Let's take the example of health care: if private health insurance companies or the national healthcare system were allowed to discriminate between individuals, for instance on the basis of genetic data or the person's current state of health, someone with

cancer or genes indicating potential health problems could not obtain medical insurance at an affordable price. This is an old theme in economics: information kills insurance. That is why in many countries, the law prohibits conditioning medical insurance fees to information regarding the individual concerned.

Similarly, there is no reason the market will lead to a socially desirable distribution of incomes. Inequality is expensive for two reasons, one connected with justice and one with efficiency. In a market economy, inequality might be viewed as no more than a failure of insurance. "Behind the veil of ignorance" (that is, before we know anything about our own future) we would want to reward effort to incentivize people to create wealth for society, but we would also want to ensure that we would be able to live in decent conditions if we have the bad luck to be among the most unfortunate. In this sense, the social contract can be seen simply as an insurance policy. This is the foundation for redistribution through the tax system. In sum, there is no reason why access to insurance and the distribution of the income and wealth created by the market corresponds to what people would want behind the veil of ignorance, before knowing their place in society.

Moreover, in addition to this "destiny risk" (as one might describe it), inequality can also be dysfunctional.[4] It distorts social bonds and so can create externalities from which the whole population suffers, including those who have prospered because of their work or background. These externalities include civil insecurity, ghettos, and groups vulnerable to radicalization. The disturbing sight of gated communities shows clearly that the negative effects of inequality cannot be summed up simply as a failure of insurance against "destiny risk."

THE COMPLEMENTARITY BETWEEN THE MARKET AND THE STATE AND THE FOUNDATIONS OF LIBERALISM

Public debate often pits advocates of the market against advocates of the state. Both parties assume the market and the state compete. And yet, the state cannot ensure its citizens a (decent) life without a market; and the market equally needs the state to protect free enterprise, to guarantee contracts through the judicial system, and to correct market failures.

The organization of society is traditionally (and implicitly) based on two foundations. The first, the invisible hand of the competitive market, described in 1776 by Adam Smith in *The Wealth of Nations*, uses the pursuit of self-interest to achieve economic efficiency. The idea is that the price of a good or service, which results from matching supply and demand, encapsulates a lot of information: the buyer's willingness to pay and the seller's cost. In fact, an exchange occurs only if the price the buyer is willing to pay matches or exceeds the price he is asked to pay; similarly, the seller will agree to sell only if the price he receives exceeds his production cost. Putting these two observations together, the buyer will purchase only if he is prepared to pay more than the seller's production cost. In a competitive market, buyers and sellers are too small to manipulate prices; if the market is in equilibrium, the price is such that the demand at this price is equal to the supply at this price. All the possible gains from trade are realized.[5] The result is an efficient social allocation of resources.

The second foundation is that the state corrects the many market failures just spelled out. It makes economic agents accountable for the consequences their choices have for others and is responsible for social cohesion. The classical liberal approach is to leave the greatest possible number of economic decisions to individuals and firms, not the state, so as to make use of decentralized information; but for this to work, individuals and firms must be held accountable for the consequences of their decisions for society. One of the clearest defenders of this idea was the English economist Arthur Pigou (Keynes's professor at Cambridge), who in 1920 introduced the "polluter pays" principle in his book *The Economics of Welfare*.

I would like to emphasize the coherence of this framework before going on to analyze its limits: the state defines the rules of the game and the agents' responsibilities; they then may (and even must!) pursue their own self-interest. Take the case of the environment: instead of the state deciding which businesses must decrease their pollution (which it can only do blindly because it lacks the necessary information), it might say: "If you emit a ton of CO_2, you will be charged fifty dollars. You decide." Having been made responsible for the impact of its choices, the firm can concentrate on producing efficiently while meeting the constraints that society wishes to impose on CO_2 emissions.

Taken together, Smith's and Pigou's work is the foundation for shareholder value and for liberalism, but for a kind of shareholder value and liberalism that differ from their common interpretations. Economic liberalism tends to be identified with an absence of state intervention and with the individual struggle for survival. But on the contrary, the keystone of the edifice is that agents must be responsible for the social cost of their choices.

FAILURES OF THE STATE

This analysis shows that the market and the state are not alternatives but, on the contrary, are mutually dependent. The proper functioning of the market depends on the proper functioning of the state. Conversely, a defective state can neither contribute to the market's efficiency nor offer an alternative to it. Like markets, however, the state often fails. There are many reasons for these failures. Regulatory capture is one of them. We are well aware of the friendships and mutual support that create complicity between a public body and those who are supposed to be regulating it (witness the revolving door through which politicians and civil servants obtain jobs in the firms they once regulated). But this is only a small part of the equation. The essence of political motivation is the desire to be elected or reelected, and this can distort decision making in two ways.

First, there is a temptation to exploit the prejudices and lack of knowledge of the electorate; we shall return to this subject later. Second, the costs of policies advocated by a hypermobilized pressure group are often not obvious to the rest of society (for example, to taxpayers and consumers), although their benefits are very clear to the group. This asymmetry of information, sometimes reinforced by a deliberate choice to obscure the favors,[6] distorts public choice. An important example of a policy whose benefits are more visible to the beneficiaries than the costs are visible to others is the job-creating clientelism often practiced by local and regional authorities, which leads to them becoming excessively large.

Making political action responsive to the public interest is complex. Electoral sanctions work in some domains, but not in others. For instance, the failure of a public transport system is very visible. But borrowing by state and local authorities (and especially its off-balance sheet forms aiming to disguise the debts), along with inefficient public sector job creation (creating, de facto, another long-term debt in the form of their life-long salaries, also off-balance sheet) are far less visible to the electorate.

To return to a point made in the introduction to this chapter: those who criticize politicians should first reflect on what they would do, in the politicians' shoes. Understanding the implications of this analysis instead of assuming that the failures of the state are just the failures of the individuals involved (even if politicians actually do differ in courage and quality of management), might discourage us from moralizing, or being too eager to condemn the entire political class.

Finally, market failures cannot always be effectively corrected due to the geographic limitations of particular jurisdictions: governments cannot make policies for other countries. Without an international agreement, regulation must be national. While any country can encourage its businesses, its citizens, and its administrations to reduce CO_2 emissions or prohibit child labor,[7] it can do little to regulate such activities in other countries.

POLITICIANS OR TECHNOCRATS?

It is not enough to insist that state intervention is necessary; we must also address how to organize it. In many countries, there are few subjects as sensitive as the division of labor between elected decision makers and independent administrative bodies run by administrators or technocrats. This tension between accountability and independence is universal, and has been manifesting itself in populist attacks on "expertise" in a number of countries, including the United States, the United Kingdom, and France.

Independence from political power is certainly not a new idea (for example, the independence of judges from the British crown dates from the Act of Settlement of 1701,[8] and the separation of powers is written into the 1787 American Constitution). But the reforms carried out over the past thirty years and the attacks on independent administrative authorities in France, or the recent verbal attacks by politicians on the independence of the judiciary in Britain and America, or on central bank independence around the world, mean we must revisit its foundations.

The independence of judges in a healthy democracy is a good illustration of a fundamental point: the setting of objectives belongs to the domain of politics and societal decision making. But however society defines "justice," its impartial application is best guaranteed by independent judges. The same goes for decision making in economic policy. Economics is a science of the means, not of the ends. Consequently, an independent authority should be trusted with a general mandate within which it can evaluate options and find technical solutions, a mandate that guarantees coherence in that authority's policies and its independence with regard to pressure groups.

The Need for Independent Authorities

I repeat: It is unproductive and irresponsible to blame politicians for the limits of political action. Instead, it is important to realize that politicians, like all of us, react to the incentives they face.

In the case of politicians, the incentives are strongly influenced by the need to be elected or reelected. This has the advantage of forcing elected officials to take public opinion into account. This benefit, however, is also the Achilles' heel of the democratic mechanism. While the goal of representative democracy is to delegate decision making to people who are better informed than the electorate, these are often transformed into pollsters who exist to follow public opinion, or at least public opinion as shaped by the media. Many prefer not to sacrifice their political careers by embracing a cause that is generally unpopular or would raise objections from special interest groups. Sometimes a politician dares to be clear sighted and ignores public opinion. For example, François Mitterrand's abolition of capital punishment in France in September of 1981 went against majority opinion. However, the personal risk was diminished by the fact that Mitterrand was at the very beginning of his first seven-year term (voters have noticeably short memories). Besides, the fact that this act of political courage struck many observers of French politics only confirms my point that such behavior is the exception rather than the rule. An American example of a courageous-because-unpopular policy choice is the Affordable Care Act (Obamacare), for which (according to some polls) the margin between those against and those in favor was about 10 percent between 2010 and 2016.

Independence can be viewed as a reaction to the derailing of regulatory decisions to further electoral goals. All over the world central banks have gained independence as a result of politicians' habit of "pump priming"—increasing public spending before an election to create a short-run boom while triggering future inflation, to the detriment of the long-run health of the economy. Telecommunications, energy, and other network industries generally also have independent regulators (government agencies and, in some countries, judges). The motivation for independent sector regulation is the political temptation, when a minister is the regulator, to keep prices artificially low. This compromises investment and the viability of long-term networks (consider how often elected representatives call for lower prices for electricity and gas).

The devolution of competition policy and sectoral regulation to independent authorities also reflects the ministries' desire to avoid conflict with the management and employees of politically sensitive industries, who obviously see their sector as a private preserve and want to avoid, at any cost, the introduction or increase of competition. For example, the abuse of a dominant position or a merger endangering competition in a market used to involve closed-door discussions with a government official. The terrain was political, and the outcome depended as much on personal relationships as it did on the economic validity of the argument. The shift of the application of competition law to independent authorities has completely changed the game. There is little room for backroom deals, and all parties involved must have solid arguments and facts. Economic reasoning plays a much greater part. I am not always in agreement with the decisions these authorities make, but that is not the point. The guidelines and hearings are subject to debates that bring out the merits of the arguments rather than power relationships: the decisions made are of a higher quality than before. If we want to improve the quality of the decisions these authorities make, it is up to us as economists to improve our research and do a better job of explaining it, and it is up to the regulatory authorities to continue to sharpen their analyses.

Another example shows the dangers of politicization: the crises in banking (and sometimes even sovereign debt) caused by the real estate market. In countries all over the world, political leaders from the conservative George W. Bush to the socialist José Luis Zapatero have sought to increase home ownership. There is nothing wrong with this, in theory. In practice, policies encouraging individuals to buy homes have included a relaxation of the criteria for financial institutions to grant real estate loans. Loans were made to households that were barely solvent, and when they hit either personal problems or macroeconomic problems (such as a rise in interest rates or a decline in housing prices), they were unable to make their loan payments and were evicted. Undercapitalized banks had to be rescued by the state.

Much has been written about the subprime crisis, which involved these very risky real estate loans in the United States and many other countries. Until 2008, Spain experienced a real estate bubble that, when it burst, had terrible consequences for borrowers, the construction sector, savings banks, and the Spanish people in general. Bailing out the banks increased its national debt (which was low, below 40 percent of GDP before the crisis) and damaged the economy to the extent that Spain had to ask the IMF, the ECB, and the European Union for financial help. Spain seesawed between austerity and plans to jump-start the economy. Unemployment rose quickly, particularly among young people, and the crisis had a high social cost.

The fragility of the banks was therefore a decisive factor in the crisis in Spain. Suppose I told you that the Spanish banking supervisors were among the most qualified in the world, according to their peers? These supervisors had identified early, around 2005, the risks the real estate bubble posed for banks. They were the first in the world to require banks to maintain additional reserves during prosperous times (one can only imagine what the Spanish crisis might have been like had they not). This anticipated the reforms adopted within the Basel framework[9] after the crisis, which introduced the requirement for banks to increase their capital in good times. However, once the central bank had diagnosed the problem in 2005, the decision about whether to force the banks to reduce their real estate exposure was in the hands of Spanish politicians. Their desire to please won out over regulatory prudence.

Increase the Primacy of Politics?

When should decision-making power be granted to politicians? In theory, the political process seems more appropriate for making the societal choices understandable to the electorate as a whole (on the condition, of course, that the majority does not threaten to oppress the minority). On the other hand, technical decisions are likely to be poorly understood by the electorate, which is problematic for the democratic process. How many voters get a doctorate in economics to improve their understanding of monetary policy or of local loop unbundling in telecommunications, and to thereby inform their vote? How many voters study for a doctorate in history and geopolitics to improve their ability to assess their government's policy in the Middle East? How many voters analyze their local public transit system's productivity, or know the data on the effectiveness of alternative education or housing policies? How many voters make a serious effort to become familiar with the details of scientific subjects such as GMOs, fracking, or global warming? These are all difficult questions even for the experts who have PhDs. The consequence of citizens' lack of expert information is that technical decisions are vulnerable to regulatory capture by the most powerful (in terms of financial and media resources) or the best organized interest groups.

This is not to blame ordinary citizens any more than politicians. I could not do so with good grace, as I often evaluate political choices with sketchy information as well. I simply want to draw attention to the consequences of this information gap, which we must take into account.

Democracy was conceived as, "the worst form of government except for all those other forms that have been tried from time to time," in the famous words of Winston Churchill. The modern state that has emerged from the philosophy of the Enlightenment seeks to be independent of special interests. Limiting the influence of elected officials on the career paths of the civil servants who are answerable to them is part of this philosophy. The creation of independent authorities is another instrument that allows democracies to respond to considerations other than short-term polls and to limit pandering to interest groups. The French Republic's web page[10] sums up the advantages of this independence concisely:

> The independent administrative authority has sought to meet three needs: providing public opinion with a greater guarantee of the impartiality of state interventions; allowing greater participation by persons of diverse origins and competencies, especially professionals in the sectors supervised; ensuring a rapid state intervention suited to the evolution of needs and markets.

This encapsulates neatly Tocqueville's admiration for the tradition of administrative independence he observed in the early nineteenth-century United States.[11]

INDEPENDENT AUTHORITIES ARE NEVER FULLY INDEPENDENT

If decision makers who are not subject to electoral sanction (judges in many countries, or economic regulators) act with greater freedom, the opposite side of the coin is the absence of accountability if they behave badly. To limit the risks of independent agencies drifting away from serving the common good, independent and respected people must be selected to run them, must submit to appointment hearings focused on their qualifications, and if possible should be appointed with bipartisan support. Favors or loyal service to a party or a politician should never be taken into account. Once in place, consultation, transparency, and the requirement that their opinions be based on sound arguments all create incentives to make socially justified decisions; publishing an evaluation of those decisions by experts who are independent of the agency can expose misjudgments.

An "independent" authority must not be (and never is) totally independent: a suitable legislative supermajority must have the power to suspend the leaders of this agency on the basis of their overall conduct (and not on a specific, hot political question). Finally, potential conflicts of interest must be taken into account and dealt with directly and explicitly through procedures that limit their impact.

Explain, Don't Complain ...

The prevailing hostility to independent agencies often owes much to the electoral calendar. For example, the anti-ECB rhetoric in Europe is in some ways political posturing that has few direct consequences, since the bank's independence is written into multilateral international agreements, and no member country has much chance of convincing its European partners to put the ECB under political supervision. [12]

But the indirect consequences are more serious. For one thing, the bashing of independent agencies may eventually subordinate them to political power. What's more, populists who attack institutions that were set up expressly to avoid vote-seeking excesses can only increase their fellow citizens' distrust of public life. To take another European example, the French and Dutch no vote in the 2005 referendum on the proposed treaty establishing a consolidated constitution for Europe showed the impact of several decades of scapegoating and "Brussels bashing." True political courage would consist of trying to reconcile citizens to modern democracy, in which independent authorities have an important role to play.

REFORMING THE STATE: THE EXAMPLE OF FRANCE

A New Concept of the State

The concept of the state has changed. Formerly conceived in many countries as a provider of jobs through the civil service and a producer of goods and services through public enterprises, in its modern form the state ideally sets the rules and intervenes to correct market failures, rather than substituting itself for the market as a mediocre manager of enterprises.[13] When markets are failing, the modern state regulates. It assumes the responsibility for creating equality of opportunity, healthy competition, and a financial system not dependent on bailouts using public money. It finds a way of making economic actors act responsibly with regard to the environment, of establishing equality in health insurance coverage, of ensuring protection for employees who do not have the information that would empower them (safety in the workplace, the right to high-quality training), and so on. In its operations, it is nimble and reactive.

However, this transition requires a return to fundamentals (what is the state good for?) and a change of mindset. Bureaucrats must no longer be "in the service of the state"—an unfortunate expression that completely loses sight of the public interest—but rather "in the service of the citizen."[14] Countries in which the state is still perceived as a provider of employment and a producer of goods and services may need to evolve toward the model of the state as arbitrator.[15]

The modern state must have the financial means to sustain the social welfare system to which its citizens have become attached. On this subject, France could take inspiration from other countries just as attached to their social systems, but appreciating that its continued existence requires rigorous management of public finance.[16] France's public spending is currently among the highest in the world: government expenditure is more than 57 percent of GDP![17] In 1960, during the *trente glorieuses*,[18] the proportion was 35 percent.

Rising public expenditure is not inevitable: between 1991 and 1997, Sweden decreased its public expenditure by 10 percent of GDP. Thanks to private contracting, the number of government officials fell from 400,000 to 250,000 in the 1990s. Sweden retained only a few hundred officials in its ministries, with a mission to define strategy, compare budget options, and enable debates. The Swedish government delegated operational activities to about one hundred specialized agencies making independent decisions about recruitment and remuneration. It was able to rationalize its services. For example,

A PROCESS FOR STATE REFORM

In countries plagued by a bloated public administration,[19] required reforms have long been identified: reduce the number of and reallocate public sector employees, substitute open-ended labor contracts for lifelong jobs, eliminate duplicates,[20] reduce the number of political layers,[21] empower public-sector managers in exchange for a strict ex-post evaluation and interference if these objectives are not met, and so on. Yet reforms frequently fail, despite the best of intentions. A few principles may increase the chances of success.

1. *Use benchmarks to convince.* Compare with the best international practices and understand the reasons for the difference. How do students perform in comparison to students in other countries? Can income taxes be collected at lower cost? Do hospitals offer the best care possible given the funds at their disposal—or, in an equivalent way, are they spending only as much as they need for the quality of the care provided?

2. *Identify the best way to address the problem.* The Canadian reform process, when the federal government set its public finances in order by slimming down by 19 percent between 1993 and 1997, is emblematic in this respect. For each program, Canada asked the pertinent questions: Is the program in the public interest? If so, could it be provided by another branch of the public sector or by the private sector? Is the cost affordable and are there alternatives? Straightforward questions like these can lead to creative solutions. Nothing is off limits, but there is a dialogue with the public to adjust and explain the program.

3. *Do not cut across the board.* Identify what is essential as well as what is not, what works as well as what doesn't. In Canada, social welfare programs (healthcare, the judicial system, housing, immigration) were not much affected, but subsidies for businesses fell by 60 percent and the budget of the Ministry of Industry and Transportation was cut in half.

4. *Monitor the conformity of policies with objectives.* Reforms can go awry. For example, the regrouping of structures to eliminate duplicates often has the opposite effect in France. Instead of producing savings, it ends up creating additional jobs and structures to coordinate authorities that remain unchanged. Detailed plans should be presented to an independent authority that would have the power to ask the actors to go back to the drawing board if there are no real savings, and that would provide follow-up monitoring.

underused postal services in rural areas were transferred to grocery stores and service stations, producing cost savings but also allowing some of these businesses to survive, thus combatting the flight to cities.

Germany, the Netherlands, the Scandinavian countries, and Canada are all countries with social-democratic traditions that have preserved a high level of public services and social welfare protection. They have succeeded in reducing costs while maintaining services. They have also succeeded in making reforms by packaging them together. Isolated reforms are difficult to carry out: single-issue lobbyists focus on stopping them, while the (usually numerous) potential beneficiaries are either not aware of what they would gain, or perceive their potential individual gain to be small, and therefore free ride. A comprehensive reform offers an overall view of a larger pie and assists the losers.

"But This Is Not the Right Time"

Several general lessons can be learned from efforts around the world to reform the state:

1. Broad reforms are possible.

2. They must be planned for the long haul. Although bipartisan support can prove hard to achieve in some cases (think of US health care reform), in many countries, the opposition party has publicly supported, or at least not attempted to derail, government efforts to sustain reforms in the national interest, such as the fiscal sustainability of the social welfare system. The opposition has continued the reforms when it returned to power, providing a good example of the proper functioning of these democracies. Many reforms of the state have been implemented by the left: by Jean Chrétien in Canada, Gerhard Schröder in Germany, the social democrats (particularly Göran Persson) in Sweden, and Michelle Bachelet in Chile, for example. The reforms were subsequently respected by the right.

3. If they are well explained and made early enough, these reforms are often rewarded by the electorate. Jean Chrétien remained in power for thirteen years and Göran Persson for ten.

4. In France, and elsewhere it is often objected that the time is not right to introduce reforms, as a struggling economy makes it hard to compensate the losers of reforms. And yet the great majority of the reforms mentioned here were made precisely under difficult conditions. The Swedish reforms were adopted in an especially difficult context. After the bursting of the financial bubble and the banking bailout in the early 1990s, and despite a devaluation, Swedish GDP fell by 5 percent between 1991 and 1994, unemployment rose from 1.5 to 8.2 percent, and the budget deficit reached 15 percent in 1994! Finland's almost simultaneous reforms were decided upon in an equally difficult economic context, against the background of the collapse of the Soviet Union, Finland's most important commercial partner. Schröder's Germany was also in a difficult situation; it was having a hard time coping with reunification and was facing demographic prospects catastrophic for welfare programs. In the 1990s, Canada was also in bad shape: the total public debt (the federal government, the provinces, and the municipalities) was approaching 100 percent of the GDP, and repaying it was beginning to make itself painfully felt.

Examples could be multiplied: a difficult economic situation can help, not hinder, reforms.

SEVEN
The Governance and Social Responsibility of Business

After exploring the governance of the public sphere, we turn in this chapter to that of business. To be sure, the focus on these two spheres is reductive. It ignores organizational forms such as voluntary associations, NGOs, cooperatives, and collaborative development (as in the case of open source software). [1] It also neglects the role of management and labor outside the firm, in important codetermined semipublic bodies, such as those managing continuing education, social security, and employment tribunals in France. But it is worth taking a moment to look at a key and somewhat puzzling question relating to the predominant model for governing the firm in our market economies: Why is investor ownership and control so widespread throughout the world? Under what circumstances can modes of organization other than capitalist enterprise—cooperatives or employee-managed firms, for instance—emerge and prosper?

A company's governance is at the heart of its management. Governance refers to those who control the company and make the major decisions: the management of human resources, research and development, strategic choices, mergers and acquisitions, pricing and marketing, risk management, regulatory affairs, and so on. The dominant form—capitalist governance—grants decision-making power to investors, or more precisely to shareholders (or de facto to creditors if debts are not repaid). These investors delegate decision-making power to a management team over which they in principle exercise oversight and whose decisions they can overturn if they are not in their interests, but which is better informed than they are. We will examine how to resolve the problem of the separation between ownership rights and decision-making control. Finally, we will analyze the concepts of corporate social responsibility (CSR) and socially responsible investment (SRI). What do they mean? Are they incompatible with a market economy, or are they a natural extension of it?

MANY POSSIBLE ORGANIZATIONS
... BUT FEW ARE CHOSEN

It is surprising, a priori, that the capitalist model of management is so widespread. A firm consists of many stakeholders or groups affected by its decisions: the investors who provide its capital, of course, but also the employees, subcontractors, and customers, the local authorities and countries where it operates, and others, such as the neighbors who might suffer if it causes pollution. We can therefore imagine a multitude of organizations in which stakeholders share power in different configurations (each with more or less voting power on the board of directors), creating various forms of joint management.

In fact, there are modes of governance that differ from the capitalist model. *Cooperative governance*, in which the users of a service own it and agree how the service will be managed and shared, exists in many sectors. For instance, agricultural cooperatives provide their members with services (loans of equipment, storage, processing, marketing). The reader may be surprised to learn that the very capitalist United States has many cooperatives: buyers' cooperatives, moving companies, investment banks,[2] and mutual insurance companies among them. The examples even included, until recently, Visa and MasterCard: these were jointly controlled by the issuers of bank cards (your bank, for example) and the acquirers (the financial institutions that manage merchants' credit and debit card activity), and (like mutual insurance companies) did not distribute dividends.

All over the world, professionals participate in cooperatives, such as medical clinics or auditing, consulting, and tax advisory partnerships. Businesses in the social enterprise sector are often also managed by consensus and votes by members. In these businesses, profit is a means (it enables the business to survive or to invest), not an end. A small portion of the profit is given to members and another portion is reinvested. Unlike nonprofit corporations, these enterprises may pay dividends to their associates, but only within limits (for example, up to a third of the profits). Nor do their investors exercise control, although they often receive a limited number of votes.

There are many other possible forms of governance, such as *employee-run firms*, which were common in Tito's Yugoslavia and existed occasionally elsewhere. In France, as in many other countries, universities are largely self-managed; although they are subject to constraints imposed by the relevant ministry, in practice elected representatives of the faculty, the students, and the staff control their governing boards.

In a much more limited way, employees may contribute to decision making in a business by attending board meetings.[3] A number of countries (such as China, Norway, and Sweden) indeed require employee representation on the board. The emblematic example is Germany, where businesses have a two-tier governance: an executive board and a supervisory board that monitors it. Legally, employees must constitute one-third of the supervisory board in any company with more than five hundred employees, and one half if the company has more than two thousand employees (in this case, the vote of the president, generally elected from among shareholder representatives, is the tiebreaker). The latest empirical studies suggest that this form of governance is not neutral in its effect: companies required to have an equal number of employee representatives on the board have a lower market value but more stable employment and pay, as well as a tendency in reaction to create incentives for the managers that favor shareholders (such as compensation more closely linked to shareholder value and greater indebtedness).[4]

In reality, a healthy economy requires a range of modes of governance, so that the structure of each business is adapted to the challenges posed by its particular context. Since this flexibility exists in practice, nothing prevents a company from adopting the kind of governance it wants, whether self-management (especially when it is first formed),[5] a cooperative, a capitalist structure, or any other.

The mode of organization we observe is therefore the result of competition between different governance models (if this competition is not distorted by fiscal or regulatory incentives favoring a particular form). So we might be surprised that economic activity is overwhelmingly organized around firms that entrust supervisory rights to a single stakeholder—the investors, to whom the management is formally accountable. These investors are, moreover, usually external to the firm.

The dysfunctions associated with this model, and regularly reported in the press, make its predominance all the more surprising. Examples include the tenuous connection between a company's performance and the remuneration of its managers, cases of dividends being paid shortly before declaring bankruptcy, accounting manipulations such as those of Enron,[6] short-term thinking to the detriment of long-term profitability, and insider trading. Luckily, most company managers behave nothing like this. Nonetheless, the governance of a business, like any economic or political institution, cannot be based on an assumption of general benevolence. These dysfunctions are costly for investors who see their savings go up in smoke, for stakeholders who haven't had an opportunity to speak out about the company's management, for the employees who lose their jobs, for local authorities who see job opportunities in their area deteriorate, and for the taxpayers who will have to pay for unemployment benefits or for cleaning up pollution at abandoned sites.

This chapter thus concerns the heart of our economy's organization: Why is business typically governed this way? Is this structure socially desirable? Is there a failure of competition among possible forms of governance? If so, is it up to the state to intervene, or should business itself adopt socially responsible behavior?

The Driving Need for Finance

Every firm, from large corporations to small and mid-sized companies, needs funding for growth or, more modestly, to get through a rough patch. In the absence of abundant liquidity or of nonstrategic and easy-to-sell assets, the company has to raise money from shareholders or creditors. However, these financiers (or *investors*—we will use these two terms interchangeably) will not provide additional money unless the return they expect to receive from their investment is at least equal to what they could obtain from other investments. This is why the company has to adopt a governance structure and commitments that reassure its investors about the return on their investment. Let us first consider the consequences of allocating control to investors and to employees, respectively, and then analyze other governance choices that impact the investors' decision to fund the firm.

Decision-making power granted to the financiers. To simplify, let us concentrate on two stakeholders in the company: labor and capital, the employees and the investors. If investors hold the decision-making power, the interests of the employees will not necessarily be represented or taken into account; the business may make decisions that endanger the jobs of its employees, at a considerable cost to them (especially in a country with a rigid labor market, like France). Of course, it is often good for investors, even from the narrow point of view of profit, to take a long-term view of the company and treat employees fairly. A company that treats its employees badly to increase its short-term profits acquires a bad reputation, and in the long term will have difficulty attracting and motivating recruits. Penalizing employees ultimately penalizes shareholders too. But that does not mean that financiers will be sufficiently concerned about the interests of employees, so we need to ask how these interests can be protected.

Decision-making power granted to the employees. If, on the other hand, employees have decision-making power, investors' returns need to be protected. Indeed, they may fear that employee self-governance would deprive them of enough of a return on their investment. Even if this return is guaranteed contractually—suppose it is debt with a specified, predetermined repayment to the creditors—the employees may use current income to increase their salaries instead of investing, or decide to decrease their work effort, or give priority to hiring their relatives and friends. Any of these actions would endanger future investor returns. Anticipating these risks, financiers would be reluctant to invest their capital in the self-managed firm. They would prefer to spend rather than save, or they may invest their money elsewhere (in real estate, government bonds, other companies, or abroad). In the end this would harm the employees, who would no longer be able to finance the company's growth (or even ensure its survival).

Furthermore, even if the financiers could ensure that retained profits would be reinvested by the employees, reinvestment in the firm would not necessarily be a wise choice. Consider a major brand of cigarettes for instance: manufacturing cigarettes might not be an attractive opportunity for investment, despite very high current revenues (and might be increasingly less attractive, thankfully, for reasons of health regulation). It is important—and this applies to all forms of governance—that capital is put to its best possible use. This best use need have nothing to do with past performance, and may require investing in completely different areas of the economy: growth opportunities often lie in new products and companies.

The idea that governance prioritizing the wishes of investors may be beneficial for employees too is counterintuitive. In the first instance, we see only direct consequences: notably the increased return for investors. Over the long term however, the company's access to finance, and the resulting growth and employment, are at stake. A governance model favoring employees by giving them decision-making power in a company with a significant need for financing may be counterproductive: the resulting shortage of capital would reduce their productivity, decrease their income, or even put them out of their jobs.

To repeat, though, this point about the hazards of self-management is not a normative judgment: a free enterprise economy must accommodate all forms of governance and let organizations pick whatever fits best in their context. Instead, these observations start to explain why a company might adopt—or not—a capitalist form of governance. A professional services company like KPMG is composed essentially of human capital, and can operate as a cooperative, whereas the companies with the greatest need for finance will tend to give control to their investors.

As Henri Hansmann noted in his famous work *The Ownership of Enterprise*,[7] however, some cooperatives have a great deal of physical capital. For example, Visa and MasterCard, before they went public on the New York Stock Exchange in 2008 and 2006 respectively, were cooperatives with large investments in physical networks, software, and marketing. Were they exceptional? Not really. In his book,

Hansmann makes a crucial observation that applies to many other aspects of our social life: collective decision making works well when the interests of the members of the community (in this case the cooperative) are aligned. So long as the banks belonging to the payment card cooperative had the same objectives (the same demand for services that the cooperative provided, similar time horizons), the cooperative functioned in a broadly unified way, and setting aside reserves for investment was not a problem. The cooperative could then adapt if there was a strong demand for capital investment.

On the other hand, when interests begin to diverge, a majority may make decisions against the minority's interests.[8] Also, the minority will not feel very involved, knowing that its proposals have little chance of being accepted. The members will start to distrust one another and information will cease to circulate. Finally, unhappy members who are not tied to the organization will look for other horizons. The alignment of goals is therefore important for the healthy functioning of any organization.

THE SEPARATION BETWEEN OWNERSHIP AND CONTROL: WHO ULTIMATELY DECIDES?

In every business, the management team has access to information and makes day-to-day decisions. The advantage the insiders gain from having this information makes external supervision of the company by the board of directors or participants in the annual general meeting (AGM) of shareholders[9] tricky. For the sake of brevity, suppose that the investors have the decision-making power. The separation between investors and management raises the question of how the management can commit to guaranteeing the investors a return. (The following points apply more generally to any situation in which actual decision making is separated from ownership rights. The members of a cooperative or an association, for example, would have the same concerns about the alignment of the management team's goals with their own objectives.) Managers may balk at making difficult choices, pay insufficient attention to internal risk management, get involved in outside activities that are not profitable, over invest, fail to select the most competent business partners, give priority to relatives and friends, or even engage in illegal activities (like insider trading, cooking the books, stealing from the pension fund, or transferring assets when they have a conflict of interest).

Information theory and game theory can help us understand power or authority using two concepts:[10]

- *formal* authority over a decision or a class of decisions, given to its holder through a contract;
- *real* authority, acquired by an agent who does not have formal authority, thanks to 1) privileged information relevant to a decision, and 2) trust the formal authority holder may have in him or her because their interests are somewhat aligned.

As in Max Weber's work, the key to the distinction between the two concepts is asymmetry of information. The firm's AGM may have formal authority but still not run the show if the board of directors withholds information. Similarly, the board of directors can simply rubber stamp the decisions made by the managers, who only hand out information when it suits them.[11] So, for instance, although certain decisions such as a merger or the choice of the next CEO fall under the formal authority of the board of directors or the AGM, this may not prevent the current CEO from having a strong influence on the decisions—at least if he or she is trusted to serve the interests of the shareholders. The connection between real authority and the alignment of interests is empirically valid.

In practice, how do investors ensure that the management team's behavior does not deviate too much from their interests? The answer takes several forms: governance consists of a series of institutions that, individually, are not enough to ensure an alignment of interests. When combined, they usually—though not always—succeed in doing so.

The Role of the Financial Structure

In a famous, provocative article published in 1958, Franco Modigliani and Merton Miller suggested that the financial structure of an enterprise has no impact on how it is run, and thus no impact on its value. In a nutshell, the ways to share a pie of fixed size (the company's future profits) between the various sources of finance (shareholders and creditors) do not affect the size of the pie, and thus do not affect the total price that investors are prepared to pay for the entirety of the company's equity capital and debt; put differently, the dividends and capital gains on stocks and the principal and interest on bonds and bank loans add up to a fixed amount determined solely by the firm's choices, and the division of the resulting cash flows is irrelevant.

But Modigliani and Miller's hypothesis is not very satisfactory: the size of the pie is not fixed, because in reality the creation of value depends on financial structure and governance. An overindebted firm will often see control pass into the hands of creditors, who tend to be cautious and may sell assets or break up the firm to make sure that the debt is repaid. Conversely, the managers of a cash-rich firm (one with little debt) can enjoy a quiet life. They do not have the pressure of paying back debts that have fallen due. They may come under pressure to pay dividends, but that is a looser constraint.

To simplify, as long as everything is going well, the shareholders control the company. They are therefore responsible for its management, and in the event of financial problems, they are the first to lose their money. The holders of company debt, who are usually passive agents in managing the firm, have two ways of protecting themselves. The first is (for certain creditors) to obtain guarantees. For example, a bank will demand that the company pledge some of its assets (real estate, inventory, or equipment, for example) as collateral, which the bank would seize if the debt were not repaid; similarly, a covered bond is in principle guaranteed even if the firm defaults.

The second kind of protection is to take de facto control of the company when it is overindebted and cannot make up for the shortfall of money by issuing new shares. This transfer of control in dire straits from shareholders to debt holders serves a dual purpose: It prevents shareholders from risking all in a last desperate attempt to make a profit (gambling for resurrection). It also keeps managers on their toes; they usually do not welcome the creditor-led change of track and therefore have an incentive to avoid a transfer of control away from shareholders.

Balance Sheet Structure and Governance

Theory predicts, and econometric studies confirm, a systematic relation between balance sheet structure and the "concessions" made to investors. A company with a fragile balance sheet (that is, one with little cash, few tangible assets to pledge as collateral, great uncertainty as to future revenues, and a reputation in the making) ought logically to offer more concessions to investors. For example, the company may have to trim its investment plans, accept a shorter maturity on its debt—allowing the creditors to exit faster if there is a problem—or offer stricter governance or a proportionately higher level of collateral. These concessions are costly but essential for a company that wants to finance growth.

A large enterprise with available cash, the ability to offer guarantees, and an established reputation will be able to get the money it needs on the bond markets at a relatively low cost of credit, but small and medium-sized enterprises depend on bank loans, as this relationship with a bank reduces the asymmetry of information between the company and the investors lending it money. Similarly, a startup in biotechnology or software (without liquid assets, without collateral, and without a reliable cash flow) will have to submit to strict supervision of its refinancing, its governance, and its investment decisions by a business angel and later a venture capitalist. Its managers will be constrained in their choices and constantly in the ejector seat.[12]

Incentives for Managers

The creation of shareholder value is also based on a complex juxtaposition of incentive mechanisms, each very imperfect, aiming to align the managers' interests with those of shareholders. Variable pay for the managers calculated on the basis of the company's financial performance (shares and stock options[13]) to incentivize them to act to improve the share price, is often criticized. The criticism is about both the level of these variable rewards, and also the fact that they do not always reward good management—as, for example, when a CEO cashes in profitable stock options a few months before revealing that the company is on the verge of bankruptcy. Criticisms regarding the way many variable reward schemes are implemented are fully justified. When they are well structured, however, and in particular when they are phased in over time, contingent on sustained performance (or else are subject to "clawback provisions"[14]) and properly indexed to share prices in the sector or the stock market, stock-based incentive pay schemes can encourage managers to adopt a long-term outlook. Let us dwell a little longer on these points.

During the 2008 financial crisis, some brokers and financial institutions were accused of short-termism because they had been taking big risks designed to increase short-term profitability. This dysfunctional behavior was attributed in particular to the mechanisms for compensating managers and to the infamous bonuses (variable pay based on year-end results) that encouraged them to maximize short-term profitability at the expense of the future. Basing managers' variable pay on an allocation of shares instead of giving annual performance bonuses is already an improvement: if a manager's inflation of company revenues comes with a long-term cost greater than the short-term gain and the stock market notices this, the share price will decrease—even if profits do increase in the short run. The manager will not benefit from an increase in the value of his or her shares, while he or she would have made a lot of money under a bonus system. But there's a catch: the market has to be aware of this substitution between present and future, of this quest for immediate profitability—and it is not always aware.

As we hinted above, it is therefore advisable that the profits achieved by managers be subject to "clawbacks": the company has to be able to take back a manager's variable pay if the short-term gains prove to be a flash in the pan; in other words, putting managers' bonuses on ice for a period discourages the quest for short-term profitability. It was in this spirit that, after the financial crisis, the Basel Committee on Banking Supervision (which defines worldwide guidelines for the prudential oversight of the banking sector) required that the pay of managers and traders in the banks should be oriented toward the long term.

These principles are useful, but they may not be enough. In chapter 12, we shall see how, in the case of finance, several factors have combined to bring about forms of remuneration that are undesirable for society. These factors include lack of attention from regulators; taxpayer-funded bailouts, which encourage banks to take risks (because they can continue to refinance themselves until the last minute, even when things are going wrong) and encourage shareholders to create corresponding incentives for the management; connivance between remuneration committees and the managers whose pay they set;[15] competition for talent and the culture of bonuses.

External Views

A multitude of countervailing powers can help highlight insufficient shareholder value creation: independent board directors, block shareholders, corporate raiders, auditors, shareholders at the AGM, ethics committees, the media, and regulators. In the abstract, these all collect information about the company's performance and strategy, and some of them act on this basis by intervening in the company's management. These complex gears and cogwheels, their interactions, and the determinants of companies' financial structures are the subject of much debate: Who supervises these supervisors? Are they seeking to create value for the company or only for themselves?[16]

AND WHAT IS BUSINESS'S SOCIAL RESPONSIBILITY?

As we saw in chapter 6, our dominant economic institutions, which are continuously evolving, are based on two principles: *the creation of value* and *accountability*, notions dear to the economists Adam Smith and Arthur Pigou. Accountability means that the firm is sensitized to and "internalizes" the cost of its decisions for different stakeholders. An example is environmental taxation, whose aim is to confront the firm with the social impact of its pollution.[17] Its analogue in the labor market is experience rating, which uses rewards and penalties in unemployment insurance (instead of legal restrictions on redundancies) to force the firm to consider the cost of a layoff on the unemployment insurance system.[18] Both seek to make the enterprise accountable, either for its environmental impact or the way it manages human resources. More generally, the aim is to protect stakeholders who do not control the decision-making process, so that those who do have control (the shareholders and managers) do not impose too many externalities on others through the choices they make to benefit the business. Facing the right economic signals, the business can then concentrate on a simple mission: creating value for its investors.

The protection of stakeholders is often imperfect, however. Contracts and regulations cannot foresee every possibility, so they will be incomplete. The problem of government failure discussed earlier complicates matters further. Ultimately, the elegant social construct represented by the protection of stakeholders (and the maximization of capitalist profit this justifies) will spring a few leaks.

According to the European Commission, the social responsibility of businesses is "a concept whereby companies integrate social and environmental concerns in their business operations and in their interaction with their stakeholders on a voluntary basis."[19] In addition to the interaction with the stakeholders (employees, customers, suppliers, local authorities, NGOs, and so on), the word "voluntary" is central to this definition. Quoting the European Commission again: "Being socially responsible means not only fulfilling legal expectations, but also going beyond compliance and investing "more" into human capital, the environment and relations with stakeholders." Thus, a socially responsible enterprise emits less CO_2 or hires a disabled person, not because it is forced to do so by the law or encouraged by a subsidy or a tax, but because it thinks it has a duty to society to behave well.

Corporate social responsibility is an old concept. For example, noting the low degree of public authorities' involvement in the age's pressing social issues, Christian employers in the late nineteenth century developed social policies (housing, family support payments) in France, Germany, and the UK. Today, the socially responsible enterprise is the object of renewed interest. This concept, however, has many meanings, and it is sometimes difficult for citizens to grasp. We can think of an enterprise's social responsibility in three ways, not mutually exclusive: the adoption of a more long-term view compatible with sustainable development; ethical behavior desired by the firm's stakeholders (customers, investors, employees); and philanthropy initiated from within. Let us look at each of these alternatives.[20]

A Sustainable View of the Enterprise

Many private and sovereign investment funds emphasizing socially responsible investment stress a long-term perspective. Like economists, they argue that profit is an intertemporal concept, that is, a long-term one. Thus, socially responsible investment funds put sustainability at the heart of their thinking, either by choice or because they are politically directed to do so (for example, the Norwegian parliament requires Norway's sovereign wealth fund to act in a socially responsible way).

How is this perspective related to socially responsible business? Isn't it a simple question of better governance? The answer lies in the correlation between businesses' short-term behavior and behavior harmful to society. Let's take the case of a bank's choice of a risky portfolio that will most likely allow it to make a high profit, but at the risk of a catastrophe. The collapse of the bank after taking excessive risk harms not only its shareholders (who may nonetheless have been happy to take this risk before the event), but also its depositors, or most often the deposit insurance fund guaranteeing their deposits. Ultimately, it is the public finances that suffer, as is shown by the aftermath of the Spanish and Irish real estate crashes. In the case of banks, the risk is exacerbated because governments habitually rescue them when they get into difficulty. They opt to do this to avoid failure spreading to other banks, and the costly consequences for small and medium-sized enterprises that bank failures generate. But the prospect of a government bailout means the bank can continue to take risks by raising new finance from creditors who don't need to worry much about being repaid, despite the bank's poor state of health.

There are other examples: a company that cuts its safety and maintenance spending too much, or introduces a product whose dangers it does not understand, may make more money, but it is taking the risk of bad news (an oil spill or a scandal affecting a new drug, in these cases) that will not only ruin the company, but also leave the victims and the government to pay the bill. Its bankruptcy would also leave its employees out of work. Similarly, the employees of a company that does not respect them will, in the future, be less likely to support its plans, and new employees will be harder to recruit. This explains why social responsibility often involves thinking about sustainable strategy.

Therefore, it is desirable that socially responsible investment funds behave like active investors, monitoring management and intervening within the board of directors or during AGMs to ensure that the company's policy is sufficiently oriented to the long term. Responsible funds can also "vote with their feet" and not invest in firms they believe do not meet the criteria for a socially responsible enterprise.[21] There are debates, though, about the definition of such criteria. For example, suppose the fund does not want to invest in an energy company that emits large quantities of greenhouse gases. Should the fund completely exclude such enterprises from its portfolio? Or should it select the companies in the sector that make the most efforts to reduce their pollution (a "best in class" approach to encourage good behavior if we cannot do without this sector, at least in the short term)?

"Delegated Philanthropy"

As we saw in chapter 5, people do not always seek only their own economic interest. For one thing, they may have sincere empathy with other people and may be prepared to sacrifice a little of their personal economic interest for the benefit of others. For another, they might also want to demonstrate to others or to themselves that they are "good people": part of our altruism is not pure, but is motivated by our concern with what we appear to be, with our social and personal image. This desire for pro-social behavior can also be expressed in stakeholders' desire for business to behave virtuously. An investor might not want his savings to be invested in an enterprise that deals with countries that do not respect human rights, or subcontracts with suppliers who use child labor or produce weapons or tobacco; to avoid doing so, the investor might be prepared to sacrifice a bit of his return. Similarly, a consumer might be happy to pay a little more for fair trade coffee, or an employee might sacrifice income to work for an NGO supporting children in sub-Saharan Africa, and thus feel a certain pride.

In this case, the company makes itself the vector of a demand for pro-social behavior. It adopts social responsibility on behalf of the stakeholders (investors, consumers, employees). Once again there is no conflict with Adam Smith's ideas. This may seem surprising, but a chain of coffee shops does not sacrifice its profit by offering fair trade coffee. It is simply responding to a demand from its customers, who are prepared to pay a bit more for their latte. It is maximizing its profit.

Delegated philanthropy is a simple concept, but it faces challenges if it is to realize its full potential. One challenge is *free riding*: we are all prepared to make a small effort to emit less greenhouse gas, but reluctant individually to make the major efforts necessary to limit global warming to 1.5 to 2 degrees Celsius. Our fellow citizens all say that they are ready to make sacrifices to limit global warming, but there is resolute opposition to even minimal carbon taxes. People hope that others will make most of the effort.

Another challenge involves the information available to stakeholders. To select a company to invest in, buy from, or work for, savers, consumers, and employees need enough information to know whether it really does behave in a pro-social way, which gives us three further issues.

Information. First, the company's stated corporate responsibility commitments may not be credible. Independently collected data are therefore essential for stakeholders to be well informed about the company's true behavior. For example, do the company or its subcontractors use child labor? The longer the subcontracting chain, the greater the information shortfall.[22] Does it engage in "greenwashing"—over-hyped but insignificant actions claimed to protect the environment—rather than giving priority to other efforts that would have much more environmental impact? CSR (also called extrafinancial, or environmental, social, and governance—ESG) rating agencies have been created to provide relevant metrics for stakeholders.[23]

Weighing objectives. The second issue is how to aggregate the dimensions of nonfinancial performance, with respect to the environment, the company's own sustainability, its employees, the tax authorities, and so on. Companies can be good in some dimensions and bad in others; one of the challenges that confront CSR rating agencies is therefore to find a methodology to synthesize these different dimensions of corporate responsibility performance in a single index. How should we evaluate the closure of a factory that emits a lot of CO_2 but provides jobs for a local community? Can a multinational corporation compensate for the damage it does to the local environment by financing a school, a clinic, or a garbage disposal facility in the community? This debate is particularly striking today, when many multinationals are undertaking socially responsible actions while simultaneously pursuing a policy of aggressive tax avoidance.[24]

What is socially (ir)responsible anyway? Ultimately, because it reflects public demand, corporate social responsibility inherits the strengths and weaknesses of the democratic process. In the preceding chapter, I emphasized that the adoption of good public policy often depends on the voters having a satisfactory understanding of the relevant question, or at least an absence of bias. Similarly, consumers, employees, and investors will push the company to behave ethically only if they clearly understand the effects of this behavior.[25] Of course, this analysis in no way diminishes the merits of philanthropy by delegation, but it shows that we need to reflect collectively on how to make it more effective.

CORPORATE PHILANTHROPY

Pro-social behavior can reflect a company's own desire to engage in causes it considers just (such as subsidies for disadvantaged neighborhoods, jobs for young people, art, or medical research) rather than simply profitable. Obviously, it is empirically difficult to draw a clear distinction between the enterprise's philanthropy (sacrificing profit) and delegated philanthropy (not sacrificing profit), to the extent that socially responsible actions may also generate a financial benefit by projecting a good image of the business.

This form of philanthropy has been attacked from both the right and the left. In a famous article written in 1970, Milton Friedman argued, in substance, that companies should not engage in charity with shareholders' money, and that managers and board directors should use their own wealth for that purpose. At the other end of the political spectrum, Robert Reich suggested that companies should not substitute themselves for the state.

Of course, the evaluation of these arguments depends partly on another evaluation: the quality of public management in the area where corporate philanthropy occurs. This is an empirical question and one cannot expect a single answer to be valid for all countries. We do not know much about this—the object of these remarks is precisely to encourage deep reflection on the subject. In practice, pragmatism has won out in many countries, which have left a free space (through tax deductions for donations) for philanthropy.

Finally, corporate social responsibility, socially responsible investment, and fair trade are compatible with a market economy. They represent a response that is both decentralized and partial (because of the free rider problem) to the question of how to provide certain public goods. They would have less place in a world in which the state was effective and benevolent, representing the citizens' will; but in the real world, there is a place for these ethical initiatives on the part of citizens and enterprises, and I hope I have helped to clarify it.

PART IV

THE GREAT MACROECONOMIC CHALLENGES

EIGHT
The Climate Challenge

WHAT IS AT STAKE IN CLIMATE CHANGE?

Rising sea levels affecting islands and coastal cities, climatic distur-bances, heavy rains and extreme droughts, uncertain harvests: we are all aware of the consequences of climate change. The costs will be both economic and geopolitical, leading to migrations and deep resentment on the part of the populations most affected. Unless the international community acts vigorously, climate change may well compromise, in a dramatic and lasting way, the well-being of future generations. Although the precise consequences are still difficult to quantify, the result may well be catastrophic if we fail to act. Whereas specialists agree that an increase of 1.5 to 2 degrees Celsius in aver-age global temperature is the upper limit of what we can reasonably accommodate (implying a likely sea level rise of 80–90 cm), the fifth (2014) evaluation report issued by the Intergovernmental Panel on Climate Change (IPCC) estimates that (on current trends) the average rise will be 2.5 to 7.8 degrees Celsius before the end of the twenty-first century. Our emissions of greenhouse gases (GHGs), such as carbon dioxide and methane,[1] have never been as high. The limit of 1.5 to 2 degrees Celsius thus represents an enormous challenge, especially in a context of sustained global population growth and the desire of many lower income countries to achieve the living standards of developed countries.

This challenge is partly summed up in figure 8.1. The graph on the left shows the path of GDP and CO_2 emissions from 1960 to 2010; as it indicates, technological progress has led naturally to lower emis-sions of CO_2 per unit of GDP. But this improvement is relatively slow.

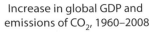

Increase in global GDP and
emissions of CO_2, 1960–2008

Projected growth up until 2050
of global GDP and emissions of CO_2
based on a scenario of 1.5° to 2° C

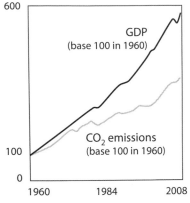

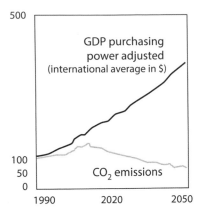

Figure 8.1. Relative development of carbon emission and production. *Source:*
Report of the Pascal Canfin-Alain Grandjean Commission, June 2015.

The graph on the right depicts the likely path of global GDP to 2050, as well as the path for CO_2 emissions needed to contain the temperature increase to a virtuous 1.5 to 2.0 degrees Celsius. A comparison of the two graphs shows that the amount of CO_2 emitted per unit of GDP must decrease dramatically to reach the environmental objective. Thus, behavior and technology will have to evolve substantially in the next thirty-five years. To succeed, we will have to transform radically the way we consume energy, the way we design, build, and heat our houses, the way we transport people, produce goods and services, and the way we manage our agriculture and forests. To these "climate change mitigation" policies, intended to reduce GHG emissions, we need to add measures to "adapt"—that is, actions to combat the impacts of global warming. Reducing the vulnerability of social and biological systems to climate change might include setting up networks to warn of floods, raising the bridges, protecting wetlands, making changes to agriculture, and migrating.

Obviously, there is nothing very new in this. Indeed, we have to remember that the international community has warned against the hazards of climate change since at least the Rio Summit of 1992. In particular, the Kyoto Protocol of 1997 was an important step. But its defects, to which we shall return, prevented any significant effort to reduce GHG emissions. The subsequent major meeting, in Copenhagen in 2009,[2] was distinguished by its lack of ambition.

Figures 8.2 and 8.3 show other facets of the challenge. The estimates of total emissions[3] in figure 8.2 show that while the majority of anthropogenic emissions (that is, those caused by human activity) are due to countries that are now developed, emerging economies will play a central role in future emissions. China provides some forewarning; it is now by far the greatest emitter, even though it still has a long way to go to bring the whole of its population up to developed-world standards of living; India and other emerging and poor countries will follow in terms of living standards, we hope, but they will have a substantial impact on global warming.

Top 10 emitters

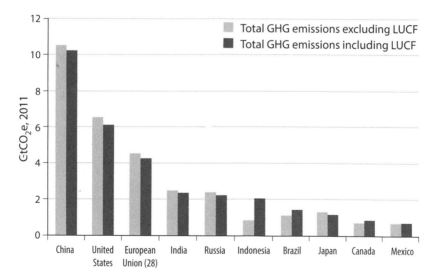

Figure 8.2. Emissions by country. LUCF (land-use change and forestry) refers to emissions resulting from the change in allocation of land and forests. *Source*: World Resources Institute.

Emissions intensity of top 10 emitters

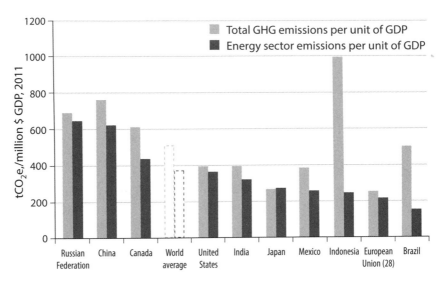

Figure 8.3. Emissions related to production, by country. *Source*: World Resources Institute.

Figure 8.3 shows great divergence in environmental performance, measured in emissions per unit of GDP (whether for all emissions or focusing on the energy sector only). It also suggests that opportunities for limiting GHG emissions are not uniformly distributed around the world. Though it is not very virtuous, Europe probably has much less room to maneuver than other regions.

Across the world, nations are content to wait and see. Not only are they making inadequate efforts to reduce the use of carbon in their industries, transport systems, and homes, but new power stations burning coal (the most polluting fossil fuel) to generate electricity, are being installed. Some countries even subsidize fossil fuel energy sources (gas, coal, petroleum), which are responsible for 67 percent of GHG emissions (80 percent of CO_2). According to the Organization for Economic Co-operation and Development (OECD),[4] 141 to 177 billion euros are still spent around the world each year to subsidize these types of energy generation. The subsidies take the form of income tax deductions and reductions in value-added taxes for specific groups and professions (farmers, fishermen, truck drivers, airline companies, low-income households, and so on), plus tax credits for major infrastructure investments. Of course, it is difficult to calculate the net subsidies when taxes on fossil energies are in place (and furthermore are subject to many exemptions). Whatever their exact amount, these subsidies throughout the world reinforce the idea that "national interest" takes priority over the environmental imperative.

How did we get to this point? How can we explain the scant progress made in international negotiations during the past twenty-five years? Can we limit global warming? These are central questions to which this chapter will try to offer some answers.[5]

REASONS FOR THE STANDSTILL

We can call for dialogue, we can dream of a different world in which economic agents—households, firms, public bodies—change their habits and decide to behave in an environmentally friendly way. We should explain what is at stake, and make people aware of the consequences of our collective behavior. But that still risks not being nearly enough. In reality, this debate has been going on for more than twenty-five years, and has been reported in the media so many times that no one is unaware of it. While most of us are prepared to make small gestures for the environment, we are not willing to give up our cars, pay much more for electricity, restrict our consumption of meat, or moderate our air travel to distant places. And while local sustainable development initiatives are praiseworthy, they will absolutely not be enough by themselves. In reality, we would like everyone else to do these things for us—or rather for our grandchildren. As irresponsible as it may be, our common policy is easy to explain. It is the result of two factors: *selfishness with regard to future generations* and *the free rider problem*. In other words, the benefits of reducing climate change remain *global* and *distant in time*, while the costs of that reduction are *local* and *immediate*.

The Free Rider Problem ...

Every country acts first of all in its own interest, on behalf of its people, while at the same time hoping to benefit from efforts made by other countries. For an economist, climate change is a "tragedy of the commons." In the long term, most countries would benefit enormously from a reduction in global GHG emissions, because global warming will have large economic, social, and geopolitical effects. The incentive for each individual country to undertake this reduction, however, is negligible. In reality most of the benefit from efforts made by any country to attenuate global warming will go to other countries.

A given country bears 100 percent of the cost of its green policies—for instance, the costs of insulating homes or replacing polluting energy sources like coal with cleaner but more expensive sources. On the other hand, to simplify, if a country represents only 1 percent of the world's population (and is near average in its exposure to the risks of climate change), it will receive only 1 percent of the benefits of its policy. So its environmental policies will primarily benefit other countries. It's as if you had to choose between spending one hundred dollars today or to save that amount, all the while knowing that ninety-nine dollars of these savings will be taken away and given to strangers. Moreover, most of the benefits of this policy do not go to individuals who are currently of voting age, but rather to future generations (who have no vote yet).

Consequently, countries do not internalize the benefits of policies to reduce emissions: these policies remain inadequate, emissions remain high, and climate change accelerates. The free rider problem leads to the tragedy of the commons. This tragedy is exemplified by many case studies in other domains. For example, when several livestock farmers share a common pasture, the result is usually overgrazing. Each farmer wants to profit from having an extra cow, without considering that his profit creates a loss for the other farmers whose animals will have less grass to eat. In the same way, hunters and fishermen do not internalize the cost to others of increasing their yield. Overfishing and overhunting, frequent subjects of international disputes, have in the past contributed to the extinction of many species ranging from the dodo, Mauritius's emblematic bird, to the bears in the Pyrenees and the buffalo on the Great Plains of North America. The evolutionary biologist Jared Diamond has shown how the deforestation of Easter Island led to the collapse of a whole civilization.[6] We find other examples of the tragedy of the commons in air and water pollution, traffic jams, and international security.

Elinor Ostrom, a political scientist who won the Nobel Prize for economics in 2009, has shown how small, stable communities can, under certain conditions, manage their common local resources without falling victim to this tragedy. This is thanks to informal mechanisms of incentives and sanctions.[7] These informal methods of limiting the free rider problem are obviously not applicable to climate change, because in this case the stakeholders are the seven billion individuals who live on our planet, plus their descendants. Finding a solution to the problem of global externalities is complex, because there is no supranational authority able to implement and enforce the standard approach for managing a common good by internalizing external costs (often used at the national level and explained below), as recommended by economic theory.

... IS AGGRAVATED BY THE PROBLEM OF "CARBON LEAKAGE"

The problem of "carbon leakage" may further discourage any country or region that wanted to adopt a unilateral strategy of alleviation. Taxing carbon emissions imposes additional costs on national industries and undermines their ability to compete if these industries emit large quantities of GHGs and are exposed to international competition. In any given country, a carbon tax high enough to contribute effectively to the battle against climate change would thus lead some companies to relocate their production facilities abroad—to regions of the world where they could pollute more cheaply. If they did not do this, they would lose their markets (domestic or export) to companies located in countries more lenient about emissions. Consequently, a unilateral policy shifts production to less responsible countries, which leads, de facto, to a simple redistribution of production and wealth without any significant environmental benefit.

Similarly, "virtuous" countries that increase by taxation the domestic price of gasoline or fuel oil to reduce the demand for them tend to cause the worldwide price of fossil fuels to fall, which in turn leads to an increase in the demand in other countries for fossil energies and therefore in GHG emissions elsewhere. The phenomenon of carbon leakage thus reduces the net climatic benefit of the efforts made in this domain.

The "Clean Development Mechanism" (CDM) set up in Kyoto in 1997 provides another example of the risk of "leakage." This mechanism gives credits to companies in countries where carbon emissions are penalized (for example, European countries) whenever the companies carry out projects to reduce emissions in other countries (such as Indonesia) that are not subject to these constraints. The company's effort is measured by the yardstick of the price on existing carbon markets—de facto, the market for tradable emissions permits in Europe (which explains, by the way, why the CDM was halted by the fall of prices on this market, a subject to which I shall return). At the time, my first reaction was positive. This mechanism creates aid for much-needed economic development, as well as a way to evaluate projects consistently with other climate change policies: a price for carbon equal to what a Western company has to pay for its emissions (the argument for the consistency with carbon permits is that the emission of a ton of carbon has the same environmental impact no matter who emits it, or where).

But I realized that my heuristic thinking was mistaken, as was that of the negotiators of the Kyoto agreement. On reflection, the CDM is not as virtuous as it seems. For one thing, it is complex to administer (to obtain carbon credits, you have to show that the project is "additional," that is, that there would not have been a reduction in pollution in the absence of the CDM program, which is logical but involves an unobserved counterfactual).[8] For another thing, it probably often has only a small net environmental impact: for example, a project to preserve a forest somewhere in the world leads to deforestation elsewhere because of supply and demand in the market for lumber or soybeans, which created the deforestation in the first place. In this example, the virtuous choice to preserve this one forest increases the price of lumber or soybeans, encouraging deforestation in other parts of the world.

This problem of leakage provides further proof that only a global accord can resolve the climate question: countries that do not penalize carbon emissions pollute a great deal, not only producing goods for their own consumption, but also for export to more virtuous countries. This has caused some observers to argue on empirical grounds that the Kyoto Protocol has not led to lower emissions, even though some countries have introduced carbon pricing.[9]

... AND BY INCENTIVES TO DELAY REFORMS

Finally, the free rider phenomenon has been aggravated by the common belief that countries that do less today will obtain more in future negotiations. Both theory and experience with other pollutants suggest that the stronger a country's reliance on carbon-based fuels today, the better its bargaining position will be to demand compensation for joining in a global agreement tomorrow. In fact, since the role of carbon fuels in their economies is so great, they are less motivated to sign an agreement, and the international community will find itself obliged to grant them larger transfers (either financial or in free negotiable emissions permits) to convince them to join in the agreement. This is exactly what happened within the United States when a sharp reduction in acid rain pollutants (SO_2 [sulfur dioxide] and NO_x [nitrogen oxides]) was negotiated in the 1980s. The highly polluting Midwestern states opposed such a policy and ended up being brought on board in the 1990 law[10] by generous allocations of free tradable emission rights. A sad reality, but one to reckon with.

MODEST PROGRESS, ALL THE SAME ...

For all that, we mustn't conclude that no progress has been made.

Tradable emissions permits. Markets for tradable emissions permits already exist in Europe (since 2005), the United States, China, Japan, South Korea, and many other countries (more than forty in all), regions, and even cities.[11] A market of this kind is one way to make economic agents responsible for their GHG emissions. The principle is the following: the public authority sets a ceiling for the amount of pollution it is prepared to tolerate; in the case of climate change, this is set at a global level and is the maximum number of tons of CO_2 we can still emit without warming the planet by more than 1.5 to 2 degrees Celsius (this quantity is sometimes called the "CO_2 budget"). Then the authority issues a corresponding number of permits, which are called "tradable emission rights" (or sometimes, pejoratively, "rights to pollute"). Any economic agent—an electricity producer for instance—must then be able to present, at the end of the year, permits that correspond to its emissions during the year. If it does not have enough permits, it will be forced to buy additional ones at the market price on the permits market or else pay a penalty (in principle, this will be far higher than the market price). If it has excess permits, it can resell the surplus at the market price. Thus, carbon emissions cost the same for everyone. The possibility of buying and selling these permits explains why in international negotiations this approach is often called "cap and trade."

Carbon tax. Other countries have chosen a carbon tax, imposed by the government for each ton of CO_2 emitted. Sweden has pursued the most ambitious policy by establishing in 1991 a carbon tax of 100 euros per ton of CO_2[12] for households (though with many exemptions for businesses, to avoid the problem of leakage discussed above). In 2015, France adopted a carbon tax on fossil fuels of 14.5 euros per ton of CO_2.[13] Outside Europe, there are a few modest carbon taxes, for example in Japan and in Mexico.

With the exception of the Swedish tax,[14] all these schemes set a price for carbon that is much lower than the price that would make it possible to remain below the 1.5 to 2 degrees Celsius limit. The carbon tax counterpart to an amount of tradable emissions permits equal to the CO_2 budget consists of setting a tax equal to what is called the "social cost of carbon"—that is, the price that will generate enough effort on the part of economic agents to put us back on track to limit global warming to 1.5 to 2 degrees Celsius. Carbon taxes are almost always significantly lower than this social cost. To mention just one estimate, the key report intended to guide the French carbon policy[15] estimated that carbon's social cost (that is, the price level that, were it applied worldwide, would make it possible to remain in conformity with the IPPC's recommendations) would be 45 euros per ton of CO_2 in 2010, 100 euros in 2030, and between 150 euros and 350 euros in 2050.[16] But today the price of carbon on the European or American market is between 5 and 10 euros, and in many countries it is zero.

Why do countries take unilateral action? Any action in favor of the climate is surprising if one considers that, as always in geopolitics, national interest comes first. Why would a country sacrifice itself in the name of humanity's well-being? First, if there is a "sacrifice," it is tiny: current measures remain modest and will not be enough to avert a climate catastrophe. Second, it may not be a sacrifice if the countries concerned gain other benefits from an environmental policy. Green choices can help reduce emissions of local pollutants—that is, pollutants that mainly affect the country itself. For instance, coal-fired power plants simultaneously emit CO_2 (a GHG), SO_2, and NO_x. The last two are local pollutants responsible for acid rain and for fine particulates that are believed to have serious health effects. Improving the energy efficiency of coal plants benefits the country, independent of any climate change consideration. In the same way, the replacement of lignite ("brown coal," which is particularly polluting) with natural gas and petroleum in Europe after the Second World War was a spectacular public health and environmental advance, one of whose notable effects was to eliminate smog in London. But again, the choice had nothing to do with the fight against climate change, which anyway was not a public issue at that time; instead it was dictated by local imperatives. Similarly, some countries could encourage citizens to eat less red meat, not to fight emissions of methane (a GHG), but rather to reduce cardiovascular disease. These "cobenefits" create an incentive—very inadequate but an incentive all the same—to reduce emissions.

Finally, the partial internalization of CO_2 emissions on the part of large countries such as China (which has almost 20 percent of the world population and is very vulnerable to climate change), the desire to appease an environmentally concerned public opinion, and to avoid international pressures are factors that may lead to action—even in the absence of a binding international agreement. Countries are therefore likely to take some unilateral measures even if concerned solely with their national interest. Actions to reduce the carbon content of production do not necessarily signal awareness of the impact of emissions on the rest of the world. These unilateral measures are called "zero ambition" measures.[17] "Zero ambition" refers to the level of commitment that a country would choose solely to limit the direct effects of pollution on the country itself. In other words, it is the level the country would have chosen in the absence of any international negotiation. These measures are insufficient to keep global warming under control.

... But Sometimes at a High Cost

In addition to tradable emissions permits and carbon taxes, many countries use a variety of "command and control" approaches (which I will come back to). Some of these measures are too expensive given their limited effectiveness in reducing global warming. While well-meaning, establishing nonquantified environmental standards or requiring public authorities to choose renewable energy sources often leads to a lack of consistency that substantially increases the cost of reducing emissions. States sometimes spend as much as a thousand dollars per ton of carbon avoided (this used to be the case particularly in Germany, a country that does not have a lot of sunshine but installed first-generation solar power systems) when other measures to reduce emissions would cost just ten dollars per ton. This is a policy described as green by the vast majority of observers, but it is not: for the same cost, emissions could have been reduced by one hundred tons rather than a single ton! I shall return to this question when considering economic efficiency as an environmental imperative.

NEGOTIATIONS THAT FALL SHORT OF THE STAKES INVOLVED

From the Kyoto Protocol ...

In the Kyoto Protocol of 1997, which went into effect in 2005, the signatory countries agreed to reduce their emissions of GHGs. The so-called "Annex B parties" (mainly developed countries) promised to reduce emissions by 2012 by an average of 5 percent compared to 1990 levels and to set up a system of tradable emissions permits. Though full of good intentions, it was certainly not ambitious enough, and its implementation was marred by serious conceptual problems. At the time they signed it, the participants in the Kyoto Protocol produced more than 65 percent of total worldwide GHG emissions. By 2012, the protocol covered less than 15 percent of worldwide emissions, given the United States' failure to ratify the protocol and the withdrawal of Canada, Russia, and Japan. Canada, for example, confronted by the prospect of its oil shale deposits windfall, quickly realized that it would need to buy emissions permits to honor its Kyoto commitments.[18] It preferred to withdraw from the protocol rather than pay. The United States Senate insisted that there be no free riders (targeting China in particular) before it would ratify the protocol. Even though, given the analysis above, the need for a global agreement is incontrovertible, the move was largely motivated by domestic politics: the US Senate was reluctant to act in the face of a public that was skeptical about climate change, and did not want to reduce its heavy consumption of carbon (see table 8.1).

Table 8.1. National Emissions per Inhabitant

Country	Tons of CO_2 per inhabitant
Uganda	0.11
Republic of the Congo	0.53
India	1.70
Brazil	2.23
World	4.98
France	5.19
China	6.71
Germany	8.92
Japan	9.29
Russian Federation	12.65
United States	17.02
Qatar	43.89

Source: World Bank.

The main attempt to establish carbon pricing under the Kyoto Protocol, the European Union's Emission Trading Scheme (EU ETS), also failed. The economic problems created by the 2008 financial crisis and then the Eurozone crisis, and the rapid deployment of renewable energy (particularly in Germany) both reduced demand for emissions permits, which led to an excess supply of permits in relation to demand.[19] Without any compensating reduction in the supply of permits, the price of a ton of CO_2 fell from its historic high of thirty euros to a price that fluctuated between five and ten euros, too low to have a significant impact on efforts to reduce emissions. It was so low that it even allowed electricity producers to replace gas with coal, which emits twice as much carbon per kilowatt hour, not to mention fine particulates. It is estimated that a price of about thirty euros for a ton of CO_2 would make gas-fired power plants more competitive than coal-fired ones. Engie (a French multinational energy company) even closed three gas-fired plants because of competition from coal-fired plants, which currently pollute almost without penalty. In contrast, the UK's imposition of a minimum carbon tax—around twenty pounds in the last two years (to be added to the price of carbon in the European emission system, about five euros currently)—had a dramatic impact on the use of coal, which quickly tumbled from 30 percent to less than 10 percent of the UK energy mix. The substitution of gas for coal brought about an important reduction in UK GHG emissions.[20]

Some see the fall of carbon prices on the emissions permits market as the market's failure. In reality the failure results from an implicit political decision not to be the only region in the world to adhere to the commitments made in Kyoto. Rather than adjusting the number of permits downward to reflect the economic situation, Europe chose to let the price fall and align itself with the even less ambitious climate policies pursued elsewhere in the world. This is the tragedy of the commons in action.

Thus, over the past twenty years, Europeans have sometimes believed that their (limited) commitment to reduce GHG emissions would lead other countries to follow their example. Unsurprisingly, this hasn't happened. Sadly, the Kyoto Protocol was a failure, and its own architecture doomed it. Because of the free rider problem, made worse by carbon leakage, only a global solution will work.

... TO THE SUBSEQUENT LACK OF AMBITION: VOLUNTARY COMMITMENTS

The Kyoto Protocol was full of good intentions, but that did not prevent countries from free riding. We can say the same of the non-binding promises made in Copenhagen, but for a different reason. The initial objective of the Copenhagen conference in December 2009 was to devise a new Kyoto Protocol with a higher number of signatories. In practice, however, the conference resulted in a profoundly different project: a "pledge and review" process. The United Nations has since merely rubber-stamped, without imposing any real constraints, the informal commitments of the countries that signed up, the INDCs (Intended Nationally Determined Contributions). This new mechanism of voluntary commitments was ratified by the United Nations Climate Change Conference, which took place in Paris in December 2015. The strategy of voluntary commitments has several significant defects, and is an inadequate response to the climate change challenge.

Greenwashing. Since the costs of reducing emissions vary from one signatory to another, it is impossible to gauge the ambition of the INDCs.[21] In reality, the system has created strong incentives to engage in "greenwashing"—appearing to be much more environmentally conscious than one actually is. This in turn makes measuring and evaluating the actual contributions more complex.

In a completely predictable way, countries choose advantageous baselines: 2005 for the United States (when shale gas became available after 2005, it reduced US GHG emissions as it was substituted for coal), or 1990 for Germany (the point at which it inherited polluting power plants in East Germany, and so found it relatively easy to reduce emissions while creating large local cobenefits). By taking years of high pollution as points of reference, countries artificially inflated the ambition of the objectives they set for themselves. The lack of comparability has been exacerbated because each commitment has its own time horizon and metric (some use peak emissions, others the reduction of emission per capita or relative to the GNP, and so on). Furthermore, some promises are contingent: in Japan, a country that uses a lot of coal, the commitments are contingent on the restoration of nuclear energy, and in many emerging or underdeveloped countries, on receiving "sufficient" foreign subsidies. In short, the INDC commitments have been a potluck to which each country brought what suited it best.

Still free riders. The INDC commitments, even if they are credible, remain voluntary, and the free riding problem is therefore inevitable. As Joseph Stiglitz pointed out, "In no other area has voluntary action succeeded as a solution to the problem of the undersupply of a public good."[22]

In some ways, the mechanism of voluntary commitments resembles an income tax system in which each household would freely choose the level of its fiscal contribution. Many observers therefore fear that the current INDCs are merely "zero ambition" agreements.

The (non)credibility of promises. Promises only persuade those who listen to them. In reality, they are not credible without formal commitments. Experience with donations for humanitarian causes (in particular for health care) has not been encouraging. This noncommitment will strengthen the temptation of signatories not to keep to their pledges, in particular if they suspect that others will do the same.

Evaluating COP 21

The latest major international meeting, the United Nations Climate Change Conference held in Paris in December 2015 (COP 21) was supposed to lead to an efficient, fair, and credible agreement. Mission accomplished? The negotiations were complex to conduct, because governments were not prepared to make binding commitments. The agreement reached displayed a great deal of ambition: the objective to be attained is now "far below 2 degrees Celsius," instead of the previous "up to 2 degrees Celsius" goal, and the world is not supposed to produce any net GHG emissions after 2050. In addition, after 2020 the funds dedicated to developing countries will exceed the one hundred billion dollars a year that had been agreed to in Copenhagen in 2009.

The diagnostic of the parties to COP 21 was correct. It recognized that the current rate of emissions is very dangerous, and that we therefore need strong action and new technologies to protect the environment. It admitted that we must reach a negative level of emissions after 2050 (the absorption of carbon by "carbon sinks" must exceed emissions by then). Poor countries would be helped. The parties also called for the creation of a system for monitoring pollution (albeit with a two-tier system, with a separate treatment for emerging countries like China—which by itself emits more than the United States and Europe combined). Even if this diagnostic was already partly embodied in the 1992 United Nations Framework Convention on Climate Change (UNFCCC), it was good that all the countries agreed to confirm that it was the correct diagnosis. On the other hand, the promises made in Paris were far from adequate; and so far as concrete measures are concerned, little progress has been made.

In terms of effectiveness in combating climate change, carbon pricing, although favored by a large majority of economists and many decision makers, was a red flag for Venezuela and Saudi Arabia—the latter even going so far as to ask for compensation if the price of oil dropped as a result of the agreement. The negotiators buried carbon pricing in the face of general indifference. As for the question of fairness, the developed countries promised an overall transfer to poorer countries, but did not specify their own individual contributions. Collective promises are never kept, since no one feels responsible for fulfilling them (the free rider problem in action again). The transfers would have been more credible if the developed countries' individual contributions had been specified. Doubts were also raised as to whether the promised transfers to poorer countries would constitute additional funds, and not just earmark existing aid to environmental projects, or be loans to be later repaid, or constitute a pledge on uncertain future revenues.

In addition, the agreement avoided making countries' commitments to reduce their emissions binding; and even so the countries' pledges fell short of what is needed to reach the 2050 cumulative emissions target. The negotiations on transparency also failed. It is difficult to understand why the global South should not be subject to the same process of monitoring, notification, and verification as the global North. The rich countries have a duty to be generous, to be sure, but not to close their eyes. This asymmetry in treatment gives rich countries a ready-made excuse for not keeping their promises in the future. Finally, the idea—unanimously applauded—that a more virtuous path would be followed by revising the protocol every five years ignored what economists call the "ratchet effect": are we really sure that a country will put itself in a better future negotiating position if it cheerfully fulfills its promises today, instead of dragging its feet? We always expect more from the best student.

The COP 21 agreement was an unequivocal diplomatic success—the 196 delegations approved it unanimously—but this consensus was achieved by yielding to various demands (as we have seen regarding the price of carbon) and thus at the price of a lack of (real, not claimed) ambition. A simple test of the truth of this reduction to the lowest common denominator is that while all heads of state went home celebrating the agreement, none of them informed their compatriots that they now had to quickly roll up their sleeves and get to work, because the era of cheap pollution was over for the country.[23]

In the meantime, new coal projects are still undertaken (for example in South Africa, where investments are sometimes financed by countries like China that have cut back on coal projects at home). Europe keeps using German and Polish coal instead of using more gas in the transition to renewable energy sources. The United States, which has almost by accident reduced its GHG emissions by using inexpensive shale gas, continues to export coal, of which it has an excess. With the election of Donald Trump, it now also has an administration supportive of the coal industry and officially skeptical about the reality of climate change. On June 1, 2017, Donald Trump announced his decision to withdraw from the Paris climate accord. In the future, other countries might fail to abide by their promises in a more discrete way, by letting their pollution slip without formally denouncing the accord.

All things considered, the newspaper the *Guardian* summed it up adequately on the day the Paris accord was signed (December 12,

2015): "By comparison to what it could have been, it's a miracle. By comparison to what it should have been, it's a disaster."

MAKING EVERYONE ACCOUNTABLE FOR GHG EMISSIONS

The heart of the climate change challenge lies in the fact that economic agents are not internalizing the damage they cause to others when they emit GHGs. To resolve this free rider problem, economists have long proposed forcing economic agents to internalize the negative externalities of their CO_2 emissions. This is "the polluter pays" principle.

To achieve this, the price of carbon would have to be set at a level compatible with the goal of limiting the global temperature rise to 1.5 to 2 degrees Celsius, and all emitters would be compelled to pay the established price: given that all CO_2 molecules produce the same marginal damage, no matter who emits them, or where or how they are emitted, the price of any ton of CO_2 must be the same. Imposing a uniform price for carbon on all economic agents throughout the world would guarantee the implementation of any mitigating policies whose cost was lower than the price of carbon.

POLICIES THAT ARE NOT ALWAYS AS GREEN AS THEY SEEM ...

A uniform price for carbon would thus guarantee that the reduction of emissions necessary to achieve the global objectives for atmospheric CO_2 would occur, and would minimize the overall cost of the efforts made to achieve it.

Environmental regulation, however, is often not based on economic instruments such as a tax or a cap-and-trade system, but on "command and control": such top-down measures include emissions limits differentiated according to the source of the emissions, mandated uniform reductions in pollution, subsidies and taxes that are not related to the actual pollution, standards differentiated simply by the age of the equipment involved, and the setting of industrial and technological standards and norms (to be clear, I am not opposed to standards; my qualm rather is that they often do not embody a cost-benefit analysis).[24]

These top-down policies create big differences in the implicit price of carbon for different types of emissions, and they increase the cost society has to pay for environmental policies. This is easily explained: take two companies, each of which emits two tons of carbon, and assume that we want to cut their total combined pollution in half, from four tons to two tons. Let's suppose that the first company has a cleanup cost of $1,000 per ton, while the second company's cost is $10 per ton. A "fair" policy might consist of requiring each company to reduce its pollution by half, thus "equitably" distributing the efforts made, and generating a total cleanup cost of $1,010. Obviously, efficiency requires that the second company should eliminate its two tons of emissions at a total cost of $20, and that the first should not do anything; thus saving society $1,010 – $20 = $990 (that is, 98% of the cost) in comparison with the top-down policy.

The economic approach, which involves setting a price for carbon in some way, makes this saving possible: with a ton of CO_2 priced at, for example, fifty dollars, the first company will not spend one thousand dollars to eliminate a ton of carbon, but rather will pay one hundred dollars to keep emitting the same amount. The second company will stop polluting altogether. Overall, the result would be a savings of $990 to society. And "fairness" and "efficiency" are not necessarily opposed: the savings achieved by moving to a carbon price would make it possible to compensate in part the losers (the tax revenue of $100 can be used as an offset for the $120 loss, while the top-down approach generated no revenue to compensate the $1,010 cost), provided that this compensation takes the form of a one-off transfer (not linked to its future choices regarding pollution).

The enthusiasm for top-down approaches originates in governments' desire to appear to be doing something to tackle climate change. Patchy but expensive initiatives that are visible to voters but concealed from consumers (because they are included in feed-in tariffs imposed on electric utilities or in the price of goods and services) are politically less costly than a carbon tax, which is very visible to those who have to pay it. Subsidies are always more popular than taxation, even if, in the end, someone has to pick up the bill for them. This is another example of how economic policy gets distorted by what is visible and what is not so visible.

It has been empirically verified, however, that top-down policies increase the cost of environmental policies considerably. To judge from experience with other pollutants, introducing a single carbon price might reduce the cost of cutting pollution by at least half in comparison with top-down approaches discriminating between sectors or agents.[25]

Western countries have made a few attempts to reduce GHG emissions, notably by directly subsidizing green technologies: high feed-in prices paid by the electrical grid for electricity produced by solar panels or wind turbines, bonus or penalty schemes favoring low-emission cars, subsidies for the biofuel industry, and so on. For every program set up, we can estimate an implicit carbon price, that is, the social cost of the program per ton of CO_2 saved. In the electricity sector, the OECD's estimates range from zero (or even less)[26] to eight hundred euros. In the trucking sector, the implicit price of carbon may be as high as one thousand euros, in particular if the trucks use biofuels. The variation in the carbon prices implied by policy measures is another demonstration of why the top-down approach is ineffective. Similarly, any global climate agreement that would not apply everywhere would be just as ineffective, because the price of carbon would be zero in the countries that didn't sign and, ultimately, very high in the countries that did.

The justification for subsidizing renewable energy sources is the "learning curve"—that is, the idea that costs decrease as companies gain experience in production. In general, this learning effect is always difficult to predict and is often oversold by lobbyists for producers seeking subsidies. But it has been important in the case of renewable energy. Dubai (a sunny country to be certain) signed a contract in 2016 for a large solar power installation at thirty dollars per megawatt hour, a price that would have been inconceivable even a short time ago. This learning curve, if it is established and can therefore be a benchmark for subsidizing, also implies that subsidies must decrease over time, because the learning effect is particularly significant when the technology is new (we refer to chapter 6 for a discussion of industrial policy).[27]

As we have seen, in the battle against climate change, it is crucial to avoid discrimination among actors. Every agreement whose implementation requires excessive mitigation expenditures will ultimately be abandoned under pressure from voters or lobbies. The green imperative will only be respected if the economic imperative is also respected. Both require a global approach and a pricing mechanism. Economic instruments (whether a tax or a market) are thus not inimical to an environmental policy. On the contrary, they are a necessary condition for one.

The Economic Approach

Most economists recommend establishing a global price for carbon. Although they differ on the exact way to implement it, this debate is secondary in comparison with the abandonment of the principle that there should be a single carbon price. Many NGOs and think tanks[28] and policymakers are on the same wavelength.[29] For example, Christine Lagarde (the general director of the IMF) and Jim Yong Kim (president of the World Bank) declared together in Lima, on October 8, 2015:

> The transition to a cleaner future will require both government action and the right incentives for the private sector. At the center should be a strong public policy that puts a price on carbon pollution. Placing a higher price on carbon-based fuels, electricity, and industrial activities will create incentives for the use of cleaner fuels, save energy, and promote a shift to greener investments. Measures such as carbon taxes and fees, emissions-trading programs and other pricing mechanisms, and removal of inefficient subsidies can give businesses and households the certainty and predictability they need to make long-term investments in climate-smart development.[30]

The same carbon price for all countries, economic sectors, and agents: Is that too simple a policy? Perhaps. Up to this point, governments have clearly preferred to make things complicated.

Two economic instruments make coherent carbon pricing feasible: a carbon tax and tradable emissions permits. Among other things, we will look at whether these strategies can enable decisions about climate policy to be devolved to individual countries. Indeed we might prefer to grant freedom to national policymakers, even if we know that they might not choose the least expensive ways to reduce emissions. Consider the example of countries that have a limited ability to collect and redistribute through taxation. Let's suppose that some of these countries favor a low carbon price for cement to promote the construction of housing for the poor; they might then want to deviate from the rule of one price. There are two arguments in favor of letting each country decide. First, it leaves governments space to convince the public. Second, other countries are interested only in the total amount of CO_2 emitted by the country in question, not the way it was emitted.

To succeed, the two alternative strategies depend on an international agreement that covers global emissions sufficiently, using an "I will if you will" approach. Both require implementation, monitoring, and verification (more generally, the precondition for any effective action to reduce emissions would be to establish credible and transparent mechanisms to measure their emissions). Economists do not agree on the choice between a carbon tax and tradable emissions permits, but in my opinion, and in that of most economists, either approach is clearly more effective than the current system of voluntary commitments.

Option 1: A Worldwide Carbon Tax

With a carbon tax, every country would agree on a minimum price for its GHG emissions, for example fifty euros per ton of CO_2, and each would collect the corresponding revenues in its own territory. All countries would then have the same price for GHG emissions.[31] For example, countries could agree on a universal minimum carbon tax, limiting the subsidiarity in national policies (except for the ability to impose an even higher tax, an option that would be unlikely to be exercised if the minimum tax were high enough). A more sophisticated mechanism,[32] in which countries would agree on an average carbon price, would enable subsidiarity. The price of carbon would then be the ratio of the receipts of this levy divided by the volume of the country's emissions. The price would be equal to the carbon tax if only a carbon tax were used; but more generally, the price could emerge from a range of policies: a carbon tax, tax credits and penalties imposed on cars based on their CO_2 emissions, etc.).

Verification of Countries' Compliance to a Carbon Price

For various reasons, the carbon tax approach and its variants raise the problem of how to verify that countries are complying with the international agreement.

Collection. At present, countries (except for Sweden) hardly tax carbon or make their citizens and businesses pay for their emissions, because—even though the public finances would benefit—most of the environmental gains would go to third countries. Whatever international accord is signed, this incentive would live on. So even if verifying domestic households' and businesses' emissions were to cost nothing (which is not the case), the authorities might nonetheless be tempted to turn a blind eye to some polluters or underestimate their emissions, thus saving the country the economic and social cost of the measures to protect the environment. This opportunistic behavior on the part of individual states in the name of national interest is hard to avert. To understand better the difficulties inherent in following up and monitoring, look no further than the ineffective collection of taxes in Greece, concerning which Greece's creditors abroad and the Greek government have different incentives.[33] To sum up: the institution of a uniform carbon price is vulnerable to free riding incentives associated with the local-costs-and-global-benefits nature of green policies. Put differently, for it to function properly, a uniform carbon price must be accompanied by a very strict system of international monitoring at the local level, which is rather unrealistic.

Offsetting measures. An agreement on an international carbon tax can fail to be implemented if countries nullify the impact of the tax by means of compensatory transfers; for example, a country can introduce a carbon tax on fossil fuel energy and reduce other taxes (or increase subsidies) by the same amount on these forms of energy, cancelling out the impact of the carbon tax.[34]

Actions without an explicit carbon price. The carbon tax approach requires finding a conversion rate to evaluate policies that have an impact on climate change but which do not have their own explicit price, such as publicly funded green R&D, standards for residential[35] or highway construction, agricultural policy, or forestation and reforestation programs. It may also be necessary to determine the conversion rates specific to each country. Construction standards, for example, have a different impact on GHG emissions depending on the climate. Similarly, new forests may increase, rather than reduce, GHG emissions in (high albedo[36]) areas of the far north or south in which trees would cover snow.

Option 2: Tradable Emissions Permits

The classic mechanism to make economic agents face the same price for polluting is tradeable emissions permits. The international agreement would define a total global emissions target and allocate a corresponding volume of permits, either free of charge or via auction. Agents who pollute more than their permits allow must buy the extra on the market. Others, who pollute less than their quota, can sell their excess permits. The cost of pollution for everyone is the market price, whether the initial allocation was free of charge or not: additional emissions deprive the virtuous company of the sale of their permits and penalize a polluting company by an amount equal to the purchase price of the additional permits.

The international agreement would cap future CO_2 emissions and thus define a predetermined number (the "cap") of emissions permits available to be traded globally. Tradable permits guarantee all countries a uniform carbon price, generated by mutually advantageous exchanges on the carbon market. The price of transferring emissions permits between states would not be determined by agreeing on a carbon price, but rather by supply and demand in this market. The scheme might begin with an initial allocation of permits between countries to ensure compensation, with the twin aims of fairness and encouraging all countries to participate.

Are private households, who do not trade in permit markets, nonetheless incentivized by the carbon price? The answer is that they are indirectly affected, as the carbon price affects the price of goods and services. As far as their energy consumption is concerned, one could apply a carbon tax as long its level was consistent with the price paid on the permits market by companies producing commodities such as electricity and cement under the system of negotiable permits. Otherwise we could follow President Obama, who applied a system of tradable rights to gas refineries and importers. These companies then pass their "carbon price signal" through to consumers.

The emblematic example of the battle against one type of pollution—sulfur dioxide (SO_2) and nitrogen oxides (NO_x), which are responsible for acid rain—originated in a law passed with bipartisan support in the United States in 1990. The law mandated a reduction in emissions from twenty million tons to about ten million tons by 1995. Each year, permits are issued with a horizon of thirty years, so at any point in time there is a thirty-year visibility for the price of permits; such a visibility facilitates the planning of investments. An ambitious environmental goal was therefore realized thanks to a market in tradable permits[37] and strict adherence to the commitments set out in the law.

Several lessons can be drawn from this experience. A single carbon price can work, even when it is not possible to treat all agents the same way. The states in the American Midwest—which, with their coal-fired electrical plants, are major polluters—vigorously resisted the 1990 law and were finally granted free permits. The market price nevertheless encouraged them to greatly reduce their pollution, which they did. Moreover, the time horizon is crucial. Economic agents (enterprises, households, administrations, states) will choose equipment that does not emit GHGs only if they anticipate a sufficiently high future carbon price. Similarly, companies will make the effort necessary to develop new, nonpolluting generations of technology only if they have an economic interest in doing so. In short, success is more likely today when we reduce uncertainty about the price of carbon tomorrow.

Should we be concerned about the evolution and possible future excesses of carbon finance? Will it lead to speculation and social harm? On the one hand, speculating on the price of carbon does not matter as long as those doing so are using their own money. On the other hand, if a bank or an energy company in the energy sector used the financial markets to take risky positions instead of using them to hedge risks (that is, to protect itself against future price changes), that is a problem because the possible losses would harm the bank's depositors or electricity consumers—and probably the taxpayer if the state ends up bailing out a failing bank or energy company. Here we are in the realm of everyday prudential regulation. The government must supervise financial market positions taken by regulated enterprises and banks, and must make sure that they insure against risks rather than increasing them. These enterprises and banks must also be forced to trade permits and their derivatives on organized markets with clearing houses so that regulators can monitor them properly. Transparent markets make positions much clearer than over-the-counter arrangements, which proved to be so toxic during the 2008 financial crisis. [38]

Managing Uncertainty

Whatever solution is adopted to combat climate change, policies will need to adjust: there is still uncertainty in climate science, in technology (with regard to the speed at which cheap, low-carbon energy sources will be developed), in the economics of mitigation (with respect to the cost of reducing carbon emissions), in the social acceptability of adaptation, and in political science (regarding countries' will to reach a sincere agreement and observe it).

Given this uncertainty, we will need to adjust the number of permits or the carbon tax to account for new developments (for example, climate change may be faster than predicted, or the worldwide rate of growth might subside, as under the secular stagnation hypothesis). The ability to make such adjustments could jeopardize the credibility of countries' long-term commitment to reducing GHGs, but there are solutions.[39] In Europe, a market mechanism to stabilize the price of tradable emissions permits will finally go into effect in 2021. In addition, allowing participants to use permits at later dates makes it possible to smooth price changes: if, for example, the participants foresee future price increases, it will be in their interest to hoard permits. This smooths the price, which rises today and falls tomorrow in comparison with a policy in which hoarding for future use is prohibited.[40]

Making Countries Accountable

It is technologically easier for the international community to monitor CO_2 emissions by country rather than to measure them at a more local level. It therefore makes sense to make countries responsible for their national GHG emissions. A nation's anthropogenic CO_2 emissions can be calculated through carbon accounting. Satellites can see carbon sinks connected with forests and agriculture. Experimental programs by NASA and ESA (the European Space Agency) to measure global CO_2 emissions on the scale of each nation look promising in the long term.[41] As is the case for current cap and trade mechanisms, the countries that have a shortage of permits at the end of the year would buy additional permits, whereas countries that have a surplus of permits would be able either to sell them or save them for future use.

INEQUALITY AND THE PRICING OF CARBON

The question of inequality arises both within and across countries.

On the domestic level, it is sometimes objected that taxing carbon will be hard on the poor. Putting a price on carbon reduces the purchasing power of households, including the poorest ones, and this might be an obstacle to implementing the policy. This is true, but it should not block the environmental objective. There must be an appropriate policy tool associated with each separate policy objective, and it is important to avoid trying to achieve many objectives with one lever (such as a carbon price). So far as inequality is concerned, the state should use income tax as much as possible to redistribute income, while at the same time pursuing a suitable environmental policy. Environmental policy should not be diverted from its primary objective in order to address (legitimate) concerns about inequality. Refraining from pricing carbon to tackle inequality would be unwise. Similar reasoning would lead us for instance to price electricity at one-tenth of its cost (hello to open windows with the radiators on, and outdoor swimming pools heated year round; farewell to insulated buildings). It would also encourage tobacco use by getting rid of high taxes on (and perhaps even subsidizing) tobacco on the ground that poor people smoke a lot. Crazy examples? Maybe, but this reasoning is often applied to carbon pricing.

The same principle applies internationally, where it is better to organize lump-sum transfers to poor countries rather than trying to adopt inefficient, and thus not very credible, policies. As Pope Francis said in his encyclical *Laudato si'*:

> Its [climate change's] worst impact will probably be felt by developing countries in coming decades. Many of the poor live in areas particularly affected by phenomena related to warming, and their means of subsistence are largely dependent on natural reserves and ecosystem services such as agriculture, fishing and forestry. They have no other financial activities or resources which can enable them to adapt to climate change or to face natural disasters, and their access to social services and protection is very limited.

Poor and emerging countries rightly point out that rich countries have financed their industrialization by polluting the planet, and that they want to achieve a comparable standard of living. Figure 8.4 and table 8.1 demonstrate the magnitude of the challenge. To simplify, we can refer to the principle of "a common but differentiated responsibility": the responsibility incumbent on developed countries now, and in the future on emerging countries, that will account for a large proportion of emissions, as indicated by figure 8.4. This has led some people to argue for a "fair because differentiated" approach: a high carbon price for developed countries and a low one for emerging and developing countries.

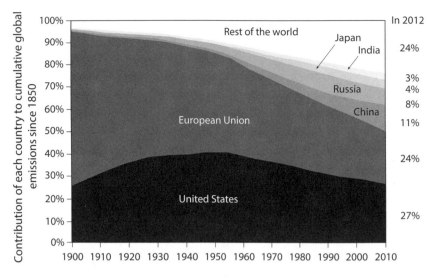

Figure 8.4. Total CO_2 emissions since 1850: the distortion of historical responsibilities. *Source*: Chair of climate economics, founded on the World Resources Institute's CAIT database.

But … a high carbon price in developed countries would have only a limited effect because they would offshore production to countries with low-cost carbon (not to mention the risk that national parliaments would exit the agreement, as happened after Kyoto). And even ignoring leakages, no matter what efforts were made by the developed countries, the objective of limiting the temperature increase to 1.5 to 2 degrees Celsius will never be reached if poor and emerging countries do not limit their GHG emissions in the future. It is impossible to exonerate lower-income countries. In twenty years, China will have emitted as much carbon dioxide as the United States has since the industrial revolution.

So what can we do? Emerging countries have to subject their citizens and enterprises to a substantial carbon price (ideally, the same price as elsewhere in the world). The question of equality should be addressed by financial transfers from rich countries to poor countries. The Copenhagen Protocol agreed on such aid, a principle reaffirmed by the COP 21 in Paris.

To sum up, international inequality raises the question of how the burden of coping with climate change is to be shared. The principle of common but differentiated responsibility reflects the idea that rich countries are generally those that have historically contributed the most to the accumulation of GHGs in the atmosphere. This observation should certainly not lead us, however, to abandon the principle of a single price, as happened in the Kyoto Protocol of 1997. In that agreement, low income countries were not subject to any price on carbon. This derailed the agreement because the US Senate would not ratify it. We should not repeat the errors made in Kyoto.

Finally, is it fair that the pollution caused, in China for example, by the production of goods exported to the United States and Europe be counted as Chinese pollution, and be covered by the system of permits to which all countries, including China, would be subject? The answer is that Chinese firms that emit GHGs when they produce exported goods will pass the price of carbon through to American and European importers so that rich country consumers will pay for the pollution their consumption induces. International trade does not alter the principle that payment should be collected where emissions are produced.

The Green Climate Fund and the Objective of One Hundred Billion Dollars a Year

Up to now, negotiations to settle the question of compensation for poor countries to gain their participation in the collective effort have failed. The 2009 Copenhagen summit promised an annual transfer of one hundred million dollars to poor countries.[42] In October 2015, the OECD[43] announced that commitments to contribute toward the goal had reached sixty-two billion dollars, a figure far higher than expected. On closer inspection, NGOs and the potential recipient countries expressed reservations about the accuracy of the data. Some of the commitments were loans, not donations. Moreover, a substantial fraction came from multilateral aid agencies (the World Bank, the Asian Development Bank, the European Bank for Reconstruction and Development) or from bilateral development agencies; since these agencies had no increase in their budgets, the question was whether this aid was additional. Was it really new aid benefiting developing countries, or just existing aid relabeled "green"?[44]

As in other domains (humanitarian aid after a natural catastrophe, or public health aid for the least advanced countries), national parliaments are reluctant to vote much money for developing countries.[45] Even an effective program like the Global Alliance for Vaccines and Immunization (GAVI)—which has a much smaller budget—got off the ground only thanks to a large financial commitment made by the Bill and Melinda Gates Foundation. At international conferences, politicians have a habit of promising financial contributions—but, once the conference is over, they reduce or reverse their pledges. Unfortunately, it is probable that free riding will endanger the progress of the Green Climate Fund.

Of course, in negotiations involving 195 countries it is difficult to agree on who is to benefit and who is to pay and how much. Each country will want to have its say and will slow down negotiations by asking to pay a little less or to receive a little more. It will probably be necessary to negotiate rough formulas based on a few country parameters (income, population, present and foreseeable pollution, sensitivity to global warming, for example) rather than trying to determine the contributions country by country. This will be difficult, but will be more realistic than an across-the-board negotiation.[46]

THE CREDIBILITY OF AN INTERNATIONAL AGREEMENT

An effective international agreement would create a coalition within which all countries and regions would apply the uniform carbon price to their respective territories. According to the principle of subsidiarity (the devolution of decision making to the lowest practical level), each country would then be free to devise its own carbon policy, by creating a carbon tax, a tradable emissions permits mechanism, or a hybrid system, for example. The free rider problem would be a challenge to the stability of this grand coalition: Could we count on the agreement being respected? It is a complex problem, but a solution is not out of reach.

Government debt is an instructive analogy. Sanctions against a country in default are limited (fortunately, gunboat diplomacy is no longer an option), which has led to concerns about whether countries are willing to repay debt. The same goes for climate change. Even if a good agreement were reached, there would be limited means to enforce it. The public debate about international climate negotiations usually ignores this reality. That said, we have to pin our hopes on a binding agreement, a genuine treaty, and not an agreement based only on promises. No matter how limited the possibility of international sanctions in the event of nonpayment of government debt, most countries do usually repay. More generally, the Westphalian tradition (that is of treaties between nation states being largely observed) gives us a nonnegligible chance of achieving it.

Naming and shaming is a good, feasible tactic, but—as we have seen in the case of the Kyoto commitments—it may remain largely toothless. Countries will always find excuses for not fulfilling their commitments: citing other measures (such as green research and development), recession, insufficient efforts made by others, a change of government, safeguarding jobs. There is no perfect solution to the problem of enforcing an international agreement, but we have at least two tools.

First, countries value free trade; the WTO might consider that the nonrespect of an international climate agreement is equivalent to environmental dumping, and impose sanctions on those grounds. In the same spirit, punitive taxes on imports could be used to penalize countries who do not participate. This would encourage hesitant countries to join the agreement and would make it more likely that a global coalition for the climate could be stable. Clearly the nature of the sanctions could not be decided by countries individually—they would quickly seize the opportunity to set up protectionist measures that would not necessarily have much connection with environmental reality.

Second, a climate agreement should be binding on a country's future governments, like sovereign debt. The IMF could be a stakeholder in this policy. For example, in the case of a tradable emissions permits system, a shortage of permits at the end of the year would increase the national debt, and the conversion rate would be the current market price. Naturally, I am aware of the risk of collateral damage that could result from choosing to connect a climate policy with international institutions that are working decently well. But what is the alternative? Supporters of non-binding agreements hope that goodwill will be enough to limit GHG emissions. If they are right, then incentive measures initiated through collaboration with other international institutions will suffice, a fortiori, without any collateral damage to these institutions.

IN CONCLUSION: PUTTING NEGOTIATIONS BACK ON TRACK

Despite the accumulation of scientific evidence that human actions play an important role in climate change, international action has been disappointing. The Kyoto Protocol failed to create an international coalition for a carbon price in proportion to its social cost. It was also a perfect illustration of the instability of international agreements that do not take the free rider problem seriously. Every international agreement must satisfy three criteria: economic efficiency, incentives to respect commitments, and fairness. Efficiency is possible only if all countries apply the same carbon price. Adequate incentives require penalties for free riders. Fairness, a concept defined differently by each stakeholder, should be achieved through lump-sum transfers. The strategy of voluntary commitments to reduce emissions is another example of a wait-and-see attitude from key countries—that is, a strategy of postponing a binding commitment on emissions to a later date.

However, this chapter should not fail to mention reasons for optimism. First, public awareness of the problem has grown in recent years, even if the economic crisis put environmental considerations on the back burner for a while. In addition, more than forty countries, including some of the most important ones (the United States, China, Europe) have created tradable emissions permit markets. Although they have generous ceilings and very low carbon prices as a result, they demonstrate a commitment to use a rational policy to fight climate change. Local carbon markets may someday connect to form a more coherent and efficient global market, even if the question of "exchange rates" will be a thorny one.[47] Finally, the sharp decline in the price of solar energy allows us to glimpse economic solutions to the problem of emissions in African and other developing and emerging countries. But all this will not be enough to attain our goals. So how can we build on these dynamics?

Although it is important to maintain a global dialogue, the UN process has shown predictable limits. Negotiations between 195 nations are incredibly complex. We need to create a "coalition for the climate" that brings together, from the outset, the major polluters, present and future. I don't know whether this should be the G20 or a more restricted group: in 2012, the five biggest polluters—Europe, the United States, China, Russia, and India—represented 65 percent of worldwide emissions (28 percent for China and 15 percent for the United States). The members of this coalition could agree to pay for each ton of carbon emitted. At first, no attempt would be made to involve the 195 countries in the global negotiation, but they would be urged to join in. The members of the coalition would put pressure on the WTO, and countries that refused to enter the coalition would be taxed at borders. The WTO would be a stakeholder on the basis that nonparticipants are guilty of environmental dumping; to avoid undue protectionism by individual countries, it would contribute to the definition of punitive import duties.

The answer to the question, "What can we do?" is simple: get back on the path of common sense.

1. The first priority of future negotiations ought to be an agreement in principle to establish a universal carbon price compatible with the objective of no more than a 1.5 to 2 degrees Celsius increase in average global temperatures. Proposals seeking carbon prices differentiated on the basis of country not only open a Pandora's box, they are above all not good for the environment, because the future growth of emissions will come from emerging and poorer countries. Underpricing carbon in these countries will not limit warming to a 1.5 to 2 degrees increase. This is so all the more because high prices for carbon in developed countries will encourage the offshoring of production facilities that emit GHGs to countries with low carbon prices, thus nullifying the efforts made in wealthy countries.

2. We also have to reach an agreement on an independent monitoring infrastructure to measure and supervise emissions in signatory countries, with an agreed governance mechanism.

3. Finally, and still in the spirit of returning to fundamentals, let us confront head-on the question of equity. This is a major issue, but any negotiation must face it, and burying it in the middle of discussions devoted to other subjects does not make the task any easier. There must be a negotiating mechanism that, after the acceptance of a single price for carbon, focuses on this question. Today, it is pointless to try to obtain ambitious promises for green funds from developed countries without that leading in turn to a mechanism capable of achieving climate objectives. Green financial assistance could take the form either of financial transfers or, if there is a world market for emissions permits, of a generous allocation of permits to developing countries.

There is no other way forward.

NINE

Labor Market Challenges

The best actor award at the 2015 Cannes Film Festival went to a Frenchman, Vincent Lindon. In *La loi du marché* (literally, "The law of the market," titled *The Measure of a Man* in English), he plays a middle-aged factory worker, Thierry, who has been fired as part of a cost-cutting exercise. Thierry takes part in one retraining program after another and repeatedly meets with counselors at the unemployment office, all to no avail. Struggling with financial problems (his home loan, a disabled son), he takes a job as a guard in a supermarket. The film tells of a store manager who distrusts his employees, monitors them, and will fire them from one day to the next for minor mischief, and of Thierry's struggle to preserve his dignity. This film depicts a deep malaise of French society—the lack of decent jobs so that many citizens are weakened or marginalized, and the sometimes very conflictual relations between employers and employees.

The film's title seems to suggest a degree of fatalism—as if this grim reality were the direct consequence of the market economy; as if it were to be expected that an employee who loses his job at the age of fifty might no longer be able to find another one; as if it were to be taken for granted that retraining programs, whose phenomenal cost is paid indirectly by the employees themselves, will not lead to anything; as if we ought to accept that a large number of workers should move from one unrewarding short-term contract to another, filling the gaps with state-subsidized jobs and unemployment benefits; as if men and women who are still young, in good physical shape, and eager to work had to be declared unfit for work and sent prematurely into retirement, a retirement financed by taxes levied on those who are still working. *Is this the law of the market or a choice made by society?*

It is not only France that has labor market problems. The British movie *I, Daniel Blake*, paints a similar picture of its lead character's seemingly inevitable downward spiral into unsatisfying jobs, dismal relations with supervisors, and inadequate welfare benefits. In the United States, many authors have documented the widespread use of short-term and zero-hours contracts, and the conflict over increases in minimum wages, leaving many people struggling to make ends meet. The details of how the labor market and the benefits system are organized differ greatly from country to country, as do their rates of unemployment: the US and UK have relatively low unemployment rates, whereas in France and other southern European countries, the jobless rate is high, especially among young people.

In this chapter, I will illustrate my points using the case of France and will therefore start by briefly reviewing the facts of its labor market. While the institutional details are specific to my own country, this chapter's lessons extend to a number of others.

First, there are some whose labor market institutions are similar to the French ones—including, for example, judicial control over redundancies, the prevalence of long-term unemployment, dysfunctional human resource management incentives for firms, the pervasiveness of short-term contracts when new jobs are created, high unemployment among the young, the old, and the unskilled, and a high cost of unemployment in terms of the government budget deficit. Southern Europe (Spain, Portugal, Italy, and Greece) immediately comes to mind.

Second, even for countries with lower unemployment or more new job creation now, the combination of globalization, technological change, and migration brings to the fore political demands to protect workers through protectionism, anti-immigration laws, taxes on "robots," and a range of labor market regulations to deal with redundancies and the "uberization" of society. The longstanding idea that workers are not "disposable commodities" is gaining new prominence in the employment policy debate, as the current technological revolution is likely to bring about an unprecedentedly rapid change in the nature of work in future.[1] Indeed, concern about the impact of automation and artificial intelligence on work in the market economy is already clear. People's fears about their work conditions and future prospects are already fueling populist movements. There is a sense that policy makers are not doing enough—and worse, that they don't even know what they should do. Politicians are being asked to wave a magic wand to assuage these concerns about job instability, degrading conditions of work, and increasing inequality. Some politicians will promise the impossible. But you do not need to be living on one of the southern European countries to understand the implications of otherwise well-intentioned job protection policies, and why it is better to protect workers than to protect jobs.

This chapter shows that unemployment is in part a choice that French society has made, and explains why. The chapter shows why mass unemployment and a dual labor market are not inevitable, and proposes avenues for reform. I will focus on employment contracts as an emblematic reform, but it is important to note that reform of the employment contract is only one part of a broader reform of labor market institutions with other, equally dysfunctional aspects. These should also be reformed in order to return to full employment, which France has not experienced for more than forty years. I will discuss some of these other aspects at the end of the chapter. I will explain why these reforms are urgent; in short, although unemployment in France and other similar countries has been slowly worsening for many years, a perfect storm of circumstances has formed that could throw them into a far more serious employment crisis. Finally, I will link the problems in the French labor market to the universal question of how to shape policies that give people in market economies a good chance of stable jobs with decent pay and conditions, particularly when globalization and new technologies seem to be threatening many people's future livelihoods.

THE LABOR MARKET IN FRANCE

Saying that France's performance in matters of employment and well-being at work is less than brilliant is an understatement. A quick international comparison clearly shows its poor performance is closer to the troubled economies of southern Europe than northern Europe.

The key facts are these:

1. Unemployment is much higher in France than in Northern European countries (Germany, the Netherlands, the Scandinavian countries) or the developed English-speaking countries (US, UK, Canada, Australia);

2. It affects mainly people between fifteen and twenty-four and between fifty-five and sixty-four years old;

3. Unemployment penalizes those with little education or training and those who live in low-income urban areas;

4. Long-term unemployment, which is by far the most harmful, is high and has been steadily increasing since 2007;

5. The French experience a serious malaise at work resulting from a lack of job mobility, conflictual relationships in the workplace, and a feeling that their jobs are not secure;

6. As a result, French taxpayers have to spend heavily on employment policy.

How many unemployed people are there in France? Answering this question turns out to be devilishly difficult. The most inherently conservative estimate stems from the definition given by the International Labor Organization (ILO).[2] It indicated 2.9 million unemployed during the third trimester of 2015, or an unemployment rate of about 10.6 percent. This was more than double the German level, for instance, and far higher than those of developed English-speaking countries or northern Europe. But this definition does not take into account almost 1.5 million unemployed persons who would like to work.[3] Statistics from the French ministry of labor[4] distinguish five types of jobseekers. The figure most commonly reported in the media is: "jobseekers expected to make active attempts to find work, but who are currently unemployed" (Category A). By this definition, there were 3,574,860 unemployed in metropolitan France in November 2015. Yet this Category A figure for unemployment also underestimates the total because it does not include the other categories of unemployed persons: those who are in training programs, doing internships, without a job but on sick leave or maternity leave, working on subsidized contracts or part time, etc.[5] Including everyone in these categories, in November 2015 there were about 6,142,000 unemployed.

Definitional issues are common to all countries, and media attention normally focuses on one rather than another, although people are quick to notice when the government tries to manipulate the figures by moving certain unemployed claimants from one category to another. Another difficulty encountered in measuring unemployment concerns unlisted unemployed persons—those who have become discouraged by the deterioration of the labor market, ranging from young people who are continuing their studies or who take a job abroad because they do not find employment in France, to older people who would like to continue working but decide instead to take retirement. Faced by this complexity in measuring unemployment, economists sometimes prefer to look at employment rates or labor force participation rates, sometimes delivering a different picture; for example, in the United States, labor force participation remained low for a long period after the 2008 crisis even as the unemployment rate declined rapidly.[6]

Who Is Most Affected by Unemployment

Two age groups suffer particularly from high unemployment in France. Those aged between fifteen and twenty-four have difficulty finding work. Their unemployment rate is 24 percent. Their employment rate (28.6 percent) is far lower than the OECD average (39.6 percent) and the rates in northern Europe (46.8 percent for Germany and 62.3 percent for the Netherlands).[7] The French labor market is thus relatively closed to new entrants, particularly young people looking for their first job. To be sure, all countries have higher youth unemployment rates than among the rest of the population. Businesses are less eager to hire employees without prior experience, and especially to pay the cost of on-the-job training for young employees who, once they have completed their training or gained enough experience, may leave the company. However, young French people pay a harsh penalty compared with northern Europe or the English-speaking countries.

A consequence of this is growing intergenerational inequality. Not only are the young unemployed at a far higher rate than older people, but they also have trouble finding housing.[8] Areas with vibrant economies, creating jobs, often also have the tightest housing markets. In fact, public policies limiting new building have worsened housing shortages, while policies unfavorable to landlords have limited the supply of rental housing, increased rents, and led to demands for large security deposits. Finally, because their employment is often unstable, many young people cannot obtain a mortgage.

People between fifty-five and sixty-four years old often take early retirement, whether willingly or unwillingly—earlier in France than in any other European country. Their employment rate (45.6 percent) is also far below the OECD average and in particular the rates in northern Europe (the employment rate in this age group in Sweden exceeds 70 percent). Those over fifty who are still active in the labor market are also the main victims of long-term unemployment; 56 percent of unemployed people aged fifty and over fall into this category. More generally, in 2016 just over 4 percent of those still wanting to work had been unemployed for more than a year, almost twice the level in northern European countries. It is commonly acknowledged that long-term unemployment is much more harmful to the individual than a short spell of unemployment. It leads to a loss of vocational qualifications, social isolation, and a stigma when trying to get back into the labor market. The fact that long-term unemployment is particularly high in France is an additional cause of concern.

Younger and older people experience higher unemployment rates than prime-age workers in many countries, but the degree to which they are penalized is higher in France than in many others.

An Expensive Employment Policy That Produces Disappointing Results

Every government spends money on its employment policies. The goals are to train workers, to help the most vulnerable, and to protect those who have had the bad luck to find themselves in a sector undergoing technological and economic change. Nevertheless, the amount France spends on its employment policy far exceeds international norms. This is, obviously, money that is not available for education, healthcare, and other public services, or alternatively (depending on one's point of view), money that weighs down public finances and increases the burden of government debt repayments. Unemployment is expensive not only for workers, but also for society in general.

What the notion of public employment policy means is a matter of debate. It may include unemployment insurance (thirty-one billion euros in 2014), assistance with coping with economic changes, and funds allocated for the vocational retraining of unemployed workers. It can also cover the cost of public employment services, subsidized jobs (in the non-profit sector, contracts combining on-the-job and classroom training, jobs in urban development zones), and what are known as general measures. These measures can encompass the reduction of employer taxes on low salaries, tax credits to encourage competitiveness and employment, and—specific to France—funds allocated to help offset the costs of capping the work week at thirty-five hours.[9] The total budgeted amount has been steadily increasing since 1993. In 2012, France was spending 1.41 percent of its GDP on "passive" policies (unemployment insurance) and 0.87 percent on "active" policies (training for unemployed workers, funding the relevant agencies, subsidized jobs, etc.).[10] If we add to this various fiscal incentives, the total reaches about 3.5 or 4 percent of GDP.[11]

The Resort to Quick Fixes

To reduce unemployment, successive governments in France (and in other southern European countries) have encouraged fixed-term contracts and subsidized jobs.

Subsidized jobs. These constitute, on the whole, a poor use of public funds, particularly for subsidized jobs in the noncommercial sector.[12] Rather than encouraging employers to use employees because it is cheap to do so, the money could be used instead to reduce social security contributions and thus incentivize companies to create the stable jobs they and their employees really need. Indeed, France has the highest social security contributions among OECD countries.[13]

Of course, I'm exaggerating a little here. Subsidizing jobs for unskilled young people may be justified on the basis of a "market failure": the company provides, at a loss, the young employee with human capital that it will gain no benefit from if the employee quits to get a higher salary elsewhere. But on the whole, the statistics show that the probability of finding a job with a permanent contract after holding a subsidized position is low, and that the beneficiaries of subsidized jobs in the noncommercial sector have less chance of being employed two years later. Thus the hypothesis that a subsidized job is a springboard to a stable job remains to be proven.

Insecure jobs. The great majority of newly created jobs in France, 85 percent in 2013, now have fixed-term (or temporary) contracts, and this ratio is steadily rising (it was 75 percent in 1999). There has also been a big increase in ultra-short-term contracts (the employee being registered as a jobseeker between two contracts with the same employer), which are not very satisfactory for the employee and very expensive for unemployment insurance.[14] Today, more than one hire out of two on a fixed-term contract is a rehire in the same company.

In reality, employment on limited-term contracts is not good for either the employee or the employer. For the former, the contract offers little protection. Since in theory (although this is frequently ignored in practice) prolonging or renewing a limited-term contract legally transforms it into a permanent contract, regulation gives the employer a very strong incentive not to do so, even if the employee's performance is satisfactory.[15] This is precisely the opposite of what regulation is intended to achieve, in terms of employee protection. In fact, within Europe, France is the country where the transition from a temporary contract to a stable contract occurs the least frequently.[16] Which means that elsewhere in Europe, a person hired on the basis of a temporary contract has a much greater chance of seeing this temporary contract transformed into a permanent job. The fact that companies resort extensively to fixed-term contracts, which neither they nor their employees like, is very revealing of the implicit cost imposed on French society by current laws regarding permanent contracts.

Nonetheless, successive French governments, knowing businesses' reluctance to use permanent contracts, have not dared alter fixed-term employment contracts. The latter serve as a safety valve for the excessively rigid rules concerning permanent contracts; it makes it possible to safeguard a minimum number of jobs and thus prevents an exorbitant rise in the unemployment figures. The polarization of terms of employment between an ultraflexible fixed-term contract and an ultrarigid permanent contract divides the labor market between those who spend more and more time trying to find a real job, and those who have been hired for an unlimited period and whose jobs are protected. In other words, this polarization is a dirty trick played on employees in general, and especially on the young.[17]

Even so, political debate is focused on dismissals of employees who have permanent contracts. Such dismissals represent only a small fraction of terminations (4.4 percent) and are supervised by the courts, with additional governmental pressure if the subject gets media coverage. On the other hand, the debate ignores almost completely the two principal causes of turnover in the labor market: resignations, which are few in number (9 percent of terminations) and decreasing, and above all terminations at the end of a fixed-term contract, which are far more numerous (77 percent) and are steadily increasing. (The rest consists of terminations by mutual agreement,[18] those at the end of probationary periods, and retirements.)

The French exceptionalism in terms of the figures does not mean that other countries lack labor market rigidities whose effects can be counterproductive. For example, Spain has a high rate of unemployment among young people for similar reasons. Countries that have more flexible labor market institutions may still encounter difficulties in delivering good jobs, especially to the young. In the UK and US, employers have increasingly been creating insecure work in the form of zero-hours contracts, while self-employment and agency work has also become more prevalent, prompting much debate about whether policies need to change. While the US experiences a low unemployment rate, one in six working-age men without a college degree is not part of the workforce.[19]

Malaise in the Workplace

For employees, unemployment and precarious employment are the tip of the iceberg. The hidden part is multiform …

Insufficient mobility and imperfect matching of employees to jobs. It is natural that employees move from one company to another. They may wish to take on new professional challenges and acquire knowledge while exploring new horizons. They may also want to leave coworkers or superiors with whom they have difficult relationships. Conversely, in a changing economy, companies may wish to reorient their activities to adapt, and seek to hire employees with skills different from those they hired earlier. The perception in France that a job with a permanent contract is a (very relative) privilege, to be clung to for fear of not finding an equivalent position, facilitates neither mobility nor the matching of employees to jobs, which entails a cost for both employees and companies.

Conflictual relationships. Relations between employers and employees are not harmonious in France. France ranks 129th out of 139 countries in terms of people's perception of relationships at work.[20] We can only guess at the causes of this unfortunate French peculiarity, which contributes to employee burnout. Perhaps the absence of mobility just mentioned plays a role. An employee whose relationship with coworkers or superiors has grown tense will normally change jobs in a fluid labor market, but in France he or she does not have that option and will remain, despite the conflict. It is not impossible, either, that some less than scrupulous employers may deliberately worsen an employee's work environment in order to give him or her an incentive to accept a mutually agreed-upon termination and to leave the company; this allows the employer to avoid a hearing before a labor tribunal.

The French report suffering from considerable stress at work. Studies conducted on the basis of international data[21] demonstrate a positive correlation between legislation protecting jobs and stress at work. This correlation is hardly surprising. As we have seen, rigidity in jobs and the scarcity of jobs damage relationships at work in several ways: employees unsatisfied with their jobs hold on to them nonetheless, and unscrupulous bosses can easily play on the fear of unemployment to intimidate employees.

A strong sense of job insecurity. Job insecurity is obviously felt by workers with fixed-term contracts, whose jobs are by definition precarious. More surprisingly, workers with permanent contracts also feel insecure, even though they benefit from what are in practice the world's most protective labor laws.[22] This observation is not as paradoxical as it seems, insofar as a worker with a "permanent" contract knows that if he is fired or his firm goes bankrupt and he becomes unemployed, his chances of finding an equivalent job are limited. This leads to a feeling of pessimism that pervades the whole of French society and paralyzes it, handicapping its ability to adapt and innovate. While the French example is extreme, it illustrates the degree to which employment laws may have unintended consequences.

The Need for Reform

One argument often advanced against the necessity of reforming labor institutions in France is that unemployment reflects a weak demand for companies' products, and that a macroeconomic reflation would reduce unemployment. There is no doubt that France, like all European countries, is suffering from an uncertain outlook and is subject to the aftereffects of the financial and European crises.[23] Favorable prospects and a well-filled order book would obviously have very positive effects on employment. But the macroeconomic argument is not relevant, for several reasons.

The most obvious of these reasons is that unemployment is structural, not only cyclical. It has not fallen below 7 percent in France for thirty years, despite an employment policy that is very costly, measures paying workers to retire several years early, and encouragement to use fixed-term contracts. It is no accident that unemployment in other countries of southern Europe, whose labor market institutions have similar origins to that of their French counterparts, is far higher than in northern Europe or the English-speaking countries. Contrast the UK, where the unemployment rate peaked at 8.5 percent after the financial crisis but has declined to 4.7 percent in 2017 despite the UK government's budget austerity measures. Secondly, although the appropriate level for the budget deficit in a period of recession can be debated,[24] we have been experiencing a Keynesian reflation resulting from the decrease in the value of the euro, lower interest rates, and a fall in the price of oil; unemployment should therefore be decreasing rather than increasing. Thirdly, we should wonder why companies' order books are not very full. This brings us back in part to the question of the competitiveness of French businesses (which includes factors other than hourly pay, such as how easy it is to match employees to the right jobs, social security contributions, or management styles). Finally, a reflation by means of a budget deficit involves less risk when public finances are sound than when they are already in bad shape (as a result of forty years of budget laxity).

AN ECONOMIC ANALYSIS OF LABOR CONTRACTS[25]

MAKING EMPLOYERS ACCOUNTABLE FOR THE COSTS OF DISMISSALS

Work contracts and rules about redundancies and layoffs have to reconcile two objectives. Employees are not responsible for and have no control over technological change or demand shocks faced by their employers; they must therefore be insured against the risk that their jobs might become obsolete or simply unprofitable. For its part, the company will insist on flexibility in its management of human resources as it copes with these supply and demand shocks. Without this, it will be reluctant to create jobs in the first place, because it will incur large losses in the event that these jobs are not very productive. Two diametrically opposed points of view? Not necessarily. But to reconcile these two aims, *the employee, not the job, has to be protected*.

The employer knows whether a job is profitable for the firm—profitability properly conceived, of course, because an employer can cope with temporary losses on a workstation or a production unit due to a temporary decrease in demand, and yet still profit in the long run by retaining the job. The employer has the information needed to manage human resources. But we also have to ask what impact his choice between keeping the employee or letting him go might have on the company's stakeholders.

In this case, there are at least two stakeholders: The first is the employee concerned, who suffers a financial cost from the loss of earnings as well as a psychological cost (for example, the loss of the social connections provided by the job, or family tensions). The externality created by dismissal is the rationale for two forms of compensation for the employee: the company grants severance pay, and government unemployment insurance provides replacement income and possibly also free training. The second set of stakeholders, often forgotten in this debate, includes those who pay for the provision of unemployment insurance, benefits, unemployed workers' retraining expenditures, employment agency costs, etc. This second set of stakeholders is largely comprised of other firms, which finance these expenditures through their payroll taxes (social security contributions), and, if the social security system is in deficit, the taxpayer.

The principle of accountability that is the keystone of our economic system in other domains would prescribe that when a company fires an employee, it should "internalize" the external cost to society: both the cost to the employee and the cost to the social system. If it does not, it will have a tendency to dismiss employees too often (here I deliberately ignore regulatory constraints on dismissal, which I will discuss in detail later on). In order for the firm to internalize the cost to the welfare system, it must pay a penalty for dismissing workers, with the money going to the social security system or government budget and not to the employee.

It should be noted that this penalty need not be an additional tax burden on businesses, but might rather take the form of a system whereby the penalty could be earmarked to reduce social security contributions paid by employers who keep their workers on: the penalty is then fiscally neutral for business as a whole. However, although today everyone finds it reasonable that the polluter should pay in environmental matters,[26] the idea that companies who fire employees should pay a penalty for doing so is not part of our economic software. Let us discuss in greater detail this unfamiliar "dismisser pays" principle.

A first question regarding this principle is how to calculate the cost of dismissals for the unemployment insurance fund. Firing a thirty-year-old software engineer in Paris who will find a job the next day costs nothing; but firing a fifty year old with few skills in a depressed job market is quite another matter. How then should we calculate the cost of the dismissal?

A clever way of calculating the penalty for dismissal consists of looking at how much the fired employee cost the unemployment insurance fund after he or she has been dismissed. This approach goes back to FDR's United States, which set up a system on this principle that is still in operation, called "experience rating."[27] This has a twofold advantage: that of applying a higher penalty for dismissing employees who will have a harder time finding a job, and that of giving the company an incentive to invest in on-the-job training, thus enriching the human capital of its employees, and so limiting the length of time that they will be out of work in the event that they are dismissed. Similarly, it provides an incentive for management and labor in the same sector to improve the quality of ongoing vocational training, because they will be sensitized to the typical length of time people are unemployed.

We will see later that the reward-penalty system has other advantages, such as eliminating collusion between employers and employees at the expense of the social welfare system, and an improved allocation of activity among sectors of the economy.

Discussion

The principle that the employer who dismisses an employee pays the associated social cost provides a general outline of how to achieve the desired accountability. It is, however, too simplistic; a few adjustments to the basic principle may be needed.[28]

Progressive rights. Although fixed-term contracts are undesirable and should be abolished, enterprises do need short-term employment for temporary tasks or seasonal activities. A single labor contract system with progressive rights for the employee is compatible with this need for short-term jobs.

Evasion mechanisms. As in the case of environmental damage, there is a danger that companies will evade regulation by subcontracting the work that is most unpredictable and thus most at risk of being terminated. By resorting to subcontractors who have no real capital and will be incapable of paying any penalty when their order book vanishes, they thus escape liability in the same way environmental cleanups can be dodged by transferring hazardous activities to subcontractors that are really empty shells. But, as in the case of environmental taxation, we can imagine ways to prevent these evasions: for example, demanding bank guarantees or tracing legal responsibility back to the parent company or the contractor (extended liability).

Selection effects. A reward-penalty system can lead enterprises to be cautious about hiring unreliable employees who are very likely not to satisfy the company's requirements. This is obviously already the case today for permanent contracts, and more generally it will always be the case in any system in which the enterprise faces a cost for firing employees. However, it is possible to envisage the use of subsidies for hiring persons who are particularly disadvantaged on the labor market, or reducing somewhat the intensity of the reward-penalty system for such employees.

PERVERSE INSTITUTIONAL INCENTIVES

A TWOFOLD INCENTIVE TO COMMIT CRIME ...

In France, a company firing its employees gives them severance pay, but it does not pay the cost of the dismissal to the unemployment insurance system, which may well be higher.[29] On the other hand, a company retaining employees pays social security contributions, which include premiums for unemployment insurance. Companies that keep their employees on thus pay for the companies that fire them. This is upside down. By making companies that do not fire their employees pay the costs of dismissals incurred by the unemployment insurance system, the current system encourages dismissals in two ways.

... A MISSION IMPOSSIBLE ENTRUSTED TO THE JUDGE

Perhaps understanding that they were creating incentives to dismiss employees by making firms who do not lay off their workers pay (rather than those doing the firing), French legislators sought to compensate by regulating dismissals. This gave the courts the power to adjudicate on dismissals. However, whatever their competence and integrity, judges do not have the information that would make them better able than CEOs to decide the legitimacy of dismissals made on economic grounds. Consequently, the outcome of legal procedures involving such dismissals is completely arbitrary and unpredictable. Our institutions have entrusted the labor courts with a mission impossible.

THE HIDDEN COSTS OF FRENCH DISMISSAL PROCEDURES

If it gets to litigation, dismissal procedures[30] result in major costs for the company far in excess of the payoffs to the employees who have been fired. The procedures are very lengthy (although they have been getting a little shorter lately). Suits relating to dismissals can be brought by the dismissed employee for up to two years.[31] After the case is submitted to a court, a decision takes on average 13.6 months in the first instance and 35 months in the event of an appeal (which occurs in two-thirds of the cases). Not to mention that in a few cases there remains the risk of reinstatement—with payment of the interim salary.

The employer has to prove that there was a "real and serious cause" for the dismissal. In France, in contrast to many countries, the redundancy of a position, employee performance, or more generally the desire to cut costs are not considered legitimate reasons. A dismissal on economic grounds can only be justified if there are serious financial problems that put the company's survival in danger, so a company that is otherwise healthy cannot stop an activity for which it no longer has a sustainable order book.[32] Unsurprisingly, the cost to the company also includes the time its managers devote to dealing with the case (which takes them away from tasks involving the company's future).

As for the employee, the process is costly, as well as unfair: those who are vulnerable and not very familiar with the complexity of the French system may be discouraged and may play the game less well than insiders[33] who know how the institutions operate. Furthermore, there is also a great uncertainty as to the final decision and important disparities between labor tribunals.[34]

These inefficiencies would to a large extent disappear with the introduction of a reward-penalty system that would penalize companies for each dismissal in exchange for a reduction in their unemployment insurance contributions and less burdensome administrative and judicial procedures for dismissal. Companies could in fact be granted more flexibility in exchange for accepting this accountability. The principle of dismissal on grounds of economic redundancy would then be accepted, as it is in the US, northern Europe, and many other countries. This would balance the interests of employees, whose sense of identity and social connection depends on their work, and those of their employers, who want to be able to adapt their human resource management to economic and technological imperatives. On average, employees would not lose job security, because those currently on fixed-term contracts would then have a more stable job, and those on permanent contracts who lost their job would have a better chance of finding a new one. A penalty based on how long the laid-off workers stay unemployed would also encourage companies to invest in the human capital of their employees, so that when redundancies are necessary, they would remain unemployed for as short a time as possible.

Finally, the courts should not be taken completely out of the picture. For example, no matter what the system, one must be able to appeal to a judge in the event of unfair dismissal, say of a pregnant woman or of an annoying trade unionist. More generally, the courts must be able to intervene if an economic rationale for redundancies is used as cover for more personal, unacceptable motives on the part of the employer.

Sectoral Misallocation

As explained above, firms are not made fully accountable for their employment decisions. One aspect of this is their abusive reliance on short-term contracts, which in France are responsible for an eleven-billion-euro shortfall in unemployment insurance payments relative to unemployment benefits paid out (the yearly deficit on unemployment insurance is four billion euros). A case in point with much media coverage is the employment regime for entertainment workers (*intermittents du spectacle*, which include media employees) where this deficit has run to about one billion euros a year for the past fifteen years. Its official goal—the promotion of culture—has been much abused (aid

ANOTHER INSTANCE OF FRENCH EXCEPTIONALISM: COLLUSION BETWEEN MANAGEMENT AND LABOR AT THE EXPENSE OF SOCIETY

Relations between employers and employees are mediocre in France … except when it comes to colluding at the expense of the taxpayer. As always, economic agents react to the incentives they confront. The real guilty parties are the French labor market institutions encouraging management and employees to manipulate the system.

First of all, employers and employees have learned to systematically transform resignations into dismissals. Unlike a dismissal, a resignation does not give the employee the right to receive unemployment benefits. Companies and their employees thus have an interest in conspiring against the unemployment insurance system by presenting voluntary departures as dismissals. So long as the employee promises to give up his rights to sue the firm and leaves the company "on good terms," this redesignation costs the company nothing, as it pays none of the unemployment benefits that the employee will receive after the "dismissal."

In fact, employers and employees do not even have to game the system now, as this collusion was made legal in 2008 through the introduction of "termination by mutual consent," a procedure that allows an employer and an employee with a permanent contract to agree on the conditions for breaking the work contract between them. This law made it easier to disguise a resignation as a dismissal. Its popularity (more than 358,000 terminations by mutual consent in 2015!) is thus not surprising.

This measure also has implications for the effective retirement age, possibly bringing it forward by as much as three years. When it was first implemented in 2009, French labor economists Pierre Cahuc and André Zylberberg noted:

> The possibility of breaking a contract by mutual consent allows an employer and an employee to separate on good terms. The devil is in the details: insofar as the employee will end up keeping unemployment payments for three years, in reality the government has just made it possible to retire at fifty-seven! An older worker will in fact be able to leave a job almost without monetary loss by having the unemployment insurance system finance what amounts to an early retirement.[35]

Let us note that this collusion against the unemployment insurance system would not take place if the company were made accountable by a reward-penalty system. This would make it expensive for a company to have a former worker unemployed or in pseudoretirement, and so there would be less of this manipulation of the system.

Another way that management and labor evade the law is the transformation of a redundancy on economic grounds (sometimes of a whole group) into a dismissal for personal reasons.[36] In this case, the termination is desired by the employer: Pierre Cahuc and Francis Kramarz observed in 2005 that

> all the testimonies obtained from CEOs, labor union officials, and directors of human resources suggest that dismissals for personal reasons are frequently economic dismissals in disguise. For the employer, the alibi of the personal motive makes it possible to avoid the procedures required for dismissal on economic grounds, even when the dismissal of a group of employees is involved; the employer is thus encouraged to adduce a personal reason for firing a worker, even if it means making a transaction with the employee so that the latter gives up his right of recourse in exchange for an indemnity. The employee then accepts particularly advantageous severance conditions.[37]

These behaviors underline the firm's lack of accountability for the cost its actions impose on the unemployment insurance system. In 2013, there were thirty-eight thousand dismissals per month for personal reasons, as compared with sixteen thousand for economic reasons. About three-quarters of the dismissals for personal reasons were undisputed.

to culture should be focused first of all on cultural works that we want to encourage—in the form of transparent subsidies rather than murky general payments). Employers in this sector welcome the system, as they are heavily subsidized by other sectors—who are of course unaware of the cross-subsidy. Audiovisual production companies use temporary workers and pay them rather low salaries. Workers oscillate between spells of short-term employment and unemployment covered by the unemployment insurance system. The political power of the sector has so far deterred politicians from reforming the scheme. In other countries, too, there are examples of powerful sectors overly reliant on badly paid short-term or contingent work, where exactly the same kind of hidden subsidies to one group of employers from others are involved.

As in any insurance system, subsidies between sectors would be justified if the goal were to insure people in a particular career against a crisis affecting only their sector. It is much less justified when there are systematic transfers, as this kind of continuing cross-subsidy distorts the allocation or activity among sectors of the economy. Finally, note that this problem would also disappear with the introduction of a reward-penalty system.

The Effect of Unemployment on Other Institutions

In the context of high unemployment, protecting jobs becomes a major concern, to the point that it affects more or less every aspect of economic policy. As an example, consider the French bankruptcy law. In relation to its foreign counterparts, France is anomalous, as its law does little to protect creditors and is very favorable to shareholders and managers. Moreover—to my point—this legislation is motivated by a desire to save jobs. The underlying idea is that if the company gets into difficulties, jobs will be more likely to be saved if control is left in the hands of the directors of the company rather than the creditors. However, first of all, there is no theoretical support and still less empirical evidence confirming the thesis that French institutions protect jobs.[38] The directors may in fact be responsible for the company's troubles. The people who have not been able to manage the company are not necessarily those best equipped to manage the fate of the employees concerned. Moreover, the partners may take undue risks (thus endangering jobs) in an attempt to overcome the difficulties. There is therefore no clear reason why the current system would preserve jobs.

Above all, job creation is actually neglected here. If the weak protection given creditors has a negative impact on the financing and growth of companies, which is likely, the law's net effect on employment is certainly negative.

In the case of other countries, it might be merger control that is affected by a misplaced idea that this area of policy can be used to preserve employment—for example, by allowing an anticompetitive merger to go ahead if the bidders argue they can save a failing company. But if the target company is in difficulties, any new management would need to look at redundancies in any event.

WHAT CAN REFORM ACHIEVE AND HOW CAN IT BE IMPLEMENTED SUCCESSFULLY?

The transition from protecting jobs to protecting employees, making companies accountable and giving them more flexibility while reducing the role of the courts, does not sit comfortably with the French tradition of economic planning. Furthermore, we must be wary of transition effects. What gains could be expected from a reform? Which factors are likely to contribute to its success? No matter how intellectually coherent it may be, the proposal to make businesses more accountable needs to be made operational. For example, reform must be socially acceptable and sustainable, and careful thought needs to be given to transition. The specifics here concern France, but the wider point is universal: labor market reform is always sensitive because it involves social relations and people's livelihoods.

WHAT IMPACT CAN BE EXPECTED FROM A REFORM OF THE LABOR MARKET?

The idea that making it easier for French companies to lay off employees could lead to a *reduction* in unemployment is counterintuitive to many. Indeed, two forces are involved: on the one hand, making layoffs easier increases dismissals of workers with permanent contracts; and on the other, employers reassured by the increased flexibility will hire more workers on permanent contracts. [39] So what are the benefits to be expected from increased flexibility?

The first benefit is better jobs. As we have seen, the current system has many inefficiencies: long-term unemployment; poor matching of employees and jobs when employees who are looking for new challenges, or who don't get along with their coworkers, or whose functions have simply become redundant, stay in the same job; the absence of a way for workers the employer wants to keep on to move from a fixed-term contract to a permanent contract; and finally the length of the legal procedures and the uncertainty that hang over both employer and employee when it comes to redundancies. Better jobs either mean more productive businesses (thus creating more jobs), or greater well-being in the workplace, or both.

The second benefit would be a lower burden on public finances and unemployment insurance. Today, the succession of fixed-term contracts and unemployment, the terminations by mutual agreement, and long-term unemployment all result either in tax increases or increases in employers' social charges, neither of which helps reduce unemployment.

Sustainable Reform

Like all major reforms, job market reform has to be maintained over the long term. If it is to be effective, employers have to believe in its sustainability. But companies might legitimately be concerned about the state's ability to make a genuine commitment to reform the employment contract. Will future governments keep the current government's promises? Companies must not fear that hires under a new system will in the near future be transformed into old-style permanent contracts when the parliamentary majority changes.

As always, the state's ability to keep its promises contributes to the success of its policies. Thus a minimal political consensus regarding the necessity of changing the employment rules is necessary. Employment is a national issue, and we can hope that a bipartisan agreement could be negotiated in order to finally remedy the problem of unemployment and social exclusion. Again, the point applies to any country making major labor market reforms. Germany's "Hartz Reforms" in 2003 did have cross-party consensus, for example; and although the reforms still have their critics, Germany's unemployment rate was just 3.9 percent in mid-2017.

The Need for a Gradual Transition

From this point of view, it is important to make sure that workers currently in a good position in the labor market (in France, those with permanent jobs) do not lose out as a result of reform. Once again drawing lessons from experiments in the area of taxing pollution,[40] it is possible to grant "grandfathered rights" to workers' existing contracts; those would hence remain under the old law concerning dismissals, whereas all the new contracts would fall under the new law. That is exactly what Matteo Renzi did in Italy in 2014.[41]

Of course, even protected by grandfathered rights, these privileged workers might still feel concern. They might fear future promotions would give priority to employees under the new contract if they did not themselves convert to the latter; and, like their employers, they might worry about the state's ability to make long-term commitments and fear, at some time in the future, the complete abolition of the old contracts, thus affecting those who had retained this status. That said, the increased likelihood of finding a new job under the new system, and better prospects for their children finding work, should overcome these concerns.

Another reason why one might want to grant grandfathered rights to employees with permanent jobs is that one could imagine an immediate wave of dismissals related to jobs that companies wanted to make redundant but have been unable to. More generally, the transition from the initial situation of the labor market, which necessarily takes time to improve following a reform, must be considered carefully. For instance, workers on the new contracts who are fired might still remain, on average, too long unemployed; it would probably be desirable to introduce the reward-penalty system gradually until unemployment has been reduced.

Educating People and Making Reform Socially Acceptable

This proposal for reforming the French labor market is less drastic than the flexi-security found in, say, Denmark (which has no reward-penalty system). Even so, one of its main attractions, the flexibility granted to employers, will also be perceived by many French people as its principal defect. And a reward-penalty system might not dispel objections. The French public's general diffidence toward economic levers (such as a carbon tax or a reward-penalty system) that make economic agents accountable for their actions constitutes an obstacle to reform. In fact, for many French people, the idea that a business might pay to fire employees is still taboo, because it seems to endorse a behavior (firing employees) that is considered immoral.

There are two responses to this ambivalence: first of all, today it is the companies that do *not* fire workers that pay most of the social cost, while those doing the firing bear only a small fraction of it (namely the severance pay). Formulating the problem in moral terms consequently leads to a slippery slope with respect to moral evaluation. Secondly, the same taboo existed twenty or thirty years ago with regard to environmental taxation, which has now become commonplace. Economists who claimed that environmental taxation (or the introduction of markets for tradable emission rights) produced environmental benefits and diminished the cost of compliance, used to hear the same refrain in response: "Paying to pollute would be immoral!" But was it more moral not to pay when one polluted? In the end, environmental taxation became acceptable for the majority of the public and is now widespread. An analogous development could, of course, be envisaged for the right to dismiss employees.[42]

The poor functioning of the labor market in southern Europe is hard to ignore, and has indeed been evident for a long time (even though it has gotten worse due to the impact of the financial and European crises). It is the economist's job to try to understand the resistance to change in light of this. When dysfunctional labor market institutions are still supported by a majority of citizens, it is not surprising that governments are in no hurry to explore controversial reforms and that they rather use the same old quick fixes to fight unemployment. It is easy for citizens to understand that their company could more easily terminate their permanent employment contracts if employers get more flexibility; it is much harder for these employees, as well as for the unemployed and employees in precarious jobs, to identify and analyze the economic mechanism that results in a more flexible system creating more numerous and better jobs.

The complexity of economic mechanisms is not the only obstacle. The prominence of redundancies made on economic grounds and their impact in the media and politics are also responsible for lukewarm public opinion about greater labor market flexibility. The employee fired in connection with redundancies has a face and experiences a tragedy (a very real one, because the labor market might never allow him or her to get another, similar job). On the other hand, the large number of good jobs that are not created every day as a result of businesses' reluctance to create more permanent positions affects nameless people: no one who is unemployed or employed on a fixed-term contract can identify with a job that has never been created. Job losses make the headlines, job creation much less so (except when politicians can plausibly take credit for them), and a lack of job creation is by its very nature invisible.

The phenomenon of the identifiable victim, much studied by psychologists,[43] refers to the observation that individuals feel much more empathy toward clearly identified victims (to the point of being prepared to help them) than toward victims defined more vaguely ("statistical victims"). For example, citizens are prepared to donate considerable sums to relieve the suffering of a person whose image and story they have seen on television, but are less disposed to help anonymous victims who have a greater need of their money. In the domain of the labor market, the identified victims are employees suffering from mass layoffs, and the anonymous victims are the unemployed for whom no job has been created.

THE OTHER GREAT DEBATES ABOUT EMPLOYMENT

MULTIPLE CAUSES OF UNEMPLOYMENT

Although it is emblematic, the character of the labor contract is not solely responsible for the current situation of high unemployment in southern Europe. For example, among other criticisms commonly directed at French institutions are the following:

- the mediocrity and cost of ongoing vocational training coprovided by management and labor, training that does not target the right categories of employees, includes only a small portion of programs that lead to widely recognized diplomas or certificates, but that, along with apprenticeships, nonetheless absorb thirty-two billion euros per year, or 1.6 percent of GDP;[44]

- the insufficient number of apprenticeships[45] and work-study programs;
- the gap between the skills provided by schools and the needs of companies (indeed, the high unemployment rate coincides with real shortages of labor for certain kinds of jobs);
- redistribution in favor of low-income workers primarily through the channel of the minimum wage (which is the highest in the European Union) rather than through the tax system—that is, through a tax credit on income from work (like the Earned Income Tax Credit in the US or the UK's tax credit system);
- the management of the unemployed (usually called active labor market policy), which is very different from that of the Scandinavian countries, for example, where the unemployed are given greater incentives to resume work. Also, the replacement rate—the ratio of unemployment benefits to earnings from employment—is around the European average, but it is much more generous for workers with high salaries (three times higher than in Germany, for instance);
- the management of the public employment service (it is symptomatic that employers resort to *Le Bon coin*—a free Internet want-ads site—to recruit employees, despite a very extensive public employment service);
- the lack of flexibility in contractual arrangements, with rules being set mostly at the sector (rather than the firm) level;
- the closed nature of certain professions (for example, taxi driving), which prevents the creation of jobs many people would want to do.

The other countries of southern Europe (Spain, Italy, Portugal, Greece), which have similar institutions and the same causes producing the same effects, have equally disastrous (or even worse) unemployment statistics than France, in particular unemployment among the young. Some of the points would apply to economies with more flexible jobs markets, but the combination explains the huge gap in unemployment rates between southern Europe (including France) and other OECD economies.

Several books would be required to deal thoroughly with all these issues. Here I will limit myself to a few remarks.

Reducing Working Hours: A False Solution

Economists widely reject [46] the fallacious claim that there is a fixed quantity of employment, a concept according to which the total number of jobs in an economy is fixed and thus must be distributed equitably (the "lump of labor fallacy"). The introduction of the thirty-five-hour work week in France in 2000, which had received no significant support from professional economists and which sought to create jobs by spreading the work around, took people by surprise. And yet the idea that employment is scarce is age old and regularly resurfaces, particularly in periods of recession. Paradoxically (given that it tends to be favored on the left of the political spectrum), the idea that there is a fixed amount of work—and so working time should be reduced in order to allow the employment to be shared—is the same one that underlies the discourse of far-right parties when they claim that immigrants "take employment away" from resident nationals. Others use it to advocate lowering the retirement age (don't older workers take work away from the young?). Still others use it in support of protectionist goals (don't foreign companies take away our jobs?). Finally, others worried about the impact on available work in 1996, when it was decided to end compulsory military service in France.

Where does the idea that work is scarce, and that the government must intervene to distribute it, come from? Indirectly, from Malthus. At the beginning of the nineteenth century, the scarce resource was still largely land. Land was more or less limited in quantity, and thus jobs working the earth were limited as well. Of course, work has always required not only labor, but also complementary factors of production, for example machine tools, premises, computers, or factories. But unlike the production factor that Malthus focused on (land), these production factors are not at all fixed in quantity, at least in the medium and long term. Even in the short term, production factors can be adjusted in certain circumstances. In a famous article,[47] David Card (now at the University of California, Berkeley) studied the impact of 125,000 Cuban migrants who came to Miami in the space of a few months in 1980. This migration, of significant magnitude in relation to the size of Miami (7 percent increase in the labor force), had practically no impact on either unemployment or on the salaries of the groups competing with the Cuban immigrants on the labor market (essentially African Americans). Work was not fixed in quantity; investments in textile production quickly created the necessary jobs.

In the case of sharing work time, the reasoning is slightly different. Suppose there is a legal obligation to reduce working time that favors employees and disadvantages companies—for instance, no change in salary (in practice, the reduction in work time is often accompanied by changes in salary agreements or state subsidies—we will return to this possibility). In the short term, it is possible that employment will increase in order to compensate for the reduction in working hours so as to meet the orders on hand and to make use of existing factors of production. However, this is a flash in the pan; in the medium term, the order book, other inputs, and employment adjust downward. Yet a sustainable employment policy has to create jobs over the medium and long term. Furthermore, the cost of public policies to compensate employers, if adopted, must be taken into account too, because taxes will have to be increased or public expenditures decreased elsewhere.

This brings me to the methodology used to measure the effects of policies, which requires rigorous econometric analyses. As we have seen, a change in labor supply or demand (such as a reduction in working time or a wave of migration) never occurs in isolation. At the same time, the economy may be growing or in recession, and thus unemployment may naturally be receding or expanding independent of the policy change; moreover, supporting measures may be introduced. Even if we limit ourselves to measuring the short-term effects, we must insulate the effect of the reduction in work time or of the resulting increase in the active population from the change in other factors influencing employment. Thus, David Card took into account the fact that the unemployment rate was increasing at the time of the Cuban exodus, along with other factors; similarly, to measure the effect of the thirty-five-hour work week, we have to correct for the effect of the economic cycle (which was favorable from 1998 to 2002), the supporting measures helping create jobs (fiscal measures, agreements on salary moderation, other dimensions of a reform package),[48] etc. Studies properly identifying the causal impact[49] of migration or policies of reducing working time (such as in Quebec and Germany, and in France in 1981 and in 2000–2002) are thus necessary. The few studies we have do not seem to show, even over the short term, job destruction related to migration, or job creation connected with the reduction of working time,[50] in contrast to what we would expect if work were a fixed quantity.

This fallacious idea that work has a fixed quantity also crops up in attitudes toward technological progress. Employment changes continually. For at least two centuries we have been afraid that automation—from weaving looms (the revolt of the Luddites in England in the early nineteenth century) to assembly lines in the 1950s, and more recently robotics—might cause employment to disappear. All these technological changes lead in fact to the disappearance of certain jobs, but fortunately not to the disappearance of employment (otherwise we would all be unemployed). Similarly, studies show that migrants bring economic benefits to a country, including for its workers in terms of more jobs and higher economic growth, with very little or no effect on earnings.[51] Needless to say, this is just a broad-brush picture, as precise effects depend on the context (such as migrants' skills, labor market and welfare institutions, and the complementarity or substitutability between immigrants and natives in the job market).[52]

Let there be no mistake: economists never take sides on the question of whether people should work thirty-five, eighteen, or forty-five hours a week. That is a choice to be made by society ... and by the persons concerned. On this last point, there is no reason why, left free to determine their working time (as is the case for independent workers), different people should make the same choice; some would rather have more free time than a higher income, while others will prefer the opposite. At the same time, the idea that laws reducing working time, lowering the retirement age, blocking immigration, adopting protectionist measures, or reintroducing military service will create jobs for others has no foundation, either theoretical or empirical.

PROTECTIONISM: ANOTHER FALSE SOLUTION

Employees affected by technological and economic change must be given help. Although these changes are inevitable, the individuals concerned nonetheless suffer major human costs in the short run. They cannot necessarily find new jobs similar to those that are destroyed. Consider the vexing issue of trade between the United States and China. While beneficial to Americans as a whole, serious difficulties have been experienced by regions like the Midwest.[53] The influx of Chinese imports has directly harmed competing American companies specializing in certain kinds of manufacturing (together with their local economies) much more than it has the American economy as a whole.[54]

This brings me to the issue of protectionism. Around the world, populist politicians are riding the wave of popular indignation against job losses or falling wages for unskilled workers. This indignation reflects real difficulties: governments have not paid enough attention to the damage caused to some of their citizens by globalization. Until 1990, international trade created relatively few losers. Since then, developing countries—notably China—have turned their backs on their earlier protectionist policies of import substitution and have opted instead for a market-driven and open economy. Simultaneously, container transport costs have fallen drastically. These two phenomena have realigned trade to take place along the global north-south axis. Whilst developed countries are winners overall, many of their workers, often unskilled, are experiencing difficulties finding jobs close to home similar to the ones that have gone. And retraining policies to increase their skills and equip them for other jobs have not kept up.

In the global south, growth helps score points in the fight against poverty. Between 1991 and 2015, GDP per inhabitant rose by 326 percent for India and 823 percent for China. This is unprecedented development in the history of humankind. But this good news brings no comfort to Americans or Britons whose salaries have stagnated during the same period, nor for the French who have lost their jobs in a depressed labor market.

Yet, protectionism can wave no magic wand. It can only encourage retaliatory measures by trading partners: if everyone looks after number one, things will not improve overall—it will even make them worse. Protectionism takes away the benefits of international specialization, and it removes the stimulus of competition, which pushes companies to improve themselves rather than profit from captive consumers. Protectionism will not deal with the challenges of digital technology either: by exploiting productivity gains, automation poses an employment problem even bigger than that associated with globalization.

THE URGENCY

French (or, more generally, southern European) labor market institutions deviate from the international norm. They are supposed to protect employees, but in fact they may weaken them by putting them at risk of exclusion and marginalization. To understand this unintended consequence, we have to look beyond appearances, and that is the first message of this chapter.

In the past, the dysfunctional nature of France's labor market institutions was not as obvious. The growth of the *trente glorieuses* (the thirty years of prosperity following World War II) made it possible to create new jobs, and the soundness of public finances allowed for government support. Today, France, along with neighbors such as Spain and Italy, is confronted by a "perfect storm"; three challenges will exacerbate the problem of unemployment.

1. *Public finances.* With a public debt of 100 percent of the GDP, France's public finances continue to deteriorate. As we have seen, current employment policy is very costly. If the country's solvency were called into question, the whole welfare state would be at risk. Reducing unemployment and thus the cost of public employment policy would help gain control over public finances.

The Complexity of the French Labor Code

In another example of France's exceptionalism when it comes to the labor market, French labor law is both complex and directive. Complex: everyone agrees. The French labor code is 3,200 pages long and continues to grow as the years go by. Even highly specialized professors of labor law do not fully master it. Hence, the adage "ignorance of the law is no excuse," which normally makes perfect sense, becomes almost laughable in this context. Do we really expect the CEO of a small or middle-sized company, who has no specialized legal department and who is busy with other tasks, to be able to master this legal corpus? Even a large company with a solid legal department is capable of violating labor law without knowing it.

The directive aspect of French labor law is more controversial. France remains one of the countries where the state and industry bodies intervene the most in contractual relationships between employers and employees. Elsewhere, there is more room for negotiations between employers and employees (Great Britain) or between sector bodies and employees (the Scandinavian countries). Some countries (Denmark) have virtually no labor law, giving contractual arrangements free rein and thus more opportunities to adapt their employment relations to the specific context of a business or sector.

To be sure, the French legislature has provided some room for negotiation at the level of sectors and enterprises. In particular, since 2004, a company-level agreement can deviate from the sector agreement if the latter does not explicitly rule it out. However, in practice there are very few such deviations from the norm, the hierarchy of rules being: 1) the labor code, 2) the sector agreement, 3) the company agreement. Sectoral agreements are systematically extended by the Ministry of Labor in such a way that the possibility of a distinct company agreement becomes moot. Sector agreements may solve the problem of free-riding in the provision of ongoing vocational training, but they also allow member companies to come to agreements among themselves and to make the final consumer pay the increase in costs (especially in sectors not subject to international competition); in the latter respect, they are bad for demand and thus for employment.[55] Because of the quasi-systematic extension of sector agreements, more than 90 percent of French employees are covered by collective conventions, compared to only 1 percent in Germany.[56]

This obviously does not mean that sectors should play no role in labor contracts. Management and labor unions in a company do not always have the expertise necessary to draw up contracts, or a clear view of their consequences, especially in small and medium-sized enterprises. The sectors thus have an important role to play as providers of services to help management and labor organize their relations better, or by conceiving sectoral agreements that are an option rather than a constraint on negotiations within the enterprise.

Finally, let us note that even when sector or company agreements are extensive, the labor code can still play an important role as in the case of a minimum wage.[57]

2. *Immigration.* The 2015 European migrant crisis has renewed many people's concerns about a shortage of jobs; no matter how considerable it seems to be, this crisis is only a prelude to what will happen if we do not succeed in controlling global warming.[58] However, migrants represent an economic as well as cultural opportunity for any country. They must therefore be welcomed as contributors to society, which requires that they not be excluded from jobs by labor market institutions—yet another reason to reform these institutions.

3. *Technology.* The digital revolution[59] will have two effects that exacerbate the social cost of rigidities. First of all, it increases the speed at which employment is being transformed and jobs destroyed and created, making the overly rigid permanent contracts even less attractive for employers than they are today, and increasing the need for better ongoing vocational retraining. Second, work is itself in the process of changing, with a growing number of self-employed people and individuals working for several employers. Many observers are calling for the creation of a worker's law rather than a more restrictive employee's law. French labor law, as massive as it is, focuses almost exclusively on the employee, and is based on a conception of work that dates from employment in factories. Consequently, France has a long way to go to prepare itself for the changes ahead. And while France

stands out for the rigidity of its labor market institutions, the same point applies to every other developed economy. Even in the flexible US, UK, or Danish labor markets, the legal and regulatory frameworks center around employees rather than workers.

While labor market institutions vary a great deal over time and between countries, the experience of France offers insights for all: All countries face legitimate concerns about the future of work and will need to resist populists appearing to wave a magic wand. All need to understand the unintended consequences of well-intentioned policies, and why it is better to protect workers than to protect jobs.

Have we really tried everything to stop high unemployment? I strongly doubt it. In this chapter, I have tried to explain why and to indicate paths toward reform. Migration, globalization, and technology all make it urgent that we take action.

TEN

Europe at the Crossroads

THE EUROPEAN PROJECT: FROM HOPE TO DOUBT

On a continent wounded by fratricidal wars, the European project to create an economic and political community on the continent aroused immense hopes. To secure peace and foster development, it proceeded over the years to thwart protectionism, ensure solidarity across countries, and modernize member states' economies. The free movement of people, goods and services, and capital, was meant to prevent protectionism. As a guarantee of solidarity, structural funds were intended to help the economic development of poor regions. Finally, the European construction responded to a less overt wish on the part of southern European countries to delegate to a supranational authority the task of modernizing the economy through reforms, such as opening up to competition, which politicians considered necessary but did not dare to advocate on the national level.

In the context of the current euroskepticism, it is useful to remember that Europe has reduced inequalities among its member states and that European Union (EU) institutions have on the whole contributed to growth. The *acquis communautaire* (the accumulated body of European Union law comprising all of the international treaties, legislation, and judgments of the European Court of Justice since 1958) is sometimes criticized, but has nonetheless forced more rigorous management on previously dysfunctional economies, to the benefit of the people.

The creation of a common currency, the euro, an optional choice progressively adopted by nineteen countries by 2015, also inspired hope. Of course, many economists noted from the outset that Europe was far from satisfying the ideal conditions for a monetary union.

The Eurozone has no fiscal mechanism to provide stability through automatic transfers from member states in good economic health to weaker ones (I shall return to this point in detail). Moreover, labor mobility is limited for cultural and linguistic reasons, and so the labor supply can only react minimally to regional demand—at the time of the euro's creation, the mobility of workers between the states of the European Union was three times less than that between states in the US.[1] These two classic stabilizing mechanisms to cushion regional shocks in federal states were absent, while the single currency eliminated the possibility of a country's currency devaluing to restore the competitiveness to an economy experiencing a foreign trade deficit.

Even so, the euro represented an extraordinary symbol of European integration. It was intended to promote trade. Far more than a simple convenience for travelers who wanted to go from Barcelona to Toulouse paying in euros, the single currency eliminated exchange rate uncertainty and thus reduced the costs of volatile foreign exchange revenues. Indeed, trade between euro area countries increased by around 50 percent between the launch of the euro in 1999 and the peak of the Eurozone crisis in 2011.[2] We know how hard it is to limit the volatility of exchange rates, as demonstrated by the spectacular exit of the British pound from the European Exchange Rate Mechanism in 1992 following a speculative attack by George Soros's Quantum Fund.

The euro was also intended to contribute to the stability of national economies by facilitating the diversification of savings across European countries: households and companies could invest abroad at lower cost, and their wealth was therefore less dependent on local conditions, which would also affect their jobs and order books. Indeed, diversification of savings is a major stabilizer across states in the United States. Finally, the euro was intended to facilitate the circulation of capital to the countries of southern Europe, strengthening their financial credibility and thus allowing them to finance their development.

Many supporters of the euro also saw it as a step on the path to greater European integration. They thought of the European Union, and then the euro, as stepping stones toward a federal Europe, either through the gradual emergence of a consensus in favor of greater integration, or because it would be difficult to reverse course—"we might as well go all the way."[3] This integration has not taken place so far, and it is doubtful that it will in the near future. Integration on this scale would have to be based on an abandonment of sovereignty far more extensive than has previously occurred, and on a mutual trust, a willingness to share risks, and a sense of solidarity—all things that cannot be forced and are barely present in the EU today. There is widespread disenchantment with the idea of Europe in general, and the euro in particular (although there are contradictions; for instance, a majority of people in the countries of southern Europe still favor remaining in the Eurozone).

How did we get here? Is there a future for the European project? To try to answer these questions, I will start by considering what led up to the euro crisis, and will then analyze the Greek crisis. Since the question of sovereign debt is so prominent, and is the source of the conflicts of recent years, I will ask more generally: How much can a country borrow while remaining in its comfort zone? Finally, I will turn to the central question: What are Europe's options? My remarks thus focus on the crisis in the Eurozone, not on the centrifugal forces (such as the departure of the United Kingdom from the EU, for instance—or, conversely, the possibility of European Union enlargement) or noneconomic aspects (such as the retreat from European values in certain EU countries, such as Hungary).

THE ORIGINS OF THE EURO CRISIS

A DOUBLE CRISIS AND A NEW CULTURE OF DEBT

During the decade that followed the introduction of the euro in 1999,[4] the southern part of the Eurozone developed two problems: competitiveness (prices and salaries increasing much faster than productivity) and excessive public and private debt.

Competitiveness

Figure 10.1 shows wage earnings from 1998 in Eurozone countries, and the striking contrast between Germany and southern European countries (France, Greece, Italy, Portugal, and Spain; France's characteristics in this regard are much closer to those of its southern neighbors than to Germany). Germany has consistently practiced salary moderation (in a relatively consensual way, because the labor unions in the sectors exposed to international competition supported it), while salaries in the southern countries exploded. In the countries of southern Europe plus Ireland, salaries increased by 40 percent while labor productivity increased by only 7 percent.[5] This divergence between salaries and productivity generated price differences: low prices for German products and high ones for those from southern Europe. Unsurprisingly, intra-European trade became massively unbalanced, with Germany exporting far more than it imported, and the southern countries doing the opposite.

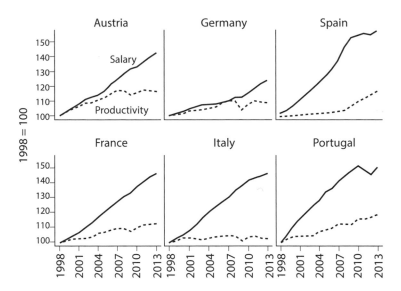

Figure 10.1. Salaries and productivity in Europe, 1998–2013. Source: European Commission, Ameco database and Christian Thimann. Note: Greece does not appear on the graph; although the increase in Greek productivity is largely comparable to that of Portugal, the increase in salaries was even greater, rising in 2008 to 180 percent of the 1998 value and thus going off the scale of the figure.

What happens when a country imports more than it exports? To finance its net imports, the country (its firms, its public bodies, its households) must sell assets overseas. These assets may be acquired by individuals, investment funds, or foreign states—for example, 50 percent of the shares in French corporations listed on the CAC 40 stock index, as well as much real estate in Paris and on the Côte d'Azur, are now owned by foreigners. Alternatively, the government, the banks, or businesses must borrow money from abroad. In any case, the country is living on credit, choosing to consume more today and less tomorrow.

Eurozone imbalances ultimately raise questions about what caused the recent impoverishment of southern Europe. Although there is no question that the growth of salaries in relation to productivity in the south was excessively rapid, many observers also attribute some responsibility to Germany's mercantilist policy. German policy has had contrasting effects on the citizens of other EU countries. On the one hand, consumers in these countries are pleased to be able to buy German goods at low prices. On the other hand, as employees of firms competing with German firms, they see their own employers struggling, not hiring, and even laying off people. The difficulties are exacerbated by the poor functioning of the labor markets in the south, reflecting policy choices in the countries concerned (see chapter 9).[6]

This is where the single currency poses a problem. If countries still had their own currencies, the German mark would have risen in value, whereas the French franc, the Italian lira, the Spanish peseta, and the Greek drachma would all have fallen. Consumers in southern Europe would have seen their purchasing power reduced by devaluation, but employees in sectors open to foreign competition would have been protected against large-scale job losses by the return to competitiveness.

Given that devaluation was not an option for the southern European countries, as they belonged to the Eurozone, the alternatives were also not very attractive.[7] One option involved trying to reproduce the effect of a fall in the currency by means of what economists call a "fiscal devaluation,"[8] which consists in raising taxes on consumption (the value-added tax, VAT) and thereby increasing the price of imports. The associated tax revenues are used to reduce the social security contributions paid by employers; this reduction in the cost of labor for domestic firms decreases the prices of domestic products and boosts exports. Such fiscal devaluation was practiced in several southern European countries, but only to a limited degree. A significant increase in VAT rates would have been necessary to compensate for losses in competitiveness ranging from 10 to 30 percent, which would have been inequitable and led to tax evasion.

The other substitute for currency devaluation, an overall reduction in salaries or prices that economists call an "internal devaluation," was implemented in countries like Spain, Portugal, and Greece. This proved very costly; while salaries moved back toward their pre-Euro levels,[9] the substantial increases that had taken place since then had created aspirations and commitments (for example, mortgage debts) in households that could not have anticipated the subsequent reduction in their incomes. Internal devaluations are also difficult to implement. States have direct control only over government salaries—they cannot guarantee that other salaries and prices will fall.

Debts

Was the crisis foreseeable? Take the case of Portugal, which experienced an economic boom in the 1990s in anticipation of joining the Eurozone. Olivier Blanchard and Francesco Giavazzi have shown that the inflow of money into Portugal during the 1990s fed the formation of a bubble rather than the development of a productive economy.[10] The widening of Portugal's current account deficit was chiefly explained by a decrease in households' private saving rather than by an increase in investment.

More broadly, the confidence created by the poorer countries' joining the Eurozone substantially lowered the interest rates paid by borrowers in these countries. The easier access to funds generated a capital inflow. This capital inflow, sometimes combined with weak regulation of banks' risk taking, fueled asset price increases and created financial bubbles, in particular in real estate.

Massive levels of debt, both public and private, are implicated in the origins of the crisis that threatens the existence of the Eurozone today. Excessive borrowing was sometimes the fault of a spendthrift public sector or a failure to collect taxes (as in Greece), and sometimes the fault of the financial sector (as in Spain and Ireland). For example, when the Irish government budget deficit ballooned from 12 to 32 percent of GDP in 2010, it was because the banks had to be bailed out.

Reduced savings and increased consumption have a counterpart: the need to either sell assets or go into debt (or both). Selling the "crown jewels" has its limits as a strategy, especially because the jewels lose value as soon as a certain proportion is owned by foreigners: for instance, domestic companies, if in large measure owned by foreigners, are unlikely to get favorable treatment in terms of tax and regulations,[11] and so foreign investors will not be willing to pay as much for them.

Debt also has its limits. There comes a time when foreign investors begin to have doubts about the ability of states—or their banks—to repay loans, and start demanding high rates of interest. They insist on "spreads," that is, an interest rate above that paid by safe borrowers, or even simply refuse to grant loans.

However, as figure 10.2 shows, until 2009 Greece was able to borrow at a rate similar to Germany, even though the international investment community was largely aware of the problems in the country's public finances. In other words, investors expected that Eurozone rules would not be observed, and bet that other Eurozone countries would bail Greece out.[12] Investors felt protected against the risk of default on Greek debt. More generally, they believed that there would be solidarity if a country in southern Europe got into difficulties. This was probably true, but only up to a point. In November 2009, the new Greek government revealed that the deficit was twice as large as the preceding government had previously announced, and that the nation's debt exceeded 120 percent of GDP. As we will see, this triggered the crisis and later led investors to take a haircut on their investment.

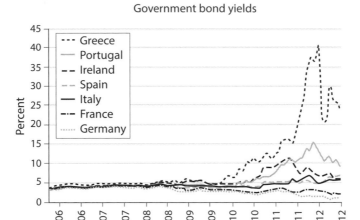

Figure 10.2. Rates on ten-year government bonds. Source: Niccolò Battistini, Marco Pagano, and Saverio Simonelli, "Systemic Risk and Home Bias in the Euro Area," European Economy, April 2013, Economic Papers 494. The data are provided by Datastream.

Tolerating, or Encouraging, the Real Estate Bubble and Risk Taking

In their classic book *This Time Is Different: Eight Centuries of Financial Folly*, economists Carmen Reinhart and Kenneth Rogoff show that mistakes repeat themselves, and that many sovereign debt crises are the result of bubbles—often real estate bubbles—that governments have neglected or even encouraged.[13] The reduction in the cost of borrowing in Spain after 1999 led to a Spanish real estate bubble that was financed by European capital. Unfortunately, it did not lead to investment in Spanish industry, which actually became less competitive. The borrowing was therefore not invested for the future. Moreover, it was a burden on the banks (in particular the regional savings banks known as *cajas*), which would later have to be bailed out by the Spanish government. The case of Spain is instructive. The large banks remained healthy,[14] except for Bankia, which the state had to inject with capital equivalent to 2 percent of GDP (thus becoming its majority shareholder). Meanwhile, the *cajas* gambled on the real estate bubble, freely granting loans. When they got into serious difficulties, they were bought and recapitalized by the state.[15]

As I explained in chapter 6, politicians both federal and regional decided to ignore the central bank's warnings, encouraging the real estate bubble. This benefited them politically, but did not put a brake on the risk taking by the *cajas*. The Spanish crisis might have been avoided if the banking union had existed at the time. The European Central Bank (ECB), which today oversees Eurozone banks, would hopefully have forced Spanish banks to slow their real estate lending. The German *Landesbanken*, which have strong political and regional ties, acted in a similar way. They too created major financial difficulties for their country.

The relaxed supervision around Europe affected private banks as much as public banks: Fortis, KBC, ING, Commerzbank, and several British and Irish banks had problems. If the Eurozone crisis had one virtue, it was in enforcing regulation of the banks at a European level, despite the reluctance of many politicians. These politicians were not only southern Europeans. Germany wanted to retain its freedom to supervise the *Landesbanken*, which were seen as a useful political tool. But national authorities supervising banking had a limited budget and supervisory teams unable to compete with those of the large banks. They could also simply close their eyes to a bubble. All of this made the case for the establishment of a single banking authority in the Eurozone, more removed from national pressures. This was implemented in 2014.

Whether because public spending was too high or banking supervision too lax, national debt reached high levels in southern Europe, as is shown by figure 10.3.

A Fragile Defense

Although the architecture of the Eurozone leaves much to be desired, the authors of its founding 1993 Maastricht Treaty cannot be accused of not having foreseen the dangers. They were aware that member countries could spend too much, or underregulate their banks, while retaining easy access to financial markets if those markets assumed

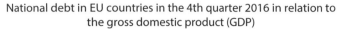

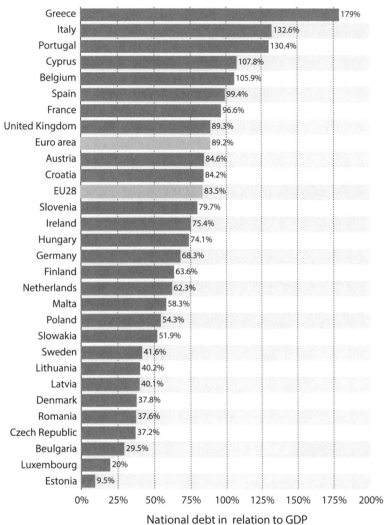

National debt in EU countries in the 4th quarter 2016 in relation to the gross domestic product (GDP)

National debt in relation to GDP

Figure 10.3. National Debt in EU countries as a percentage of GDP. *Source*: Eurostat, DebtClocks.eu.

other member countries would support them. Consequently, the treaty introduced both a limit on budget deficits (in its initial form, 3 percent of GDP), a limit on debt (60 percent of GDP), and a "no bailouts" clause. It was later decided that these requirements had to flex with the business cycle (it is reasonable to run budget deficits during recessions), but the rules insisted that a balanced budget be maintained during normal times.

These rules (known as the Stability and Growth Pact, enacted in 1997) had also provided for multilateral supervision. The European Union's economic and finance ministers would ask for remedial action by any state guilty of budgetary backsliding as soon as the country's budget deficit exceeded the 3 percent of GDP limit, other than in exceptional circumstances. In the absence of any meaningful action by the infringing country, the European Council could, in principle, levy a fine ranging from 0.2 to 0.5 percent of the country's GDP. This policy was not very credible, because levying a fine on a state that is already in financial difficulty isn't a sensible thing to do. The approach was refined in the budgetary pact of March 2012.[16]

So far, the Maastricht approach has failed. The combination of strict criteria with weak means of enforcement is an explosive mix.[17] The approach has inherent difficulties: a lack of flexibility to accommodate the national context, the complexity of measuring debt, and the problem of how to monitor and enforce the rules effectively.

The "One Size Fits All" Problem

Although it makes sense from a political perspective, given a desire for equal treatment for all, uniform constraints for all countries do not make things any easier. There is no single magic number that determines the sustainability of national debt—what is sustainable for one country may not be sustainable for another. Argentina was in great difficulty with a debt of 60 percent of GDP, whereas Japan has exceeded 240 percent but has not (yet) triggered a crisis of confidence. When is public debt sustainable?

Sustainability depends on many factors. For example, a debt is more likely to be sustainable if, a) there is a high rate of growth so that tax revenues will increase, making it easier to service the debt; b) the debt is domestic—countries don't like to default on their own citizens, banks, or central bank[18] (this is why Japan's debt, estimated at

240 percent of its GDP but with 90.6 percent held by Japanese investors, has up to this point not caused much concern);[19] c) the interest rate is low (i.e., servicing the debt is cheap); or d) the government is easily able to collect higher taxes (for a given debt, countries with a weak tax-collection infrastructure, such as Argentina and Greece, are more in danger of crises; similarly, the United States has a greater margin for maneuver when it comes to increasing taxes than does France).

Other factors contribute. The prospect of support from other countries if things get really difficult makes it easier to go into debt, as in Greece before 2009; conversely, the financial markets' perception that the federal government of the United States will not bail out a state or municipality limits how much its states and cities can borrow. The legal jurisdiction in which government sovereign debt is issued also plays a role; private creditors are often better protected, and thus more inclined to lend, if the bonds are issued in London or New York rather than in the borrowing country.

In addition, the willingness of a country to pay back its debts depends on the cost of defaulting, so this cost also determines its ability to borrow. There are several costs of defaulting. For example, the country can have difficulty borrowing again after default because it has shattered its reputation[20] (that is, markets no longer trust it), and because of the legal risk for new lenders and lenders who settle with the country to reduce its debt burden (creditors who have not been repaid and have not settled may be granted priority in repayment).[21] Other costs of defaulting can include the confiscation of government-owned assets in other countries (for example, airplanes belonging to a publicly owned company) and general difficulty in trading goods and services internationally.

Finally, the higher the debt, the more problematic the situation, and the greater the probability that what economists call "self-fulfilling panics" occur. If lenders become worried about a country's solvency, they demand higher interest rates, which in turn increases the cost of repaying the debt. This makes it less probable that the debt will be repaid, which "justifies" the market's concerns and the lenders' demand for a higher interest rate.[22]

Ultimately, although there is agreement about the characteristics that determine whether or not a debt is sustainable, and agreement that large levels of debt can be dangerous for a country, it is difficult to identify precisely a maximum sustainable level of indebtedness.

The Difficulty of Measuring Public Debt

A country's public debt consists only of financial obligations it is known for sure will materialize. This includes, for instance, government bonds and treasury bills that the government is in principle obliged to repay, whatever happens. But readers might be surprised to learn that their state pensions are not accounted for within public debt. They are "off balance sheet" to the extent that the state is not obliged to pay them (that is, governments can decide to reduce pensions, although they would certainly think twice before doing so). More than 90 percent of pensions in France are state liabilities that are not counted in public debt (as compared with 60 percent in the United Kingdom, and slightly less in the Netherlands). A recent study estimates that twenty countries in the OECD have unfinanced commitments to pensions amounting to seventy-eight billion dollars, in addition to their official debt of forty-four billion dollars.[23] These are big sums.

Governments in all countries try hard to hide their debt in the form of contingent liabilities. Auditors try to discover these ingenious devices, which include guarantees backing various debts of public bodies or public-private partnerships, underfinanced pension funds, loans to risky countries through the intermediary of European institutions (such as the ECB or the European Stability Mechanism). Another problem complicating the calculation of government debt is that it accounts for liabilities but not future revenues. This creates an incentive to sell assets, sometimes at fire sale prices, to reduce the debt.

Another important part of the state's contingent liabilities involve banking risk, as the recent examples of the United States, Spain, and Ireland clearly show. There is a limited probability that this risk will materialize, and it is therefore left off the books. What's more, the stated amount—covered by deposit insurance—is often much smaller than the true amount. If the state must bail out depositors in the event that the deposit insurance system lacks sufficient funds, in practice it also bails out other forms of bank debts, such as the deposits of small and medium enterprises and bonds issued by the bank. Much of the debate on banking reform is really the question of what, and what not, to bail out.[24] Sovereign debt issued by the state and private debt issued by banks sometimes need to be considered together. Private bank debt is partly public debt: if banks are weakened, so are the states in which they operate and vice versa. Yet for years, only public debt was considered in the Eurozone.

The Credibility of Reciprocal Monitoring

The Maastricht Treaty regarded monitoring government deficits and debts as the first line of defense, and a prohibition on bailing out member states as the second line. Neither of these has worked.

So far as *monitoring* is concerned, European finance ministers, gathered together in the Economic and Financial Affairs Council (ECOFIN), failed to punish numerous violations of the Stability and Growth Pact. There were sixty-eight violations even before the financial crisis began, and not one of them resulted in any intervention. Even France and Germany broke the rules as early as 2003. The European Union has also turned a blind eye to rule breaking in countries about to join the Eurozone or in those that became less vigilant once they joined. Italy is an excellent illustration. It made considerable efforts to reduce its debt before it entered the Eurozone, running a big primary surplus (that is, the budget surplus before interest payments), but as soon as it was in, it reduced its fiscal efforts. The damage was limited by low interest rates until the explosion of the Italian interest rate spread in the summer of 2011.

It is not surprising that mutual and reciprocal monitoring of the member states failed. A finance minister will be reluctant to anger fellow finance ministers from countries that have broken the rules by issuing a formal complaint, which is anyway unlikely to lead to any action. Political agendas also play a role. The objective of building a united Europe has often been invoked to justify turning a blind eye to dubious accounting practices, or to insufficient preparation for entering the Eurozone. Finally, every country might anticipate reciprocal favors when it needs them.

As for no bailouts, the European Union had to violate its own rules by coming to the aid of Greece. The same applies to the ECB, which acquired the public debt of countries in difficulty and accepted poor-quality collateral. For the time being, the no bailouts rule is not credible in Europe. Confronted by the fait accompli of a member state's imminent bankruptcy, Eurozone countries may show solidarity (and have shown it in the past) simply out of fear of the "fallout" that sovereign default might cause. This includes both economic fallout (trade disruption, potential losses for companies and banks that have subsidiaries or other exposure in the defaulting country, or possible runs on other fragile countries' debt) and other kinds of fallout (feelings of empathy for the troubled country, fearing for the future of the European project, or the nuisance associated with mayhem in the defaulting country).

The Comparison with the United States

To offer a comparison, in the United States (another monetary union),[25] President Obama refused to bail out California in 2009; in 2014, the city of Detroit had to settle its debts in court: it was up to the state and the city to restore budget balance without counting on a bailout from the federal government. In fact, the United States federal government has not bailed out a state or city since 1840. The rare examples of default—for example, the rescue of New York City in 1975—led to strict subsequent supervision by the federal government.

That was not the case before 1840. During the War of Independence, several states went deep into debt and were on the verge of declaring bankruptcy. Then, and for almost fifty years thereafter, the federal government repeatedly bailed out troubled states. But a political consensus developed against bailouts in favor of fiscal discipline. Eyes are currently fixed on Puerto Rico, which is very poor (45 percent of its population living under the poverty line). In 2016, the federal government created a federal oversight board to negotiate the restructuring of Puerto Rico's debt. After the negotiation with creditors failed, the federal oversight board filed for bankruptcy in May 2017, seeking the protection of US courts to reduce its debt burden.

The Cost to the People

The costs for overindebted countries begin mounting even before they default on their sovereign debt. Servicing the debt requires funds that could have been used elsewhere. The government finds it increasingly difficult to follow a countercyclical policy, allowing it to run a deficit if there is a recession or banking crisis, because borrowing to refinance its debt requires reassuring worried financial markets that it will observe budgetary rigor.

But, in the final reckoning, the total cost of borrowing is linked to the possibility of default. Like delinquent individual and corporate borrowers, defaulting countries need to renegotiate with creditors. The negotiation obviously cannot only concern a monetary compensation to creditors, since the borrower by definition is broke. Rather, the country must accept a range of concessions in terms of budget cuts and reforms, adopting policies that are meant to restore public finances, but that it would not have adopted by itself: defaulting involves a substantial loss of autonomy. When sovereign default is imminent, the hardest part for the negotiators is to make the necessary measures bearable for the citizens, while at the same time making sure that the efforts made are real. The sacrifices demanded must be fair, sparing only the most destitute. Reductions in military spending, reforms of the labor market and retirement systems, and the reinforcement and enforcement of taxation should be accompanied by an investment in export sectors, education, and productivity-enhancing infrastructure to prepare for the future.

Finally, since European institutions are too weak to create the conditions for a revival of trust in the crisis countries, recourse to the IMF was inevitable. It may be useful to restate the purpose of the IMF, because perceptions of its role are sometimes wrong. Simply put, the IMF provides services for countries in financial difficulties: no country is ever forced to use its services. Countries that ask the IMF for help generally no longer have access to capital markets—or, if they do, only at prohibitive interest rates that might trigger a spiral of high repayments, thus increasing the debt, increasing interest rates, and so on. The IMF supplies the country with liquidity. But that is not its main role, especially since its loans are almost always repaid and thus do not constitute genuine aid.[26] The IMF sets conditions for more rigorous fiscal policy. It is this conditionality that helps these countries regain their credibility, so that international investors will once again agree to lend to them. We may criticize this or that condition that the IMF imposes, but its raison d'être is to help the country that has voluntarily appealed for its help.

Revisiting Moral Hazard

Earlier in this book, I mentioned moral hazard. Generally, the term refers to a situation in which the behavior of one party affects the well-being of another party (exercises an externality on that other party), and this behavior cannot be specified, in advance and in a credible way, in a contract. In the context of sovereign borrowing, "moral hazard" refers to the choices made by a borrowing country that will reduce the likelihood of the loan being repaid to the foreign lenders.

The persistence of budget deficits and their accumulation into debt springs immediately to mind. The choice to consume rather than invest is another example. And not all investment choices have the same effect on the sustainability of debt. Investments in the production of tradable goods increase a country's capacity to repay its debt, while investment in nontradable goods decreases that capacity. This is because, to repay its debt, a country must sell goods abroad and not import too much. A (largely) nontradable good in which European countries (often via their banks) have invested is real estate, which is by definition "consumed" by residents.

Federal states like the United States or Canada have decided that the most reliable way to limit moral hazard is a rigorously observed no bailouts rule. That has been the case, as we have seen, in the United States since the 1840s, when the federal government refused to provide aid and eight states defaulted on their debts. In the twentieth century, Canada has also refused to bail out its provinces, although this has not resulted in bankruptcies. Argentina, on the other hand, bailed out its indebted provinces in the late 1980s. Ten years later, the same provinces were largely responsible for the country's massive levels of debt, leading to the famous crisis of 1998 and the sovereign default in January 2002. A similar phenomenon occurred in Brazil, and interestingly in Germany, whose federal government has continually aided some of its *Länder* since the 1980s. It bailed out the city of Bremen and the *Land* of Sarre. That did not prevent budgetary excesses afterward—quite the contrary. The *Länder* were among the agents mainly responsible for excessive debt in Germany.[27] This laxity was partly responsible for the European Stability Pact's loss of credibility, because Germany and France secured changes to the pact to avoid having to pay penalties.

GREECE: MUCH BITTERNESS ON BOTH SIDES

Following the no vote on the referendum held in Greece on July 5, 2015, and the tense negotiations that followed it, European policymakers felt somewhat relieved. The Greeks had managed to stay in the Eurozone. They accepted the troika's intrusive conditions (or stricter conditions, depending on one's point of view), but they did not manage to get the debt restructured. Tourism, the main source of Greece's export earnings, offered some relief for the country as many tourists were abandoning holidaying in North Africa and the Near East for security reasons. Countries in the rest of the Eurozone were glad that Greece had not imploded. They noted too that Alex Tsipras, the Greek prime minister, performing a volte-face in accepting conditions tougher than those he had denounced in calling the referendum, was supported by voters in elections in September 2015. After five years of crisis, with both camps stalling for time by trying to appease public opinion, European officials continued to focus primarily on the short term, with a narrow vision of the Eurozone's future.

Even just focusing on the Greek problem, never mind the global situation of the Eurozone, opinions differ considerably. As Thomas

Philippon, an economics professor at New York University, has emphasized: "Everyone seems to have an opinion about the steps that should be taken for the Greek economy and its mountain of national debt. But these opinions are for the most part arbitrary, and are often based on incomplete or incoherent reasoning."[28]

Those who take the side of the troika[29] play down the fact that Greece has undertaken reforms, hesitant and incomplete though they may be. For the first time in many years, the economy expanded in 2014. Employees had borne nonnegligible decreases in their salaries, and the government had made efforts to cut the budget deficit and to reduce the size of the overinflated public sector.[30] Those on this side of the debate also fail to acknowledge that Greece's recovery has been slowed down not only by bad policies but also by the extraordinary recession the country confronted. Investment in Greece came to a halt because investors were uncertain about demand and worried about possible expropriation in the future. They feared that their investments might later be subject to punitive taxation by a government concerned about either repaying the heavy national debt or continuing to finance public expenditure. As a result, unemployment even now remains extremely high, despite government attempts to challenge the labor market institutions inhibiting job creation. (Clearly, uncertainty as to whether these labor market reforms will be sustained has prevented them from achieving their full effect.) Some observers (although not the IMF) continue to dismiss the idea of debt relief, even though Greece is struggling to pay even the small amounts currently required (thanks to earlier restructuring of the debt, the maturities for repayment are very long and the real repayments will begin only in 2022).

Those in the anti-troika camp refuse to acknowledge that Greece has already benefited from substantial aid,[31] and don't propose any genuine economic reforms when they call for debt relief. So far, a number of reforms exist only on paper and have not yet been implemented. Tax privileges enjoyed by the wealthy, and the unequal treatment of salaried employees (who cannot escape taxation) and unsalaried individuals (who pay very little) have been criticized, but little has been done to change this. Little has been attempted to open goods markets, except for a few symbolic actions (such as relaxing regulations on the opening hours of pharmacies). There is still much that could be done on this front. Similarly, although limited progress has been made, the government continues to hold back private enterprise; international comparisons rank Greece low for the effectiveness of courts in enforcing contracts, or for making business easy to conduct. The suspension of collective agreements in certain sectors (such as public transport), along with legislation to encourage company-wide rather than branch-level union bargaining, is significant, but this decision may still be overturned. In general, the parties in power in Greece have the habit of systematically challenging what their predecessors have done, and this does not help the country.

The anti-troika camp also refuses to recognize that a certain amount of putting public finances in order (or "austerity," as this camp calls it) was inevitable. As Olivier Blanchard, the IMF's chief economist from 2007 to 2015, put it:

> Even before the 2010 program, debt in Greece was three hundred billion euros, or 130 percent of GDP. The deficit was thirty-six billion euros, or 15½ percent of GDP. Debt was increasing at 12 percent a year, and this was clearly unsustainable. Had Greece been left on its own, it would have been simply unable to borrow. Given gross financing needs of 20–25 percent of GDP, it would have had to cut its budget deficit by that amount. Even if it had fully defaulted on its debt, given a primary deficit of over 10 percent of GDP, it would have had to cut its budget deficit by 10 percent of GDP from one day to the next. This would have led to much larger adjustments and a much higher social cost than under the programs, which allowed Greece to take over 5 years to achieve a primary balance.[32]

By demanding the cancellation of the debt and the creation of the equivalent of Brady bonds,[33] the anti-troika camp correctly wonders about the country's ability to repay the debt without tremendous social cost; but it does not take into account that Eurozone countries, unlike the commercial banks that were the creditors of Latin American countries that defaulted in the 1980s, do not have the option of keeping their distance after the debt has been restructured. Their well-being is tied to Greece's, and the restructuring of Greek debt will not necessarily end their financial involvement in the country. Although I consider Greece's debt unsustainable, and very likely to weigh on the country's future, the situation is more complex than the proposal to simply forgive the debt would suggest.

A Confrontation in Which No One Comes Out a Winner

There are good reasons for concern. First of all, about economic performance. Investment in Greece may not resume in the short term. Since the banks' balance sheets are weighed down by unproductive loans to enterprises, mortgages, and holdings of government bonds, the banks need to be recapitalized (a point the ECB has started to insist on) so that they can start to fund productive investment. And foreign investors' trust must be restored.

Nor is there any guarantee that an intrusive approach will necessarily pay off. If we examine the privatizations being asked of Greece, we may agree that the management of public assets should not be left to a ruling elite. But selling them off cheaply will help neither the Greek government nor, indirectly, its creditors. Domestic buyers with cash on hand are scarce, and foreign buyers offer low prices because they fear, logically enough, that government policies intended to satisfy local interest groups or to raise funds to reimburse the debt will swallow up part of their investment. Here again the lack of long-term clarity has far-reaching consequences.

The second source of uncertainty concerns relations within Europe. The relationships between the peoples of the European Union, which the founding fathers conceived as a way to promote peace on the continent, are steadily deteriorating. With the improvement of the situation in Portugal, Ireland, Italy, and Spain, the insulting group acronym "PIIGS"[34] has disappeared, but we are witnessing a resurrection of old and very sad clichés about nationalities, in particular Germans and Greeks. Populists on the left and especially on the right opposed to a united Europe are daily winning more voters.

Agreements are also more and more often obtained by making threats. An instance of political arm wrestling occurred in July 2015. On one side was the Greek government, which used Greece's exit from the Eurozone—"Grexit"—as a threat. A Grexit would expose Eurozone countries to geopolitical upheaval in the Balkans, to a repudiation of Greece's debt (which will occur to a certain extent anyway, but whose recognition governments prefer to delay for electoral reasons), and to the blame for whatever might happen to Greece. On the other side, the rest of Europe, which won a short-term "victory," was motivated by the desire to send European populist movements the message that there is no free lunch, and to underline the potential humanitarian and economic consequences of Grexit for Greek citizens. The Greeks understood that a return to a devalued drachma (though the devaluation by itself would not be the end of the world) would involve dealing with complex legal problems and with further capital flight, balancing their budget, submitting to sanctions, suffering another short-term decrease in productivity, coping with increased inequality, and perhaps losing some of their *acquis communautaire*[35] under pressure from powerful populist parties. Leaving the euro is quite different from not joining it in the first place.

Two Extreme Scenarios: Grexit and the Entrenchment of the Troika in Athens

Prior to the 2015 referendum, the press commented extensively on the possibility that Greece might leave the Eurozone, or even the European Union. The Greek finance minister even made a contingency plan for leaving the euro shortly before the referendum, and his German counterpart spoke of a "temporary" Grexit.

The benefit for Greece of leaving the euro would be that it would very quickly recover its competitiveness; the depreciation of the drachma that would follow would make Greek goods and services cheap and imported goods expensive. This would revive economic activity and create employment. As I have said, this exit from the euro would prove very costly for Greek citizens, however, quite apart from their loss of purchasing power. First, it would lead to a default by the state and the Greek banks, which would have trouble repaying debts denominated in euros using their devalued currency. The Greek state would have to redenominate the banks' liabilities (and assets) and their contracts more generally into the local currency. Argentina did this in 2001, calling it "pesification." This is effectively default by another name, and would avoid neither international sanctions nor an additional loss of reputation for the country. Greece would be unable to borrow from foreign lenders for a while, and would have to instantly balance its budget. Greece would also lose the five billion euros it receives every year from the EU. Since it joined the European Union in 1981, Greece has been a major beneficiary of EU funds. Europe, having become its main creditor in recent years, would feel justified in withholding structural funds if loans were not repaid. Finally, Greece would see levels of inequality, already high, skyrocket. Greeks who had invested their money abroad would become much richer thanks to the fall of the drachma, whereas ordinary citizens would see their purchasing power fall even more. Reducing this inequality would require a much better performing fiscal administration.

Opinions differ regarding the possibility of contagion, the prospect that Greece's problems might spread to other European countries. This would not be through cross-exposure: unlike 2011, when the first bailout occurred and a default would have meant major losses for German and (especially) French banks, European banks no longer had many assets in Greece by 2015. The divergence in opinion instead rests on the impact that Grexit would have on other fragile countries. One camp maintains that the financial markets would panic because leaving the euro would no longer be taboo. Another, more interesting, version of the same argument is that the financial markets are learning that the Eurozone is no longer going to insure the debts of one of its members—which it had already begun to suggest by imposing losses on the Greek state's private creditors in 2012[36] and, in Cyprus in 2013, on depositors who had no deposit insurance. In contrast, others argue that leaving the euro, because it would be costly for Greece, would weaken populist movements in other countries in southern Europe exploiting anti-euro sentiment. This camp adds that firmness in negotiating with Greece benefits the countries that have made greater reform efforts, or that had not benefited from the transfers granted to Greece (Spain, Portugal, Ireland, and eastern Europe). These countries were, notably, Germany's allies in demanding firm treatment for Greece.

Grexit is a risky option, but so is business as usual. It is fine to stall for time, but to avoid eventual ruin, politicians should reflect on the bigger challenges of the Eurozone. Whatever your opinion, there should be a consensus on at least a few points:

1. The troika cannot continue to run Greece jointly with its government for the next thirty years. The Greek debt of 180 percent of GNP—characterized by a high rate of foreign holdings—is gigantic for a country with limited fiscal capacity, and has a long maturity (about twice as long as that of other national debts) and a low interest rate, following the restructurings of 2010 and 2012. Payments are due to become large only after 2022, and then will be made over many years. Can we envisage the troika in charge for such a long time? The referendum and the popular discontent in Greece have shown the predictable limits of this exercise. Besides, the IMF is generally brought in by a country in difficulty so that it can reestablish its credibility and overcome a short-term liquidity problem. Democracy requires that the IMF's intervention is temporary.

2. In Greece, investment (and consequently employment) has little chance of recovery as long as there is no long-term certainty.

3. Reforms are better than austerity, even if we have to admit that their exact nature is difficult to specify in an agreement.

4. Debt relief is necessary, but it merely creates breathing room, which makes it likely that the question of further debt relief will come up later.

5. Solidarity and responsibility go hand in hand. Europe needs a little more of both.

6. Solidarity is a political decision. The ECB plays its role by providing liquidity in a countercyclical manner (that is, when there is a recession or the threat of a recession) and punctual aid to prevent problems from spreading, but it should not be obliged to provide permanent support to struggling countries just because

an unelected body can do this more easily than a parliament. If this was allowed to happen, the ECB's (indispensable) independence could be compromised. Politicians should assume their responsibilities.

7. By providing liquidity for the Eurozone, the ECB gives it the time and the opportunity to get out of a rut. But the ECB alone cannot solve the problems that created that rut. Individually and collectively, member countries must take advantage of the breathing room accorded by the ECB to reform their institutions.

WHAT OPTIONS DO THE EU AND THE EUROZONE HAVE TODAY?

The founders of the European Union had a long-term vision for managing the potentially dangerous postwar period, and in 1957 they were able to mobilize enough political support to construct a community of states. Today, we once again need a long-term vision. For the Eurozone (to simplify dramatically) there are two strategies. The current strategy is based on an improvement of the Maastricht Treaty. It does not provide for automatic stabilizers, such as a shared budget (implying the partial or full pooling of tax revenue), common deposit and unemployment insurance, and borrowing under joint and several liability, that would make it possible to stabilize a member state economy in difficulty. This strategy implies limited risk sharing.

The second, more ambitious solution would be federalism, which implies greater risk sharing. The 2012 banking union[37] is an embryonic form of federalism. If it is accompanied by deposit insurance guaranteeing deposits of ordinary savers in Eurozone banks, which are themselves centrally monitored, it will be a major step toward sharing risks with limited moral hazard for its member states (who no longer supervise their own national banks). Although opinions on this subject differ, the banking union, executed correctly, is a game changer. Obviously, European banking supervision is still in its preliminary stages and must prove its independence from the member states and the banking sector. In addition, some characteristics of banking supervision (particularly its limited coverage in political debate and in the media) have facilitated the abandonment of sovereignty through the creation of the banking union, but may be lacking in other kinds of action moving member countries toward a federalist state. Thus it is not certain that people will so easily accept the next steps toward European federalism.

I wonder whether Europeans and their leaders are fully aware of the conditions that must be met for either of these approaches to work: one cannot simultaneously insist on more sovereignty and greater risk sharing. This is the heart of the problem.

THE IMPROVED MAASTRICHT OPTION

The Maastricht approach infringes on the sovereignty of member states only with respect to monitoring government debt and deficits by the Eurozone.[38] In theory, it excludes bailouts. In practice, when faced with a member state in difficulty, the Eurozone countries tend to stand together. As we discussed, such solidarity may be motivated by financial interest, empathy to the plight of troubled countries, or fear of geopolitical repercussions if they do not assist. Regardless of the motivation, this unplanned (or *ex post*) solidarity is necessarily limited, however, as is also shown by the heated debate over who would be the winners and losers from a German fiscal stimulus.

This limited solidarity raises the question of why countries do not create a formal insurance mechanism in which they commit to come to each other's rescue. One such scheme is the joint issuing of debt for which they would be collectively responsible under joint and several liability; if a state defaulted, its debt would be assumed by the other states. However, as I have indicated in a recent article,[39] while healthy countries can always express their solidarity *ex post* during a rescue operation, they have no incentive to tie their hands *ex ante*. That is, they have little interest in contributing more insurance to the countries that are most at risk than what they would voluntary contribute *ex post* if the latter got into trouble, because the countries at risk cannot indemnify them for the cost of this commitment without borrowing even more.

The Achilles' heel of the Maastricht structure is the management of deficits, which is economically unsatisfactory, as we have seen, but is also undermined by a lack of political will to intervene early—at a point when (fiscal) rigor would be least costly. Some progress has been achieved by reforms called the "Two-pack," which embody an external examination of budgetary policies. But their effectiveness is yet to be tested. If a country fails to respect the rules, it is not clear that anyone has the power to enforce them.

Given that the political process has little chance of producing the hoped-for results, the Maastricht approach seems to require the establishment of a highly professional and independent fiscal council that would intervene when there is an unsustainable deficit, but would not advise whether the country should decrease expenses or increase taxes to reduce it, nor suggest the appropriate composition of expenditures and revenues. A recent innovation is the introduction, in the member states, of independent fiscal councils similar to the Congressional Budget Office in the United States (they already existed in some European countries, such as Germany and Sweden). An independent evaluation by experts[40] is useful for identifying anomalies. For example, most governments make systematically optimistic forecasts for growth. This inflates their forecasts of tax revenues and underestimates the likely cost of social programs, such as unemployment benefits, and so allows them to appear not too much in deficit. Sometimes independent fiscal bodies have a broader mandate. The Swedish Fiscal Policy Council, for example, also evaluates the consequences of government policies and their viability.[41]

Unlike the national fiscal councils that were imposed on the member states in 2011, this fiscal council would have to be European (the basic problem is, after all, the "agency" that exists between Europe and its member states) and capable of requiring prompt corrective action. In addition, given that financial sanctions are not a good idea if a country is already in financial difficulties, other measures must be used, although these will only sharpen the populations' concerns about legitimacy and sovereignty. As things stand, the current impulse toward national sovereignty works against such improvement of the Maastricht approach.

To sum up, no matter how appealing it was to introduce independent fiscal councils in 2011, we should not expect miracles. It is unfortunate that their members are citizens of the countries concerned, even though the mission of the councils is to stand for European, not national interests. Above all, such bodies do not resolve the question of what to do when a country does not respond to warnings, which is far from a theoretical possibility.

The Federalist Option

A Greater Sharing of Risks

Starting with the United States at the end of the eighteenth century, many countries reacted to the difficulties of their member states by increasing the federal capacity to go into debt and by introducing systematic fiscal transfers among their members. The federalist approach inevitably implies greater risk sharing than the Eurozone countries currently allow. Full integration would make Eurozone countries jointly responsible for the debts of other member states through the issuance of euro bonds, that is, bonds issued jointly by the states of the Eurozone, the repayment of which they would jointly guarantee. A joint budget and shared deposit insurance and unemployment insurance schemes would also act as automatic stabilizers, offering more protection for countries in temporary difficulties. For example, the income tax—not least because it is a progressive tax—effects major transfers from wealthy regions to poor regions, which have expenses (retirement pensions, health care) as costly as those of other regions.

The practical importance of this risk sharing in federal countries is debated. In federations like the United States, the extent of this kind of stabilization seems empirically limited, and less important than the stabilization operating through the financial market—that is, through the diversification of the portfolios held by individuals and enterprises far beyond the boundaries of the state.[42] In any case, the sharing of risk may have helped make the no bailouts policy more credible. Recall that since the 1840s the United States federal government no longer bails out the states: the existence of stabilizers perhaps reduces the number of excuses for poor performance.

The Prerequisites for Federalism

The federalist vision requires that countries meet two preliminary conditions. First, every insurance contract must be signed behind the veil of ignorance. You wouldn't sell me insurance if you suspected that my roof had a good chance of falling in tomorrow. That is why a high degree of risk sharing is probably unacceptable for the countries of northern Europe. The asymmetry between north and south might be corrected by identifying and isolating the problems inherited from the past and dealing with them adequately. Doing so is complex, but this problem can be solved. For example, in introducing a European system of deposit insurance, the troubled assets held by banks in difficulty could be dealt with by creating "bad banks" to hold these assets in each member state.

A second and much more fundamental point is that countries living together need common rules to limit moral hazard. Common rules should concern those areas of potential mismanagement that can force a country to ask for help. We have seen that the supervision of banks should not be carried out at the country level, because the banking sector and the politicians then have too much influence over the process. The case of a common system of unemployment insurance is more complex. The unemployment rate in Eurozone countries is only partly determined by the economic cycle, which by itself would justify a mechanism of insurance among countries. It also results from choices about job protection, active labor market policies, contributions to social security, occupational training schemes, collective negotiations, and the protection of professions, among other things. Those countries whose institutions produce an unemployment rate of 5 percent will not wish to be part of a shared insurance system with those whose choices create a 20 percent unemployment rate. The same goes for pension and legal systems. Many Europeans, however, including some who claim to be federalists, are still opposed to the idea of surrendering more of their sovereignty.

The federalist approach will not be made more acceptable by the mere creation of a European parliament with extended powers. First there must be an agreement on a foundation of common laws and regulations, as was the case—in a more modest way—during the initial phase of the European project, and then in the gradual construction of the *acquis communautaire*. The countries that have undertaken painful political reforms might fear seeing their own *acquis* disappear. More generally, each member state will fear that the profound contractual incompleteness of a top-down "political Europe" will produce a result even more distant from its aspirations than what we have today. The consequences of federalism should be understood by everyone before we set out on this path.

The Limits of Solidarity

Federalism is sometimes much more than an insurance policy between regions of a single federation. In other words, transfers between regions can be more structural than conditional. In the United States, wealthy states like California and New York systematically and substantially subsidize the poor states, like Alabama or Louisiana. During the past twenty years, New Mexico, Mississippi, and West Virginia have received on average more than 10 percent of their GDP this way. Puerto Rico currently receives 30 percent of its GDP from the rest of the United States. Germany makes large, regular transfers between its *Länder*, which all receive about the same amount per inhabitant. Italy transfers resources from the north to the south, the UK from the south to the north, and Catalonia to the rest of Spain. In Belgium, Flanders transfers funds to Wallonia, whereas financial flows used to move from Wallonia to Flanders.

In the end, everything depends on the willingness of wealthy regions to finance poor regions. We still have an imperfect understanding of what would determine this willingness. Clearly a common language and nationalist feeling help generate the unidirectional transfers in Italy. It can also be argued that the strong separatist movements in regions like Catalonia in Spain and Flanders in Belgium are linked to a sense of cultural and linguistic distance. More generally, the welfare state is usually more developed in homogeneous communities.[43] What is true for regional governments is probably also true at the national and international levels. For better or worse, groups are more receptive to redistribution when the beneficiaries are close to them culturally, linguistically, religiously, and racially.

And Now

It is hard to say in advance what path Europe will take to solve its problems. Perhaps it will be a revision of the Maastricht approach, accompanied by specific—but necessarily limited—integration using the model of the banking union. But if we Europeans want to live together, we have to accept the idea of losing a little more of our sovereignty. To achieve this in an era of increased nationalistic fervor, we must rehabilitate the European ideal and remain united around it. This is no easy task.

ELEVEN
What Use Is Finance?

Few subjects in economics arouse as much emotion as finance. Since the 2008 crisis, the ranks of its detractors have swelled considerably and its defenders have retreated. Everyone agrees that finance is still a major force in the economies of the developed world. But is that a good or a bad thing? To tackle this question, we first need to understand the point of finance, its uses, its dysfunctions, and its regulation. The role of the economist is to help mitigate market failures. So, after explaining the importance of finance in our societies, I will devote most of this chapter to trying to understand how it can cause problems and what the government can do about it. In the next chapter I will turn to the diagnosis of the financial crisis and the postcrisis situation.

WHAT USE IS FINANCE?

To state the obvious: finance is indispensable to the economy. Otherwise we could spare ourselves financial crises and bailouts by simply abolishing it. Needless to say, no country has chosen to outlaw finance. Broadly, finance fulfills two functions for borrowers: First, it funds or helps to fund households, governments, and businesses (from startups to the major publicly listed corporations). It further provides borrowers with ways to insure themselves against destabilizing risks. In doing these things, the financial system also provides savings products for anyone seeking to accumulate wealth, from individual households to business and governments.

In particular, finance mediates between badly informed savers (you and me) and borrowers. Until recently, the banker's trade was essentially to take in household savings and turn them into loans to other households investing in real estate and durable consumer goods, or to small and medium-sized enterprises (SMEs) to allow them to finance their growth or simply to get through a rough patch. Traditionally, households and SMEs could only borrow from banks, whereas large companies were able to finance themselves by issuing bonds directly on the market. The financial sector directed households' money toward the most promising enterprises, thus helping the allocation and reallocation of the available funds toward their best uses. Finance is in this way an essential factor in economic growth.

By doing this, the banks transform maturity to create liquidity. In other words, they borrow short term from depositors to make relatively long-term loans (although there are many examples of banks' handling long-term saving by consumers and short-term borrowing by enterprises). Thus, our bank will give us instant access to our deposits, but it grants us a twenty- or thirty-year loan if we want to buy a house. This can lead to a potential vulnerability, to which I will return: if all the depositors at the bank withdraw their deposits at the same time, and the bank no longer has enough money coming in to cover the withdrawals, it is forced to find new money to honor its promise to return cash on deposit. It does this either by borrowing, or by selling its assets (loans it has made for real estate purchases and loans to businesses).

Finance also provides insurance for businesses, households, and governments. Just as an insurance company allows us to insure ourselves against car accidents, fires, disabilities that prevent us working, and death, so banks, insurance companies, and reinsurers allow businesses to protect themselves against events that might threaten their growth or even their survival. For example, Airbus's revenues are denominated mainly in dollars, while its expenses are denominated partly in euros; if the dollar were to fall suddenly, it could harm the company's activities. Airbus can insure itself against fluctuations in the dollar-euro exchange rate by means of financial instruments called "foreign exchange swaps."[1]

Similarly, a bank is often affected by fluctuations in interest rates. As it generally borrows short term and lends long term, if interest rates rise, the bank's costs will immediately increase, whereas much of its revenue will stay the same (loans granted to businesses and households usually specify fixed nominal interest rates not linked to changes in the market rate). The bank can insure itself against this risk by using a financial instrument called an "interest rate swap." A final example: an enterprise can be weakened if a major customer or supplier faces financial difficulties; it can insure itself against this risk by means of a "credit default swap" (CDS), which would bring in revenue in this eventuality. All these are examples of derivatives—financial products whose value depends on moves in other variables, such as exchange rates, interest rates, or a company's bankruptcy. Many derivatives offer economic agents ways of insuring themselves against events that might adversely affect them. In this respect, finance is useful to society.

Today, the activities of banks and other financial intermediaries are much more numerous and complex than they used to be. The collapse of financial intermediaries has always been costly for society, but finance as a whole has been under heavy scrutiny ever since the 2008 crisis. What happened?

HOW TO TRANSFORM USEFUL PRODUCTS INTO TOXIC PRODUCTS

To illustrate how finance can turn toxic, take two examples that played a major role in the 2008 crisis: derivatives and securitized assets. Why were these products, which in principle are useful, at the heart of the crisis? The answer lies in asymmetries of information, as in so many other examples in this book. There are externalities involved too, because these products can cause losses for third parties, such as taxpayers and investors.

THE DANGERS OF DERIVATIVES

As we will see in detail in the following chapter, derivatives have ravaged the financial sector. Consider an example involving public sector buyers of toxic products in France. There, about 1,500 local authorities (communes, departments, hospitals) had taken out toxic loans from financial intermediaries such as Dexia (a specialist in these loans, later bailed out by both the Belgian and French governments).[2]

The first problem was that these loans involved, as many of this kind did, "teaser rates" of interest that started very low but rose sharply later.[3] Did this make them toxic? Not necessarily; if the local authority had saved during the initial period, it could have afforded higher payments later. Local authorities, though, usually didn't do so. (If they had intended not to spend the extra money released by lower initial repayments, there would have been no point to the teaser rates.) The use of teaser rates allowed the authorities to maintain a fictitious budget balance during a period of high spending or a major public sector recruitment drive.

This practice obviously benefits a politician in office—come the election, he or she can point to past balanced budgets. Financial institutions are at least implicitly complicit with the authorities concerned; to win the business, they anticipate the officials' needs by offering deferred payment. Politicians, so quick to condemn teaser rates and subprime loans, all too often took advantage of these arrangements in their own localities. To be sure, the accounts of local governments are monitored (in France by the regional Court of Accounts [*Cour des comptes*], in the US by state comptrollers), but this supervision occurs *ex post*, often when it is too late. Some senior officials also warned French local authorities against these toxic loans, but their warnings were not always heeded. There is no simple method of public accounting,[4] and different countries have experimented with their own solutions. But it seems to me that greater transparency would help.[5]

A second problem may be more anecdotal but is nonetheless revealing. The loans to French local authorities were toxic in part because they were indexed to variables such as the exchange rate of the euro relative to the yen or the Swiss franc. For example, loans taken out by five hundred local authorities and hospitals were indexed to the Swiss franc.[6] In other words, the amount that had to be paid back depended on changes in an exchange rate that had no relation to the borrower's finances. When, on January 15, 2015, the Swiss National Bank announced it would no longer enforce the peg that held the

Swiss franc price of a euro to 1.2 or less, the value of the Swiss franc went through the roof and local authorities had to pay back loans at interest rates as high as 40 or 50 percent, when the ECB's key interest rate was virtually zero.

Were "Local Authorities Victims of Financial Speculators," as the newspaper headlines said? Yes and no. Clearly, some financial intermediaries were less than scrupulous, Dexia foremost among them. They knew exactly what they were doing when they structured these loans. These (expert) professionals were meant to sell financial products aligned with the interests of the community, not those of the elected officials with whom they were negotiating. They failed to meet their obligations, but the blame has to be shared. One can easily imagine that some political leaders without much training or experience might have been duped (although their inexperience in itself ought to have led them to be careful), but we can also assume that in other cases there was complicity with the finance departments of some local authorities, especially the biggest and therefore more sophisticated ones.[7]

On the one hand, the idea of low introductory rates followed by very high payments later on is easy to understand; on the other, even officials who are not experts in financial products should fathom that the yen or the Swiss franc bear little relation to, and therefore cannot hedge, the risks their local authority faces. Knowingly or not, local authorities used derivative products either to embellish their financial accounts in the short term, or to create a risk instead of eliminating one (the yen or Swiss franc indexation was pure roulette), or both. Local authorities fear being accused of speculation. They tend to vehemently criticize financial institutions when they lose money in financial deals, and yet boast about their own sound management when they gain from them. The irony of this episode is that the French state set up a compensation fund for local authorities, thus validating *ex post* certain lenders' lack of scruples and the complicity or incompetence of local government finance departments.

The case of these local government toxic loans is both anecdotal— at the global level, it represents only a small fraction of the money lost through the shady use of derivatives to take risks rather than to offset them—and emblematic of the agency problem. Too often, the risks of financial engineering are borne by third parties who lack information and have no control over the risk taking: the people living in a municipality, a bank's depositors, or taxpayers. In these cases, finance can rapidly become dysfunctional.

Derivatives also create asymmetries of information between prudential regulators and the banks, insurance companies, and pension funds that they monitor. Over-the-counter products[8] are complex, sometimes intentionally so. In a nutshell, the problem is how to distinguish between financial services used by agents who fully understand the risks inherent in a financial transaction and pose no danger to small savers and taxpayer funds, and those that specifically require detailed regulation. If Warren Buffet[9] wants to bet on a complex derivative or a risky enterprise, it is not a cause for concern. He is committing his own money, or that of other sophisticated investors. The founding principle for the prudential regulation of banks, insurance companies, pension funds, and financial intermediaries is the need to protect people who do not understand the complexity or the risk involved in financial products, or who are incapable of monitoring the transactions, on and off the books, made by financial intermediaries. By definition, this prudential regulation also protects public finances, as the threat of such an institution failing often leads to a bailout using public money.

ANOTHER EXAMPLE: SECURITIZATION

When the bank grants a thirty-year mortgage, it can choose to keep this loan on its books. It will continue to receive all the interest due and the repayment of the principal over the thirty years of the loan. But it can also move this loan off its books by selling the loan and its associated revenues to someone else, for example another bank or investment fund; in practice, it bundles together a number of mortgages and resells them in the form of a financial security whose dividends will come from repayments on the various component mortgage loans.

The bank can choose somewhere between these two extremes, securitizing part of its mortgage portfolio and keeping the rest on its books. The part kept on the bank's balance sheet (the keeping of which is known in financial jargon as having "skin in the game") serves to make the bank act responsibly, because it will be more careful in granting loans if it knows that it cannot transfer all the risk to others. Put differently, the issuer of a securitized bundle of loans loses its incentive to monitor the quality of the underlying loans, as it knows it will not suffer the consequences.[10] The danger is that the issuer will grant risky loans, and then seek to offload them through securitization, without the buyers being able to detect the lack of due diligence (although, arguably, the fact that the issuer doesn't want to keep the loans ought to tip them off). In fact, there is an increase of up to 20 percent in the default rate on mortgages that differ only in how easily they can be securitized![11] This is moral hazard in action.

Securitization is a well-established practice, and almost anything can be securitized: loans to SMEs, car loans, outstanding credit card debt, insurance or reinsurance contracts, and so on. What purpose does it serve? First, it gives lenders an opportunity to refinance themselves so they can invest elsewhere in the economy. Securitization makes it possible to bring "dead capital" back to life. Second, in cases where the lender's risk is particularly concentrated on one borrower, it helps the lender diversify and be less exposed to the nonrepayment of one particular loan. Thus, securitization is a very useful practice if it is used prudently—but, like derivatives, it was abused during the years preceding the crisis.

Lenders, who once retained a large proportion of their loans on their balance sheets, effectively started to transfer a significant part of the associated risk.[12] The proportion of mortgages securitized rose from 30 percent in 1995 to 80 percent in 2006. And, above all, for subprime mortgages (that is, mortgages with a high risk of not being repaid), the proportion securitized increased from 46 percent in 2001 to 81 percent in 2006. As we have seen, it is important that lenders do not disengage themselves entirely. The issuer of a loan should retain part of the risk, just as insurance companies do when they transfer part of their risks to reinsurers. Moreover, securitization increased significantly at a time when loans were becoming riskier (even though both theory and practice say banks should retain a larger part of their loans when these become riskier and therefore more subject to information asymmetries).

Furthermore, securitized assets should be accompanied by "certification" before being bought and sold on the market. This rite of passage, which occurs in many other institutions (for example, initial public offerings on the stock market), usually takes the form of a scrupulous examination by potential buyers and/or rating agencies. As we will see in the next chapter, buyers sometimes bought securitized mortgages without worrying too much about quality. They were trying to circumvent prudential capital requirements (which allowed less bank capital to be held against mortgages that were deemed to be high grade) and rating agencies underrated the risks as shown by the default of numerous AAA securities, which were supposed to be the most secure on the market. [13]

THE CHALLENGE OF NOT THROWING OUT THE BABY WITH THE BATHWATER

No financial instrument or transaction is bad in itself, provided that a) the risk is well understood by the parties using it, and b) it is not used to put a third party at risk (investors, guarantee funds, or taxpayers, for example) if that third party is unaware of its exposure. Properly used, financial instruments contribute to the dynamism of the economy. It is more constructive to engage in the inevitably technical debate about market failures and regulation than to reject wholesale the achievements of modern finance. But it is undeniable that these instruments make the supervision of the financial system more complex, that what is described as "financial innovation" is often no more than a way of getting around the rules and exposing small investors or taxpayers to major unwanted risks, and that the numerous abuses should be eliminated. There is no question of renouncing the principles of securitization or derivatives, but we need to get back to economic fundamentals in order to prevent the abuses that these practices can create.

Speculation: Myth or Reality?

There is no worse insult in the economic domain than being called a "speculator." In practice, a speculator is someone who makes bets on the financial markets. To be clear on one point right away, we are all speculators in our own way. Try the following experiment: one of your friends tells you about the harm caused by the international speculators who will not invest in Greece and refuse to lend to the Greek government at low spreads, depriving the Greek economy of oxygen (which is true). Then ask him if, in that case, he has converted or is considering converting the assets in his savings account or his retirement fund into Greek government bonds. Another example: if we buy a house expecting prices in the neighborhood to remain stable or increase by the time we resell the house, then we are making a bet on the price of an asset. We are speculating. The truth is that if we have any savings, all of us— private individuals, firms, financial institutions, or states—invest our money with the aim of at least protecting it, or even of optimizing returns (balancing risk and return depending on our appetite for risk).

The Role of Stock Markets

Let us leave for the moment the world of debt for the world of equity. What is the benefit to a company of issuing tradable shares that do not formally promise repayment, but will pay yet unspecified dividends in the future? These future dividends will be left to the discretion of the general assembly of shareholders (annual general meeting) at the recommendation of the board of directors. There are several possible benefits:

First, the fact that the payments to be made to shareholders are not specified in advance, unlike interest on debt, leaves the company more room for maneuver when it lacks cash. A temporary lack of cash flow, in this case, does not threaten the survival of the company. Of course, the other side of the coin is less pressure on managers to generate results. In the end, the level of indebtedness (or more precisely, leverage) will depend on the company's expected revenues. For example, a startup often generates little revenue for several years, and making debt repayments would stifle it. By contrast, the payment of regular coupons on debt liabilities is more suitable for a company that receives regular revenues and has little prospect of profitable new investments (for example, a major tobacco brand).[14]

The second benefit is connected, paradoxically, to the fact that shares are much riskier than bonds for their holder.[15] The yield on corporate bonds is independent of the firm's performance, at least when there is no concern about a possible bankruptcy. In contrast, shares' high sensitivity to a firm's performance leads stock market analysts to scrutinize shares more closely: Will the management team's strategy ultimately generate profits and thus dividends and capital gains? In this sense, a company's value on the stock market expresses the market's opinion about the quality of its management. It is a "noisy" opinion, to be sure: stock market values can be affected by bubbles (as we will see later) and are generally volatile. Executives may also try to inflate the stock value, especially in the short term, by strategically leaking information about the company. Despite its genuine defects, a firm's share price is a useful measure of performance, helping assess the management team's performance and affecting its tenure and possibly its remuneration (through the granting of shares and stock options). The value of a company's shares is a better measure of long-term performance than annual accounting data; remunerating executives with bonuses based on this year's profits generates excessively short-term behavior.

Finally, investments or divestments in a firm's shares, though motivated entirely by private interest, serve the interests of savers who would like to invest in the stock market. When informed financial market participants sell overvalued shares, the price of the shares falls. Small investors without any information will probably buy the shares—for example, through a mutual fund—at a price closer to their true value, and thus have a chance of not being ripped off. This financial arbitrage is one form of speculation that turns out to be useful.

Harmful Speculation

Nonetheless, there is also bad speculation, connected solely with the quest for rent seeking or even outright fraud. For example, speculation based on privileged information, such as the imminence of a merger or acquisition or a change in regulations. This is the notorious crime of insider trading. Becoming aware of future events through internal sources does not imply any useful insight—the facts become public knowledge a few days later anyway—and taking advantage of this inside information to buy (if the news is positive) or to sell (if it is negative) reflects nothing more than self-enrichment at the expense of small investors. Put differently, insider trading does not create economic value. It even destroys it, because it discourages small investors from using their savings to finance productive business.

A variant of insider trading is the manipulation of shares by a broker who receives a major buy order. Anticipating that this order will cause the share price to rise, he can buy shares in advance for himself (this is called "frontrunning") and sell them when the customer's order has been executed, for an almost instantaneous capital gain. It goes without saying that this is also illegal (which does not prevent it from happening) and is monitored by financial regulators—for example, by the Securities and Exchange Commission in the United States. But market manipulations using only public information are legal: that is what George Soros did when he sold short British pounds in 1992 to convince other investors that the currency was about to fall in value, which did in fact happen.

In addition to the many forms of fraud against which financial regulators are meant to protect investors, there is a question as to whether taking financial positions by buying and selling various assets is in itself sufficient to make markets efficient, a question to which I now turn.

ARE MARKETS EFFICIENT?

All financial crises, and not only that of 2008, raise the question of the possible irrationality of financial markets and of those who participate in them. Many phenomena, some very old and some more recent, suggest irrationality: rapid fluctuations in the prices of shares, commodities, or bonds; the sudden freezing of financial markets that had previously been very active; real estate and stock market bubbles;

the volatility of exchange rates and sovereign spreads; or the failure of financial institutions. In view of all of this, should economic analysis be based on the assumption that agents in financial markets are rational?

Before turning an economist's eye on this question, I must first emphasize that the idea that economists have unlimited confidence in the efficiency of financial markets is at least thirty years out of date. Economists mostly agree that the hypothesis of rationality is a starting point for analyzing financial markets, and that a good understanding of the price movements we observe requires a much richer conceptual framework. The dividing line between the extreme views (that financial markets are either fully efficient or wholly irrational) has given way to a subtler view of the way financial markets function, based on financial bubbles, principal-agent problems, financial panics, behavioral economics, and arbitrage frictions. These five approaches have been extensively researched over the past few decades, and call for a few comments.

FINANCIAL BUBBLES

The hypothesis of financial market efficiency is based on the view that the price of a financial asset reflects its "true" or "fundamental" value, that is, the value of its future yields, discounted by the interest rate (technically: the "present discounted value" of these future yields). A simple example will illustrate the notion of fundamental value: suppose a financial security will earn one dollar next year, one dollar the following year ... and so on, forever, and that the annual interest rate in the economy is 10 percent. In this case, the fundamental value of this asset is ten dollars: if you had ten dollars and you invested it at 10 percent interest, you would receive one dollar per year, forever.[16] Owning this asset would produce the same financial flows as owning and investing ten dollars in an alternative account.

The hypothesis that financial markets are efficient must have some truth: bad news about a business (a court judgment against it, the discovery of a technical defect in its products, the loss of a customer or a key manager) causes its share price to fall on the stock market—unless this news has been completely anticipated by the market, in which case it has already been incorporated into the price of the asset. Bad economic news about a country struggling to repay its debt increases the interest spread for new public borrowing and lowers the price of government bonds it has already issued. The price of your apartment rises if the construction of a nearby subway station is announced, and falls if city planners announce a lot of new residential construction nearby, which will make real estate less scarce.

Nonetheless, the price of a financial asset need not correspond to its true value. One reason can be the existence of a bubble. A bubble occurs when the value of a financial asset exceeds its "fundamental," that is, the present discounted value of future dividends, interest, rent, or amenities associated with holding this asset. In the example given above, an asset price over ten dollars would indicate the presence of a bubble.

There are many examples of bubbles. Take gold. Its value does not reflect the uses to which it could be put in medicine, electronics, or dentistry. To be more precise, if gold were treated as a raw material like any other, and the gold ingots held by central banks and individuals were used in industry, its price would be much lower. Consider the world's first stamp, the British Penny Black, which sells for tens of thousands of pounds, or its cousin, the Penny Red, which sells for about half a million pounds (there are only nine Penny Reds in the world: only one sheet got into circulation before the Post Office destroyed the printing plate). Such stamps create no value by themselves, either financial or aesthetic (not least because their monetary value means they are usually hidden away in a safe deposit box). Even a Picasso or a Chagall painting may be seen as a bubble: although their aesthetic value is undeniable, and in this sense they produce a "return" for the owner, this aesthetic value could be replicated for a few thousand dollars using modern technology, which can produce copies the naked eye cannot distinguish from the original.[17] Only the rarity of a postage stamp or a painting enables a bubble and allows it to reach a high price. Virtual currencies currently offer a textbook example of this phenomenon. If someday the market decides that Bitcoin has no value—if investors lose confidence in it—Bitcoin will in fact have no value, because there is no fundamental value behind it, unlike a share or real estate.

Stocks and real estate can also be subject to bubbles, that is, valuations that exceed their fundamental value. The collapse of the dot-com bubble in 2001 is an illustration, but fortunately its consequences were limited because the owners of Internet stocks were not, in contrast to the banks holding real estate assets in 2008, already heavily indebted. Real estate bubbles are very common. As Carmen Reinhart and Kenneth Rogoff have shown in their book *This Time Is Different: Eight Centuries of Financial Folly*,[18] banking and sovereign defaults often follow credit bubbles, especially in real estate.

There is a longstanding economic literature on financial bubbles. One branch of this literature studies the possibility of asset bubbles in a world in which economic agents are rational, showing that irrationality is not a precondition for the emergence of bubbles.[19] For a financial bubble to be sustained in a world of rational investors, the interest rate must not exceed the economy's growth rate,[20] as it can be shown that bubbles must grow on average at the interest rate (this is because holding the asset must, on average, produce the same yield as other assets).[21] An interest rate higher than the growth rate would imply an exponential growth of financial assets by comparison with the size of the real economy, in which case buyers of financial products would not be able to finance their acquisitions. Conversely, prolonged low interest rates are conducive to the emergence of asset bubbles.

At the microeconomic level, that is, taking assets individually, bubbles can only occur in assets with specific characteristics. The quantities of the asset available must be limited, otherwise the market would take advantage of overvaluation to produce more of it, ad infinitum, and the price would fall. A Picasso painting can be the object of a bubble; but a copy of the Picasso cannot, and its price will remain close to the cost of producing a copy (how close depends on competition in the market for quality copies).

Next, the asset must have a long time horizon. A rational bubble cannot occur in a bond that matures in one year. A rational investor never buys an overvalued asset to hold it: he would lose money compared to investing in other assets at the market interest rate! So he must resell this hot potato before the asset matures. To simplify, suppose that a bond includes only a final repayment of one hundred dollars on December 1 (such bonds are called "zero coupon bonds"), that the bonds can be traded only on the first of each month, and that the market interest rate is 0 percent. On December 1, the principal is repaid and the bond is no longer worth anything. On November 1, investors are prepared to pay one hundred dollars for the bond to receive a cash payment of one hundred dollars on December 1. On October 1, they again are willing to pay one hundred dollars for the bond, which they can resell at one hundred dollars on November 1, or else keep until it reaches maturity and receive one hundred dollars on December 1. And so on: the price of the bond at each date preceding maturity is equal to the fundamental (here, one hundred dollars).

There has also been much research into the conditions for the emergence of bubbles and on their impact.[22] To give only one example,[23] bubbles increase not only the value of the assets concerned, but also interest rates and the overall liquidity in the financial system. Moreover, bubbles, as long as they grow, raise the net worth of institutions that hold these overvalued assets and thereby allow them to increase their leverage (by issuing new debt) and to invest, and so boost the economy in that way too. However, when they burst, bubbles produce an inverse "wealth effect" by diminishing the value of the assets. Institutions holding assets involved in the bubble become short of funds. This creates a recession if they are highly indebted, as was the case in 2008, in contrast to when the dot-com bubble burst in 2001. This is a good reason for making sure that banks do not invest too much in a bubble. There are several ways of achieving this. The banking regulators can demand that banks hold larger reserves to reflect the risk that a bubble in an overvalued asset might burst. Regulators can also limit the demand for the asset concerned (in the case of real estate, for instance, requiring a minimum personal down payment in the form of a maximum loan-to-value ratio, or setting a ceiling on the ratio of the borrower's monthly mortgage payment to their income).

Important empirical work suggests the existence of bubbles in financial markets. In particular, Robert Shiller, who won the 2013 Nobel Prize for economics, has repeatedly issued warnings (not always heeded) about bubbles.[24] It is not easy, however, to detect a bubble. One method currently used (particularly in Shiller's pioneering work) takes inspiration from the divergence between fundamental value and the bubble: it compares the price of the asset with the dividends or other benefits that can be derived from it. For example, we can compare the cost of purchasing a real estate asset to its rental income. To be sure, owners may attach a value to living in their own home and altering it as they wish (conversely, some people prefer not to have to deal with the hassles of being an owner). And tax considerations also play a role. Even so, if the price exceeds the present value of the rents, there may be a bubble.[25]

To make the price and the rental income comparable requires, in principle, making assumptions about future rental rates and interest rates so as to compute the present discounted value of future rental incomes. But in practice, researchers often just look at the evolution of the ratio between price and rent, which can be instructive. For example, the price-rent ratio almost doubled in France between 1998 and 2006 (see figure 11.1), and today it is still much closer to the 2006 level than to the 1998 level. In fact, real estate is much

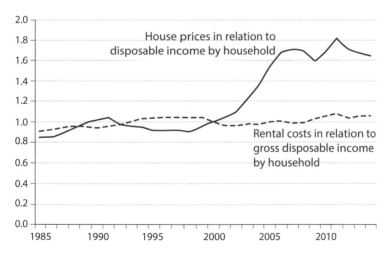

Figure 11.1. Relationship between price and rent in France, 1985–2014.
Source: Guillaume Chapelle, on the basis of data provided by the
Conseil général de l'environnement et du développement durable.

more expensive in France than in Germany, whereas it was the other way around until 2003. The price-revenue ratio is today 25 to 30 percent higher in France than in Germany. The regulators should be monitoring the solvency of financial intermediaries exposed to French real estate risk.

For shares, we can similarly look at the price-earnings ratio. A very high ratio suggests a bubble. There are again many complications: we need to have a view about future dividends (which are analogous to the path of rents in the real estate case) and the interest rate used to discount future dividends to calculate their present value. And again we can focus on the price-dividend ratio for simplicity. In 1981, Robert Shiller noticed that the price of stocks fluctuated far too much in relation to changes in dividends—that is, the fundamental value—thus suggesting the existence of a bubble varying over time.

Agency Problems: The Divergence between Individual and Collective Interest

The second perspective on the efficiency of financial markets distinguishes between individual and collective rationality. The agents in an economic system can behave rationally from their own point of view, but the result can be harmful from the point of view of the group. This classic theme in the economics of regulation has cropped up repeatedly in this book.

Consider a risky asset to which a bank is highly exposed. If things go well, the asset will produce a high yield and the bank's shareholders will receive a lot of money. If things go badly, the asset will lose part of its value, shareholders will receive nothing, and the bank's creditors, and perhaps also its employees and borrowers (the SMEs who depend on relationship lending from the bank) will suffer. This is a negative externality affecting all the stakeholders. Moreover, the bank might be able to continue borrowing, despite the risk, if lenders think the government will bail out the bank if it gets into difficulties. In this case, the divergence between individual interest and collective interest is even greater. To repeat the old adage, profits are privatized and losses socialized.

The possibility of relying on the taxpayer also explains behavior that seems irrational at first glance. Before the euro crisis, many buyers of Greek government bonds understood that Greece was not as secure as Germany, but they were convinced that Germany and other Eurozone countries would come to Greece's aid if there was a problem. Logically, they accepted very low interest rates on these bonds, rates close to those prevailing on *Bunds* (German treasury bills).

Similarly, it may not seem obvious that Richard Fuld, the CEO of Lehman Brothers, the investment bank that failed in 2008, acted rationally when, at a point when his bank was on the point of collapse, he bought even more subprime products. The toxicity of these products was well known by then. Nor does it seem logical that he was able to continue borrowing on financial markets in order to do so. But many investors who continued to lend to Lehman Brothers were counting on a federal government bailout to prevent it from failing.[26] Maintaining its access to financial markets enabled Lehman to take on more risks in the hope of keeping its head above water when it had nothing left to lose. Just as a soccer team that is losing 2-0 in the final fifteen minutes of a game takes all kinds of risks even if that means it might lose 4-0, Lehman had—like every institution in distress—an incentive to take on risk to increase, if only slightly, the probability that it would pull through. In the case of the soccer game, the 4-0 loss does little harm, except to the players' self-esteem; indeed, the club's supporters will approve this risk taking. In contrast, the bank's "gambling for resurrection" strategy is not exactly in the interest of creditors or employees.

The system of remuneration is another cause of dysfunction connected to the problem of agency. Whether due to complicity between the executives and the remuneration committee, or to the often-stated desire to attract and retain the best talent, bonuses strongly encourage short-term behavior of the kind we saw before the 2008 financial crisis. (In the next chapter, I will return to the question of remuneration and its regulation.)

As a final example of the difference between individual and collective interest, high-frequency trading is rational at the level of the institution engaging in it, but its value to society is unclear. Today, financial institutions spend considerable sums on computing and communications infrastructure so they can execute orders a fraction of a second faster than their competitors. Computers react instantaneously to news about financial markets (prices, for example) and execute orders in milliseconds, before rivals can take advantage of the same possibilities of arbitrage between the prices of different assets. It is not obvious what social gain this speed of execution produces. Many people are now calling for a waiting period, so that buy and sell orders are executed only after a slight and uncertain delay. This will put an end to this high-frequency arms race, which is a zero-sum game.[27]

Financial regulation seeks to reduce the divergence between individual interest and collective interest. It comes up against problems of information, however. Whole areas of the economics literature have been devoted to what the jargon calls "agency problems," that is, economic agents' ability to take advantage of asymmetries of information. These asymmetries of information complicate the monitoring of fund managers by investors, of traders by their bank, or of financial institutions and rating agencies by their prudential supervisors.

Hypertrophied Financial Sector

Every aspect of finance was growing before the crisis. Economists Thomas Philippon and Ariell Reshef have studied the changing nature of employment in finance.[28] They have shown, in particular, that financial deregulation has changed the makeup of jobs, which have become more highly skilled. But for a given level of education and skills, there was also a 50 percent increase in salaries between 1990 and 2006. The share of financial intermediation in the economy grew rapidly between 1980 and 2006,[29] and this phenomenon has been particularly striking in the US and the UK. This hypertrophy (excessive growth) in finance has been fueled by profits that are "too easy," attracting the well educated to the sector. As we will see in chapter 12, the authorities have turned a blind eye to risk taking and (legal) evasion of regulatory requirements, as in the case of the off-balance-sheet vehicles that allowed banks to invest with almost no funds of their own. And, of course, the safety net provided by the taxpayer has greatly encouraged risk taking, which generates very large profits as long as everything is going well. Problems of agency were thus the source of the excessive growth in the finance sector during the 1990s and 2000s.

FINANCIAL PANICS

Another potential inefficiency of financial markets is the possibility of investors acting collectively in a way that has negative consequences.[30] I touched on this subject in the previous chapter when discussing sovereign debt crises in Europe. Bank runs are another striking example (the reader might recall the humorous but apt description of the start of a banking panic in Walt Disney's film *Mary Poppins*[31]).

An essential characteristic of bank intermediation is the activity of maturity transformation, described earlier, of short-term deposits into long-term loans. If the depositors all start withdrawing their money at the same time, the bank is forced to liquidate its assets (its loans to firms) to honor depositors' demands. If these assets are not very liquid, that is, if they cannot be very quickly resold at their fair value,[32] their prices drop; the bank records losses and may not have enough money to repay its depositors. All depositors then have an incentive to rush to withdraw funds from the bank while they still can. This is known as a self-fulfilling prophecy, because in these circumstances the bank may be sound but still fail: individual rationality adds up to collective irrationality.

Today, lines of people waiting in front of banks thought to be on the brink of collapse have practically disappeared, because retail banks now have access to deposit insurance on the one hand, and to liquidity provided by the central bank on the other hand, giving them time to sell their assets at reasonable prices. The world was astonished to see lines of customers outside branches of the British bank Northern Rock in September 2007 (it was the first time since 1866 that there had been a depositor run on a British bank). The reason was that the United Kingdom's deposit insurance was ill conceived: it guaranteed 100 percent of the first £2,000 and 90 percent of the following £33,000. But any deposit insurance that covers less than

100 percent of the total can lead depositors to withdraw their money at the slightest rumor (in comparison, deposit insurance now covers €100,000 in Europe and $250,000 in the United States, in both cases at 100 percent).

Nowadays, bank runs no longer involve small-time (retail) depositors, but only big-time (wholesale) depositors who are not covered by deposit insurance schemes: this means corporate depositors, wealthy households, and participants in the interbank market and the money market (the market in short-term loans). In fact, looking beyond the media's interest in a bank run involving small-time depositors, Northern Rock's problem was that it had raised three-quarters of its funds on the wholesale market (not from retail deposits), funds which were not insured, and were also often very short term and therefore prone to a run.

Whereas the insurance schemes in each country protect the deposits of small depositors, the provision of liquidity by the central bank is meant to protect banks against the withdrawal of large deposits—though in a less automatic fashion. Traditionally, a bank lacking liquidity can borrow, short term and against collateral, from its central bank. In the crisis of 2008, many other mechanisms supplemented this traditional liquidity provision. Later, Eurozone banks were able to refinance themselves over the longer term (three years) with the ECB, thanks to Long Term Refinancing Operations (LTRO). The ECB also bought from them government bonds that had become risky on the secondary market (Outright Money Transactions, or OMT). However they do it, the central banks allow banks to buy time. If the problem is a pure shortage of liquidity, as in a bank run, the bank has more time to sell its assets at a reasonable price. If the problem is more serious and stems from the quality of the bank's balance sheet, then more drastic steps have to be taken to improve its management and reduce its risks.

Perverse coordination can also occur in the case of sovereign debt, through a different mechanism. Suppose a country is able to repay a loan if it is contracted at the market interest rate (that is, without any or with very little spread). If investors nonetheless think this country might default, they will rationally demand a higher interest rate to compensate for the risk. As a result, repaying the debt is more costly, implying in turn a higher budget deficit, increased debt, and a greater risk of default. In turn, this may increase the concern felt by investors, who will reasonably be likely to demand even higher interest rates, and so on. There can be an equilibrium of distrust, rather than of trust. Again, this is a case of individual rationality and collective irrationality.

The provision of liquidity to a country is more complex than providing it to a bank, and in practice we see many approaches. In Europe, the ECB has played the role of provider of liquidity across the Eurozone since the statement made by its governor, Mario Draghi, on July 26, 2012: "Within our mandate, the ECB is ready to do whatever it takes to preserve the euro." More generally, countries can turn to the IMF to obtain liquidity and bring in other investors in exchange for conditions imposed on the country's finances. In addition, instead of proceeding *ex post*, after the difficulties have been acknowledged, a country can establish early lines of credit either with consortiums of international banks or with the IMF.

Behavioral Finance

"Behavioral finance" aims to incorporate into the analysis of financial markets cognitive biases and other departures from the model of the rational agent (behavioral economics incorporating psychology into economic analysis has progressed more generally during the past two decades).[33] In this case, it is not necessarily a question of the contrast between individual rationality and collective irrationality, but rather of better understanding individual "irrationality." There are too many aspects of this to cover in detail here: overoptimism (for example, the tendency of fund managers to think they are better than their colleagues), limited attention and—at the same time—excessive attention to certain types of risks,[34] erroneous beliefs (due to poor comprehension of Bayes's law or to certain other biases), aversion to losses, endogenous morality (due to the existence of room for maneuver over what is socially acceptable), and more.

There is both empirical and theoretical research in this domain. In terms of empirical results, researchers have documented a large number of small anomalies in the pricing of assets, which are not always "arbitraged": agents are not aware of some correlations or causal links, or they categorize assets in groups that are too crude. Here we see the subtle distinction between rationality (agents are rational, but make a trade-off between more sophisticated analysis and the cost of undertaking this analysis) and irrationality (agents have an incorrect understanding of the financial environment).

To give only one example of the theoretical research, I will mention the work of Roland Bénabou (a professor at Princeton) on the persistent state of denial that has, in his view, been instrumental in creating a collective illusion regarding subprime loans.[35] Bénabou incorporates emotions (such as anxiety) that are created by high stakes and uncertainty; for example, we all prefer not to think about stressful prospects. An agent may be induced by his or her emotions to ignore real hazards, even at the price of making bad decisions. Human memory and attention are limited and malleable, which makes it possible to update our beliefs in a biased way: encoding (the transformation of information so it can be stored into memory) and selective forgetting of the signals received, post hoc rationalization, and so on. These hypotheses are based on many empirical studies that draw attention to the fact that we treat good and bad news asymmetrically, or even prefer not to know the truth.[36]

Bénabou also systematically examines how the nature of economic or social interactions between agents shapes the patterns of thinking emerging in general equilibrium. This analysis of "groupthink" shows that a whole community can be involved in a contagious denial of reality.[37] The results help explain the recurrent cases of enterprises, institutions, or political regimes that self-destruct through collective blindness. This blindness is at the heart of the book (and the film) *The Big Short: Inside the Doomsday Machine*, to which I will return below.

FRICTIONS IN FINANCIAL MARKETS

Differences in analysis. Finally, a particularly active area of research over the past thirty years concerns the difficulty of arriving at the "right" price in a financial market in which information is not uniformly disseminated. This research has its source in the works published in 1970 by George Akerlof, winner with Michael Spence and Joseph Stiglitz of the Nobel Prize in 2001 for their contributions to information theory. In brief, we do not want—or at least we should not want, in our own interest—to trade with someone who is better informed than we are, unless the gains from that exchange would be very large. Suppose, for example, that I offer to sell you a financial security whose true value I alone know (we are not in frequent contact, so that there is no trust established between us). The security could yield fifty dollars or one hundred dollars with equal probability. Should you be prepared to pay seventy-five dollars? You should think about it in the following way: if the true value of this security is one hundred dollars, then I would keep it for myself rather than selling it to you for seventy-five. You should not be willing to pay seventy-five dollars because, if I am willing to sell it for less than one hundred dollars, it is a signal that the security must be of poor quality, and therefore is worth fifty dollars. In this example, the price will be fifty dollars, because you know I will only sell you the security if it has low value, is a "lemon." This reasoning seems complicated when you are not used to it. But professionals are well acquainted with this phenomenon, whether they deduced it or learned it through painful experience.[38]

Whenever there are asymmetries of information among the participants, financial markets are not as liquid as they should be. Sometimes they even freeze up entirely: we say "there is no longer a price in the market." To be precise, there are no longer any transactions in the market, because the only prices that could generate transactions would not be acceptable to the sellers. Thus, many markets disappeared from one day to the next during the 2008 crisis.[39] More generally, studies of the microstructure of financial markets emphasize the information frictions that prevent these markets from operating as smoothly as the efficient market theory predicts.

The limits to arbitrage. Market prices can fail to reflect correctly the information available about the true value of assets if those who have the information do not have the necessary financial resources to trade on a large scale. Some people may be aware that certain assets are undervalued or overvalued, but they may be unable to act on the information (which, if they did, would tend to correct the pricing error) because they lack the cash to do so. Today, we understand the "limits of arbitrage" a little better (in general, it is due to the problems of agency already mentioned, which prevent those who have the information from raising the necessary funds to arbitrage the difference between price and true value), although our knowledge of this subject would be worth refining further.

A good illustration of this phenomenon is found in the book (and film) *The Big Short*, where a group of financial traders sell the real estate bubble "short." They were convinced that financial assets whose return depended on the repayment of risky mortgages were overvalued, and that the rating agencies had not done their work properly when giving these assets investment grade ratings. Selling a security short means promising to deliver the counterparty a given quantity of the security concerned at a given future date (in a month, in six months, or whenever) without actually owning it now. If the value of the security falls before that time, the seller makes a capital gain when buying the security for cash to make good on their commitment; the counterparty, who is now holding a security that has lost value, loses out. If, on the other hand, the value of the security rises, the short seller loses money. And if the short seller doesn't have enough money and goes bankrupt, the counterparty does not receive the profit it should have received. Hence in such a contract, as in many loan contracts, the counterparty requires the seller to deposit collateral, here called a "margin call." The problem for arbitragers is that even if they are correct and the security is overvalued, they do not know when this will be corrected. So long as the correction does not occur (that is, as long as the price does not fall), their counterparties constantly demand more collateral to cover themselves, and short sellers run out of money before their bet proves right. That is what happens in *The Big Short*, where the arbitragers' diagnosis of subprimes is confirmed, but the price correction is so slow in coming that they come within a hair's breadth of losing their whole investment.[40]

WHY REGULATE IN FACT?

Financial regulation has two components: regulating stock exchanges and financial markets, and monitoring the solvency of financial institutions. These two tasks often involve different regulators (in the US, the Securities and Exchange Commission and the Federal Reserve; in the UK, the Financial Conduct Authority and the Prudential Regulatory Authority). The purpose of market regulation is to avoid harmful behavior in the financial markets in order to protect investors from being manipulated and swindled.

Prudential regulation, on the other hand, concerns primarily the solvency of financial intermediaries. Its primary goal is to protect badly informed creditors (depositors, insurees, and savers, for example) in their dealings with financial intermediaries (banks, insurance companies, and pension funds). To the extent that the government may have to bail out financial intermediaries that are in difficulty (especially large institutions such as Bear Stearns or RBS), its task is to protect taxpayers' money too.[41] The prudential authority's principal responsibility is thus to represent the interests of small investors.[42]

The second main function of prudential regulation is to limit domino effects, known as "systemic risk." This refers to fears that the failure of one financial institution might cause contagion as other institutions lose money on the loans they made to the first institution, or when the distressed institution sells assets at fire-sale prices in a saturated market. This regulatory aim may coincide with the first, because the supervisors want to avoid domino effects involving commercial banks and other regulated institutions, but it has a broader significance in terms of maintaining the integrity of the financial system as a whole. This second justification of systemic stability is also invoked when rescuing an institution that does not have small depositors, such as an investment bank. For example, in 2008, even though neither had any small depositors, the financial conglomerate AIG (American International Group) and the investment bank Bear Stearns were bailed out by the US government because their default could have had a systemic impact.

To understand the philosophy of banking regulation, it is useful to closely examine an earlier international regulatory framework, which has now been superseded. In the 1980s, the international community tried to limit a regulatory race to the bottom, whereby countries could enable their banks to expand rapidly internationally without sufficient equity of their own, or by going into excessive debt. In the case of retail banks (also called "commercial banks"), the regulation that emerged from the 1988 Basel Accord, known as Basel I, required every bank to have enough capital (its own equity) to make it highly probable that it could cover the risks of loss. This minimal level of equity capital was standardized among countries.

The rules governing the capitalization of banks have to achieve a compromise. On the one hand, banks must be sufficiently capitalized to ensure that the small saver (or more often the taxpayer) does not suffer when it sustains losses. On the other hand, equity standards that are too severe can make credit scarce and prevent financial intermediaries from fulfilling their economic mission: for example, banks should be financing businesses (and particularly SMEs) so they can invest, and providing liquidity for firms and markets.

Greater regulatory rigor also requires monitoring the development of the "shadow" financial sector (which theoretically has no right to either deposit insurance or to access to central bank liquidity). This migration of activities out of the regulated banking sector (which we currently see in "shadow banking" in China) is likely to pose problems in the future, just as was the case, as we shall see, with the five great investment banks (Lehman, Bear Stearns, Merrill Lynch, Goldman Sachs, and Morgan Stanley) in 2008. They were monitored by a grand total of six people.

Table 11.1 shows an extremely simplified balance sheet for a retail bank, that is, a bank centered essentially on the traditional activities of making loans to individuals and to small and medium-sized enterprises on the assets side, and taking deposits on the liabilities side.

The first international agreement on minimum prudential standards, the Basel I accord described above, focused on the risk of default, requiring that a bank's lending be backed by enough of its own funds (equity capital), the amount depending on the riskiness of its loans.

Table 11.1. Simplified Balance Sheet of a Retail Bank

Assets	Liabilities
Loans to small businesses	Own funds (common stocks, retained earnings)
Mortgage loans to households	Supplementary capital: general loan loss reserves, hybrid debts that count as capital ("tier 2"); subordinated debts, convertible bonds, preferred stock
Other assets (loans on the money market, financial market investments)	Uninsured deposits (say, individuals over €100,000, small businesses, borrowing on the money market)
Secure assets (treasury bonds, government loans, etc.)	Insured deposits (say, individuals up to €100,000)

Note: To calculate the capital needed on the right-hand side of the balance sheet, the amount called "basic" or "tier 1" (common stocks plus undistributed profits) was distinguished from those funds called "complementary" or "tier 2" (for instance, bank's debts that are relatively stable, such as long-term subordinated debt or hybrid securities). Tier 1 capital was supposed to constitute at least half of the total (thus at least 4 percent of the value of the weighted assets).

For example, a secure loan (such as holding a treasury bond) required no capital to be held against it, while a loan to a private company had to be backed by eight cents of equity capital per dollar of loan. More generally, each element of the bank's assets was given a weight between zero and one: 0.2 for a relatively safe loan to a local authority or another bank, 0.5 for a mortgage loan secured on property,[43] and 1 for loans to businesses and other riskier securities. The total amount of reserves a bank needed to hold had to amount to at least 8 percent of its total liabilities, weighted by risks in this way. So, for instance, a loan to a local authority had to be backed by 1.6 cents of capital.

Regulators knew, however, that this system implied major limits on their understanding of banks' risks. Capital requirements did not differentiate between loans to businesses according to their quality (as captured by, for example, their ratings). Nor did the rules involve a measure of the available liquidity. The capital requirements also ignored market risks and the correlations between markets. Indeed, the formula to calculate capital requirements was simply additive: the total requirement was obtained simply by adding up the capital required for every loan; no attempt was made to measure the correlations between the risks (the correlations usually stemming from macroeconomic factors, such as fluctuations in interest rates, exchange rates, counterparties, real estate prices, and so on). Were they offsetting or in fact amplifying each other? Ignoring this question created incentives for banks to take correlated positions so as to make their balance sheet riskier, especially if they were already in difficulties.[44]

The next set of regulations at the international level (Basel II), was conceived in the 1990s and implemented by 2007. It was intended to be more precise in its measurement of risk. First of all, it allowed banks to use the ratings of certified agencies to adjust their capital requirements according to the quality of the various financial assets.[45] In the same spirit, Basel II enabled the use of "mark-to-market" values, that is, measuring the current value of some of the bank's assets by applying the values of similar assets traded on sufficiently liquid markets. (The traditional method of accounting—in "historical costs"—was to register them at their purchase value, and not to revise this figure except in the case of a serious event, usually the borrower's default.)

Finally, Basel II authorized (large) banks to use regulator-approved internal models to measure their total risks and thus the capital requirements, allowing the regulator to intervene by requiring the bank to raise more capital or restrict certain activities when the signals turned red. A structured dialogue between the supervisors and the banks on their watch was organized in the framework of what was called "Pillar 2" (Pillar 1 being capital requirements, modified as described above). Finally, "Pillar 3" increased the transparency of banks' activities to the market, so that market forces would limit lending to a fragile bank (of course, this monitoring by the market does not work if participants anticipate that the bank will be bailed out by the state, such that lending to the bank is implicitly guaranteed).

The transition from Basel I to Basel II illustrates the classical dilemma between opting for mechanical rules and greater flexibility. Basel I set up a system of mechanical requirements for capital reserves, requirements that were often distant from economic reality. But Basel I's rigidity limited manipulations. Basel II allowed the banks much more flexibility, which enabled them to make a better evaluation of the risks if the process had integrity, but required stricter supervision to be effective. Internal models, even if validated by bank supervisors, create degrees of freedom for less scrupulous banks. Banks have private information, and they can deceive a regulator regarding how big their risks really are. Similarly, the extensive use of ratings only works if the rating agencies do not collude with the industry in a way that leads to ratings inflation.

Economic theory suggests a few commonsense rules. Any increase in the flexibility of supervision must have as its counterpart a greater distance between those doing the evaluating (the rating agencies, the regulators) and the entities being evaluated (the banks). Greater flexibility increases the stakes for those who are supervised, and thus increases the danger of pressure on or complicity with the regulators. Conversely, if we fear for the integrity of supervision and evaluation, we will have to return to mechanical rules.[46]

TWELVE
The Financial Crisis of 2008

It's awful. Why did nobody see it coming?
—Her Majesty Queen Elizabeth II[1]

The financial crisis of 2008 has had lasting effects on economic output and employment. Although economic growth has now returned to normal in the United States, with unemployment down to 5 percent and economic confidence restored, it took many years for output to recover to its precrisis level. Europe—admittedly struggling with other difficulties in addition to the financial crisis—is stuck in a complex economic situation with large-scale unemployment in the countries of southern Europe. The crisis has also placed a heavy burden on public finances, diminishing the ability of governments to intervene in any future crises.

August 9, 2007, was the date of the first intervention by the Federal Reserve and the European Central Bank. No one that day—economists included—remotely imagined that whole swaths of the banking system were going to be bailed out by governments. Or that five of the largest investment banks would disappear in their existing form (Lehman and Bear Stearns disappeared completely, Merrill Lynch was bought by the Bank of America, and Goldman Sachs and Morgan Stanley survived by asking to become regulated retail banks in order to receive liquidity assistance). Nor could anyone have predicted that successful commercial franchises like Citigroup, the Royal Bank of Scotland, and Union Bank of Switzerland (UBS) would need government support as a result of foolish risk taking; that an insurance company and two institutions guaranteeing real estate loans would receive around $350 billion from the US government; that a little more than a year later, the US government would have committed the equivalent of 50 percent of its GDP to the recovery efforts; that US and European governments would loan substantial sums directly to industry; or that central banks would use unconventional monetary policies, enter into an era of extremely low interest rates, and go far beyond their mandate by supporting governments.

In Europe, the UK, Belgium, Spain, Iceland, and Ireland all experienced massive banking problems.[2] Some other countries, such as France, the Scandinavians, and Japan, fared relatively well in this context, although some of their banks benefited from the US taxpayer bailouts of institutions such as AIG, to which they were exposed. Was this relative stability due to the lessons learned from earlier errors, which led in the 1990s to the bankruptcy of Crédit Lyonnais in France and widespread banking crises in the others?

What caused the financial crisis? Have we learned its lessons? Are we safe from another? To tackle these questions, I will begin with an analysis of its causes before discussing the postcrisis situation. Finally, I will examine the responsibilities and role of economists in preventing crises. This chapter, which is a little more technical than the others, is also the only one that is not completely stand-alone: reading the preceding chapter, though not essential, would be advisable.

THE FINANCIAL CRISIS

There are many excellent accounts of the economic crisis,[3] and here I can touch only briefly on the subject. One thing is for sure: the 2008 crisis is a textbook case for the theory of information and incentives courses taught in economics departments. At every link in the chain of transfers of risk, one of the parties had more information than the other (asymmetry of information), and this distorted the proper functioning of financial markets and their regulation.

Market failures due to asymmetries of information are a constant, although the introduction of new and often complex financial instruments, and participants' and regulators' lack of familiarity with them, certainly made the information failures worse. So we cannot explain the crisis by this cause alone. There were two other factors contributing to the market failures. First, inadequate regulation and a laxity in enforcement—especially in the US, where the crisis originated, but also in Europe—created incentives to take risks, ultimately at the expense of the public. Second, market failures and lax regulation had a bigger impact because the context had never been so favorable to taking risks.

An Excess of Liquidity and a Real Estate Bubble

Crises often have their origin in a lack of discipline during good times. The Federal Reserve's maintenance of abnormally low interest rates for several years early in the new century provided very cheap liquidity—at times the short-term rate was 1 percent. When combined with investors' desire to find yields superior to the low market interest rates, this monetary policy fed the real estate boom.[4]

What's more, in the decade before 2008, there was an influx of money looking for investment opportunities to the US. Financial markets in the United States are highly developed. They create many tradeable securities, which makes them attractive for people with money to invest. Some of the surplus savings from sovereign wealth funds in the Middle East and Asia, plus foreign exchange reserves accumulated by export surplus countries (such as China) were invested in the United States because they could not be recycled in their own financial markets. This international savings glut enabled financial intermediaries to invest in real estate. In turn, this strong demand for securities, along with favorable regulatory treatment not corrected until after the crisis, encouraged the securitization of debt. These macroeconomic conditions created a permissive environment that encouraged actors to plunge into the breaches created by market and regulatory failures.

Abundant liquidity and low interest rates led to a big increase in risky real estate loans granted to US households with only limited ability to repay them;[5] these loans usually had a very low fixed interest rate for the first two years, followed by a variable interest rate with a high margin levied by the lenders. The lenders also often failed to verify the information (for example, about income) provided by prospective borrowers.[6] The subsequent stagnation in real estate prices, which precluded the easy refinancing associated with rising property values, and a rise in interest rates in the mid-2000s led to defaults on these loans with upward-varying interest rates. Many households simply could no longer make their loan payments, whereas others, protected by American personal bankruptcy laws, decided to walk away from their loans when the market value of their houses fell below the outstanding balance on their mortgage. The danger posed by risky real estate loans was thus that a macroeconomic downturn might lead to repossessions, the eviction of property owners, and major losses for lenders when the property was put back up for sale on the market. The losses suffered by lenders were all the greater because other lenders were doing the same thing, leading to a decline in real estate prices.[7]

What was the US government's reaction to this real estate lending? It took the same political decision that led to a banking crisis in some other countries (like Spain at the same time). The US administration encouraged more households to become home owners. During the 2000s, the government let the real estate bubble inflate, and, more damaging, allowed its banks to become exposed to it. It would have been better to reduce the tax subsidies available for home purchase (the tax deductibility of interest paid on real estate loans) and the implicit guarantees on home loans provided by semipublic agencies such as Freddie Mac and Fannie Mac. It would have been advisable to impose stricter borrowing criteria, such as capping the real estate loan-to-value ratio and the borrower's annual debt repayment-to-income ratio. But the political imperative won out.

Of course, risky lending made it possible for less well-off people to become home owners. But many of these households lacked a proper understanding of the risks they ran if interest rates went up, or if real estate prices stalled, preventing them from taking out a new loan to cope with higher payments. Institutions making real estate loans have always played on households' desire to own property to sell risky mortgage contracts. At a minimum, the US federal government should have helped ensure that there was symmetric information between lenders and borrowers about the risks, since few states regulated the conditions on mortgages or discouraged abusive practices.

The government can tackle the asymmetry of information between lenders and borrowers by giving additional information to borrowers, whose freedom of choice is then respected. Alternatively, borrowers can be protected in a more "paternalistic" way, although there are some dangers inherent in this approach. The justification for paternalism is that people yield to temptation and tend to overconsume compared to what they would choose in a cooler state of mind. This rationale underlies some kinds of policy interventions (see chapter 5). From this point of view, the state should set ceilings on the loan-to-value ratio on a property and on the borrower's annual debt-repayment-to-income ratio and prohibit seemingly attractive "teaser rate" loans with very low promotional interest rates during their early years.

Excessive Securitization

Recall that good securitization requires two conditions: 1) the bank making the loans must keep skin in the game (i.e., enough of the risk of nonrepayment) on its own books to encourage it to monitor their quality, and 2) the rating agencies evaluating the investment quality of the loan portfolios must find it to their advantage to do due diligence. In the last chapter we saw that prior to the financial crisis banks retained too small a proportion of the risk to have enough of an incentive to grant only good loans.

In the United States, rating agencies are essential actors in the process of securitization.[8] Recall that banks' equity capital requirements depend on the riskiness of their assets. After 2004, when the Basel II accord was implemented in the United States, the banks were able to measure this risk using assessments made by the rating agencies. If a bank buys a securitized product, it will need to hold much less equity capital if the rating of the product is AAA than if it is BB. It is essential for government regulators to be able to trust the rating agencies, which are truly auxiliary regulators.

The main problem at the time was that the rating agencies were giving AAA ratings to securitized products that were much riskier than the AAA bonds issued by businesses or local authorities. Was this due to unfamiliarity with the securities—or due to a conflict of interest? It's hard to say, but the agencies' incentives were not fully aligned with the regulators' objectives. The agencies received fees proportional to the value of securitized assets issued, thus creating an incentive to give higher ratings (just as if our salaries as professors increased with the grades we give our students' papers). The desire to keep happy the investment banks that were major clients of the rating agencies was also part of the problem.

Excessive Transformation

As the last chapter explained, a bank borrows short term to lend long term. This can expose it to a bank run, in which the bank's depositors, fearing that it might turn into an empty shell, all try to withdraw their money at the same time. In the years before the crisis, many financial intermediaries—not only retail banks—took substantial risks by borrowing very short term on wholesale markets (the interbank and money markets). This strategy is profitable as long as short-term interest rates remain very low, but it exposes the bank to a rise in interest rates if it has not covered itself against this risk. If the interest rate is 1 percent and rises to 4 percent, the financing costs of an institution that is financed almost exclusively using short term borrowing (as was the case for the vehicles created to securitize real estate loans) roughly quadruples.

Banks that have no retail deposits are particularly exposed to this risk (since the introduction of deposit insurance, individuals' deposits are very safe and therefore not subjects to runs). As we have seen, the five big US investment banks either went bankrupt or teamed up with retail banks to get support from the government. But retail banks, whose funding is, a priori, more stable than that of investment banks, had also increased their reliance on short-term wholesale funds.

This generalized risk taking through substantial maturity transformation puts the monetary authorities in a delicate situation. Either they do not act on interest rates to keep them low, in which case the financial system may collapse, or they keep interest rates artificially low and then indirectly bail out the vulnerable institutions. If they bail out these institutions, they validate the risky behavior, creating costs that I will explain below. Thus, the excessive transformation of short-term funds to long-term lending trapped the monetary authorities. This was particularly clear immediately after the crisis. (The problems today are different. This is true both for the central banks, which cannot make interest rates fall much below zero—because if they did, economic agents would prefer to hold cash, which would at least give them a zero interest rate, ignoring transaction costs—and for the banks, which suffer from low yields across all maturities.)

A Way of Getting around Regulatory Requirements for Equity Capital

Regulated financial institutions (retail banks, insurance companies, pension funds, brokers) are subject to requirements regarding the minimum level of equity capital, as explained in the last chapter. For banks, the Basel accords set out the general principles at the international level. The idea is to maintain a buffer, the bank's "capital," which makes it likely that the bank can absorb most risks it faces. This protects the depositors' insurer, the deposit insurance fund, and, if public funds are employed to bail out the bank, the taxpayer. For a given size of its balance sheet, the bank, on the contrary, has an interest in reducing its equity capital (or even, in extreme cases, minimizing it to match the regulatory requirement). In effect, holding less equity capital means a higher return for the shareholders who provide it.

The supervisors in charge of financial regulation have a complicated task. For one thing, bank balance sheets and financial techniques are continually evolving; for another, supervisors have limited means to carry out their supervisory tasks or to attract the most talented staff (who have the choice of working instead for the regulated institutions, insurance companies, investment banks, or rating agencies). The supervisors' task is also complicated when they compete with each other. Prior to the crisis, banks in the United States could sometimes choose their regulator by defining their principal activity in order to obtain the most lenient supervision (for example, selecting "real estate" meant they would face a less intrusive regulator). Incidentally, the

very fear of a regulatory race to the bottom in terms of equity requirements by national regulators motivated the Basel accords, which set
an international minimum standard.

Before the crisis, many financial institutions exploited the flaws
in the regulators' analysis of their risks to understate their need for
capital and thus increase the return on their own equity capital. For
example, they made loans requiring little capital to be held against
them to vehicles containing assets they had themselves securitized,[9]
even though the risk for the financial institutions was equivalent to
what it would have been if they had left the securitized loans on their
balance sheets; put more simply, moving mortgages from the balance
sheet to another entity, which it insured against refinancing problems
through a line of credit, reduced the bank's capital requirement substantially. In the end, the regulators were unable to, or didn't know
how to, restrain such dangerous behavior.

EXCESSIVELY VAGUE BOUNDARIES OF THE REGULATED SPHERE AND A SOMETIMES-UNHEALTHY MIXTURE OF PUBLIC AND PRIVATE

Simply put, the prudential regulation of banks involves give and take.
Retail banking is supervised, involving equity capital requirements
and other constraints. In exchange, it gets access to central bank
liquidity and to deposit insurance, two factors limiting its exposure to
risk. Deposit insurance dissuades small depositors from fleeing if its
financial difficulties become public. Thanks to the central bank's provision of liquidity, the retail bank can calmly choose between selling
assets at a reasonable price and reconstituting its own funds by issuing
new equity. Unregulated banks (known as "shadow banks"—investment banks, hedge funds, money market funds, and private equity
firms) do not have this privilege. At least, not in theory.

The 2008 crisis showed that failure to regulate the mutual exposure
of the regulated and unregulated sectors can compel the authorities to
rescue unregulated entities by pouring in capital, buying up assets, or
simply keeping interest rates low. So the unregulated sector had access
to the taxpayers' money and central bank liquidity without having

to submit to the discipline of prudential supervision. This interdependence between the regulated and unregulated sectors is illustrated by the debate about the US authorities' refusal to rescue Lehman Brothers in 2008. Taxpayers' money had already been used to save another investment bank, Bear Stearns.[10] A few days after Lehman Brothers went bankrupt, the US government also bailed out another large unregulated entity, AIG, a large insurance company that had become, de facto, an investment bank. Later, much more public aid was given to retail and investment banks. It is difficult to estimate the cost of this aid at the time that it was granted. In the United States, it proved, ex post, to be modest: the banks ended up paying back most of the funds they received. Obviously, things could have turned out worse, as they did in some European countries.

To return to the case of AIG: a priori, there is nothing abnormal about rescuing a large insurance company. However, AIG's insurance activity was viable and capitalized separately, precisely to protect it from the collapse of the parent holding company engaging in risky activities. The holding company could have gone bankrupt without serious consequences for its insurance business. Although it seems odd that AIG's holding company was able both to escape supervision and to have access to the taxpayers' money because of its bad management, the interlinking of this institution with regulated institutions— through over-the-counter markets in derivatives, for example—created a systemic risk that "justified" its rescue.[11]

The boundary between the public sphere and the private sphere was as blurred as the border between regulated and unregulated sectors. In September 2008, two semipublic real estate credit agencies, Fannie Mae and Freddie Mac, which insured or guaranteed 40 to 50 percent (by 2007, 80 percent) of the outstanding real estate debt in the United States,[12] were rescued. Real estate again was the problem, but these two companies were anomalies. Since they were private, their profits did not benefit the taxpayer.[13] On the other hand, they had a US government guarantee (in the form of lines of credit with the US Treasury) and were counting on the general belief that the government would bail them out if they got into difficulties. So it proved. Once again, profits were privatized, losses nationalized.

Ultimately, they had not been rigorously regulated.[14] Strikingly, these agencies still play a major role in guaranteeing real estate loans in the United States.[15] In Europe, by comparison, the European Commission limited this phenomenon by successfully using the State Aid Law to prevent EU member governments[16] from subsidizing private businesses through implicit state guarantees.

THE NEW POSTCRISIS ENVIRONMENT

The crisis left at least two legacies: low interest rates and the search for new forms of regulation.

HISTORICALLY LOW INTEREST RATES

This particular legacy was supposed to be temporary. Very soon after the crisis began, the US, European, and British central banks provided much liquidity and thereby reduced interest rates to close to zero—in other words, to negative levels allowing for inflation (that is, in real rather than nominal terms). Japan has had an interest rate below 1 percent since the mid-1990s; in 2017, it is zero. Interest rates in Japan and Europe are expected to remain close to zero for a while, while the United States is beginning to raise rates very cautiously.

Low interest rates in downturns have a clear rationale. In particular, low short-term rates allow financial institutions to refinance themselves at low cost and ease the financial sector's problems.[17] In the end, only the state can provide liquidity for the economy. It can do two things that markets never can: first, mortgage the future revenue of households and businesses (even those that don't yet exist), or more precisely, the taxes that the public authority will levy on this revenue. This sovereign power of taxation underlies the state's role in macroeconomic regulation. The ability to tap into the future income of economic agents allows the state to issue national debt and to provide liquidity to the banking system.[18] The state can jump-start banks and businesses today in exchange for an increase in taxes tomorrow. Second, the central bank can create inflation, and in that way change the real value of contracts that are denominated at face value, both loans and nonindexed wage agreements. (Currently, central banks struggle to create expectations of even moderate inflation, so this second approach has no effect.)

The primary goal of providing liquidity is of course not to save banks that imprudently get themselves into difficulty and need refinancing; it is to keep alive the financial intermediaries so essential for the economy to function. Small and medium-sized businesses do not have access to financial markets (they cannot issue bonds or commercial paper to finance or refinance themselves) because they do not have an established reputation in the financial markets, have few assets to pledge, and are not diversified. They depend on banks to monitor them and ensure that the collateral these businesses offer is of good quality. When the banks are in difficulty, small and medium-sized enterprises are the first to suffer, as we have seen in all credit-crunch events.

Yet low interest rates, no matter how necessary they may be in a crisis, are not without costs:

- They lead to a massive financial transfer from savers to borrowers. In fact, this is exactly what a monetary bailout of banks is intended to do. But low rates please other investors, not just those in the regulated banks, because a decrease in interest rates increases the price of assets such as property or shares (the future yields on these assets are attractive in relation to the low yields offered on the bond market). This redistributes wealth because the owners of these assets, whether regulated or not, receive more when they sell them.[19] Low rates thus have gigantic redistributive effects, some desired and some not.
- Financial bubbles tend to emerge when interest rates are low, as we saw in the preceding chapter.
- Low interest rates encourage financial institutions that have guaranteed higher yields to their customers to take additional risks. This is a problem in Germany, for example, where insurance companies have promised investors in life assurance funds yields as high as 4 percent. The yield on ten-year German government bonds, which varies between 0 and 1 percent, makes it very difficult to make good on this guarantee unless the funds

are invested in high-yield and therefore riskier (even "junk")
bonds.[20]

- Low short-term interest rates could lay the foundation for the
next crisis by encouraging banks to borrow even more short-
term funds. This argument is currently less persuasive for two
reasons: 1) "quantitative easing" has had just as big an influence
on long-term rates, which are now often as low as short-term
rates, so banks' prospects are not as attractive as their low financing cost would suggest, and 2) regulators are currently setting up
liquidity requirements so as to limit banking institutions' short-
term indebtedness.

- There is a fifth cost: when we get to zero nominal rates, they can
fall no further, because people will prefer to hold cash, which
keeps its nominal value (that is, it offers a nominal rate equal
to zero).[21] This is what economists call the Zero Lower Bound
(ZLB). The central bank can no longer boost the economy by
lowering interest rates to negative levels; this can quickly lead
to a recession and unemployment. In this situation, central
banks have to turn to a toolkit of complex, imperfectly mastered
instruments[22] that I will not discuss here.

Low Interest Rates over the Long Term?

Until the crisis, the consensus among macroeconomists was that
we were in a period called "the great moderation." Monetary policy,
sometimes accompanied by fiscal policy (in a "policy mix"), seemed
to have done remarkable work during the twenty years preceding the
crisis. It aimed at price stability by targeting a stable target inflation
rate (2 percent, for instance), and adjusting monetary policies to
reflect the economic situation and unemployment level. Today, this
consensus regarding the primacy of monetary policy no longer exists,
in part because this policy mix is not viable at the Zero Lower Bound.

What if low interest rates were not merely a temporary phenomenon associated with the crisis? What if we were fated to live for a
long time in an economy with low interest rates, in which monetary
policy is unable to reenergize the markets and prevent recessions and

unemployment—a phenomenon that is a piece of what is sometimes called "secular stagnation"?[23] Economists disagree as to whether this is the situation today. What is certain is that there has been a decrease in interest rates on safe assets (say, government bonds) since the 1980s. In real terms (that is, once inflation has been deducted), these interest rates were around 5 percent in the 1980s, 2 percent in the 1990s, 1 percent until the Lehman Brothers bankruptcy in 2008, and about minus 1 percent since then. What are the reasons?

The first structural reason concerns the supply and demand for safe assets. If there is little supply and much demand, the price of these assets will necessarily be high. For a financial asset, a high price corresponds to a low yield (intuitively, the owner of the asset pays a high price if he only acquires the right to get a low yield in the future). There are several other symptoms, in addition to the low interest rates, of this excess demand. Before the 2008 crisis, there was a frenzy of securitization whose goal was to create safe financial assets (although ultimately this securitization created risky assets, as explained above, which was not how it was described at the time). Another sign is the emergence of bubbles.

The *demand* for safe assets has increased. First because of an overall higher level of savings. Since emerging economies (such as China) and countries with raw material revenues (such as the petroleum-producing countries when the price of oil was still high) did not have developed financial markets, they tried to invest their money in developed markets. This led to the "savings glut" mentioned earlier. Another factor contributing to higher savings is the increase in inequality, because well-off households save more than poor ones. Greater savings tend to reduce the yield paid to savers.

Savings have also exhibited a "flight to quality": a shift in savings composition in favor of safe assets. Since the crisis, tougher prudential regulation has penalized risk taking. As a result, banks, insurance companies, and pension funds now have more appetite for safe assets, that require them to hold relatively little capital. Individuals are also taking refuge in uncertain times in safe assets. The French invest almost 85 percent of their long-term life assurance savings in "euro funds" (that is mainly in bonds issued by governments and by highly rated companies); most of these euro funds are guaranteed in nominal terms (i.e., there is no risk of a loss of principal). They do not tend to invest in riskier assets, such as shares.

The *supply* of safe assets seems to have decreased: diversified real estate portfolios and the sovereign debt of OECD countries, which used to be considered completely safe, are now risky. This has led to a significant worldwide fall in liquidity. According to Ricardo Caballero and Emmanuel Farhi, the supply of secure assets had fallen from 37 percent of worldwide GDP in 2007 to 18 percent in 2011.[24]

Finally, lower population growth is often invoked to explain low rates.[25] Demography has complex effects, but many researchers agree that it is a factor. For example, it decreases labor supply relative to capital, and thereby the yield on capital, causing interest rates to fall. In a pay-as-you-go pension system (that is, with pension benefits financed by contributions levied on active workers rather than funded by pension funds' assets), the demographic slowdown also translates into a reduction in the relative number of active workers, an increase in private savings to offset the reduction in pensions, and, ultimately, lower interest rates.

So it is possible that low interest rates may be here to stay, in which case we will have to rethink macroeconomic policies.

The New Regulatory Environment

Nothing is without risk. Although we need to respond vigorously to the failures of regulation, and to reduce the frequency and scale of crises, we cannot completely eliminate the danger that they will happen. Just as a person who has never missed the beginning of a movie, never been late for a meeting, and never missed a train is probably overcautious, an economy in which people acted in such a way as to make a crisis inconceivable would probably be one functioning far below its potential. To avoid all crises we would have to constrain risk taking and innovation. We would also need to invest in the short term rather than over the long term, because the long term is more uncertain, and so riskier. The goal is therefore not to completely eliminate crises, but rather to get rid of incentives that encourage economic agents to adopt behaviors harmful to the rest of the economy. This requires limiting the externalities the financial system imposes on savers and taxpayers.

Prudential regulation and supervision are more art than science, because it is in fact difficult to assemble the data needed to measure precisely the effects predicted by theory. Yet there are still some general principles we can use, although it is hard to quantify the relevance of each of them. In 2008, a number of economists, including myself, recommended[26] protecting regulated institutions against the risk of contagion from the unregulated sector; increasing their levels of equity capital and putting greater emphasis on liquidity; making regulation more countercyclical; monitoring the pay structures of senior bank officers; allowing securitization, but supervising how it is used; monitoring the rating agencies; rethinking the "regulatory infrastructures"; and, in Europe, creating a supervisor on the European level within the ECB (this has since happened—see chapter 10). What is the situation today?

Having Your Cake and Eating It Too

Regulators, central banks, and governments have been forced to intervene to rescue financial institutions they did not regulate through bailouts, buying up toxic products, and loosening monetary policies. As we have seen, one illustration of this phenomenon is the recent history of US investment banks, particularly Bear Stearns and AIG. The only denial of aid to an investment bank (Lehman Brothers) created a serious panic in financial markets, halting consideration of further private sector bail ins.

The fear of systemic risk played too big a role in the formulation of public policy. This was partly because there was a lack of transparency about mutual exposures between financial institutions. The regulators had little information regarding the exact nature of the mutual exposures and the counterparty risk involved in the trades in over-the-counter markets. More generally, it is almost impossible for a regulator to calculate mutual exposures, direct and indirect, in the global financial system, especially since some of the financial institutions concerned are either not regulated or are regulated in other countries.

Thus, it is a question of keeping as many harmful financial products as possible out of the public sphere. In this case, the public sphere corresponds to the regulated sphere, which in theory is the only one that can be bailed out. Reforms have been implemented to make this containment more likely in practice.

The first of these reforms is the *standardization of the products and their trade on organized (rather than over-the-counter) markets.* Although it is important for the financial system to be able to tailor products to various specific needs, this makes it much more difficult for supervisors to assess the corresponding commitments and valuations. There is clearly no question of banning financial innovation or tools suited to specific needs, but the migration of regulated intermediaries toward standardized trade on exchanges should be encouraged (through a judicious choice of equity capital requirements). Unregulated intermediaries should, of course, remain free to put the accent more on over-the-counter trading. As explained in the preceding chapter, businesses and banks primarily need insurance contracts against straightforward risks—changes in macroeconomic variables such as exchange rates or interest rates, and the default of counterparties to which they are most exposed.[27] These standardized products can be traded on derivatives platforms that limit mutual exposures: regulators need to have a clear picture of regulated institutions' exposure to default by another institution. The use of well-capitalized clearing houses that demand guarantee deposits from their participants, along with the centralization of supply and demand, could potentially achieve this.[28] The new, postcrisis Basel III accord has moved in this direction. It penalizes over-the-counter contracts by demanding that more capital be held against them. It would be desirable to go further. At the same time, clearing houses must be subject to strict prudential rules too, otherwise the regulator would merely be diminishing the risk of (direct) bank failures by increasing the risk that the clearing houses default.

A more drastic version of the idea of insulating the retail banks is one that structurally separates retail banks from investment banks, a proposal made in different forms by Paul Volker, the former head of the Federal Reserve in the US, and by Commissioner Liikanen for the European Union. It was stated in its most drastic form by John Vickers, a prominent British economist, in the recommendations of the report from the UK's Independent Commission on Banking.[29]

The Countercyclical Character of Equity Capital Requirements

There are good theoretical justifications for a countercyclical solvency ratio, that is, capital requirements that are higher during booms but fall during a banking crisis. For one thing, periods when banking equity capital is in short supply go hand in hand with a credit crunch, making life difficult for businesses depending on the banking system; in particular, small and medium-sized businesses either must pay high interest rates or are refused loans. For another, policymakers should aid the financial system at times of scarce liquidity, especially for those liquidity shocks that are rare (as this makes it too costly for the private sector to hoard liquidity just in case). Loosening solvency constraints in such periods is one way to provide this aid, alongside monetary policy.[30] The Basel III agreement has provided for banks' capital buffer to be countercyclical, reflecting macroeconomic conditions.

The Regulation of Liquidity and of Solvency

Before the crisis, there was no unified regulation of liquidity, whether in the Basel accords or at the European level, and the liquidity requirements placed on banks were low. In theory, regulators should enforce both a liquidity ratio and a solvency (or capital) ratio, but the practice is more complex. It is notoriously difficult to construct a good measure of the liquidity of a financial intermediary. The liquidity of a bank depends, on the asset side of the balance sheet, on the possibility of reselling, when necessary, securities (treasury bonds and bills, certificates of deposit, securitized products, stock shares, bonds) without too much discount (this is market liquidity). On the liabilities side, it depends on whether the institution can raise funds (such as sight deposits or certificates of deposit) rapidly and on reasonable terms (this is funding liquidity). A bank's liquidity also depends on its reputation, which affects the value of the assets it tries to sell and its ability to raise new funds.

The Basel Committee is putting the final touches on two new ratios: The Liquidity Coverage Ratio requires banks to hold liquid assets, such as treasury bonds, in an amount equal to or larger than its net cash loss over thirty days in case refinancing could not make up for a massive withdrawal of (essentially uninsured) deposits. The Net Stable Funding Ratio has a similar flavor, but looks at a horizon of one year.

Calculating equity capital requirements will always be a work in progress. The correct level depends on the risk the regulator is prepared to tolerate, on the volatility of the economic environment, on the quality of supervision (are the rules being properly applied?), on the composition of the bank's assets and liabilities, and on the danger of activities migrating into the unregulated, shadow banking sector. With the necessary data hard to get, it is difficult for an outsider to estimate with precision the right level of equity capital. There will always be some trial and error, but we know this much: banks were not holding enough equity capital before the crisis.

Basel III has increased the requirements: The required Tier 1 capital[31] rose from 4 percent to 7 percent, to which can be added the countercyclical buffer (when there is high credit growth in the economy) of between 0 and 2.5 percent. An extra capital requirement of up to 2.5 percent is required from banks that are deemed systemically important. The total requirements for Tier 1 and Tier 2 capital rose from 8 percent to up to 13 percent. There is also a new minimum leverage ratio, the philosophy of which is based on a vision that supervisors have an extremely limited ability to gauge the risk; according to current proposals, banks will need to have at least 3 percent of their risk-unweighted exposures (on and off balance sheet, as well as those related to derivatives and securities financing) in Tier 1 capital, with a possible surcharge for large banks deemed to be systemically important.

Will that be enough?[32] It's difficult to say, but the increase in capital requirements is an important step forward.

A Macroprudential Approach

The current reforms tend to be "macroprudential": they are rooted in the idea that the solidity of a bank depends not only on its own equity and liquidity, but also on the solidity of other banks. There are many reasons for this.

Banks can be interdependent through their mutual exposure, which raises the fear of contagion if one of them goes bankrupt; they are also dependent on each other in a more indirect way, because if they encounter difficulties at the same time, they will try to sell off their assets concurrently. The wave of orders will cause asset prices to fall (in so-called "fire sales") and reduce each bank's market liquidity.

Bank failures have different consequences in times of crisis than in periods of stability. There is more likely to be a systemic impact if the other banks are also affected by a macroeconomic shock. Furthermore, a possible bailout by the taxpayer is more expensive if the government has already been forced to rescue other banks. Finally, we have already observed that, in the case of excessive transformation (borrowing short and lending long) by financial intermediaries, the central bank will have no choice but to reduce interest rates. All this implies that a bank should hold more capital when its strategy means its risk of failure is strongly correlated with macroeconomic shocks.

Remuneration

Remuneration in banking circles is the subject of two debates. One concerns the amount: the amount of remuneration in finance, in particular in the US and the UK, is high. High levels of remuneration in themselves do not justify ad hoc treatment of the financial world: whatever the state's preferences about redistribution, it should redistribute income through taxes, not decide whether a banker deserves less than a television anchor, a successful entrepreneur, or a soccer player. The other debate concerns whether high remuneration packages reward good performance or, on the contrary, create bad incentives. Large bonuses received by managers[33] who later fail, stock options received before share prices collapse, or golden parachutes[34] that reward underachievement are shocking not only from an ethical point of view, but from the point of view of efficiency. These outcomes do not create good incentives.

The bonus culture is pertinent both to the excesses of finance and to the question of inequality. Systems for remunerating managers are in fact too often focused on overachievement and the short term, and thereby encourage excessive risk taking. This is particularly true when there is a small risk of extreme loss ("tail risk"). A risky strategy that is profitable with a probability of 95 or 99 percent, but may produce a catastrophe otherwise, then secures (most of the time) a generous remuneration for the manager, and leaves the high—but improbable—losses to shareholders, creditors, and taxpayers.

Why are shareholders likely to go along with such compensation policies? The first answer is that they also profit so long as the downside risk is not realized, even if they would lose their shirts if it did. A second answer is that the banks tend to give priority to short-term remuneration to attract talented employees. This was particularly apparent during the years preceding the 2008 crisis. Unrestrained competition for talented employees is conducive to bonuses and short termism; bonuses do not result only in higher-than-average pay, but also a wide dispersion of profit-based compensation among managers or traders (because the increase in remuneration due to competition to attract and keep talented employees occurs through variable remuneration, not fixed salaries).[35]

Why do banks' creditors agree to lend under such conditions? They do not always know about the risk taking, but, above all, banks are able to take these greater risks thanks to the state's explicit or implicit safety net, which enables them to continue raising new funding even in the face of bad omens. That may be why finance is different. The television anchor, the entrepreneur, or the soccer player do not call on public money when they get into financial difficulties.

Thus, it seems legitimate for the state to regulate compensation in the private sector, at least the part of it that is liable to be bailed out with public money. The state can insist on compensation schemes that induce bank managers to take a long-term perspective. A case in point is deferred compensation, in which the managers' compensation is vested over time and granted only when it becomes clear that the managers' performance was not a flash in the pan.[36] In addition, the second pillar of Basel II allows regulators to require an increase in equity capital if the system of remuneration encourages short termism and excessive risk taking. Of course, deferring remuneration by just a few years may not be enough: certain risks materialize only much later, because they are taken over a long period (for instance, the risk of longevity in life insurance). Over very long periods (ten years, say) it is difficult to distinguish the contribution made by one manager from that of successors.[37] A compromise must be found.

Finally, it is entirely possible that the remuneration committees of banks indulge senior management. It's not clear that this is peculiar to finance. Problems of governance exist in all sectors of business. Regulation specific to finance cannot be grounded in this argument alone.

Opponents of regulating bankers' remuneration have two arguments:

The first relates to the importance for a bank, as for any business, to be able to attract the best talents to lead it. Let us suppose, to pursue this argument, that a bank could increase its value by 0.1 percent by attracting a CEO who is a little more talented than others. If this bank has a value of a hundred billion dollars on the stock market, this increase represents a hundred million dollars. The bank would rightly be prepared to pay a lot to acquire the services of this more talented manager.[38] A variant of this argument maintains that the bank has no choice because of the competition from unregulated intermediaries, such as hedge funds and private equity companies, offering generous remuneration to those they consider to be the best managers. Failing to match these employers would deprive retail banks of the best talent.

The second argument is that the excesses of finance will not be corrected by regulating pay and bonuses. Hubris may be as important as a cause of dysfunctional behavior as is profit.[39] Recall the immoderate ambition of CEOs such as Richard Fuld, who wanted his bank, Lehman Brothers, to beat Goldman Sachs; and Jean-Yves Haberer, who wanted to transform Crédit Lyonnais into a world leader; or the personal ambition of rogue traders such as Jérôme Kerviel (Société

Générale) and Nick Leeson (Barings). If hubris is the main driver of risk taking, regulating remuneration would have little effect, and only classical prudential supervision could limit it.

In conclusion, questions about excess pay seem to go beyond the regulatory framework for finance. They raise the general question of the *level* of redistribution the government wants to see, whether in banking or in any other sector. The question of the *structure* of remuneration and incentives seems to be more specific to banking, insofar as the failure of a bank can lead to the demand for public funds. Controlling remuneration that encourages risk taking and is oriented toward the short term must therefore be part of the supervisory framework.

Basel III created some relevant guidelines (the exact regulations depend on how these guidelines are implemented in different countries). They reduce the proportion of variable pay (for example, variable remuneration such as bonuses is not to exceed fixed remuneration); in addition, the guidelines introduce a deferral period (usually three to five years) to penalize behavior that is profitable in the short term but costly in the long term. As in the case of the increased equity capital requirements, these reforms are difficult to calibrate. But they seem to be heading in the right direction.

RATING AGENCIES

The crisis also raised questions about the rating agencies. These agencies play a central role in modern finance by informing individual and institutional investors, as well as regulators, about the risks of financial instruments. They failed to do this in the case of subprime mortgages. The major argument in favor of regulating the rating agencies is that over time their judgment has become an integral part of the regulatory assessment of risk, and that they earn major revenues from this. The capital requirements of regulated institutions (banks, insurance companies, brokers, pension funds) go down significantly when they hold highly rated debts. The privilege that rating agencies enjoy has to be counterbalanced by supervising their methodology and conflicts of interest. On the other hand, there is no basis for regulating the activities of rating agencies that are not involved with prudential regulation (unless these activities lead to a conflict of interest).

Basel III and the new prudential regulations for insurance companies ("Solvency II") retain the principle of using ratings to estimate risk, while regulators in the United States are now far more circumspect about using ratings.

REGULATORY INFRASTRUCTURES

The crisis put in question not only the regulations, but also the supervisory institutions that apply the regulations. Could supervisors take prompt corrective action before getting to the point of either closing or bailing out a bank? Could coordination be achieved between different national supervisory authorities or between the authorities in several countries? When it comes to international cooperation, the main problem is transnational financial institutions. The systems for guaranteeing deposits and for transferring assets, and the laws governing bankruptcies, differ from one country to the next. Supervision (the monitoring and implementation of capital requirements) and the management of crises (bailing out institutions or accepting their bankruptcy, buying up toxic assets, and so on) offer textbook cases of free riding and countries' ability to game the system. Unfortunately, I do not have room to explore this important issue further here.

IS THE FINANCIAL SYSTEM NOW SECURE?

As I have said, the current state of our knowledge and, in particular, the limited availability of the data that would allow supervisors (or economists) to calibrate capital and liquidity requirements precisely should encourage us to be humble. However, as long as the reforms are implemented and not derailed, the financial system will prove to be less risky than it was before: the Basel III reforms seem to be headed in the right direction. An increased requirement of equity capital, the introduction of a minimum liquidity ratio, the inception of macroprudential measures in the form of countercyclical equity capital buffers, a greater use of centralized exchanges instead of over-the-counter markets, institutional reforms (for example, the creation of the European Single Supervisory Mechanism)—all are genuine improvements.

There are still, however, major areas of risk. Some of these are connected to the macroeconomic environment; they are based on slower global growth, more volatile financial markets, and the challenge of how to exit low–interest rate policies without compromising growth. Other concerns stem from the combination of geopolitical risk and local economic conditions—for example, in Europe political shocks such as the UK's Brexit vote, the political uncertainty over the European Union, the structural weakness of certain economies, the significant proportion of unproductive loans still on European (especially Italian) banks' balance sheets, and the intimate connections between banks and sovereign states.[40] There is uncertainty about how China will transition from a catch-up economy to one on the frontiers of technology and institutional design (including managing its credit bubble and reforming financial markets). In the emerging economies, overindebtedness in foreign currencies (usually in US dollars) may put businesses and banks in difficulty if the local reliance on commodities (natural resources, agricultural products) is associated with inadequate risk management.[41] Finally, economists still do not know enough about how prudential regulation ought to operate, including the extent to which investors should be held responsible for their investments in regulated institutions (i.e., bailed in, in case of default)[42] and, of course, about the proper calibration of capital and liquidity requirements.

I will end by discussing a particular issue: shadow banking. As regulation becomes more rigorous, banking activities tend to migrate toward "parallel" banks that are either lightly regulated or not regulated at all. There is no objection to this as long as the migration does not take place at the expense of vulnerable actors (small depositors and small and medium-sized enterprises) or taxpayers. Now, as we saw in 2008, the shadow banking sector can benefit in practice from public liquidity and bailouts. At the time, this was because the regulated banks were exposed to the shadow banks if they got into distress, either directly through liabilities owed them by shadow banks, or indirectly because the latter might trigger fire-sale prices for some types of assets, thereby making it harder for regulated banks to raise cash by selling their own assets; but we can imagine other factors that could lead to resorting to public finances in case of bank distress, for example if individuals put their money in shadow banks, or small businesses started to depend on borrowing from them (both true today in China).

WHO IS TO BLAME? ECONOMISTS AND THE PREVENTION OF CRISES

In the end, the financial crisis of 2008 was also a crisis of the state, which had been disinclined to do its work as a regulator. Like the euro crisis discussed in chapter 10, the 2008 crisis had its origin in the failure of regulatory institutions: failure in prudential supervision in the case of the financial crisis, and failures of state supervision in the case of the euro crisis. In both cases, lax supervision prevailed as long as everything was going well. Risk taking on the part of financial institutions and countries was tolerated until the danger became obvious. Contrary to what many people think, these crises were not technically market crises—the economic agents were reacting to the incentives they faced, and the least scrupulous among them exploited gaps in the regulation to swindle investors and take advantage of the public safety net. Rather, the crises were symptoms of a failure of national and supranational state institutions.

Economists have been roundly reproached for not having predicted the crisis[43] and even for being responsible for it. In reality, most of the causes of the financial crisis were connected with hazards that had been studied before it occurred: asset bubbles, the impact of excessive securitization on the issuers' incentives, the growth of short-term indebtedness and the possible lack of liquidity in financial institutions, poor measurement of banking risk, the moral hazard of rating agencies, the opacity of over-the-counter markets, the drying up of markets and the disappearance of market prices, herding behavior in financial markets, and the procyclical impact of regulation.

Nonetheless, although academic research provided some keys to understanding several of the factors that led to the crisis, it had little success in preventing it. We must acknowledge that economists had little influence during the period leading up to the crisis. Four factors contributed to this situation:

First—and this is an essential point—it has to be understood that economists will always be more comfortable identifying the factors likely to lead to a crisis than predicting whether it will occur, or on what date, just as a physician will be more comfortable identifying factors that might cause an illness or a heart attack than in saying exactly when they will occur.[44] Just like epidemics and earthquakes, financial crises are difficult to predict, but we can identify likely causes. Since financial data are very imperfect and the world is continually changing, there will always be great uncertainty about the magnitude of the effects concerned, not to mention the self-fulfilling factors (like bank runs[45]) that are, by definition, unpredictable because they are, in Keynes's words, based on "the feeling … in the mind of the investor."[46]

Second, the diffusion of academic knowledge was very piecemeal. The blame for this falls both on the researchers, who often did not make the effort to share their knowledge and make it more operational, and on policymakers, who pay little attention to gloomy warnings from economists when things are going well. Researchers cannot expect policymakers to read technical articles (even if knowledge is often transmitted by economists working for regulatory authorities); they have to extract the essence, make research comprehensible, and show exactly how to make use of it. These are things that top economists are often loath to do, because they prefer to devote their time to creating rather than disseminating knowledge—not to mention the fact that their academic reputation depends on the approval of their peers, not that of policymakers. To facilitate the dissemination of scientific knowledge, it can only be beneficial to train excellent applied economists who will work for regulators rather than embarking on academic careers, and will share research insights in conferences organized with regulators, central bankers, and bankers.

Third, almost all researchers were unaware of the extent of the risks that were being taken in the financial sector; for example, they did not know the amount of off-balance-sheet commitments or the size and correlations of over-the-counter contracts. To be sure, supervisors had only partial knowledge too; but outside their small circle, very few knew what was going on. Should academic economists have been better informed? I have no good answer to that question. On one hand, it would have been useful if policymakers had listened to economists. On the other hand, economists specialize: research and teaching are distinct from applied economics, even if they nourish each other.

Fourth, a few economists, either by inner conviction or because of conflicts of interest, underestimated the importance of financial regulation or oversold the virtues of over-the-counter markets or of financial innovation. Their arguments were quickly exploited by interested parties. Charles Ferguson's 2010, well-researched film *Inside Job*, while certainly polemical, shows the dangers of complicity between researchers and the subjects of their research. The issue of conflicts of interest is not very different from the problems that arise in other sciences when private or public interests intrude into the world of research. The difficulty is immediately obvious: those with the information that could have the greatest relevance for public policymaking are often connected with those who have a stake in regulation. There is no miracle solution. To help mitigate this problem, most research groups, universities, and public organizations now have an ethical charter requiring researchers to declare potential conflicts of interest. This is useful, but researchers must ultimately be bound by personal ethics.

PART V

THE INDUSTRIAL CHALLENGE

THIRTEEN
Competition Policy and Industrial Policy

Going beyond the sterile dualism of state and market, it is now clear that intelligent government regulation can reduce market inefficiencies while limiting the negative impact of its interventions on innovation and creativity. The complexity of the interactions between economic actors, information asymmetries, uncertainty, and a multiplicity of contexts means it takes a great deal of reflection to find the best way to manage competition and design regulation. Advances in theory, confirmed by empirical work, have led economists to recommend numerous reforms in the way markets are regulated and organizations are managed.

Even in a market economy, the state is at the heart of economic life in at least six ways. Through *public procurement*, it is a buyer and therefore organizes competition between suppliers for the construction of public buildings, for transport (such as highways, railroads, and mass transit in cities), for hospitals, for defense, and for other government activities. As the *legislative and executive power*, it gives permission to open supermarkets, issues taxi licenses, grants landing rights to airlines, and licenses spectrum to telecommunications, radio, and television operators. This indirectly influences the prices that consumers pay for shopping, travel, phone calls, or their favorite programs. As a *referee of markets*, it encourages competition, thereby guaranteeing innovation and affordable products for consumers. It sets the rules through competition law, it works through the competition authorities to prevent abuses of dominant position, and it prohibits agreements and mergers that would cause prices to rise too much.[1] As a *regulator* of sectors such as telecommunications, electricity, the postal service, and railroads, it ensures that monopolies or highly concentrated markets do not translate into the exploitation of users. As a *financial supervisor*, it ensures that banks and insurance companies do not take too many risks to increase their profits at the expense of savers—or of taxpayers if the financial institution has to be bailed out. As a *signatory of international treaties* (especially those dealing with world trade), it determines the exposure of sectors of industry to foreign competition.

The state might not fulfill these functions properly (as the financial crisis showed), either because it is negligent or, more often, because of the strong influence of organized lobbies. Rather than protect users or taxpayers, who represent the majority of stakeholders but are often apathetic because they are disorganized and not well informed, the state prefers to remain in good favor with the lobbies—or at least to avoid too brutal a confrontation with them.

One area in which special interest groups are particularly influential concerns restrictions, or even prohibitions, on competition. It is natural that established businesses—from the shareholders to the employees—want to block new competitors or to get financial compensation from the government if they lose their exclusive access to a particular market, but it is more surprising for the state to give in to their demands. Yet politicians are not always well disposed toward competition, either because they want to grant favors to the lobbies seeking protection against it, or because they resent competition as a restraint on their political action and power. Once again, the victims of this lack of competition—consumers who have less purchasing power as a result—are poorly organized and ignorant of the impact of the public decisions that they either do not follow or do not understand. This is true everywhere, but especially so in France, where, surprisingly, consumers and consumers' associations exhibit a wariness of competition, against their own best interests.

In all countries, consumers and taxpayers have little influence compared to special interest lobbies. This is why, for example, European legislators gave a leading role in the European Union's body of law (the *acquis communautaire*) to pan-European competition rules and other regulations governing economic activity. These rules have made it possible for many countries to modernize their economies by protecting their politicians from the power of interest groups. A striking example of this are the contrary trajectories of Poland (inside the European Union) and Ukraine (outside the EU), countries that were economically at about the same level when Poland joined the EU, and whose levels of GDP have since totally diverged, even before the recent conflict in Ukraine. In Poland, EU competition law made it possible to prevent monopolies from forming when the economy was liberalized, whereas in Ukraine the opposite happened when privatizations took place, partly because of political corruption. (Estonia is probably an even better example than Poland, because it went further still in liberalizing its markets.)

WHAT IS THE PURPOSE OF COMPETITION?

Economists have always praised the merits of competition in markets where it is possible. However, competition is rarely perfect; markets have flaws, and market power—that is, a firm's ability to set its prices substantially above its costs or to offer poor-quality services without losing many customers—has to be checked. Advocates of competition, as well as its detractors, sometimes forget that competition is not an end in itself. It is only an instrument in the service of society. If it leads to inefficiency, it must be eliminated or corrected.

How does competition serve society? There are three main arguments.

AFFORDABILITY

The most obvious benefit of competition is lower prices for consumers. A monopoly or cartel can increase its prices and, up to a point, will only lose a few of its customers. The dominant company—whether it is private and seeking a profit, or public and (often) seeking revenues to cover high production costs—will not resist the opportunity to charge high prices or offer poor-quality goods and services. The result is that people have less purchasing power and consume less. The entry of competitors makes consumers less captive, and puts downward pressure on prices.

Take the case of the taxi industry in France, with its high prices, poor-quality service, and frequent shortage of available vehicles. Unless they are well off or have the cost reimbursed by their employer, individuals in France rarely take taxis, whereas many of them could do so if they lived in Barcelona or Dublin, where deregulating the taxi market to introduce competition reduced fares and increased supply. The entry of Uber, although controversial, has increased competition in the taxi market in many French cities. Similar observations could be made with regard to intercity bus transport in France, whose partial liberalization was the goal of the Macron Law (named after its sponsor, who was then minister of the Economy, Industry, and Digital Affairs).

The cell phone or the Internet in African countries is another example of the virtues of competition. The (landline) telephone service used to be a cash cow for some members of the elite, and was only used by the affluent. Service was sparse in rural areas, and the monopoly operators charged exorbitant prices. As a result, most Africans not only did not use telephones, the vast majority did not even own one. This situation has totally changed, thanks to competition from and between cell phone companies. Millions of people with low incomes can now access medical or financial services (and free online education and other services provided by charities in partnership with businesses) thanks to competition between companies providing more affordable telecommunications.

In most developed countries, citizens have much more often had access to telephones, but made little use of them. Before these markets were opened up to competition, people rarely made long-distance or international calls because they cost too much: competition has led to much lower prices, and much greater use of the telephone.

An example of the adverse effects of restricting competition—one so self-defeating that it might be amusing if not for its consequences for households, especially the least well off—is provided by France's Raffarin and Galland Laws of 1996. The Raffarin Law made it illegal to open a new supermarket of more than three hundred square meters without government authorization. The opening of large supermarkets was in fact blocked for ten years.[2] This law was supposed to restrain the power of large supermarkets, but immediately the value of shares in these big chains went up, because investors understood that the legislation would limit competition among them, and so would benefit the incumbents. The same year—again supposedly to restrain the expansion of big chains that could get better deals from suppliers—the Galland Law banned supermarkets from passing on to consumers the price reductions they obtained, thus leading in practice to a rise in prices as big supermarkets stopped discounting. As I live in the city center, I like having small stores nearby, even if I have to pay more. But the lesson that I learned from this episode is that these laws privileged consumers like me at the expense of many of my fellow citizens (and there might have been other ways of keeping small stores alive in the city center).

A final example is protection against international competition. In the early 1990s, the French automobile industry was far behind its competitors, particularly the Japanese. Costs were high and quality inferior. But there was scant pressure of competition. Opening the European market to competition from imports drastically changed the organization of the industry and productivity. Renault and Peugeot-Citroën sharply increased their efficiency in comparison to the best international practices.[3] China's accession to the WTO in 2001 is another example of the impact of international trade on efficiency and innovation. Economists have shown that there was a sharp increase in innovation and productivity in textile companies threatened by this new competition.[4] The effects of such competition are not negligible for consumers. In France, a quarter of consumer goods imports come from countries where wages are low. The monthly gain per French household is between one hundred and three hundred euros.[5] Of course, a significant part of these gains is due to the difference in wages, and not solely from exposing French monopolies or oligopolies to competition.

INNOVATION AND EFFICIENCY

Competition is not only reflected in lower prices. It encourages businesses to produce more efficiently and to innovate. It promotes a diversity of approaches and experiments, giving rise to new technologies and business models, as we now see online. Productivity gains can be broken down into gains in existing businesses, which improve when spurred by competition, and gains through "creative destruction" as inefficient enterprises disappear and are replaced by more productive new startups. In both the United States and France, at least a quarter of the growth in productivity is estimated to be attributable to this kind of renewal.[6]

A lack of competition makes life easy for companies, their executives, and their employees, who enjoy a tranquil existence in a protected market; in economic jargon, they enjoy monopoly rents. Monopolies not only tend to have high costs, but they usually generate little innovation. By innovating they would cannibalize their existing activities (what they gain on new products they lose in part through lower sales of existing products), and they really don't need to innovate anyway because their executives face no criticism for being less dynamic than a competitor.

These phenomena are not new. Innovation in products and customer service are not simply due to extraordinary technical advances. To go back to the taxi example, companies such as Uber, SnapCar, Lyft, and others using a mobile app to link drivers and passengers have introduced simple ideas for which users are voting overwhelmingly with their feet and wallets. Geolocation makes it possible to follow the driver's route to the destination and work out how long it will take to arrive. This traceability protects the consumer. Paying with a preregistered debit card using an app that sends an electronic receipt direct to the user simplifies the payment process and makes it easier for business travelers to reclaim their expenses. Another "innovation" is feedback that allows drivers and users to build a reputation for courtesy and punctuality. Providing a bottle of water or letting passengers recharge their cell phone are hardly technologically revolutionary. Yet taxi companies had either never thought of these innovations or just did not to bother to introduce them.

INTEGRITY

Another important benefit of "free" competition is linked to the adjective "free." When there is competition, companies cannot obtain monopoly rents through government regulations. Consequently, they do not spend large sums on rent seeking, an activity that imposes costs on society. Corruption represents the extreme quest for rents. One of the scourges of import controls in developing countries is that import licenses are granted by government officials who have powerful friends and enrich themselves at the expense of everyone else. If the goal is to limit imports, it would be better to levy a tax or allocate quotas to the highest bidder through a government auction. The revenues from the auction would go to the state.

In less flagrant cases, the absence of free entry into markets may also lead public officials to favor local suppliers for reasons of friendship or political calculation. We instinctively think that buying from local suppliers is a good thing, and sometimes it is, but only if there is no bias in favor of these suppliers.[7] The disadvantaged nonlocal supplier is also a local producer in another community, region, or country. Such territorialism is rightly condemned by market access regulations both at the national level, and internationally by the WTO. Importantly, this kind of territorial favoritism is not a zero-sum game with ultimately offsetting effects, i.e., local firms everywhere substituting for nonlocal firms. Competition gives people access to the best the world has to offer. Decision makers who privilege local suppliers do so at the expense of the taxpayer or the consumer, who will pay more or receive lower-quality services.

Finally, in a democracy, actions seeking to influence public decision making increase in frequency with the power of the state and have a social cost, whether they are discreet (lobbying in Paris, Brussels, or Washington) or highly visible (blocking highways or disrupting public services in France).

INDUSTRIAL ECONOMICS

Industrial economics studies the exercise and regulation of market power. It does this by creating models that extract the essential elements from each situation. The predictions of these models can then be tested econometrically, in the laboratory, or even in the field. Ultimately, any model must rest on reasonable hypotheses and make robust predictions supported by empirical evidence. Then economists can confidently make policy recommendations or suggest business strategies.

Industrial economics has a long tradition. It began in France, with the work of the economists Antoine Augustin Cournot (1838) and Jules Dupuit (1844), who tried to construct an analytical framework that would help them better understand some specific problems. Dupuit, a civil engineer, devised a method to calculate how much the users of a road, bridge, or railroad would be prepared to pay for their services. This concept (called "consumer surplus" in the jargon of economics) is fundamental, because we can say whether a provision would be justified by comparing it with the costs of providing the service. Dupuit also raised questions relating to pricing. He wondered why the third-class carriages on trains offered such poor quality (they didn't even have roofs), when the company could have offered much higher quality service without paying much more to provide it. His answer was in retrospect obvious: if the company did that, second-class passengers would have traveled third class. Then the quality of the second-class service would have to be improved or its price decreased, which would have led first-class passengers to travel second class, requiring in turn an improvement in quality of service or a price reduction for first class. This partial but pioneering analysis later gave rise to a sophisticated theory of market segmentation, and to a vast field of applications extending from transportation to computer software.

Industrial economics turned then to public policy when the Sherman Antitrust Act was introduced in the United States in 1890, along with other competition law and regulatory jurisprudence around the same time. Lawmakers sought to limit anticompetitive behavior. This interventionist approach was later supported by the descriptive studies produced by what is known as the Harvard School (proponents of the structure-conduct-performance paradigm),[8] advocating public intervention in the organization of markets. A counterrevolution took place in the 1960s and 1970s, when the Chicago School rightly criticized the lack of a theoretical basis for many areas of competition law and challenged the whole edifice. The economists behind this critique of competition law did not develop a rival doctrine, perhaps because they were wary of regulation in general. By the late 1970s and early 1980s, the ideas underpinning competition law and regulation had to be rethought. The resulting body of work made it possible to build a more solid case for public intervention.

Is Competition Always Good?

The answer to this question is unequivocally no. For example, competition can lead to a duplication of costs. Just imagine three or four electrical distribution networks, several parallel railroad lines between New York and Boston, or multiple Oxford Circus Stations. In practice, there are large "fixed costs" for infrastructure, such as railroad tracks or stations—costs that depend little if at all on traffic volume. There may also be "network effects": even if a competitor of Boston's MBTA could build a second line between Wonderland and Bowdoin competing with the Blue Line, if it could not connect at State to go to Forest Hills there would be no hope of competition on journeys to Forest Hills or anywhere on another line in the network.

These fixed costs and network effects make it difficult and even undesirable to establish true competition in infrastructure provision. Infrastructure then represents a bottleneck operated by a monopoly provider. The regulator controls the prices that the provider charges to suppliers of complementary services who require access to the infrastructure (e.g., train operators needing access to tracks and rail stations); "open access" forces the infrastructure owner to provide competing operators with nondiscriminatory access to it. Examples of this in France include SNCF Réseau, which is part of the French national railroad system, or Orange, which owns the infrastructure for and also competes on adjacent telephony and Internet markets.

It is important to ensure that the existence of a natural monopoly at one point in the value chain does not turn the whole sector into a monopoly. If there is a danger of that happening, it may be desirable to further separate the service from the infrastructure to allow fair competition in the potentially competitive segments. An illustration of this "structural separation" strategy is the dismantling of AT&T in 1984 into the "baby bells"—the local infrastructure owners—and a long distance phone company (AT&T) that was in competition with other long distance companies. Other illustrations are provided by municipal and national airports, which are usually completely separated from the airlines who use them, and by the UK's National Grid, which owns and manages the gas and electricity grids.

There are also examples of competition being introduced for ideological reasons. A famous instance was the competition between urban bus companies introduced in the UK in 1986. This resulted in "bus wars": buses racing to pick up passengers before other buses, and blocking rivals. A combination of consolidation in the sector and the inability to get the benefits of operating whole networks largely (although not entirely) put an end to the experiment. But it still happens in Manila today, while in Santiago, Chile, bus drivers receive no fixed salary, being paid only for the number of passengers they pick up—their buses are nicknamed "yellow monsters."

But the absence of competition *in* the market does not necessarily imply a total absence of competition. Competition *for* the market (bidding for a concession contract) then replaces everyday competition: this often occurs in public services such as water supply or sanitation, or licenses for the right to operate a bus or rail line.

Finally, if there is competition, it must benefit users. It must not be distorted by dirty tricks played by firms attempting to beat rivals by means other than attractive offers, investment, and innovation. This supervision of behavior in markets is an essential part of competition law.

COMPETITION AND EMPLOYMENT

People often associate competition with job destruction. Clearly, this cannot be generally true: a priori, more competition implies lower prices, higher quality, or both, more customers as a result, and ultimately a larger market with net job creation. Logically, therefore, competition increases employment overall. As an example, a larger number of taxi licenses would increase the availability of taxis and reduce the price of journeys (exactly as the entrance of Uber has opened up taxi services), increasing demand and so ultimately creating jobs.

But there is a legitimate concern. The introduction of competition is accompanied by restructuring and adjustments that are costly for the employees concerned. Competition arouses reactions similar to those that often accompany technological progress. In one famous episode, a group of British textile workers in the early nineteenth century, known as Luddites, reacted to the introduction of labor-saving looms by destroying them. Although such extreme actions are rare, technological innovations have often aroused understandable fears among employees in the affected sectors.

Liberalizing infrastructure industries to introduce competition is likely to lead to downsizing by the incumbent operators, who can no longer afford redundant staff or services. If the new operators do not create enough jobs to compensate for those that have been lost, this is a human problem—one that will be significant in the short term even if the restructuring ultimately improves prospects for the industry, the jobs it provides, and the service for its customers. Several responses are necessary, including recruitment freezes (rather than dismissals), retraining, and so on. As always, it is particularly important to protect the person, not the job.[9]

One can also envisage a phased opening up to competition, to give existing firms a chance to adapt slowly—on condition, of course, that the transition does not become a pretext for indefinitely deferring competition. A 1991 European directive provided for the introduction of competition between railroad operators. Germany, Sweden, and the UK all introduced competition and saw their freight and passenger traffic rise (although the process has not been uniformly smooth); but France is still talking about a possible introduction of competition in 2019, even though, despite some efforts at improvement, its rail sector is languishing.

WHERE DOES INDUSTRIAL POLICY FIT IN?

Industrial policy refers to the channeling of public funds (or tax breaks) to benefit certain technologies, sectors, or even specific firms, or to support small businesses.

Any industrial policy must begin with the question, "What problem are we trying to solve?" Thinking about state intervention must start with reflection about the nature of the "market failure" involved. But a simple analysis of market failure is not enough. Take the case of the environment.[10] There is a market failure to the extent that economic agents do not internalize the negative effects their polluting activities have on others. The economic approach to reducing emissions, however, consists of taxing these emissions, rather than deciding between different ways of reducing pollution. Alternatives in the case of CO_2 emissions include developing electric cars, investing in renewable energy, capturing and sequestering carbon, saving energy, and others. Suppose we decide that developing the electric car is an excellent idea: What technology should we choose? The same goes for renewable energy. Renewables will be indispensable for low carbon generation, but which ones should we choose? Should we favor wind power over solar power, putting all our eggs in one basket? Should we diversify our choice, or favor some different alternative energy sources? Just think of the misuse of public money to promote biofuels.

All these questions lead to another: Wouldn't it be smarter to create conditions favorable to investment in all such forms of energy rather than "picking winners" in advance? "Let a hundred flowers bloom, let a hundred schools of thought contend!"[11] Taxing carbon is a policy that does not distort competition between the alternatives. The evidence suggests that industrial policies creating the fastest growth have been competitively neutral.[12]

The rationales for an industrial policy include:
- the difficulty small and medium-sized enterprises (SMEs) have in raising funding;
- the lack of research and development in the private sector, particularly upstream research, because its results cannot be completely appropriated by those funding the R&D—other enterprises partly benefit from the knowledge thus acquired without having to pay for it (similar to the argument that on-the-job training benefits competitors because of worker mobility, so firms will underinvest in it);

- an absence of coordination between complementary businesses that could form a geographical cluster or an industrial network (to give an example borrowed from the traditional economy, between a factory using a certain kind of coal or steel and the production of that coal or steel).

The first two difficulties can justify what are called "horizontal policies" (such as subsidies for R&D or for SMEs), which do not favor one business, technology, or location over others. But let's begin with industrial policies that seek, on the contrary, to target their assistance.[13]

Targeted Industrial Policy

The question of the state's role in organizing industry is a longstanding political debate. Some politicians are sensitive to the demands of business leaders who want access to public funds. Others sincerely think that attempting to develop or save specific industries that they consider, rightly or wrongly, to be creating wealth and jobs is acting in the general interest. The lack of enthusiasm shown by most economists toward industrial policy (with a few notable exceptions, in particular Dani Rodrik at Harvard and Joseph Stiglitz at Columbia) astonishes them. So why are economists skeptical?

A Blind Approach ...

Picking winners. The main reason for this skepticism is that politicians and voters lack information about the technologies, sectors, and businesses that will produce tomorrow's economic wealth. Decision makers, whatever their professional qualifications or integrity, cannot predict where breakthrough innovations will occur (and their decisions will be all the more disastrous if they are too closely connected to lobbies). Commissions assigned to make these policies often produce rambling lists of desirable actions, usually without any convincing arguments for government backing of the selected technologies: no serious cost-benefit analysis, or even technological feasibility study. States have no particular talent for detecting future successful sectors and activities. At best, they choose more or less at random; at worst, they favor certain pressure groups.

In support of this view, there are many examples of white elephant projects like the Anglo-French Concorde (finally taken out of service in 2003), Groupe Bull (a French computer company that aimed unsuccessfully to compete with IBM's supercomputers and was kept alive by public funds), or Malaysia's unsuccessful BioValley project.

Industrial policy was easier in the postwar period, when it was a question of reconstruction in many countries. At that time, it was clear that investment was needed in infrastructures, which were based on familiar technology and for which the demand was evident (transportation, electricity, steel production). But today's structurally important industries (such as data processing, biotechnology, and nanotechnology) no longer meet the same criteria.

Clusters. Many countries have invested in industrial clusters with the laudable goal of promoting a specialist research and industrial complex (again, in fields like biotechnology and medicine, software, or nanotechnology) in a small geographical area. There are economic arguments in favor of clusters. A cluster can create critical mass and thus a deeper labor market, which is a nonnegligible benefit in sectors that are rapidly evolving with a lot of labor mobility between companies. Infrastructure is shared. Technological spillovers occur thanks to proximity, which encourages informal interactions and the exchange of know-how.[14] Yet these government interventions too often fail to achieve their objectives, which are frequently too numerous,[15] resulting in a scattering of resources, more often in response to local authorities' demands rather than as part of a clear strategy.[16]

We must face the fact that the most important hi-tech clusters usually form spontaneously. One remarkable example is the Kendall Square area near MIT, which is now the temple of biotechnology. MIT had no medical school, but it did have several famous biologists on its faculty, such as Phillip A. Sharp, David Baltimore, and Salvador Luria. Sharp (who received the Nobel Prize in 1993 for his work on ribonucleic acid) cofounded Biogen in 1982. The quality of the research conducted at MIT attracted leading thinkers from all over the world. Students, often with the help of their professors, founded startups that are now in the vanguard of research and economic activity in this area: for example, Amgen, Biogen and Genzyme (which now belongs to Sanofi). The great pharmaceutical companies such as Astra-Zeneca, Novartis, Pfizer, and Sanofi have also established research laboratories there, in the hope of benefiting, like the startups, from the academic research centers and the positive externalities they create.

If we look to the future, it seems obvious that significant technological innovation will be necessary to limit climate change to a tolerable level. It is equally clear that no one really knows which technologies will achieve this. I have a hard time imagining governments choosing the winning technology in these conditions. The same goes for nanotechnology, biotechnology, and future technologies in general.

I will close this section with a different kind of critique of industrial policy. Whether they are publicly or privately funded, bets on technology are inherently risky, so it is not surprising that governments sometimes make the wrong choice. There is no such thing as zero risk, and anyway it would not be desirable: we would never do anything. On the other hand, it is important to recognize our mistakes and not to continue to support projects that are failing; the money could be much better used to finance other investments.

Governments often yield to the temptation to solve problems by throwing money at them, whether to show that they were right after all or to satisfy the very pressure groups they helped create thanks to the financial manna of public support. It is very difficult to stop public projects. This is equally true when the initial project succeeds. This is one of the criticisms of public subsidies. From an economic point of view, it may be reasonable to subsidize a nascent technology to "pump prime" and benefit from learning by doing in the industry (this is the idea that costs decrease with production experience). The problem is that the beneficiaries of subsidies end up organizing to prevent the flow of money from drying up, even when the subsidy is no longer justified. In this area, private financing has an advantage. It knows when to stop funding what is no longer fruitful or necessary, and when to redeploy the money to more promising uses.

… Or a Visionary Approach?

The examples of the failures of industrial policy mentioned above are anecdotal, which is a problem. Unfortunately, there are few *ex post* evaluations using rigorous statistical analysis of these policies. The success stories told by the few defenders (among economists) of industrial policy are just as anecdotal. For example, the latter cite the success of Airbus, a result of European industrial policy. The logic behind Airbus was different—the goal was to maintain competition in a market that might otherwise have been completely monopolized by Boeing. Without Airbus's entry into the market, Boeing would probably have been able to impose very high prices on airline companies, and thus indirectly on travelers. Twenty years ago, Damien Neven and Paul Seabright showed that the competing subsidies for Boeing in the United States and for Airbus in Europe actually benefitted the entire world. With or without subsidies, the competition between the two manufacturers allows airline companies to buy better-quality airplanes at lower prices, and so also benefits consumers.[17]

The supporters of industrial policy also like to cite DARPA, a federal defense agency that supports advanced research projects. It was responsible for the development of the Arpanet network, the precursor of the Internet, and of the Global Positioning System. Supporters also cite the contribution of industrial policy to the development of economies such as South Korea and Taiwan.[18] Finally, they note that although many of the great American universities (such as MIT, Caltech, Harvard, Stanford, Yale, Princeton, and Chicago) are private, the state plays a fundamental role by granting (competitive) financing; I will return to this example later. For now, I will point out that in Europe, as in the United States, successful government interventions are rarely motivated by considerations of industrial policy. Much more often, they are motivated by other national objectives, such as defense.

WHICH INDUSTRIAL POLICY?

Given the lack of rigorous evidence, what should we conclude? Dani Rodrik, one of the economists who has supported some kinds of industrial policy (but certainly not all), has made the following commonsense point: whether or not we like industrial policies, governments will continue to pursue them. Whatever our opinion of them, we have to try to make such initiatives as successful as possible, accepting that our knowledge about them will continue to evolve. My experience leads me to propose seven guidelines:

1. identify the reason for the market failure, in order to be able to respond more effectively;
2. use independent, appropriately qualified experts to select projects to receive public funding;
3. pay attention to the supply of research capability as well as the demand for it;
4. adopt a neutral industrial policy that does not distort competition between companies;
5. evaluate interventions after they have taken place, and publish the results; include a "sunset clause" which ensures support can be withdrawn if the policy is not working or is no longer needed;
6. involve the private sector closely in the risk taking;
7. bear in mind how the structure of the economy is evolving.

The first recommendation, the necessity of identifying the market failure, has already been mentioned and requires no further commentary.

The second recommendation bears on the need to make an *ex ante* evaluation. The government should make its choices using agencies that are highly professional and protected from political interference. The cited examples of successful industrial policy in the United States (DARPA, university research) use peer review. From the same point of view, Rodrik notes that the rapid, state-sponsored growth of salmon farming in Chile in the 1990s involved quasi-independent professionals. It is certainly not always easy to find evaluators who are competent, available, and independent—the best ones are usually very busy and are likely to have been employed by the industry concerned. But this procedure is the most reliable. Beyond the technology, officials also need to call on specialists on the funding side of things by hiring experts in venture capital or seeking private cofinancing.

For the funding of academic research, the best scholars are mobilized to prioritize projects and provide a ranking that cannot be challenged for political reasons; this is the principle of peer review. For example, the National Science Foundation and the National Institutes of Health function as autonomous agencies respecting the opinions of experts. The same goes for the European Research Council, which was created in 2007 and has built an excellent reputation for competence and impartiality. Of course, it is important to identify the best experts, and then to ensure that any remaining conflicts of interest (for example, evaluating proposals made by close collaborators) are eliminated or managed. Competition between researchers, teams, and universities has very beneficial effects on innovation.[19]

The third recommendation, which suggests looking at the supply of researchers, proceeds from the observation that too often the state or the local authority identifies an area of research that it (often legitimately) considers important (the environment or biotechnology, for example) but whose conditions for success it does not investigate. It is, however, pointless to spend money if there are no researchers of international stature to carry out the work. This problem arises with scientific research and also, for example, the creation of clusters. There is a danger that the government will construct facilities or finance research without much realistic potential, hoping that success will follow automatically.

This is what I call the *Field of Dreams* mentality: if you build it, they will come. That may be true in a baseball movie, but the key actors in economic and scientific development will not rush to join every new project or cluster that gets funding. Identifying the key experts who can attract their peers and the best students seems crucial to the success of a project that seeks to expand the technological frontiers.

The fourth recommendation, not distorting competition, has already been mentioned. It is desirable not only on economic grounds, but also because it protects against officials who might favor a particular company or a recipient of public funds.

Ex post evaluation, the fifth recommendation, is difficult to carry out, because no one has much enthusiasm for drawing up a post-mortem assessment. That said, it is a useful way to learn lessons from past errors and identify those responsible for white elephants. Of course, *ex post* evaluations are really needed for all public policies, not only industrial ones.[20]

The sixth recommendation means structuring private cofinancing in such a way that it shares the risk. If the private investor is not prepared to take a risk, that is probably because the project is not viable. Private investors' desire to make a commitment should be taken as a signal of whether the envisaged project is in the public interest.[21]

Finally, we need to try to anticipate the way the economy will change. In some countries, including the US, the UK, and France, there is a certain nostalgia for the manufacturing industry. Obviously, good industrial projects should not be ruled out. Germany, for example, has benefited from the dynamism of its industrial sector. But looking backward could lead to difficulties in the future: taking that perspective suggests that the reduction in the manufacturing sector from 18 percent to 12 percent of French GDP requires a national strategy of reinvestment; but this fails to identify the real question. It is more important to ask why this decline happened than to assume the renewal of manufacturing per se is the right objective. And to return to the star exhibit for supporters of industrial policy, South Korea, let us note that its experience[22] has involved applying many of the principles set out here: ensuring competition between companies, using peer review, a limited duration for programs, the identification of companies that export successfully, and risk sharing with the private sector.

"Industrial renewal" is more a slogan than a strategy. At least in developed countries, twenty-first-century economies will be based on knowledge and services. If we focus on industrial renewal, it risks not only using public money, but also steering the country toward activities with little added value, which will ultimately impoverish the population. (On the other hand, strategies for high-value niches, driven by businesses themselves, as in Germany, make sense.) This does not mean that we should abandon industry. The surest way to create good industrial projects with high added value is to create an environment for businesses that favors their financing and development, and to ensure that they are integrated in a culture of innovation.

Europe's Industrial Weakness

The weaknesses of the industrial fabric in France are well known: the lack of fast-growth SMEs and (connected with this) the lack of new entrants into the elite club of big business. France is not alone—other European countries suffer the same longstanding weaknesses. Fifteen years ago, a report[23] issued by the French Council on Economic Analysis noted that, in a list of the 1,000 largest companies worldwide, among the 296 American companies on the list, 64 (22 percent) had been created after 1980, whereas among the 175 European companies only 9 (5 percent) had been created since 1980. The average age of companies on France's CAC 40 Index is 101 years. The average lifespan of a company in the S&P 500 has decreased from 61 years in 1958 to 18 years.[24] By way of contrast, there is a great deal of inertia in Europe, whose only two "champions" born in the second half of the twentieth century are the UK's Vodafone and Germany's SAP.

The SME problem is particularly significant in France: only 1 percent of its businesses have more than fifty employees, as opposed to 3 percent in Germany. There are 12,500 middle-sized businesses in Germany, as opposed to only 4,800 in France.

What Support Should There Be for SMEs?

Should SMEs be given special support? The justification for doing so is that they have inadequate access to credit. It is easier for big businesses to finance themselves, because they have established reputations and assets that they can put up as collateral when they borrow. Accordingly, they have access to the bond market. This is not generally the case for smaller companies, which are usually dependent on bank loans in the EU. This explains why EU law does not consider "horizontal" arrangements—such as the R & D tax credits or guarantees for bank loans to SMEs—as state aid (which is normally prohibited).

It is debatable whether SMEs need additional sources of financing, given current arrangements. In many countries, including France, they now enjoy numerous forms of public support and tax breaks for borrowing. Besides, the complexity of the system and the multiple tax loopholes transform companies into deal hunters. The systems of support for innovation can be staggeringly complex. Companies spend a lot of resources trying to identify sources of public funding for projects they would go ahead with anyway. This situation destroys more value than it creates, and SMEs do not even have the resources to play this game well.

Generally speaking, SMEs would benefit from reforms eliminating the obstacles that the government puts in their way, for example:

- *Threshold effects.*[25] These arise from defining SMEs as having fewer than a specific number of employees, which is frequently denounced by economists who see this as holding back companies' growth. For example, French companies that exceed the thresholds of ten, twenty, or fifty employees are subject to costly additional constraints: accounting obligations, a rise in their social security contribution rates, works councils, the requirement to have a job preservation plan in the event of redundancies, and so on. Moving from forty-nine to fifty employees creates thirty-four additional obligations for the company. A company that is confident about its future growth will go ahead, because it will not really have a choice. On the other hand, a company uncertain about its future will think twice before crossing the threshold (relying instead on overtime, outsourcing, or the creation of new companies). Threshold effects create an "SME trap." Figure 13.1 shows the striking distortion created in France by the fifty-employee threshold, in the form of a precipitous decline between the number of firms with forty-nine employees and the number of firms with fifty. But such threshold effects exist almost everywhere, including in the United States (for example, in the form of subsidies reserved for companies with fewer than fifty employees). They are particularly strong in countries like France, Italy, and Portugal, where, moreover, the effect creates additional unemployment because of the local labor market. Some studies[26] suggest the cost of threshold effects could amount to a few percentage points of GDP.

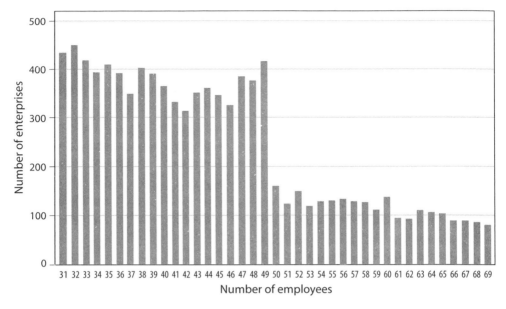

Figure 13.1. The number of French enterprises in relation to the number of employees (from 31 to 69 employees). *Source*: Ficus (fichier fiscal), 2002.

- *Complexity.* The extreme complexity of labor laws, of the fiscal system, and of access to public procurement (as in the case of policies supporting innovation) particularly penalizes SMEs without specialized management expertise.
- *Payment delays.* In France, public sector customers and large companies can be slow in paying their bills for services provided by SMEs.
- *The treatment of bankruptcies.*[27] France is unusual in its legal treatment of distress and bankruptcy. It gives a great deal of power to shareholders and managers in circumstances in which they may have failed. Contrary to what happens elsewhere in the world, French creditors are not well protected if the company encounters problems. It should be no surprise that French SMEs have a hard time borrowing under these conditions.
- *Labor and tax regulations.* Other obstacles to SME growth in France include constraints on human resource management

associated with the quasi-systematic extension of sector-level agreements to individual firms[28] and taxation favoring business transfers to family members or nonresidents.[29]

Removing obstacles such as these, versions of which exist in all countries, would be more useful than additional financial assistance for SMEs.

FOURTEEN
How Digitization Is Changing Everything

We increasingly shop and do our banking online, read our news on websites, use Uber, carpool using BlaBlaCar, and reserve accommodations through Airbnb. The digitization of society is at the heart of economic and social changes in the twenty-first century. It will have an impact on all human activities, just as it has already changed trade, finance, the media, and the travel and hospitality industries.

Everyone will have to adapt, including some surprising organizations. Confronted by the decline of the press and the traditional media, in 2014 National Public Radio (NPR) in the United States transformed itself into the Spotify of radio: its app NPR One asks you to rate its programs, examines the length of time you spend listening to each of them, analyzes your podcast downloads, and eventually provides you with tailor-made programming suited to your interests. This is only the beginning. Digitization will turn insurance, health care, energy, and education upside down. Professional medical, legal, and fiscal services will be transformed by intelligent algorithms based on machine learning,[1] just as robots will transform a number of other services.

Economic interactions are only one dimension of this change. Digitization influences personal relationships, civic life, and politics. Businesses are preoccupied by the way the structure of industry is changing, by changes in the nature of work, and by fears about cybersecurity and ransomware. Digitization has an impact on intellectual property rights, competition law, labor law, taxation, and regulation in general. The digital economy is bringing extraordinary technological progress that is giving us better health, as well as more time and purchasing power, but it also creates dangers we cannot ignore. The goal of this chapter and the one that follows is to analyze a few of the biggest challenges so that we can understand better and prepare ourselves for this profound transformation of business, the world of work, the system of regulation—in short, society in general.

This chapter focuses on the strategies of digital companies, and the challenges involved in regulating these markets. Two-sided platforms are the hub of the analysis. They enable different sides of the market (we might call them "supply" and "demand," or "sellers" and "buyers") to meet and interact. They are large and growing in their importance. Today (August 2017), the five largest global companies (by market capitalization) are two-sided platforms: Apple, Alphabet (Google), Microsoft, Facebook, and Amazon. Seven of the ten largest startups are also two-sided platforms. This chapter will analyze their business model and consider whether these businesses are making us better off.

PLATFORMS: GUARDIANS OF THE DIGITAL ECONOMY

Your Visa card, your PlayStation, the Google search engine, the instant messaging service WhatsApp, and the real estate agent on the corner have more in common than you might imagine. They are all examples of "two-sided markets."[2] That is, a market in which an intermediary (Visa, Sony, Alphabet, Facebook, the real estate agency) enables sellers and buyers to interact. These "platforms" bring together different communities of users seeking to interact with each other—for example, players and developers of games in the case of the video-game industry; the users of operating systems (Windows, Android, Linux, or OSX on your Mac or iOS on your iPhone) and application developers; users and advertisers in the case of search engines and media; or holders of bank cards and merchants in the case of card transactions. These platforms bring both groups together and also provide a technological interface allowing them to interact. Which is worth a little further explanation.

THE ECONOMICS OF ATTENTION

For a long time, economists assumed economic progress meant inventing new products, producing them at lower cost, and trading them

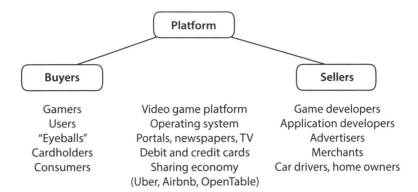

Figure 14.1. Two-sided platforms.

more efficiently by reducing transaction costs, often the transportation costs and customs duties that hindered international trade (empirical studies testing "gravity models" of international trade show that levels of trade between and within countries rise as transportation costs fall).

Fifty years ago, someone who wanted to read or listen to music could access only a limited number of references. A reader bought a newspaper for information about current events. To read a book or listen to a record, the reader was restricted to the catalogue of the local library. A wealthier household might put together a proprietary library, but it would be relatively small. When shopping, consumers were limited to their neighborhood stores. Someone who wanted to make friends or find a partner was dependent on relationships in the village or community.

In contrast, the cost of sharing information and transporting a *digital* good from one side of the planet to the other is almost zero. Catalogues are now limitless. While, for many millennia, our ancestors had trouble finding trading partners, now our problem is identifying, among the millions of partners with whom we could trade, the one that best corresponds to our expectations. We suffer from too much choice, not too little. Our problem now is how best to allocate time and attention to this plethora of potential activities, trades, and relationships. The economics of attention fundamentally changes behaviors and interactions. We need the combined insights of economists, psychologists, and sociologists to understand the consequences.

Thus, the most significant transaction costs are no longer transportation costs, but rather assessing what is on offer and choosing who to do business with, along with the signaling costs (seeking to convince potential trading partners of one's reliability). Our almost infinite sources of information, and the limited time we have to process and understand them, put the intermediaries and platforms that help us find these partners at the heart of the economic process. The more the other costs (transportation, customs duties, listing) fall, the more important costs associated with signaling, reading, and selecting become, and the more we need sophisticated platforms to match the buyers and sellers.

These platforms supply precious information about both the quality of what is on offer and who would be the best match, by communicating the reputations of vendors (the ratings of hotels on Booking.com, resellers on eBay, or Uber drivers) and providing advice about the products best suited to our tastes (through recommendations on Amazon or Spotify). They put us in contact with partners who are either more reliable or just better suited to our needs. They enable us to find a way, at low cost, through the maze of offers.

What is known as the sharing economy falls into this category. Its logic is to take better advantage of underused resources: apartments (Airbnb), private cars (Drivy or UberX), private planes (Wingly), or empty space on car trips (BlaBlaCar) or delivery vehicles (Amazon On My Way, You2You). But intermediaries are necessary to help each side identify what they would gain from taking part—for example, the trade between a tourist looking for a particular type of apartment on a particular date, and a householder who will be away from home at that time and wants to earn extra income. The user lost in a gigantic maze of information will need to trust the intermediary: trust the impartiality and quality of the recommendations, have confidence that personal data will be protected and deleted when promised, and believe that this data will not be transmitted to third parties. I will return to these points in the next chapter.

The ease of finding suppliers leads to trade that would otherwise be unimaginable. It often also causes prices to fall by putting suppliers in competition with each other. This is not always the case, however. Glenn and Sara Ellison at MIT have shown that the prices of rare secondhand books, for which there is little demand, are often more expensive online.[3] Those who are actively searching for "niche products" like these are prepared to pay a lot to acquire them, whereas those who come across them by chance in a bookshop or a garage sale tend not to be prepared to pay as much. The higher price online is not necessarily a sign of economic inefficiency, however. Without search engines and platforms, the buyer would probably never have been able to find the rare book.

Technological Platforms

Unlike Google, eBay, or Booking.com, payment card platforms such as PayPal or American Express do not put sellers and buyers in direct contact with one another: instead, they work on the basis that we are already engaged in a transaction with a merchant, and are simply looking for a way to pay rapidly, safely, and without having to go to an ATM or make a bank transfer.

Similarly, we do not need PlayStation or Xbox to inform us about the products the videogame developers have designed for their consoles. There are independent information channels (including advertising, reviews in newspapers, displays in stores, and keywords on Google's search engine) to tell us about new games. Rather, the consoles manufactured by Sony or Microsoft allow us to play the videogames developers design in the same way Windows allows us to use applications, commercial or not, compatible with the software on our computers. More generally, a second function of platforms is not so much to match and recommend buyers and sellers who would not know about each other, but rather to supply a technical interface so as to allow interactions to be as smooth as possible between users; in the same spirit, Skype or Facebook allow us to stay in contact with our family and friends through a convenient and congenial interface.

TWO-SIDED MARKETS

The economics of two-sided markets provide a theory that sheds light on the behavior of companies in all these—apparently disparate—markets. This theory is regularly used as much by management consultants as by competition authorities.

THE BUSINESS MODEL

These platforms have two communities of users, and the challenge is to find a viable economic model that ensures that both participate. Every two-sided platform faces a chicken-and-egg problem. A manufacturer of videogame consoles must attract both players and developers of videogames. Players want a wide choice of games, while developers want to reach the broadest possible market. The console manufacturer wants to stimulate enthusiasm on both sides. Media organizations (newspapers, television channels, websites) have the same problem, because to create a sustainable business model they must capture the attention of audiences and also interest advertisers. For payment systems such as American Express, PayPal, and Visa, the goal is to attract consumers and simultaneously ensure that merchants will accept their method of payment. All these activities make it essential to get two categories of customers onboard by taking advantage of their respective interests.

After a certain amount of trial and error, a new business model has emerged. I will use the language of economics to explain it first before turning to some familiar examples. The economic model depends on the *elasticity of demand* and on *externalities* between the different sides of the market. First, for each side of the market, the elasticity of demand is a measure that reflects how many users (in percentage terms) the platform loses when it raises the price by 1 percent. In all industries, two-sided or not, the elasticity of demand is a key concept when it comes to setting prices. A high elasticity of demand enforces price moderation, whereas a low elasticity encourages price increases. This is a theoretical concept, but it corresponds to everyday business experience and explains why competition generally makes prices fall: in increasing its price, a business will lose more customers, because they can defect to its competitors rather than just stop consuming.

Second, and more specific to two-sided markets, users benefit from the presence of those on the other side of the market—there are externalities between the two groups. If one side of the market benefits a lot from interactions with the other side, then the platform can charge more to the former and, in a "seesaw" pattern, will want to charge less to the latter side to make it attractive to join. The platform provider thus needs to know which side of the market is most interested in the service (has the lowest elasticity of demand, and is therefore likely to pay more without ceasing to consume), and which side brings more value to the other side.

Platforms often grow thanks to very low prices on one side of the market, which attract users on that side, and indirectly enables the platform to earn revenues on the other side. The structure of prices between the two sides of the market takes full advantage of the externalities between them. The basic idea is simple: the real cost imposed by a user is not the straightforward actual cost incurred in serving them. The user's presence creates a benefit for the other side of the market, which can be monetized—thus, de facto, reducing the cost of serving this user. In some cases, one side of the market might not pay anything, or might even be subsidized, the other side paying for both. Many newspapers—particularly free papers like *Metro* and *20 Minutes*—, radio stations, and websites do not ask their audiences to pay anything in exchange for the information and entertainment they supply. All their revenue comes from advertising. The PDF software for reading a file can be downloaded free of charge, but anyone who wants to create more than a very basic PDF file must pay for the professional version of the software. Why? Because the person who writes and distributes the document generally has a greater desire to be read than a potential audience has to do the reading. In contrast, readers of books willingly pay for a best seller.

Similarly, users of Google benefit from its numerous free services (search engine, email, maps, YouTube, and so on). The presence of the users (along with the information obtained during searches, from sent emails, and through other activities on the Google platform, as well as the information collected by other websites and purchased from data brokers) attracts advertisers, who can present their wares on the platform in a targeted way. Advertisers pay very large sums for this privilege.[4] This model is often replicated by platforms in other sectors.

For instance, OpenTable, an online restaurant reservation firm that manages twelve million reservations per month, does not make consumers pay—but charges restaurants one dollar per guest.

The payment cards sector is particularly interesting. When a consumer makes a payment by American Express card, American Express makes a profit from the commission it charges the seller—say, between 2 and 3 percent. This commission, also called the "merchant fee," is deducted from the purchase price (a bank that is a member of Visa or MasterCard also receives a percentage of the transaction, but indirectly through the "interchange fee" paid by the merchant's bank to the cardholder's bank). This explains why cards are often provided for free (or even at a negative price if they also give air miles or rebates in cash to the card user). The business model consists in providing consumers with cheap debit or credit cards and making merchants pay a percentage on each transaction. Even though the merchant fees are high (0.5 to 2 percent for Visa and MasterCard, around 3 percent for PayPal) the merchants have an interest in accepting the cards, because otherwise they risk losing customers. This is especially true for American Express, which benefits from an up-market image and many business clients, allowing it to charge higher commissions.

As we have seen, platform price structures are often favorable to one side of the market and very unfavorable to the other. Are these predatory prices (that is, abnormally low) or abusive prices (abnormally high)? It is far from clear—even companies that are not at all dominant in their markets (unlike Google) use this kind of price structure. We will return to this when discussing competition policy in two-sided markets.

When the Egg Comes before the Chicken …

Two-sided platforms have another problem if one of the sides using them needs to invest before the other side arrives in the market. In this case, expectations matter. For example, when a new videogame console is launched and there is no established customer base, independent game developers start work well before they are assured of the console's success. They assume the risk of developing (at great

Table 14.1. Asymmetric but Efficient Pricing

Low price side	High price side
Consumers (search engine, portal, newspaper)	Advertisers
Cardholders	Merchants

cost) videogames created for a platform that might not attract enough customers to make their investment profitable. To reassure developers, the console manufacturer generally announces that it will levy a royalty of five dollars to seven dollars on each game sold. These royalties increase the platform's stake in a wide diffusion of the console, and so will encourage the platform to put consoles on the market at a low price to attract new users: the platform gets not only the console's sale price, but also some commission on the subsequent sales of games. By contrast, if the platform's only source of revenue came from selling consoles, it would sell them at a high price, way above the manufacturing cost. Few consumers would buy the console and the game developers would sell few games. The royalty levied on the sales of games gives the platform some skin in the game, so to speak, and somewhat aligns the platform's incentives with the interests of game developers, who are then reassured that the console will not be too expensive.

Indeed, console manufacturers such as Sony or Microsoft often sell their consoles at a loss of up to a hundred dollars per unit.[5] Given this assurance, game developers may be willing to create titles long before the console is on the market. The platform can also develop its own games before the console goes on the market, as Microsoft did with Halo when it launched the Xbox in 2001.

The example of videogames is an extreme one because one side of the market lags far behind in adopting the platform. But the same problem is found elsewhere. Microsoft's Halo strategy, in which the company produced its own applications when it did not yet have a large user base, is frequently used. When the iPhone was launched in 2007, Apple did not yet have its App Store, so it produced its own applications. Netflix now produces its own programs and offers them in addition to the films it has bought from external content providers. A recent book by David Evans and Richard Schmalensee describes the importance of getting timing right in two-sided market strategies.[6]

Compatibility between Platforms

In many cases, consumers in these two-sided markets can choose between several platforms. Should the platforms cooperate so that they are all interoperable? In telecommunications, this cooperation is mandated by regulation. It is unthinkable that a subscriber to one mobile phone network would not be able to call a friend who has subscribed to a different one. But interoperability may be voluntary: real estate agencies often share listings to provide more choice for all their customers.

Other platforms choose not to be compatible. It is not possible to pay a merchant who accepts only Visa and MasterCard with an American Express card. An application written solely for Windows cannot be used with the Linux operating system. Incompatibility may lead users on one side of the market to increase their opportunities to engage with more users on the other side by joining several incompatible platforms, a practice called "multihoming." This happens, for example, when consumers have several payment cards, or when merchants accept different cards. Videogame developers can port the same game to different console formats. People wishing to buy or sell an apartment can approach several agencies simultaneously if the agencies do not share their listings.

Applications for mobile phones are another example. This is a market characterized by a fairly stable Apple-Android duopoly.[7] As one might imagine, multihoming is most widespread for the most popular applications. In this case, the application needs to be developed for each operating system, and the cost of marketing must be duplicated too—it is important for an application to be among the "most popular" of the ecosystem to be noticed by consumers. The same four applications are the most popular on both systems (Facebook, Pandora, Twitter, and Instagram). More generally, 65 percent of multihomed applications are found among the most popular.[8]

This kind of behavior has an influence on the choice of business model. User multihoming influences the way platforms set their prices. In the United States, for example, American Express had to cut the commissions merchants pay it following the appearance in the early 1990s of no-annual-fee cards on the Visa and MasterCard platforms. American Express's customers decided it was better to have a second payment card that cost nothing, which they would be able to use if their American Express card stopped working or was rejected by the seller. Then merchants reasoned, "Since my customers with an American Express card now also have a Visa or MasterCard, and these cards charge me less, I can refuse American Express cards without losing or antagonizing the customer." At that point, American Express was forced to reduce its merchant fees to keep retailers on its platform.

Opening Up

Sometimes a platform can decide that it will itself act as one of the two sides of the market. Then it conforms to the standard model of the firm, which has only to attract final consumers. Apple is a well-known case.[9] In the personal computer market, Apple limited the applications and hardware that would work on its operating system in the 1980s. Apple made the computers itself and set a high price on access to the software development kit, which made it a quasi-closed system. By contrast, Microsoft, with its DOS system (and later Windows), which became dominant in the 1990s, decided very early on to be open[10] by distributing development kits almost free of charge and not manufacturing computers itself. Apple has subsequently learned its lesson from this episode of competition between ecosystems, and has opened up (today, there are 1.5 million downloadable applications on the App Store); but it still keeps control not only over its operating systems (macOS and iOS), but also over the manufacture of computers (Mac) and mobile phone hardware (iPhone). Google's Android mobile phone operating system is more open than Apple's, even though Google has been accused, as Microsoft was earlier, of limiting access to other competing products.

In addition to the question of possible barriers to entry, to which I will return, the choice of whether to have an open system or not can be analyzed as follows. Apple's decision to be closed gave it better control over the hardware, but limited consumer hardware choice and raised hardware prices, thus potentially making the Apple brand less attractive. In France, the Minitel, a precursor of the microcomputer, developed a closed model for its applications— and very quickly lost the battle. As we have seen, another consideration is how established the platform is.[11] A new platform does not always have a choice; even with an open architecture, it can be led to produce hardware and applications itself, or to sign agreements like the one Bill Gates signed with IBM in the early 1980s (so that IBM computers ran on DOS). It is only with time that platforms get the full benefit of openness.

A DIFFERENT BUSINESS MODEL: PLATFORMS AS REGULATORS

CLASSIC AND TWO-SIDED ORGANIZATION

To understand why platforms differ from classic markets, let's take the example of the "classic" or "vertical" business model of the pharmaceutical industry. Increasingly, innovative drugs are produced by entrepreneurial biotech companies. However, these companies have no comparative advantage in development, clinical trials, securing approval from the regulatory authorities (such as the Food and Drug Administration in the United States), manufacturing, or marketing. So they sell their patents, grant exclusive licenses, or are acquired by a large pharmaceutical company such as Aventis, Novartis, Pfizer or GlaxoSmithKline.

In every case, a single pharmaceutical company will market the drug, because if there were multiple licenses, competition between pharmaceutical companies would lower the price that could be charged, decrease the value of the patent, and so reduce the revenue from licensing it. A biotech firm will therefore take care to create a downstream monopoly that maximizes profits from selling the drug.

Compare the platform model (figure 14.1) with the vertical model (figure 14.2). In the vertical model, the biotech startup has no contact with the end customer, and transacts only with the seller—the pharmaceutical company. The startup has no direct interest in whether the pharmaceutical company sets low prices that would increase consumption of the drug. That does not mean that the pharmaceutical company, which (in contrast) deals with both the startup and the customers, plays the role of a platform: the startup and the customers have no interaction with each other. This distinction between the vertical model and the platform model has important consequences.

Another illustration of the difference between vertical and platform organization is the comparison between a fruit and vegetable market (which is a platform, because the sellers interact directly with customers, but need the marketplace to do so) and a supermarket (where food suppliers have no interaction with customers, but instead sell their products directly to the supermarket, which then retails them to customers). In a fruit and vegetable market, sellers are not only concerned by such things as the conditions for acquiring a stall, or what share of their revenues they have to pay to the market's

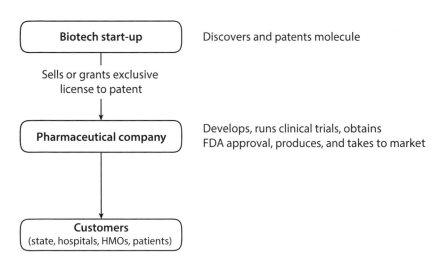

Figure 14.2. The vertical model.

owners, but also in whether the market will be able to attract buyers. A supermarket supplier, on the other hand, has a contract to provide a certain number of units at a given price. It does not care how many customers visit the supermarket.

These examples show that platforms are not a phenomenon peculiar to the digital era, even if digital technology has made them pervasive. And the organizational choice (classic vs. two-sided) is not cast in stone: when it began in 1994, Amazon was not a true two-sided platform, but a vertical (although digital) retailer: it bought books from publishers and resold them on the web.

PLATFORMS AS REGULATORS

A two-sided platform interacts both with the seller and the customer. This means that it cares about the customer's interests. This is not philanthropy. A satisfied customer will pay more to the platform, or will be more inclined to return. This underlies the uniqueness of the two-sided platform business model.

Competition among sellers. The first implication is that, unlike a holder of a pharmaceutical patent, a platform is usually not hostile to competition among sellers. For instance, many operating systems, such as Windows, have built their success on opening their platforms to external applications. These applications are often in competition with each other, and also with applications produced by the operating system owner itself.[12] This competition drives down prices and improves quality, making the platform more attractive to consumers. It is as if the platform has granted licenses to several sellers. It is more concerned with protecting the buyer's interests than the biotech startup of the vertical model.

Price regulation. Similarly, platforms sometimes regulate the prices that sellers can ask. The music sales offered online in 2007 by Apple's iTunes Store limited the charge for downloads to $0.99 per track and $9.99 per album; likewise, payment card platforms frequently forbid merchants from charging extra for payments by card.

Monitoring quality. To protect their customers, platforms also try to keep undesirable counterparties from accessing the platform.

Nightclubs and dating agencies screen their customers at the entrance. Stock markets set solvency requirements (more precisely, they demand collateral) to prevent a member's bankruptcy from having negative effects on other members. They also prohibit unethical behavior, such as "front running," a practice close to insider trading in which a broker buys or sells for himself before executing a major buy or sell order for a client. Apple monitors the quality of the applications on the App Store, and Facebook employs numerous people (although perhaps not enough given the concern about "fake news" and other issues) to keep an eye out for offensive content and behavior. Many platforms do not release the buyer's payment to the seller until the buyer has received the purchased item and is happy with it.

Providing information. Finally, platforms protect users by providing them with information about the reliability of sellers through a rating system. Sometimes they also have a quasi-judicial function by offering conflict arbitration—for example, sites that auction used cars do this.

The sharing economy that we hear so much about these days has adopted all these strategies. A platform like Uber verifies a driver's background, requires the driver to provide quality service, has users give ratings, and stops drivers with a bad reputation from accessing the platform. Sharing economy platforms also sometimes offer mediation, and guarantee to reimburse dissatisfied customers.

THE CHALLENGES TWO-SIDED MARKETS POSE FOR COMPETITION POLICY

REVIEWING THE SOFTWARE OF COMPETITION POLICY

What should we think about two-sided platforms' technology and marketing practices? Today, competition authorities in every country face this question. The traditional reasoning set out in competition law is no longer valid. Remember that it is common for a platform to set very low prices on one side of the market and very high prices on the other side. Offering goods at a low price (or even for free) on one side of the market naturally creates suspicion among competition authorities. In classic markets, it could be a predatory act against weak competitors. In other words, it may be a strategy to put rivals out of business by weakening them financially, or simply by signaling the intention to be aggressive. Conversely, a very high price on the other side of the market may suggest monopoly power. But in practice even small firms entering the market, such as a new website or a free newspaper funded by advertising, practice this asymmetric type of pricing. A regulator who does not bear in mind the unusual nature of a two-sided market may incorrectly condemn low pricing as predatory, or high pricing as excessive, even though these pricing structures are adopted even by the smallest platforms entering the market. Regulators should therefore refrain from mechanically applying the classic principles of competition policy where they are simply not applicable. New guidelines for competition policy as adapted to two-sided markets would require instead that the two sides of the market be considered together rather than analyzed independently, as competition authorities still sometimes do.

Farewell to Competition Law in These Sectors?

Although applying competition policy to two-sided markets requires care, it would be wrong to conclude that the sectors they serve should be abandoned to a sort of legal no-go zone into which competition law does not venture.

Making Competitors' Customers Pay …

Many platforms have a practice that affects us all indirectly: they require the sellers not to charge the platform's customers more than they would pay using any other channel. Often, the buyer has alternatives to a platform in buying from the seller. But the merchant is not authorized to charge more for a transaction via the platform than for one that bypasses it. Put differently, platforms require that the merchant fee they levy on the seller is not passed on to the end customer. (In economic jargon, we say the price is "single" or "uniform," that there is "price coherence," or that the platform user enjoys a "most favored nation" clause.)

For example (see figure 14.3), American Express charges merchants a transaction fee, but the consumer can pay merchants using cash, check, or another payment card instead. In the absence of specific regulation, American Express requires that the merchant not charge a higher price to consumers using their AmEx card. Similarly, a night in a hotel or a plane ticket can be reserved either through an online reservation platform, such as Booking.com or Expedia, or directly with the hotel or the airline company. The online reservation platform requires that direct purchases not be cheaper: the price of a room at an Ibis, Novotel, or Mercure hotel must be the same whether the room is reserved directly thorough their parent company (Accor) or through Booking.com or Expedia.[13] Amazon too implements this policy for its suppliers (such as book publishers) in many countries, although regulators in some others, including the United Kingdom and Germany, have ruled that platforms cannot insist on price coherence.

In the case of payment cards, competition authorities in some countries have insisted that merchants be free to levy surcharges on payments by card. Yet price uniformity also has two virtues. First, it avoids captive customers facing unexpected additional fees at the last moment.[14] We have all been on websites where we have found the plane ticket we wanted, entered all our information, only to discover at the final screen a ten dollar surcharge because we want to pay by card. Sometimes this online experience has equivalents in physical stores, in those countries that have freed merchants from the obligation to charge a single price (the United Kingdom, the Netherlands, the United States, Australia, and others); the surcharges are then much greater than the merchant fee levied by the card platform. In practice, though, surcharges are relatively rare, especially in stores with repeat customers. Second, for reservations made through a platform such as Booking.com or other online travel agencies, uniform pricing also has the advantage of preventing a consumer from finding the hotel they want on the platform's website, and then going directly to the website of the hotel or another website for a lower price, leaving no revenue for the entity that helped them find the hotel in the first place.

A compromise is needed. Uniform pricing is not necessarily good for the consumer. The reason is simple: high commission charges

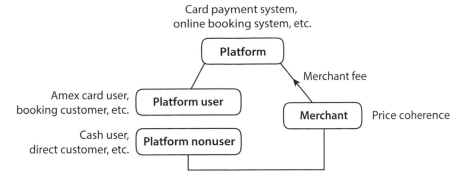

Figure 14.3. Price coherence in payment cards, online reservations, and other two-sided platforms.

levied by the platform are passed on to third parties—the customers who do not use the platform. Thus, the 15 to 25 percent commission charged to hotels by Booking.com is paid in part by customers who do not use Booking.com. Given that 20 percent of all hotel reservations pass through Booking.com, the site's customers pay only a small portion (20 percent) of what the hotel is charged by the online reservation platform, while 80 percent is paid by customers who do not use the platform. This is in effect a private tax levied on non-platform customers.[15] It is not all that surprising that excessive sales commissions can be charged.[16] In this case, the market failure is not an asymmetric price structure (which, as we've seen, is typical of two-sided markets), but the negative externality imposed on those who do not use the platform.

There are other examples of this problem. The question for the future will be whether we should regulate sales commissions, and if so, how. Uber clearly creates added value; but is it worth the 20 or 25 percent levied on the driver? Is there enough competition between platforms to keep their profits in check?

Platforms must create value, and not be parasites. But services that put the two sides of the market together might seek to extract an economic rent, either in the form of excessive sales commissions or, on the consumer side, by abusing advertising and lower-quality service.

We've all had the experience of looking for a little restaurant on the web, but we can't find its website—in any case, not on the first page of the search engine's results—because several platforms interpose themselves between us and the restaurant.

The economic analysis of these issues, whether in regard to sales commissions or other platform practices, is in its infancy, but it will provide the principles of regulation in this type of market. In the case of payment cards, for instance, economics suggests that merchant fees should be based on the principle of the internalization of externalities, as described in several chapters of this book;[17] the merchant fee should be equal to the extra profit the merchant derives from accepting a payment by card, as compared to an alternative method of payment.[18] The consumer, in choosing the method of payment, then imposes no externality on the merchant. This principle is now the one adopted by the European Commission to regulate the open Visa and MasterCard systems.

In this domain, as in others, neither *laissez-faire* nor a hasty set of regulations is warranted. A thorough economic analysis is required.

When Sellers Fight Back …

Platforms are not always in control. Sometimes they face something stronger than they are. One example is the price comparison sites for air travel in the United States.[19] The business model of these price comparison sites depends on access to airline data on prices and seat availability (so they only offer a price if there is a seat available). The airline sector is very concentrated in the United States, and the larger airline companies have tried to keep price comparison sites (especially smaller ones) from gaining access to the data they need. Why do they refuse to be listed on these comparison sites?

The airlines want to retain control over their customer data so they can target individuals with advertising and offers suited to them. Sometimes, they do not wish to pay the sales commission charged by the site (which indeed can be high and end up hurting consumers, but refusals to list happen even when there isn't a commission to pay). They are reluctant to admit, though, that they also do not want travelers to compare prices easily. In other sectors, when consumers can easily compare prices there is downward pressure on them. If an airline is known to have many flights to a destination, it is probable that the traveler will go to its website if it is not listed on the price comparison platform. A refusal to be on the platform may be anti-competitive.

Contestability

It does not take long to notice that information technology markets are highly concentrated. Often, one company (Google, Microsoft, Facebook) dominates the market. There is nothing abnormal about this; there will inevitably be a concentration of users on one or two platforms, but there are still grounds for concern about whether competition is functioning properly. There are two reasons for this concentration.

The first reason for the concentration is a network externality: we need to be on the same network as the person with whom we want to interact. That is Facebook's model. If our friends are on Facebook, we need to be there too, even if we would really prefer another social network. We want to be on Instagram to share our photos with others who are on Instagram. When the telephone was invented, the initial competition among (noninterconnected) networks ended with a monopoly, because ultimately users wanted to be able to call one another. When competition was reintroduced into the telephone industry in the 1980s and 1990s, it was necessary to ensure that the networks were interconnected, and thus gave one another access—without regulation, incumbent operators would not have given this access to new, smaller entrants.

Network externalities can be direct, as in the case of Facebook, or indirect, as in the case of a platform for which many apps or games have been created—the more people use a platform, the greater the number of apps, and vice versa. Or a greater number of users may increase the quality of service by allowing better predictions, as with search engines (Google) and GPS-based geographical navigation apps (Waze); for instance, while competing search engines can rival Google's for the most common requests, they do not have access to enough data to satisfy unusual search requests. Thus, a platform user benefits from the presence of other users on the same platform, even if there is no direct interaction with them, in the same way that a city dweller can benefit from the presence of other city dwellers who, although forever strangers, are the reason for amenities, such as bars or cinemas.

The second reason is linked to what are called "economies of scale." Some services require large technological investments. Designing a search engine costs roughly the same, whether there are two thousand search requests a year or two trillion (in the case of Google's). But obviously, the value of the user data from these two search engines, and what they could charge advertisers, would not be the same at all: they scale up.[20] The forces at play lead to a "natural monopoly." Because of network effects and economies of scale, the online economy is often a case of winner takes all. The browser market was dominated by Netscape, then by Internet Explorer (Microsoft), and now by Chrome (Google).

There are, of course, exceptions: economies of scale and network externalities are not always paramount, and the market is not always covered by one or two companies. There are many online platforms for music and film, such as Apple, Deezer, Spotify, Pandora, Canalplay or Netflix (although they are differentiated, for example, by their degree of interaction with the listener).

The concentration of digital markets again raises the question of competition. If one company has a dominant position, it creates a serious risk of high prices and a lack of innovation. New enterprises must be able to enter the market if they are more efficient or more innovative than the established monopoly; in economic jargon, we say that the market has to be "contestable." If it is not possible to have vigorous competition between companies at a point in time, we must be satisfied with dynamic competition—or "creative destruction" as Schumpeter called it—in which today's dominant firm is replaced by another that has made a technological or commercial leap.

This problem of contestability resurfaces regularly. In 1969, an antitrust suit in the United States forced IBM to separate its software activity from its hardware activity, an area in which IBM was dominant. It arose again with Microsoft and the dominance of its

Windows operating system (a 1996 lawsuit in the United States and another in 2004 in Europe sought to unbundle the Microsoft operating system from its other services, such as Internet Explorer and the Media Player), and most recently with Google. These antitrust suits often relate to the tie-ins enforced by a dominant company—in other words, either adding another service at the same price (software, in the IBM example) or, more generally, selling this additional service at a very low price, so that the purchasers of the basic service buy both of them anyway.

The question of why these free or low-price add-ons are a problem is more complex than it seems. Suppose IBM's software is inferior in quality to that of its competitors. A priori, IBM would have an interest in letting its customers use competitors' software, thus reinforcing the attractiveness of its hardware, which it could sell at a higher price. Following this line of argument, the practice of tying IBM software to hardware suggests the software must be superior to that of its competitors—otherwise IBM wouldn't have had an interest in tying the sales—in which case there would be no reason to be concerned. On the contrary, preventing IBM from pushing its software onto the market would only damage the user experience.

In antitrust suits, the dominant company will give various reasons—sometimes legitimate—for tying sales. One is the attribution of responsibility: If the product doesn't work, how does the user know who to hold responsible? Do web searches fail to deliver because of the browser or because of the search engine? Another reason sometimes given is the protection of intellectual property, if compatibility with the products of competing companies requires giving them trade secrets. Another justification often given is the segmentation of markets: IBM used this argument, asserting that the tied sale of punch cards—a potentially competitive additional service—allowed it to distinguish between casual users and intensive users so that it could charge the latter more. A similar argument was used in the 1990s in several "aftermarket monopolization" lawsuits. Primary market manufacturers (car manufacturers, Xerox, Eastman Kodak) refused to supply ISOs (independent service organizations) with parts for repairs or cartridges, arguing that this allowed them to price discriminate between high- and low-usage customers; this allowed them to charge higher prices for repairs and cartridges, thereby lowering the total user cost for low-intensity users and raising it for high-intensity ones. Finally, there is the argument that distribution costs are not duplicated when there is a single vendor, although this is a less convincing argument in the digital era, where many products are distributed over the Internet.

The contestability imperative makes it possible to understand why the practice of tie-in sales can be a problem. It is, in fact, essential that markets be contestable. Entrants into online markets often begin with a specific product, as part of a niche strategy, rather than with a complete range of products. It is only later, after successfully entering the market with one product, that they fill out their range. Thus, Google began with only its search engine before it became the company we know today; Amazon started by selling books. But to be able to get into the market at all, entrants must be able to sell their original product if it is better than the competing one offered by the incumbent. The dominant company may then wish to block even partial new entry to the market—not to improve its short-term profits, but because it might prevent the newcomer from later competing in areas in which the established company occupies a monopoly position.[21] In this case, the practice of tie-in sales is anticompetitive.

This analysis clearly shows that it is impossible to formulate a one-size-fits-all policy. There is no predetermined answer to the question of whether competition authorities ought to forbid a dominant company from imposing tie-in sales or anything resembling them (rebates for multiple purchases, for example) on its customers. Such commercial practices may be justified, but they may also serve only to consolidate the dominant position. The only valid way to ensure that competition enables the digital sector to realize its potential is to approach these questions on a case-by-case basis, deploying a rigorous economic analysis.

FIFTEEN
Digital Economies: The Challenges for Society

The digital revolution is rich in opportunities. Like it or not, this revolution is inevitable. All sectors of the economy will be affected. We have to anticipate the many challenges that the digital revolution presents so that we can adapt to them rather than merely enduring them: concerns about the trustworthiness of web platforms, data confidentiality, sustaining a health care system for all, fears about the destruction of work and greater unemployment, and the difficulties involved in implementing an increasingly complex tax system. These challenging questions underline the high economic stakes involved and the urgent need for a framework for analysis.

I start by discussing the need for Internet users to have confidence in the digital ecosystem. This trust must apply at two levels. As I showed in the last chapter, there is too much choice, too much information, too many people to interact with nowadays. Platforms are there to guide us and make up for our limited capacity to pay attention. This raises the question of the reliability of their recommendations. The second issue is the use made of personal data. This data is now a powerful economic and political asset for those who possess it. It will not always be used as we would wish, which raises the complex question of property rights over this data. Then I will explain why information could destroy health insurance systems, which are based on the mutual sharing of risks, and I will sketch out a regulatory response to this danger.

The digital revolution also raises fears about the future of employment and how it is organized: Which jobs are disappearing, or will disappear? Will there still *be* jobs once intelligent software and robots have been substituted for both skilled and unskilled workers? Will the jobs that remain be "Uberized"? Is society moving toward the end of conventional salaried employment, replaced by independent or "gig" labor? Any detailed predictions would prove wrong, so here I simply raise some of the main questions and try to provide elements of an answer.

TRUST

If we are already online through our computers, our smartphones, or our tablets, tomorrow the "Internet of things" (IOT) will make us even more connected. Home automation, connected cars, sensors (connected wristwatches, intelligent clothes, Google Glass), and other objects linked to the Internet will keep us constantly connected, whether we like it or not. This prospect inspires both hopes and fears. Whereas some of us now worry about cookies on our computers,[1] soon public and private websites will have far more detailed profiles thanks to rapid progress in things like facial recognition software. It is natural under the circumstances to worry about constant surveillance, like Big Brother in George Orwell's *1984*. The social acceptability of digitization depends on us believing that our data will not be used against us, that the online platforms we use will respect the terms of our contract with them, and that their recommendations will be reliable. In short, it is based on trust.

TRUST IN RECOMMENDATIONS

In many areas, we depend on the advice of better-informed experts: a physician for our health, a financial adviser for our investments and loans, an architect or a builder for the construction of houses, a lawyer for wills and probate, a salesperson when choosing products. This trust can be built on reputation, as it is with a restaurant. We rely on customer ratings, our friends' advice, or guide books. In the case of a neighborhood restaurant, if we are not satisfied we simply won't go back. Reputation, however, forms a basis for trust only if the quality of the recommendation can be evaluated afterwards.[2] If not, regulation may be necessary to improve the way the market functions.

Trust is linked both to competence and to the absence of conflicts of interest (such as sales commissions, friendships, or financial ties to a supplier). These conflicts of interest may lead the expert to recommend something not in our best interest. Just as the salesperson at the mall might recommend a particular camera or washing machine to get a bigger commission, it is reasonable to ask whether a website recommends products to suit our tastes and give value for money, or because it will get a share of the profits if we make the purchase. Nowadays, doctors are increasingly expected to reveal conflicts of interest, such as gifts or commissions from a pharmaceutical company that might lead doctors to recommend a less effective or more expensive drug, or to send us to an inferior clinic for treatment. In the future, the same problem will arise with medical apps on the Internet: Can they be both judge and judged? This problem is obviously not peculiar to medical services. More and more professions (including research) are subject to the requirement (whether imposed by law or self-imposed) to divulge potential conflicts of interest.

Trust in the Confidentiality of Personal Data

We trust our doctor because he or she is bound by a vow of professional confidentiality that is almost always honored. Can we be sure that the confidentiality of the personal information collected by the websites and social networks we use will also be respected? The question of confidentiality is as important for digital interactions as it is for medical data, but the guarantees online are much weaker.

Websites do have confidentiality policies (which few people read); they tell us about putting cookies on our computers and try to be transparent. Nonetheless, the contract between us and the websites is, in the jargon of economics, an incomplete contract. We just cannot know exactly what risks we are incurring.

First, we cannot evaluate the quality of any website's investment in security. Numerous recent examples, widely reported, show that this is not just a hypothetical issue: from the theft of credit card information (forty million Target customers in 2013, fifty-six million Home Depot customers in 2014, eighty million customers of health insurer

Anthem in 2015) to the theft of personal information held by government agencies (in the United States, for example, the Office of Personnel Management in 2015, the National Security Agency in 2013, and even thirty thousand employees of the Department of Homeland Security and FBI in 2016), not to mention the sensational theft in 2015 of emails, names, addresses, credit cards, and sexual fantasies of thirty-seven million clients of Ashley Madison[3] (a platform for extramarital affairs). Companies do invest large sums in online security to avert reputational damage, but would invest much more if they fully internalized the cost of such security breaches to their customers.

With the IOT, connected cars, household appliances, medical equipment, and other everyday objects will be partially or entirely managed remotely, and the opportunities for malicious hacking are going to increase. Though these technological developments are desirable, we must be careful not to repeat the mistake of constructing digital security for personal computers only in reaction to failures; security must instead be an integral part of the initial design of a device.

Moreover, clauses preventing the resale of customer data to third parties are unclear. For example, if a company transfers this data free of charge to its subsidiaries, who use it to provide us with services, has it broken our contract? The issue of data sharing is very sensitive. In general, any company that collects data should be at least partly responsible for any harmful use subsequently made of it by others, whether they obtained it directly or indirectly. (It is a bit like when a company's first- or second-tier supplier pollutes the environment or exploits workers. The company at the top of the supply chain can be held responsible either through legal mechanisms, such as extended liability, or through reputational consequences.)

What happens to our data when the company holding it goes bankrupt? Online or offline, when a company is in default, creditors can recover part of their investment by acquiring or reselling its assets; this is how businesses get access to credit in the first place. If data is a major economic asset, creditors naturally want to exploit it. Is this transfer desirable if the company's customers are relying on confidentiality? This too is not purely hypothetical: the American electronic products chain RadioShack had promised not to share its customers' data, but this data was sold when RadioShack went bankrupt in 2015.[4]

An additional problem is that users do not always have the time and expertise to understand the consequences of a confidentiality policy whose implications are complex and sometimes seem remote (most young people who post photos and other personal information online do not think about the use that might be made of it when they apply for a job or a loan).

Thus, we might ask whether the "informed consent" that we give websites is genuinely "informed." Just as in the case of commercial transactions offline, it is important to protect the consumer by regulation. When we park our car in a public lot, the ticket we take at the entrance specifies (legitimately) that entering the lot implies that we accept certain rules. We never read these tickets because it would be a waste of time and would block the entrance to the parking lot. But the law must protect us against one-sided clauses, that is, clauses that attribute disproportionate rights to the seller (such as the owner of the lot). The same goes online. Users cannot be expected to dissect complex documents every time they register with a website.

WHO OWNS DATA?

The processing of data will perhaps be the main source of value added in the future. Will we have control over our own data, or will we be hostage to a company, a profession, or a state that jealously retains control over access to it?

Today, many people are concerned about the entry of companies like Google, Amazon, Facebook, Apple, and Microsoft into territories such as health care. This reaction (outside the US at any rate) is partly envy of the fact that one country, the United States, has been able to create the conditions for state-of-the-art research in companies and universities in areas such as information technology and biotechnology—the dominance of the United States and a few other countries is not just luck. Still, it is legitimate to worry about the barriers to entry facing other companies that do not already own large amounts of data in these sectors.[5]

Digital companies can use the data they have gathered about their customers to offer them more targeted, suitable products. In theory, there is nothing wrong with this (bearing in mind the point made above about the possible use of this data for purposes that were not part of the original deal). It is better to receive relevant than irrelevant advertising. The problem comes if would-be competitors cannot make similarly attractive offers because they do not have the same information; the incumbent with the data is in a dominant position and can increase its profits at the expense of the consumer.

This raises the following fundamental question: Does the company holding customer data have the right to make money from the possession of that information? The commonsense reply, also discussed in chapters 16 and 17, is that if the data was collected thanks to an innovation or a significant investment, then the company ought to be able to profit from retaining and using it. If, on the other hand, it was easy and cheap to collect, the data ought to belong to the individual concerned.

To illustrate this point, take the simple example of personal data entered by the customer of a platform, or by counterparties (consumer, seller) transacting on the platform. We are rated by the purchasers when we use eBay to sell goods, Uber drivers are rated by passengers (and passengers by drivers), and restaurants listed on TripAdvisor are rated by their customers. In these cases, there is hardly any innovation, because decentralized evaluation is natural, and commonplace online. Such data should belong to the user: we want to have the option of using a platform other than eBay if it raises its prices or provides inferior service, but we don't want to start over again, without the reputation we laboriously built up for our eBay persona. Similarly, an Uber driver may want to transfer their rating when he or she leaves to go to work for Lyft. But the reality is different: from social networks to online stores, digital companies appropriate our personal data, albeit with our formal consent. Even health data garnered by implanted medical devices and Internet-connected wristwatches is usually transferred to the supplier's website, which claims the property rights to it.

If there were a clear separation between data provided by the customer and the subsequent processing of the data, the right policy would be simple: the data should belong to the customer and be portable—that is, transferrable to third parties at the wish of the customer.[6] Thus, since 2014, American patients have had access to their medical data, stored in a standardized and secure manner. Using an application called Blue Button,[7] a patient can access his or her medical file and choose to share it with medical service providers. On the other hand, processing this data represents an investment on the part of the company, so that processed data should, in theory, become its intellectual property. It seems natural to draw a distinction between the data, which belongs to the individual users, and the processing of it, which belongs to the platform.

In practice, however, the boundary between data and processing can be hard to establish.

First, the quality of the data may depend on efforts made by the company. One of the major challenges for sites like Booking.com or TripAdvisor is to guarantee the reliability of data against attempts to manipulate it, for example by hotels employing people to post fictitious favorable ratings (or unfavorable ratings for competitors). Similarly, Google needs to ensure that its PageRank algorithm, which decides on the order in which links to sites appear onscreen (and which depends in part on their popularity) is not distorted by searches targeting a particular site in order to artificially boost its ranking. If there were no attempts to manipulate ratings on Booking. com, it would not really have any justification for claiming ownership of the hotel ratings data. It is only because Booking.com has invested heavily to improve the reliability that it cocreates economic value (the individual reputations of hotels) and can therefore claim a property right to it.

Secondly, the collection and processing of data may be connected. The type of data collected may depend on the use that will be made of the information. In this case, it is harder to draw a clear distinction between data—which belongs to the user—and processing —which belongs to the company.

People often argue that platforms should pay for the data we give them. In practice, many sites do pay. This payment does not take the form of a financial transfer, but rather of services provided free of charge. We provide our personal data in exchange either for useful services (search engines, social networks, instant messaging, online video, maps, email) or in the course of a commercial transaction (as in the case of Uber and Airbnb). Online businesses can often argue that they have spent money to acquire our data.

There is one other angle to the problem. The transfer of data from the company to the user (possibly to be sent to another enterprise, as with Blue Button) needs data portability standards. Who will choose which kinds of data will be assembled and how it will be organized? Could standardization stifle innovation? As data is at the heart of value creation, defining rules governing its use is an urgent task. The answer will be complex, and it must rest on careful economic analysis.

HEALTH CARE AND RISK

The health care sector provides a good illustration of the way digitiza-tion will disrupt business and public life in the future.

Health care data has always been created through contacts with the medical profession: in a doctor's office, at the hospital, or in a medical laboratory. In the future, people will also be generating data nonstop, thanks to smartphone sensors or Internet-connected devices (as is already the case for pacemakers, blood pressure monitors, and insulin patches). Combined with knowledge of our genetic herit-age, health data will be a powerful tool for improved diagnosis and treatment.

Big Data, the collection and analysis of very large data sets, pre-sents both an opportunity and a challenge for health care. It is a marvelous opportunity insofar as it provides more precise diagnoses, which are also less costly because they limit the expensive time highly skilled medical professionals have to devote to each patient. Examina-tions and diagnoses will soon be carried out by computers. This frees the doctor and the pharmacist from routine tasks.

As in other areas, machines could replace human beings for some tasks. Compared with a human being, a computer can pro-cess a far larger quantity of a patient's data and correlate it with the symptoms and genetic backgrounds of similar patients. A computer does not have human intuition, but this will gradually be overcome by machine learning, i.e., the processes through which the machine revises its approach in the light of experience. Artificial intelligence (AI), by imitating humans while also trying to discover new strategies, has enabled computers to dominate the game of chess for the past twenty years; in 2016, a computer defeated the world Go champion. Computer scientists and researchers in biotechnology and neuroscience will be at the heart of the value chain in the medical sector, and will appropriate a significant part of its added value.[8] This may be speculative, but one thing is certain: the medical profession of tomorrow will not resemble the current one at all. Digital health care will improve prevention, which remains less developed than curative medicine. Technology might also help answer the question of how to provide equal access to health care, now endangered by the combination of higher treatment costs and weak public finances.

So the opportunities for society are magnificent. But so is the challenge to the mutuality and risk sharing that characterizes health care systems; let us first review the underlying insurance principles, which apply to all health care provision systems.

The Key Principles of the Economics of Insurance

The distinction between what economists call "moral hazard" and "adverse selection" is crucial here. Moral hazard is the common propensity to pay less attention, and make less effort, when we are covered by insurance and will not be fully responsible for the consequences of our actions. In general, moral hazard refers to behaving in ways that are harmful to others when we are not going to be held fully responsible: we leave the lights on or water our lawns too much when we aren't paying the full costs. Another example is risk taking by a bank that knows it can always borrow more from lenders, when those lenders expect a government bailout if the risks don't pay off. Yet another is an agreement between a company and an employee made to camouflage a dismissal as a termination, which in turn generates a right to unemployment benefits paid for by taxpayers.[9] The examples could go on.

Some events, on the other hand, may not be our fault: the light-ning that strikes our house, the drought that destroys our crops, a longstanding ailment or congenital illness, a car accident for which we are not to blame. We want to secure insurance against such risks, whose costs are best spread across the population. Such risk pooling may be limited, however, if different individuals face different proba-bilities of such a mishap, and if there are asymmetries of information about these probabilities. Insurers are accordingly concerned about the possibility that their offers attract risky insurees, but not low-risk ones, either because low-risk individuals self-select out of the market or because other insurers have "cherry picked" (attracted the most profitable insurees). For instance, healthy individuals may not want to pay the insurance premium appropriate to an average citizen, and therefore self-select out of the market; or well-informed insurance companies may offer lower premiums to these healthy individuals, denuding the market (to uninformed insurers) of all but those likely to experience poor health. When this happens, we say there is adverse selection in the market.

The principles guiding insurance for the common good are simple: risks that are not under the control of those concerned should be fully shared. When, on the other hand, people's actions affect the risks, they must be held partly responsible, to give them an incentive to behave in the collective interest rather than only in their own interest. If an individual builds a house in a flood zone because the land is cheap, they should not get government support when the house is flooded.[10] But the loss can rightly be fully covered if the damage is due to an unpredictable event. In health care, this principle means fully insuring the costs involved in treating a serious medical con-dition, but making patients act responsibly with regard to drugs or treatments with minimal therapeutic effects, or unnecessary consul-tations and tests.

In practice, things are a little more complicated. It isn't always easy to distinguish the scope of moral hazard from that of bad luck, so we can't be sure how far to hold people responsible: Was the harvest small because the farmer did a bad job, or because of unexpected problems with the soil or the climate? Do we get a second opinion from a doctor (imposing additional cost in countries with state health insurance) because we think the first doctor wasn't sufficiently careful or competent, or because we are hypochondriacs? [11]

This inherent uncertainty about responsibility explains why (in any type of insurance) the insured and the insurer often share the risk. Deductibles are often used to achieve this. So, for example, in French health care, copayments established when the public health care program was first set up were high: 30 percent for a consultation, 20 percent for hospitalization. These copayments were then covered in full by supplementary insurance policies, so other copayments have been reintroduced to try once again to make patients share responsibility. Patients must now make minimum contributions to the cost of health care, though not on longstanding ailments, cancers, or other major health risks. [12]

TODAY ...

Sometimes, the insurance market does not need to be regulated. Home insurance allows us all to pool our risks (if my house burns down, your insurance premiums will pay part of the cost of rebuilding it, and vice versa) without serious problems of risk selection: in other words, I can get a policy specifying a reasonable premium to insure my house because the chances that my house will burn down are about the same as the chances that your house will burn down.

This is not the case for health, where there are great inequalities among individuals. Without regulation, there would only be minimal risk pooling. There is a strong incentive for insurers to select "good" customers (those whose risk of illness is low). In France for example, half of all health care expenses are incurred for the treatment of only 5 percent of those insured. An individual with a longstanding medical condition will not find a private insurer prepared to sell health insurance at a reasonable price. (This question of preexisting conditions was an important issue in the US's Affordable Care Act and the debate about replacing it.) The selection of risks—an insurer's ability to target people with low risks and to offer them advantageous terms not available to riskier individuals—would generate huge inequalities, based solely on factors that individuals cannot control (the good or bad luck of being in good or bad health). Information kills insurance. [13]

That is why most of the world's health care systems, whether public or private, forbid selection based on risk characteristics, at least for basic insurance (the US will be an exception if it reverts to the situation before the Affordable Care Act). In France, the public health care system is universal, so the problem of the selection of risks for basic insurance does not arise. In Germany, Switzerland, and the Netherlands, basic health insurance is provided by private businesses, who compete and are forbidden to cherry-pick insurees: they are not allowed to use questionnaires to identify less risky customers—they are in fact obliged to accept all potential subscribers. Their rates must be the same for everyone (although with variations allowed for a choice of deductible and sometimes based on age group). Of course, there are indirect ways of selecting low-risk customers who will probably have little need for medical treatment, for example by directing less advertising toward high-risk groups, but it is up to the regulator to intervene if there is abuse. In Switzerland, compensation for risks among insurers is also provided for; this further diminishes the incentive to select low-risk customers. [14]

The same may not be true for supplementary private health insurance. While other countries have chosen a coherent overall system—whether wholly or almost wholly public (as in the UK) or private (as in Germany, Switzerland, and the Netherlands)—France uses a hybrid system: public basic insurance with additional insurance coverage provided by the private sector. People therefore have two insurers, which doubles administrative costs and complicates the task of controlling medical costs. Furthermore, on the supplementary health insurance front, the French state encourages the selection of risks by subsidizing collective contracts provided through employment. [15] Employees being, on average, in better health than the rest of the population, this works against the unemployed and the elderly, who are often forced to pay higher premiums to gain access to complementary insurance. [16]

... AND TOMORROW

The greater availability of information affects risk sharing. One of the positive aspects of this is that it will be easier to control moral hazard. Cheap monitoring of our behavior (such as the number of miles we drive, or our efforts to look after our health) will allow insurers to lower premiums and deductibles for those who behave responsibly. It will also enable them to recommend healthier behavior. On the other hand, the digitization of the economy and the progress of genetics, as exciting as they are, also create new threats to mutuality.

Genetic background is the typical example of a characteristic that is not subject to moral hazard: we do not choose it in any way, whereas we can, through our behavior, influence the probability of a car accident (by driving carefully) or the theft of our vehicle (by parking it in a garage or locking the doors). Without regulation, individuals whose genetic tests suggest that they will be healthy for the rest of their lives would be able to use these results to obtain cheap insurance. There's nothing wrong with that, you'll say ... except that there is no free lunch. The cost of insurance for those whose genetic makeup suggests, on the contrary, a long-term malady or fragile health will see their insurance premiums rise to extremely high levels: farewell to mutuality and risk sharing. Again, information destroys insurance.

Prohibiting discrimination among customers based on genetics and health data is not enough to reestablish the mutuality that makes insurance possible. That is where the digitization of the economy can hurt. Our habits of consumption, our web searches, our emails, and our interactions on social networks reveal a great deal about how healthy our lifestyles are, and even perhaps about our illnesses. Twitter, Facebook, or Google, without having any access to our medical histories, can predict—approximately, to be sure—whether we have preexisting medical conditions, behave in risky ways, take drugs, or smoke. Digital companies can select people who are good risks very precisely by offering individualized or collective contracts based on the information they gather. Axa's future competitors will probably no longer be called Allianz, Generali, or Nippon Life, but Google, Facebook, and Amazon.

We need to think about the future of insurance for health risks and plan for these developments, rather than merely endure them. This is a challenge for governments, but also for economists.

THE NEW FORMS OF EMPLOYMENT IN THE TWENTY-FIRST CENTURY

NEW FORMS OF EMPLOYMENT?

Many people are concerned about the changing nature of work. This has some distinct aspects: the development of independent working, and the outlook for unemployment. It is difficult to forecast what the organizations or work of the future will look like, but the economist can contribute a few things to think about. Let us begin with the organization of labor.

Independent work is ancient: farmers, merchants, and many members of the professions are self-employed and usually own their means of production. Temporary workers, freelance journalists, performers, and consultants have always worked for several employers. Second sources of revenue have also become very widespread: high school math teachers tutor students at home, students have part-time jobs, and so on.

The function of economics is not to make value judgments about how work is organized; on the contrary, it is important for people to be able to choose the kind of employment that suits them. Some people prefer the relative security of salaried employment and the comfort of being part of an organization managed by someone else. They may also fear the isolation associated with working independently—which helps explain why self-employed people share work spaces, such as "fab labs" (fabrication laboratories) or "makerspaces" for computer sciences and hi-tech entrepreneurs. They do it to share ideas, but also to preserve human contact. Other people prefer the freedom associated with working for themselves. To each according to their tastes.

The amount of self-employment is increasing, along with the fragmentation of labor into microjobs. Many platforms allow someone—perhaps an employee or a retiree—to work a few hours a day to earn a bit of income. Amazon Flex allows people to deliver packages, perhaps in the course of a trip they were planning to make. The idea is that private individuals replace delivery companies for short journeys. Through the Mechanical Turk platform, which Amazon launched in 2005, people can perform small tasks in return for small payments. Some people make a full-time job out of this, while others work only occasionally. Today, there are supposed to be five hundred thousand of these "Turkers" throughout the world. On TaskRabbit, a platform for handyman services, we can hire people to mow our lawns, construct our websites, do house repairs, or help when we move.

There is nothing conceptually novel about all this, but digitization makes it easier to break production up into simple tasks and to connect users. As Robert Reich, President Clinton's secretary of labor and a critic of this development (which he has called the "share-the-scraps economy"), points out: "New software technologies are allowing almost any job to be divided up into discrete tasks that can be parceled out to workers when they're needed, with pay determined by demand for that particular job at that particular moment."[17] Supporters retort that it improves the efficiency of a market by matching demand with supply, an exchange in which everyone is a winner. Wealthy households can afford to pay for numerous services that did not exist earlier, or were more expensive. But so can the middle classes, as experience with ride hailing companies shows. In cities such as Paris and London, taxi rides are expensive and relatively few people use them—the well-off and those with expense accounts.[18] Many people who hardly ever used this form of transportation have begun to do so since lower-cost services like Uber or Lyft appeared.

What Should We Think about Uber?

The very mention of Uber triggers fierce debates.[19] This is just as true in France (where UberPop, with its nonprofessional drivers, was banned in 2015 after protests by taxi drivers) as in the US (where some cities have introduced restrictions) and the UK (where London's famous black-cab drivers have staged protests and lobbied for restrictions). How should an economist respond? I will limit myself to a few reflections.

1. First, whether for or against Uber (I will return to arguments pro and con), it has certainly brought a technological advance. This advance is simple enough, which shows how harmful an absence of competition (true of many taxi markets before Uber) can be to innovation. What are the innovations adopted by Uber? Automatic payment by a preregistered card, which enables users to leave the taxi quickly; rating both drivers and customers; not having to call and wait for the despatcher to send a taxi; geolocation, monitoring the taxi's itinerary before and during the trip and so enabling a reliable estimate of the waiting time and journey time; and finally, and perhaps counterintuitively, surge pricing that raises fares when vehicles are scarce. These are almost trivial "innovations," but no taxi company had thought of them or bothered to implement them.

The most controversial of these innovations is surge pricing; and although one can imagine abuses (in theory the algorithm could raise prices dramatically when a storm is forecast, although in practice Uber refrains from such price gouging by capping fares in emergencies), having pricing respond to supply and demand is, overall, a good thing. The pioneer of peak load pricing was EDF, France's state-owned energy company, which has long used a pricing scheme thought up by a young engineer called Marcel Boiteux, who went on to become the company's CEO. Today, this idea is applied under the variant of "yield management" to plane and train tickets, hotel rooms, and ski resorts. It makes it possible to fill rooms or unoccupied seats by charging low prices at off-peak periods without compromising the company's finances. To return to taxis: when there is a shortage, instead of making users wait endlessly for a car, surge pricing encourages those who can walk, take the subway, or hitch a ride with friends to do that instead. This leaves the rides available for those who have no alternative.

2. Existing businesses may resist new technological developments, but the defense of established interests is not a good guide for public policy. In this case, the status quo is unsatisfactory. In many cities, taxis were expensive and often unavailable. The limited market meant many potential jobs were not created—jobs that could have been done by the people who needed the work most. It is interesting to

note that in France, Uber created jobs for young people from immigrant backgrounds in a country where labor market institutions have not worked well for this group.

3. There are two arguments that support the case of traditional taxi drivers. The first is that competition should be on an equal footing; this is a crucial argument. We should calculate whether a traditional taxi and an Uber taxi pay the same social security charges and taxes. Examining these figures would ensure that there was no distortion of competition. This debate is purely factual, and could be conducted objectively—something that was not done in the dispute in 2015 that resulted in the banning of UberPop in France.

The second argument results from a blunder many taxi regulators have made in the past. They granted individuals, free of charge, taxi licenses that were very valuable because they were issued in limited numbers. In theory, these official authorizations cannot be passed on, but in practice they are often resold. The state is responsible for the current fraught situation. Some independent taxi drivers have paid high prices for their licenses, and the new competition is destroying their future retirement savings. This raises the issue of whether the state should compensate them for their capital loss (whereas if there had been no reselling of licenses, the problem would not have arisen, because a right to make income acquired free of charge could legitimately be revoked). In Dublin, the authorities found a clever solution, giving a new license to everybody who already had one as the means of compensation, while doubling the number of taxis. That was the right policy, until the technological progress brought about by ride-hailing platforms.

The Challenge of Innovation

Employment needs businesses. France has a disturbing shortage of new enterprises at a global scale. All the companies on the Paris CAC 40 stock index—which are often very successful internationally—are descended from old companies. That is not the case in the United States, where just a small proportion of the one hundred biggest listed firms existed fifty years ago. To create jobs, France (and other

countries) need to develop an entrepreneurial culture and environment. Globally successful universities are also needed to take advantage of this turning point in economic history, a point at which knowledge, data processing, and creativity are going to be at the heart of
creating value. In fact, universities are a sort of condensed version
of all the ways businesses will need to transform: more horizontal
cooperation and multitasking, an emphasis on creativity, and a desire
to realize oneself through work. For its part, the working culture in
Silicon Valley or in Cambridge, Massachusetts, has been inspired by
American universities, the world their young creators know best.

The End of Salaried Employment?

Is "contingent work," such as self-employment or gig work, and the
disappearance of salaried employment, likely to become the norm, as
many people predict? I don't think so. I would bet instead on a gradual move toward people working independently, not on the complete
disappearance of salaried jobs.

This gradual change will happen in part because new technologies
are making it easier to put independent workers in contact with customers and to run a back office. Even more important, independent
contractors need to create and be able to promote their *individual*
reputations at low cost. Customers used to rely on a taxi company's
reputation, or choose a washing machine by the manufacturer's brand,
rather than rely on the reputation of the employee who happened to
drive the taxi or make the machine. Now, as soon as an Uber customer is matched with an available driver, the driver's reputation is
available at once, and the customer can reject the transaction. A firm's
collective reputation, with the concomitant control of its employees'
behavior, is becoming gradually less important than individual reputations.[20] This individual reputation, as well as digital traceability of
the service provided, is one answer to the question of trust raised at
the beginning of this chapter.

But technology can sometimes have the opposite effect and favor
standard salaried employment. George Baker and Thomas Hubbard[21]
give the following example: In the United States, many truck drivers

work for themselves, which causes some problems. The driver owns his own truck, which is a substantial investment. Drivers are investing their savings in the same sector as their labor, which is risky—in a recession, income from work and the resale value of the vehicle decrease at the same time. Common sense suggests that people's savings should not be invested in the same sector as their employment. In addition, owner-drivers have to pay for repairs, during which time their only source of income is unavailable.

In that case, why aren't truck drivers employees of a company that buys and maintains a fleet of trucks? Sometimes they are, but moral hazard limits this: an employer needs to worry about the driver not being careful with the vehicle, whereas the independent trucker has every incentive to take good care of it. Computerization can alleviate this problem. The trucking company can monitor the driver's behavior using onboard computers.

More generally, several factors explain why conventional jobs still exist. First, the investment required to set up a business may be too large for a single worker, or even a group of workers. Even if the investments are affordable, some people prefer not to put up with the risk and stress of running a business, such as doctors or dentists who choose to be employees of a medical clinic rather than set up on their own.

Second, from the perspective of a business owner, having someone work for other people may be undesirable for several reasons. If the worker has access to manufacturing secrets or other confidential information at work, an employer is likely to insist that people work for the one firm exclusively. When the work involves teams, and the productivity of each individual worker cannot be measured objectively (unlike that of a craftsman who works alone), the worker is not always free to organize work as he or she likes. In this case, having several employers could generate significant conflicts over the allocation and pace of work. Third, it may be the case that individual reputations based on ratings do not function well. As Diane Coyle notes,[22] the quality of the individual consultants may be hard to monitor, at least immediately, by the clients; whereas a traditional consultancy employing individual consultants may be more efficient at "guaranteeing" quality.

In short, I believe that salaried employment will not disappear; but there are good reasons for thinking that it will continue to become less important over time.

A Labor Law Ill-Suited to a New Context

France, like many other countries, conceived its current labor law with the factory employee in mind.[23] It consequently gives little attention to fixed-term labor contracts, and still less to the teleworker, the independent worker, or the freelancer. Labor laws were not written for students or retirees working part time, freelancers, or Uber drivers. In France, 58 percent of employees outside the public sector still have permanent employee contracts, but this proportion is falling. In many countries, such as the UK and US, the number of salaried employees is declining, whereas the number of self-employed workers is increasing. We need to move from a culture focused on monitoring the worker's presence to a culture focused on the results. This is already the case for many employees, especially professionals, whose presence is becoming a secondary consideration—and whose effort is in any case hard to monitor.

Confronted by these trends, legislators often try to fit new forms of employment into existing boxes, and to raise questions in similar terms: Is an Uber driver an employee or not?

Some people would answer yes, arguing that an individual driver is not free to negotiate prices, and is subject to various requirements for training, type of vehicle, or cleanliness. For some drivers, all their income comes from their Uber activity (others may drive for other ride-hailing platforms, or may have other entirely different jobs, for example, in a restaurant). Finally, drivers with poor ratings may be terminated by Uber.

Yet restrictions of various kinds also do apply to many self-employed workers, who are limited in their freedom of choice by the need to protect a collective reputation—such as that of a profession, a brand, or a wine region's appellation. In many countries, an independent physician cannot choose the price he or she charges, and must follow specific rules or risk losing accreditation. Even an independent winemaker must respect certification rules.

Others would argue that Uber drivers are free to decide how much they work and where, when they work, and where they go. In addition, they bear the economic risks. So the status of an Uber driver (or others working for similar platforms) is a gray area. They have characteristics of both independent contractors and salaried workers.

In my view, this debate goes nowhere. Any classification will be arbitrary, and will no doubt be interpreted either positively or negatively depending on one's personal prejudices about these new forms of work. The debate also loses sight of why we classify work in the first place. We are so used to the current framework that we have forgotten its initial purpose, which was to ensure the worker's well-being. The important thing is to ensure competitive neutrality between different organizational forms: the dice must not be loaded in favor of either salaried employment or self-employment. The state must be the guarantor of a level playing field between organizational forms and not choose policies that make the digital platforms unviable just because they are unfamiliar and disruptive. If there is something wrong with the labor market, policy intervention should fix it, and not cherry-pick a specific organizational form.[24]

One thing is certain: we will need to rethink our labor laws and the whole work environment (training, retirement, unemployment insurance) in a world of rapid technological and organizational change.

INEQUALITY

Digitization may also exacerbate inequality. First, inequality between individuals. The share of income going to the highest-paid 1 percent of the population in the United States rose from 9 percent in 1978 to 22 percent in 2012.[25] As Erik Brynjolfsson and Andrew McAfee have noted, the big winners of the digital age are "the stars and superstars."[26] In the last forty years, labor economists have analyzed the path of earnings, especially in the United States. The earnings of people with graduate degrees have shot up, while the earnings of college graduates have also risen significantly, although not as much. The earnings of all other groups of workers have stagnated or even decreased.

This polarization is likely to get worse. Innovative, highly skilled jobs will continue to get the lion's share of income in the modern economy. The problem of distribution will become more difficult; governments will need to ensure a certain level of income for all individuals, and to that purpose will need to choose between regulations that keep wages at a level above the market rate (and thereby cause unemployment) and direct payments (also called universal income or negative income tax). Are we moving toward a society in which a nonnegligible proportion of the workforce will be unemployed, and will have to be paid an income financed by a "digital dividend"? (Compare this to the "oil bonus" that each resident of Alaska automatically receives from the state.)[27] Or are we creating a society in which this part of the population will hold low-productivity public service jobs (as happens today in countries like Saudi Arabia)? These solutions however may contravene individuals' desire to gain dignity through work, and will also require countries to be able to access the digital manna.

There indeed may also be substantial inequality between countries. Let us sketch out an extreme scenario to illustrate the danger of this trend. In the future, countries that can attract the most productive people in the digital economy will disrupt the value chain in every sector and appropriate immense wealth, while the other countries will have only the scraps. This inequality could result from differences in public policy concerning higher education and research, and from innovation policy more generally. But it will also result from fiscal competition. The mobility of talented people—a labor market that is now completely globalized—will lead many of these wealth creators to migrate to countries that offer the best conditions, including the lowest tax. This also relates to the inequality of individual incomes. Countries not taking part in this global competition for talent will not be able to redistribute wealth to the poor, because the poor will be all that they have. While this scenario is too simplistic (and exaggerated for effect), it illustrates the problem. Unlike oil manna, digital manna is mobile.

THE DIGITAL ECONOMY AND EMPLOYMENT

The Jobs Most in Danger

Not a day passes without an article appearing in the press, fretting about the mass unemployment that will be created by the digitization of the economy. One example is the furor over a statement in 2014 by Terry Gou, the CEO of Foxconn, a Taiwanese electronics company with 1.2 million employees located mainly in Shenzhen and elsewhere in the People's Republic of China. Gou said that his company would soon use robots in place of humans, in particular to assemble new iPhones.

Machine learning and AI will also change the employment structure. To some extent, this will just accelerate an ongoing trend. Many jobs involving routine (and thus codifiable) tasks, such as the classification of information, have been eliminated: banking transactions are digitized, checks are processed by optical readers, and call centers use software to shorten the length of conversations between customer and employee, or even replace humans with bots. Book and record stores have disappeared in many cities.

These changes are concerning. Most emerging and underdeveloped countries have counted on low salaries to attract outsourced jobs from developed economies, using this route to escape poverty. Robots, AI, and other digital innovations substituting capital for labor threaten their growth. And what about developed countries? If even Chinese labor is becoming too expensive, and will be replaced by machines, what will happen to better paid jobs in these countries?

David Autor, a professor of economics at MIT, and his coauthors have studied the polarization over the last thirty years resulting from technological change in the United States, Europe, and other countries.[28] Digital technologies tend to benefit those employees, generally highly trained, whose skills complement the new digital tools; obviously, it also means fewer jobs for those whose work can be automated, and "hollows out" the distribution of jobs into either high-paying skilled positions or low-paying basic service positions. The kind of jobs being found more often are, at the bottom of the salary scale, those for nurses, cleaners, restaurant workers, custodians, guards, and social workers, for example, and, at the top of the salary scale, for business executives, technicians, managers, and professionals. Jobs offering middle-level salaries—for administrative personnel, skilled laborers, craftsmen, repairmen, and so on—are now relatively less available. In the United States, the difference in salary between those who hold university degrees and those who left right after high school has grown enormously in the past thirty years.

Computers can easily replace humans for certain tasks. Deductive problems require applying rules to facts: the particular is deduced from the general rule in a logical way. An ATM verifies a card number, the PIN code, and the bank account balance before issuing money and debiting the account; programing these operations replaced many of the earlier functions of bank tellers. Nonetheless, total employment in banking rose even as the ATM network spread, because demand grew and teller jobs were replaced by new tasks.[29]

On the other hand, induction, which starts with specific facts and works toward a general law, is more complex. There has to be enough data for the computer to discover a recurrent pattern. But great advances have been made on this front. For example, algorithms could predict the United States Supreme Court's decisions about patents as well as any legal experts. Similar techniques are enabling automated facial recognition, voice recognition, medical diagnosis, and other tasks that previously only humans could perform.

The hardest tasks for a computer arise with unforeseen problems that do not match any programmed routine. Rare events cannot be analyzed inductively to generate an empirical law. Frank Levy (MIT) and Richard Murnane (Harvard), one of whose diagrams I reproduce in table 15.1, give the following example: Suppose a driverless car sees a little ball pass in front of it. This ball poses no danger to the car, which therefore has no reason to slam on the brakes. A human being, on the other hand, will probably foresee that the ball may be followed by a young child, and will therefore have a different reaction. The driverless car will not have enough experience to react appropriately. This does not mean, obviously, that the problem cannot be solved eventually, because the machine can be taught this correlation. But this example illustrates the difficulties still encountered by computers.

Table 15.1. The Disappearance of Jobs

Increasingly Difficult to Program

$\longrightarrow$

	Rule-based logic	Pattern recognition	Human work
Variety	Computer processing using deductive rules	Computer processing using inductive rules	Rules cannot be articulated and/or necessary information cannot be obtained
Examples	Calculate basic income taxes	Speech recognition	Writing a convincing legal brief
	Issuing a boarding pass	Predicting a mortgage default	Moving furniture into a third-floor apartment

Source: Frank Levy and Richard Murnane, Dancing with Robots, NEXT report 2013, Third Way.

The challenges for humans and computers are therefore different. Computers are much faster and more reliable when processing logical and predictable tasks. Thanks to machine learning, computers can increasingly cope with unforeseen situations, provided they have enough data to recognize the structure of the problem. On the other hand, the computer is less flexible than the human brain, and is not always able to solve some problems as well as a five-year-old child. Levy and Murnane conclude that the people who will do well in the new world will be those who have acquired abstract knowledge that helps them adapt to their environment; those who have only simple knowledge preparing them for routine tasks are most in danger of being replaced by computers. This has consequences for the education system. Inequalities due to family background and education are likely to increase further.

The End of Work?

Although the current changes are occurring faster than previous technological advances, what is happening to work nonetheless shares the same characteristics. I have already mentioned the well-known episode at the beginning of the nineteenth century in Britain, when the

Luddites (skilled textile workers) revolted by destroying new looms that less-skilled workers could operate. The Luddite revolt was brutally suppressed by the army. Another example of dramatic change is the reduction in demand for agricultural labor in the United States; in less than a century, the proportion of workers employed in agriculture fell from 41 percent to 2 percent of the total. Despite this massive loss of agricultural jobs, unemployment in the United States is only 5 percent. This illustrates the fact that the destruction of some jobs is compensated by the creation of new, different jobs.

Technological progress destroys jobs and creates others, normally not harming employment in aggregate. For digital technology, the most visible jobs created are those connected with computer science and the digital sector. After more than two centuries of technological revolutions, there is still little unemployment.[30] The alarmist predictions of the end of work have never been realized. As Erik Brynjolfsson and Andrew McAfee note,

> In 1930, after electrification and the internal combustion engine had taken off, John Maynard Keynes predicted[31] that such innovations would lead to an increase in material prosperity but also to widespread "technological unemployment." At the dawn of the computer era, in 1964, a group of scientists and social theorists sent an open letter to U.S. President Lyndon Johnson warning that cybernation "results in a system of almost unlimited productive capacity, which requires progressively less human labor."[32]

To return to the question of inequality, the right question is not whether there will still be work. The real question is whether there will be enough jobs paying decent wages. This is difficult to predict. The recent developments suggest not. On the other hand, most individuals want to be useful to society—work, remunerated or not, is one way to do so. As Erik Brynjolfsson and Andrew McAfee note, employment is one way we construct the social fabric. Perhaps people will be prepared to accept low pay in return for this social bond. In the shortest term, however, the destruction of jobs is costly for those who lose them. The acceleration of creative destruction raises three questions: How can workers, with jobs or not, be protected? How can we prepare ourselves for this new world through education? How are our societies going to adapt? Burying our heads in the sand is not a strategy.

THE TAX SYSTEM

Finally, the digitization of the world of work confronts us with new fiscal challenges and exacerbates existing ones, both within countries and internationally. I will just mention them here.

National Aspects

One issue at the national level is the old one concerning the distinction between commercial transactions and barter. The demarcation between the two is subtle, but they are treated in radically different ways for tax purposes. If I employ a construction company to paint my home, my payment is subject to value-added tax, and the employee and the employer are taxed depending on their status (social security charges, income taxes, corporate taxes, and so on). If I ask a friend to do the job, and give him a case of good wine in return, no taxes or social security contributions are levied. This is not only because the tax office would find it hard to spot this transaction, but also because it is a noncommercial exchange, and so not liable for tax. But where does the noncommercial stop and the commercial begin? Trade with one's family and friends, or exchange in clubs or small-scale cooperatives, meets most criteria for a producer-consumer relationship. So is it really noncommercial? Why does this classification mean the transactions are treated differently for tax purposes? These questions are particularly important in a country like France, where labor is heavily taxed (60 percent on average for the social security contribution, 20 percent for the VAT, and an income tax that can be high if one does not benefit from the many loopholes). The questions are fundamental for the sharing economy: Is my membership in a car club "sharing" a simple commercial relationship? As with labor law, we owe it to ourselves not to simply try to put the new economy's activities in preexisting but arbitrary boxes; we need to rethink our tax system.

INTERNATIONAL ASPECTS

International taxation also poses many challenges. Practices such as the use of transfer pricing between the divisions of a multinational company to locate profits in a country with low corporate taxes are now pervasive. A company might make a subsidiary in a country that has a high corporate tax pay a gold-plated price for services or products provided by a subsidiary in a country with a low corporate tax. It does this to empty the high-tax subsidiary of taxable profit. This fiscal arbitrage, designed to reduce corporate tax liability, has always existed. Such practices are inevitable when there are no international accords on tax harmonization. Multinational companies like Starbucks and Amazon are thus regularly criticized in Europe for their intensive fiscal "optimization."

The fact that digital business is dematerialized makes this arbitrage even easier. We no longer know exactly where an activity is located. It is easier than it used to be to place profitable entities in countries with low corporate taxes, and vice versa, and to shift profits using transfer prices. Intellectual property rights to a book or a design or software can be established in any country, independent of where they are consumed. Advertising fees can be collected in Ireland, even if the target audience is in France. Large US corporations use a complicated structure based on a technique known as the "double Irish," which grants intellectual property rights to an Irish corporation located in Bermuda (in Ireland, there are no taxes on the profits of offshore branches, and thus on the profits of branches located in Bermuda).[33] The United States Treasury does not profit from this either, because overseas profits of US companies are taxable in the US only when they are repatriated. Therefore, the money is left in Bermuda and only ever repatriated when there is a tax amnesty in the United States. It is estimated that the five hundred largest American firms have two trillion dollars parked abroad.

The Internet has no borders, which is good. But countries need to cooperate on taxes[34] to prevent tax competition for overseas investors (the question of the "correct" level of taxes on corporations is different; I will not take that up here).

An example of an agreement to end tax competition is the 2015 agreement on the value-added tax on online purchases within the European Union. This authorizes the purchaser's country to add value-added tax to the online purchase; previously the value-added tax was levied on the supplier, encouraging companies to locate in countries with low value-added tax rates, and to sell to consumers located in countries with high value-added tax rates. The new system is a satisfactory regulatory response for business models such as Amazon's, which bill the individual consumer. But it does not resolve the problem of platforms like Google, which technically does not sell anything to the French consumer, but charges advertisers who do. Regulators are discussing this problem, because the tax base in this case is much less clear than in the case of a sale of a book or a piece of music.

Digitization represents a marvelous opportunity for our society, but it introduces new dangers and amplifies others. Trust, ownership of data, solidarity, the diffusion of technological progress, employment, taxation: these are all challenges for the economics of the common good.

SIXTEEN
Innovation and Intellectual Property

THE IMPERATIVE OF INNOVATION

Classical growth theory starts from the premise that economic growth results from the accumulation of capital (such as machinery or energy supply) and increasing labor power (through population growth, along with improvements in health care and education). Yet, in a famous article in 1956, Robert Solow showed that the accumulation of capital and labor explained only part of measured growth, leaving an important role for other factors,[1] such as technological progress, in explaining a nation's economic growth. Today, even more than in 1956, technological innovation is at the heart of the mechanism of growth. The twenty-first century economy is called a knowledge economy, and it is certainly an economy of wide-ranging technological change.

The older view is more applicable to "catch-up economies."[2] Japan experienced three remarkable decades following the Second World War; so did France with its *trente glorieuses*. China has done the same since 1980. But a time comes when imitating foreign practices and techniques, and accumulating capital and labor, deliver decreasing yields and are no longer sufficient to drive growth. Then countries have to find a new approach and expand the "technological frontier."

Economies on the technological frontier require a different culture and institutions from those of catch-up economies. Universities must provide high-quality training, pursue state-of-the-art research, and encourage their students to be entrepreneurial. Lending should no longer be available only to big companies and traditional small and medium-sized businesses, but must also be partly devoted to financing innovative enterprises. For Schumpeter's "creative destruction" to work (new innovations making old ones obsolete), independent competition authorities need to eliminate artificial barriers to market entry. The stakes are high, because value creation is increasingly based on innovation. The wealth of nations increasingly depends on their ability to locate at the top of the value chain.

This leads me to the controversial topic of intellectual property. What do we mean by the term? What are the benefits and the dangers of intellectual property? What challenges do governments face in this area? Later, I will examine a particular—but fundamental—challenge: that of the patent "thickets," which hold back technological progress. Economic analysis suggests concrete solutions to this problem, permitting a wider diffusion of technologies without diminishing the incentives to innovate.

Alongside the financial crisis affecting the Eurozone for some years now, a source of concern in western Europe has been a weaker rate of innovation than the United States,[3] and perhaps soon weaker than that of Asian countries, which are investing heavily in the knowledge economy. Innovation requires favorable culture and institutions. I will examine the characteristics that encourage innovation.

Finally, I will discuss a collaborative model, an alternative to intellectual property, or rather one based on a different concept of intellectual property: open source software. This model is an unusual mode of organization; we will try to understand how it differs, and study the strategies adopted by economic agents who use it.

INTELLECTUAL PROPERTY

INSTITUTIONS

Say you complete your studies in biotechnology and want to go into applied research with the goal of discovering a new vaccine, producing biofuels using microorganisms, or developing disease-resistant crops that require less water. You will need investment finance, which you will get only if your project offers the prospect of a profit from which to repay investors. But the knowledge you are going to generate is what is called a "public good." Once created, it can be used by everyone in a nonexclusive way at a negligible cost. Once the chemical formula and uses of a molecule are known, every business can use this formula and market the product (vaccine, biofuel, seed), leaving tiny profit margins to the person who has invested in the research and development (R&D). Here once again is the free rider problem we saw in chapter 8, on the environment: if every discovery fell immediately into the public domain, and could be used free of charge by anyone, most people would wait for others to shell out the money for R&D. The incentives would encourage a wait-and-see approach instead of creative activity. Intellectual property is a necessary evil that seeks to stimulate R&D and artistic creation by providing an income for the creator. That is why it appeared very early. The first patents date from ancient Greece, and then developed in Florence and Venice in the fifteenth century.

Intellectual property takes many forms:

- The patent, which guarantees its holder an exclusive right—a monopoly on the use of the knowledge thus generated. The grant of a patent includes a defined period (usually twenty years from the date of issue), after which the knowledge falls into the public domain. Only a discovery that is not obvious and is not covered by "prior art" can be patented, and it must also be useful. Patenting is a public process and allows patent holders to manage their intellectual property as they wish, for instance to sell exclusive licenses if they do not want to exploit the innovation themselves.
- Copyright, which protects a form of expression (such as a book or a film) for a given period (in the United States, the author's whole lifetime plus seventy years after death).
- A trade secret, which (as the name suggests) protects the inventor only against the theft of his intellectual property. Trade secrets relate to information that benefits the firm and that the firm will strive to keep secret. In general, trade secrets concern an innovative production process: a new product is usually public information, and so cannot be kept secret. The (unpatented) Coca-Cola formula is a famous example of a trade secret.

  Note that the abolition of patents would lead innovators to use trade secrets to protect their inventions, though this would oblige them to integrate vertically with producers if they were not manufacturers themselves. Unlike patents, the trade secret makes it very difficult to grant licenses because someone buying a license will legitimately want to know the nature of the knowledge that is for sale. Once this knowledge has been revealed, the licensee can use it without paying. In practice therefore, only patented inventions are licensed.

- The trademark, which protects an enterprise's symbol, permitting it to distinguish its product from competitors' similar products.

What do these different intellectual property institutions have in common? All of them grant the inventor market power, that is, an opportunity to profit financially from the invention, either by selling licenses or by earning profits above the costs of production if making and selling the final product. If the invention fell into the public domain, however, someone who wanted to use it would not have to pay to acquire a license, and competition among producers using the invention would reduce above-cost margins to low levels. The cost of intellectual property protection is obvious: in order to create an incentive to innovate by allowing the inventor to profit from it, the government establishes a monopoly. It thereby increases the cost of using the invention and limits its diffusion: there will simply be fewer users.

This fundamental trade-off is inherent in the institution of intellectual property. It is also the reason why many countries have sought alternatives. In the seventeenth and eighteenth centuries, Britain and France created competitions, the prizes for which were granted by the crown. Once the inventor had won the prize, the intellectual property represented by the invention fell into the public domain. For example, in the seventeenth century, France organized a competition for the invention of a water wheel. In the late sixteenth century, Spain and the Netherlands held competitions promising a reward to anyone who could find a sufficiently precise method for measuring longitude at sea. The competitions had no winners. In 1714, the British Parliament offered a similar prize for the measurement of longitude. Most of the prize money was finally granted, after much controversy, to John Harrison. Harrison began working on the problem in 1714, but did not receive the complete payment until fifty-nine years later!

Granting prizes or awards is a complex procedure, because it requires specifying in advance exactly what is to be invented. Very often, the peculiarity of creative work is that we don't know exactly what we're going to find. If we could describe an innovative scientific article or a symphony in advance, the creative work would clearly be redundant. But sometimes we can define a desirable outcome without knowing how it will be possible to attain. Then the question is how much the reward should be. Does the prize undercompensate the research effort, in which case it risks failing to attract talented entrants? Or does it overcompensate, resulting in an unreasonable commitment of public funds? Recently, the mechanism of rewarding by prizes has been revived[4] for vaccines and drugs specific to developing countries, which can be too poor to attract the private research needed. The prizes set an objective for the vaccine, while specifying maximum acceptable side effects.

Currently, the protection of intellectual property is hotly debated.[5] I will just look at a few key points, concentrating on patents, but some of the debate concerns other forms of intellectual property. For example, the retroactive extension of copyright length (that is, extending the copyright period for works that have already been produced) is particularly astonishing. If, logically, intellectual property is a necessary evil to provide incentives for R&D or artistic creation, it has to remain true to that objective. But when the creative investments have already been made, strengthening intellectual property rights has no incentive effect at all: it's too late! It reduces diffusion without contributing to creation. Nevertheless, the US legislature has twice extended the duration of copyright, first in 1976, extending it to fifty years after the author's death, and again in 1988, when the period was lengthened to seventy years after the author's death. The latter law, known as the Copyright Term Extension Act, is sometimes called the "Mickey Mouse Protection Act," in reference to the Walt Disney Company. Walt Disney was in danger of losing the copyright to its still-profitable films and derivative products, and lobbied for the extension.

The number of patents has increased considerably over the past thirty years for several reasons. There were incentives for patent offices to do so (especially in the United States, where, before the

America Invents Act of 2011, the Patent and Trademark Office was indirectly encouraged to grant patents rather than to refuse them). Governments broadened the definition of patentable inventions to include software programs, biotechnology, and life sciences, as well as business methods. This proliferation would not be serious if the superfluous patents were inconsequential, such as the patent awarded for a watch for dogs—which runs seven times faster than an ordinary watch to reflect the canine species' lifespan. The Internet is full of websites listing ridiculous patents.

However, in other cases the economic consequences of the proliferation of patents can be considerable. Some patents have the potential to capture economic value without representing a major advance for society. For instance, Amazon's 1999 US patent[6] on "1-Click Ordering," which protected Amazon's sole use of the idea that an online retailer could keep information about customers (delivery and billing addresses, credit card numbers, and so on) so as not to have to ask for them again when the customer makes another purchase. This was a simple replica of practices already well known in many traditional brick-and-mortar stores.[7] Even if this practice had not already existed, it was sufficiently obvious not to merit a patent (and did not get one in Europe). Of the three criteria for patentability, this patent fulfilled only one: usefulness. Fortunately, the patent was eventually (in 2007) partially invalidated by a court, but we can imagine the income that Amazon might have received if the court had decided to validate the patent instead!

The second danger—which is worth examining here—is the multiplication of gatekeepers for a given technology and the accumulation of licensing fees users have to pay as a result.

MANAGING ROYALTY STACKING

The biotech and software sectors are characterized by a multitude of patents of varying importance, held by different owners, who become gatekeepers for the technology. These "patent thickets" lead to an accumulation of royalties that have to be paid for licenses ("royalty stacking" or "multiple margins" in economic terminology).

"Coopetition" and Patent Pools

To understand the problem of the accumulation of royalties (which was brilliantly formalized in 1838 by Antoine Augustin Cournot and more recently by the Berkeley economist Carl Shapiro),[8] it may be useful to draw an analogy (represented in figure 16.1) with medieval Europe. In the middle ages, navigation on rivers was made difficult by a series of tolls. In figure 16.1, four toll collectors collect a toll, one after the other. To travel the whole length of the river, a user needs the permission of each of these toll collectors. As such, we describe the navigation rights obtained by paying the tolls as complementary: if any of these four tolls were not paid, then the user would not be able to travel from the river's source to its mouth. For example, there were sixty-four tolls along the Rhine in the fourteenth century.[9] Each collector set a toll with a view to maximizing revenue, without worrying about the consequences for river users or for the revenues of other toll collectors (a higher toll reduces traffic on the river and so penalizes other collectors). This is the "tragedy of the commons" in action,[10] the same tragedy that leads to overuse fishing grounds and pastures or to an excessive emission of greenhouse gases. Europe had to wait until

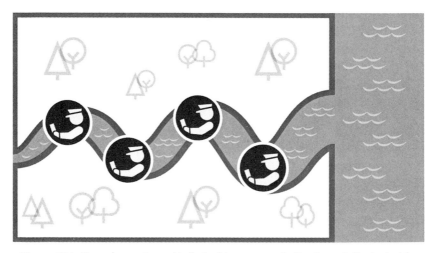

Figure 16.1. Complements and toll stacking: co-marketing is socially desirable.

the Congress of Vienna in 1815, and the laws that followed it, to see the end of this practice of accumulating tolls. [11]

Today, hi-tech industries try to eliminate multiple margins. New guidelines have recently been adopted by competition authorities around the world to encourage the use of patent pools. A patent pool is an agreement among different firms to jointly market licenses for a group of patents related to the technology concerned and belonging to members of the pool. This approach allows technology users to acquire a comprehensive license, whereas otherwise they would be forced to obtain licenses for five, ten, or fifteen patents. If they attempted this, they would run the risk that each patent holder could make excessive demands and so block access to the technology. The formation of a pool is an example of what economists call "coopetition" (an amalgamation of "cooperation" and "competition"). In a pool, companies that are potentially in competition cooperate to market their patents together. Like an agreement among the toll collectors in figure 16.1, a pool reduces the total cost of the patent licenses when the patents are complementary, that is, when the user needs the whole set of licenses to be able to create value using the technology. The owners of the patents come to an agreement to moderate their own royalties because this will allow demand to increase. The agreement therefore benefits patent owners and consumers alike.

Unfortunately, patent pools—and joint marketing in general—can also offer companies an opportunity to *raise* prices. Consider two substitutable patents, either one of which meets all the user's needs. To return to the river transport analogy, imagine two toll collectors on two branches of the river (figure 16.2). The user can take either the northern or the southern route, and gains nothing by having access to both. The two toll collectors will be eager to avoid direct competition, and will both be able to raise their profits if allowed to jointly market users' downstream access. In the case of substitutable patents, the owners can increase the price of their licenses by forming a pool and then acting like a cartel or a monopoly resulting from the merger of the firms. Thus, there are good pools (which make prices decrease) and bad pools (which make prices rise).

Figure 16.2. Substitutes: co-marketing amounts to merger to monopoly.

Some more history may be useful here. People often do not know that, before 1945, most of the major industries—aeronautics, railroads, cars, television, radio, the chemical industry—were organized around patent pools. But in 1945, the fear that joint commercial exploitation might conceal the formation of cartels provoked the United States Supreme Court to become hostile to patent pools. Competition authorities discouraged patent pools, which were, it is true, sometimes used to eliminate competition among holders of functionally similar patents. For fifty years, patent pools more or less disappeared. [12] In hindsight, this is regrettable; technological developments were becoming increasingly complex during that period.

Couldn't the competition authorities simply have prohibited bad pools that increased prices, and authorized the good ones? Unfortunately, the authorities do not have the relevant data to make this distinction. They often have scant historical data on which to estimate future demand for licenses. Moreover, the characteristics of substitutability or complementarity evolve and vary, depending on the use to which the technology is put. [13]

Nevertheless, simple regulations that do not require the competition authorities to have any information can make the distinction

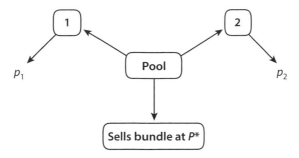

Figure 16.3. Individual licenses.

between good and bad pools. First, the pool can authorize individual licenses—that is, allow the owners of each patent to continue to sell licenses independent of the pool (see figure 16.3, which takes the example of two patent holders, each of which has one patent). As shown by an article I coauthored with Josh Lerner of the Harvard Business School,[14] individual licenses recreate a competitive situation when a patent pool would have increased prices. They therefore neutralize bad pools, while at the same time letting good pools reduce prices.

A simple case of two patents that are completely substitutable for each other illustrates this. The competitive price for licenses is then approximately zero (the cost for a holder of intellectual property rights to authorize a user to have access to his technology): each company is prepared to reduce its price in order to win the market, so long as there are profits to be made. A pool has the potential to destroy this competition, and to increase the price until it reaches the level a monopoly would charge, which is defined as the price that maximizes the joint profit of the two owners of intellectual property rights—i.e., the cartel price.[15]

But introduce the possibility of individual licenses, and suppose that the pool tries to set a supracompetitive price P (for example, a price equal to the monopoly price) and share the profits equally.[16] Rather than receive half the pool's profits as their share, each patent holder could price an individual license at a level slightly below P, the pool price, capture the entire market, and receive (almost) the whole profit.[17]

You might think it is naive to suppose that patent holders will behave in a competitive way and reduce their prices below the high pool price. In the short term, a price reduction increases the profit of the company that introduces it, but it might provoke an aggressive reaction by the other company, which will lower its price in turn. The resulting price war may not be worth the trouble. That is why economists and competition authorities are concerned about "tacit collusion"[18] or, in the terminology of competition law, coordinated effects. In these circumstances, the firms may not want to compete individually with their pool's offering for fear of starting a price war.

To guard against this threat of tacit collusion, a second regulation, called "unbundling," that also does not require specific information, must be added. If the pool is forced to unbundle its offer, users can buy each license from the pool individually, and the price charged by the pool for a set of licenses is the sum of the prices of the individual licenses (see figure 16.4). The combination of individual licenses plus unbundling prevents a pool from increasing prices.[19] In fact, these requirements effectively limit the role of the pool to fixing a ceiling on the price of each license.[20] Thus, the formation of a pool will have no harmful effects (it will not lead to price increases). If the patents are complementary, it will allow users to acquire their licenses

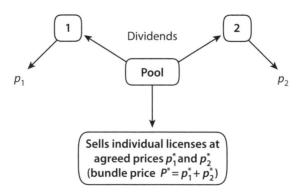

Figure 16.4. Individual licenses plus unbundling.

for less than they would without a pool, and allow patent holders to derive more profit from them, creating an additional encouragement to innovate. Note that both of these ideas, based on economic theory and not requiring the competition authorities themselves to have any information about the patents, have been incorporated into European guidelines (in 2004 for individual licenses, and in 2014 for unbundling).

Technological Standards

I would like to round off this discussion of the consequences of the proliferation of patents with a few remarks about standard setting. In information technologies in particular, the users of the technology have to coordinate if they want to interact. In the absence of compatibility among networks, I can't call you with my cellphone if your phone operates on a different network. Similarly, the developers of apps for my smartphone have to conform to the technical standards set for Google's Android or Apple's iOS. Interoperability requires convergence on specific standards. How does this convergence take place? Sometimes, a company is so dominant that it succeeds in imposing its technology as the standard for the rest of the sector. More often, however, the standard is dictated by a standard-setting organization that considers the possible alternative technological approaches and then establishes a standard, consisting of a set of functions that users (such as computer or smartphone manufacturers, infrastructure suppliers, telecommunications, cable, or satellite communications companies, or developers of applications) must incorporate into their technological choices.

When a standard is being set, there is in general more than one way to solve a given technological problem. Each of these paths may be equally viable, but the standard-setting organization will often choose just one of them. The problem is that this choice of a single standard may create monopoly rents because it might make a particular patent indispensable, even if it was previously not very important, thanks to the availability of alternative technological choices that offer the same result. Such patents become "standard-essential": they

Figure 16.5. The creation of a monopoly.

are essential only because they have been selected. The owner of a standard-essential patent can then claim large royalties, even though other patents could have had the same value if a different technical standard had been selected.

To pursue the river transport analogy (see figure 16.5), a decision to improve the waterway on the northern branch or to locate an important trade fair there, might have made this branch more attractive. Once decided, however, the toll collector on this northern branch could charge a monopoly price, whereas previously the two options were equally attractive.

To prevent patent holders from taking advantage of the sheer luck of being included in a standard that makes them essential, standard-setting organizations often ask patent holders to promise ex ante to provide licenses on fair, reasonable, and nondiscriminatory terms (FRAND). But these promises are ambiguous, as it is not clear how to define a fair and reasonable rate. In fact, there are now major legal actions challenging the meaning of these commitments all over the world—actions involving Apple, Google, Microsoft, Samsung, and many others. These companies complain that their competitors are charging excessive license fees for patents, breaking the commitments of the FRAND promise made during the standard-setting process. The stakes and the sums demanded in these suits are gigantic, and it is very hard for a court to judge whether a demand for a license fee is "reasonable." The court simply does not have the information to do that. Another idea that has emerged from economic theory, which again would not require data, would be to obtain the patent holders' commitments not to exceed a price ceiling (of their choice) for their licenses, and to do so before the standard was finalized. The standard-setting organization could then define its norm on the basis of the information revealed by this choice.

No one would build a house on land without knowing the price of that land. The same goes for technologies. Josh Lerner and I proposed that owners of intellectual property make commitments regarding the conditions for granting licenses before the standard is chosen. We also tried to explain why it is unlikely that this precommitment obligation will occur if there are competing standard-setting organizations (as patent holders will be able to shop around for one that does not try to impose this kind of obligation on them).[21]

THE INSTITUTIONS OF INNOVATION

Innovation needs both inventors and finance.

COMPANY R&D VERSUS INDEPENDENT R&D

Innovation happens more and more in small entrepreneurial start-ups rather than in large companies. There are many reasons for this. Researchers in large companies sometimes face resistance from their superiors, who do not want to cannibalize existing profits by developing better new products, and who might abandon the project if it turns out that cannibalization is likely. Researchers also sometimes have difficulty convincing their superiors that their preliminary ideas are well founded. Finally, researchers do not generally have the same financial incentives as an entrepreneur.[22] Even when companies reward employees who have made major innovations, these rewards often remain incommensurate with the importance of the contributions. For example, Shuji Nakamura, who won the Nobel Prize in physics in 2014 for his invention of blue LEDs (from which we benefit every day, because they were the missing link for producing white light) initially received from his employer, Nichia, for whom he had brought in hundreds of millions of dollars, just a hundred and eighty dollars for his contribution.[23]

Of course, large companies would like to reproduce the advantages of the entrepreneurial approach through corporate venture capital (the direct investment of corporate funds in external startup companies). According to Sam Kortum and Josh Lerner, these corporate funds have (like internal company R&D funds) not always met with success. Because the company's management continues to worry about possible cannibalization, researchers and external partners still fear that the project might be halted. Besides, the constraints on remuneration within the company limit the ability of these funds to attract the best people.

A startup has a competitive advantage compared to a big company's internal research department when the intellectual input is more important than the capital needed to back it—that is, when the initial funding needed is modest. Competition between potential customers also protects independent innovators against the whims of a single user of that innovation, and thus favors entrepreneurship. Different ways of organizing entrepreneurship have different origins. In some hi-tech cases, for example, the quality of the science is vital, and thus entrepreneurship originates in the academic community.

But innovation does not always require high-level science; as Edmund Phelps remarks,[24] innovation is not the preserve of educated elites. To take only a few emblematic nineteenth-century innovators, Thomas Edison (the inventor of the electric light, power utilities, and sound recording) came from a modest background; George Stephenson (who built the first steam railway) was illiterate until the age of eighteen; John Deere (inventor of the steel plow) was a blacksmith; and Isaac Merritt Singer (who improved the sewing machine) was a mechanic and an actor. In France, at the same period, Lafarge, Michelin, Schneider, and many other companies that would eventually be major listed corporations were founded by entrepreneurs who were not technology leaders of the time.[25] Today, Uber, Facebook, Netflix, and Airbnb are built on an intelligent approach to identifying niches and services that are unexploited, but do not require being pioneers of science.

Entrepreneurial firms can therefore emerge on a university campus, but it is not necessarily the case. A culture of entrepreneurship matters more. In addition, many innovative semiconductor companies emerged through spawning (spinning off further startups) from companies that were themselves entrepreneurial—a phenomenon which is common for this type of enterprise.

FINANCE

Inventors working inside a company do not have to look for outside finance; they simply need to convince their superiors that their ideas are well founded. In contrast, startups are often based, at first, on a small amount of personal funding (the entrepreneur's savings and sometimes contributions from family and friends). If it looks promising, the new business will soon need further financing: first from business angels—rich individual investors who have often been successful entrepreneurs themselves and have experience in spotting the best potential projects—and then venture capital from venture capital structures. Such structures are composed of VCs or general partners, who monitor the startup and invest money from their funds, as well as more passive investors (the limited partners), such as pension funds, mutual investment funds, insurance companies, endowments, foundations, or semi–public sector companies, which are attracted by the certification brought about by the venture capitalists but do not demand returns as high.

The role of the venture capitalist is not just providing investment funds. By selecting the most promising projects, the VC reduces the risk of adverse selection faced by passive investors who do not know where to put their money. Once these promising projects have been identified, the VC has a managerial role, improving governance and supervising the investments assiduously. In this process, VCs play an important advisory role. For example, an entrepreneur who is a scientist may lack expertise in management and in marketing products. Investment funding is given to the entrepreneur gradually, conditional on hitting agreed targets ("stage financing"). Finally, venture capital retains control rights. VCs can replace the entrepreneur or some of the collaborators if objectives are not met. If the entrepreneurs hit their targets, on the other hand, they earn more autonomy.

A few additional points will conclude this rapid overview of financing innovation. Startups often produce no profit for years; it is therefore not advisable for them to get into debt, because they would quickly face repayments that they could not make. Instead, investors buy preferred stocks (which are a kind of debt, but the payment can be deferred as long as no dividend is distributed to stockholders), convertible bonds (which can be transformed into stocks, either at the request of their holders or of the company), or sometimes common stock.

One of the important elements of the initial contract is to foresee when the financiers will be able to realize some of their returns. If the business succeeds, it can go public on the stock market, which on the one hand allows the company to gain access to other sources of capital, and on the other hand allows investors to cash in, at least in part. This withdrawal returns capital to the initial investors, which they can use to invest in new startups. It is impossible to set an IPO date in advance; it depends both on the progress made by the company, and how much money is available on the stock market: VCs and startups try to "time the market," i.e., to pick an IPO date when there is plenty of liquidity in the market so that the shares will fetch a high price. For that reason, IPOs tend to "cluster" in up times for the stock market.

Venture capital also has limitations. It requires professionals who can make a personal financial contribution. The fact that these professionals are investing their own money in the startup (they have "skin in the game") makes their action credible and leads other passive investors (who provide most of the necessary financing) to follow their example. The available VC funds, however, fluctuate greatly. During the Internet bubble, IPOs raised large amounts of money, and venture capitalists received a great deal of it, which they could later invest. In contrast, cold-issue periods (when there are only a few IPOs) lead to lower amounts of available VC funds. VC financing has the drawback of being cyclical. Funding from limited partners may also fluctuate; for instance, new regulations limiting the risks that pension funds can take may discourage them from buying shares in IPOs.

Venture capital also has a public component in many countries. Public financing can be a useful complement to private sources, but only under certain conditions. It has to be in line with the analysis of industrial policy outlined in chapter 13, involving experts and limiting political influence. For example, the United States Small Business Investment Research Fund is reputed to finance not very promising projects as a result of political pressure. Ideally, public investment would complement private venture capital rather than competing with it, and adopt a countercyclical policy—but that is easier said than done.

COOPERATIVE DEVELOPMENT AND OPEN SOURCE SOFTWARE

The process of production and innovation in open source software is very different from what economists might first expect. Traditionally, a company pays its employees, defines their tasks, and appropriates the intellectual property they create. In an open source software project, many contributors are not remunerated. Their contributions are voluntary, and the programmers are free to work on the subprojects that they believe are the most interesting or the best suited to their competencies. The way that open source software is organized, however, is not at all anarchic. Project leaders break the work up into well-defined modules and accept contributions in an "official" version so that contributions are functional and coherent and the project does not veer off course or fork into incompatible versions. Finally, the intellectual property is limited: for example, the license for open source software may specify that anyone who uses it must make available, under the same conditions, any improvements to the original software.

Open source software now plays an important role in many sectors. The best known to the general public are Linux[26] (an operating system for computers that competes with Microsoft's Windows and Apple's MacOS) and Android (an operating system for mobile phones whose principal competitor is iOS, for iPhones). But open source products are also very prominent in software managing servers (the market for web server software, used by computers that publish on the Internet, has been dominated by the Apache open source project since the mid-1990s), scripting languages (Python, PERL, PHP, etc.), web browsers (Firefox and Chromium, which is the open source counterpart of Chrome), databases (MySQL), email (Thunderbird), office software (LibreOffice), the cloud (OpenStack), and Big Data (Hadoop).

What are the incentives and roles of the various players in the open source process?

What motivates programmers. Working on the development of open source software costs a programmer a lot of time. A programmer who works as an independent also foregoes the monetary compensation they would have received working for a business or a university. For a programmer affiliated with an employer, the opportunity cost of working on open source software is that it may be impossible to complete other tasks. For example, the production of academic research may fall off, or a student's progress on a thesis may slow down.

At the beginning of the 2000s,[27] Josh Lerner and I were fascinated by the growing success of open source software. We were unconvinced by the arguments advanced to explain the reasons for this success and also the strategies that it was proposed commercial software developers should pursue in response. At the time, there were two dominant explanations for programmers' participation in the development of open source software. The first was that these contributors were intrinsically more generous or less eager to make money than their counterparts in the commercial world. Pro-social behaviors do play a nonnegligible role in many domains of economic life. This hypothesis was at least coherent. But it raised the question of whether, in practice, commercial software programmers are less concerned about the public good than open source programmers. It is a question on which we have little information (the results of surveys about motivations cannot be trusted, because it is well known that respondents give self-serving answers).

The second tentative explanation was much more alien to economic reasoning. It maintained that contributors to an open source software project expected their contribution to trigger a virtuous process based on generalized reciprocity. The resulting influx of many other contributors would make it possible to develop an open source product that could be used by the contributor, making the individual decision to contribute seem rational. This explanation (based entirely on personal self-interest) runs counter to the theory of public goods, as well as to empirical observations of free-rider behaviors seen in other contexts; as we have already seen, for example, countries, businesses, and households generally do not limit their greenhouse gas emissions in the hope that their individual behavior will trigger a series of reciprocal reactions that will make it possible to solve the problem of global warming. (Europe has tried to set an example, but it has not had the slightest success in starting a virtuous circle, even though it represents 10 percent of worldwide greenhouse gas emissions).

Lerner and I maintained that several other motives for open source collaboration are possible. First, people may improve their job performance by contributing to open source software development. This is particularly relevant for system administrators looking for specific solutions for their company. Studies later showed that many open source contributors were indeed motivated by meeting the needs of their organizations. Second, the programmer may take intrinsic pleasure in choosing a "cool" open source project, and may find it more enjoyable than a routine task imposed by an employer. Third, open source contributions offer programmers an opportunity to demonstrate their talents.

On this third point, the economic theory of signaling suggests that programmers have more incentives to participate in an open source project when the contribution is more visible to the audience they are trying to impress. In this case, the audience concerned may be, as in the academic world, peers: programmers, like members of any profession, want to be recognized by their community. But many open source programmers target other audiences too, including the job market (commercial software companies recruit among contributors to open source software who have distinguished themselves through their contributions) and the venture capital community, which will in certain cases—especially where the leaders of open source projects are concerned—finance commercial applications constructed around open source software.

Open source software lends itself well to this kind of signaling. Breaking a task into modules makes it possible to identify their difficulty, the quality of the solutions, and the people responsible for them. The information collected is even more useful if an individual programmer takes responsibility for the success of a subsidiary project without interference from a superior. Projects define levels of recognition (such as programmer, project manager, or member of the board of the Open Software Foundation). Reinforcing the differentiation in this way enhances signaling. An indirect confirmation of the signaling hypothesis is that commercial software companies, aware of the desire for signaling, have tried to emulate open source software by recognizing the individual contributions made to elements of their software by their programmers.

The strategies of commercial companies. This leads us to discuss the question of the strategies adopted by commercial software companies confronted by competition from open source software. At first they were hostile, but they have adapted to the phenomenon and have even found opportunities in it.

- As we have seen, they may want their employees to work on open source projects to identify the best talents in their segment of the industry, and possibly recruit them.
- They may wish to share their source code with users who have signed a confidentiality agreement so they can benefit from the external work of debugging.
- They may wish to make commercial source code available through academic licenses (as Microsoft has done) so that it can become familiar to programmers. It may be used in schools and universities for pedagogical purposes, thus creating an "alumni effect" and emulating the benefits of open source software such as Linux.
- Above all, a business may decide to make money not on the code itself, but on complementary segments, developing and

exploiting expertise in goods and services based on the open source program. Google distributes Android free of charge as an open source program, and derives profit from the data it harvests from Android users (complementing data harvested through its search engine, Google Maps, or YouTube, and data purchased from data brokers). IBM made open source software central to its strategy, charging for consultancy. Commercial enterprises like Red Hat for Linux and Scientific Workplace for LaTeX,[28] offer tailored or easier-to-use versions of open source programs.

Contributors to an open source project are not always paid (as is typical for projects inspired by the personal desire to "scratch one's own itch"[29]), but some are. Companies often largely finance projects that are important for their business by employing the main contributors. Linux is typical. Android, as we have seen, is essentially developed by Google, MySQL by Oracle, and so on.

Java used a different strategy. When it was released in 1995, Sun licensed Java for a fee to other companies, who were free to modify it for their own purposes. This created dependencies on proprietary code and threatened fragmentation of the Java ecosystem, which was a threat to their core business. In 2006, Sun created a single, open source implementation (OpenJDK) under a GPL license (see below) to fight the fragmentation.

Many challenges arise when a profit-making enterprise seeks to be at the center of an open source development project. The commercial entity may not sufficiently internalize the open source community's objectives. It may not be able to make a credible commitment to keeping the source code in the public domain, or to adequately highlight important contributions. For example, as new versions come out, Android becomes increasingly dependent on Google's services; a manufacturer who wants to produce an Android mobile phone but does not have an agreement with Google (notably, to gain access to Google Play's app store) finds itself with an almost nonfunctional product. It is not clear that these fears will inevitably be realized (because it is not impossible that Google might want to build a reputation for neutrality), but they exist.

These difficulties explain why Hewlett-Packard has published some of its code through Collab.Net, a firm founded by open source programmers that organizes open source projects for enterprises who want to open up their software. Collab.Net offers a kind of certification to the effect that the enterprise is truly committed to the open source character of the project.

The choice of intellectual property. Open source programmers' motivation also depends on the license governing the open source project. The project must be protected if it wants to remain open source. Some licenses, such as BSD (Berkeley Software Distribution), are permissive: the user retains the possibility of using the code as he or she wishes. These licenses allow programmers to develop marketable proprietary software, but they create the risk of the project splitting into multiple variants that may not be compatible with one another.

It is interesting to note Google's strategy for Android here. To make this open source software attractive by authorizing users to modify it in a proprietary manner, and at will, Google chose a very permissive license.[30] But incompatibility as a result of the choices made by smartphone makers and telecommunications operators would be catastrophic. When Android was launched,[31] Google put together a coalition of manufacturers, operators, and software designers that made a commitment to maintaining a common base as Android evolved.

Conversely, a license like the General Public License (GPL)[32] restricts interaction with commercial software. It obliges the parties to ensure that the community benefits from any modified version, unless the modification has been made for strictly personal use. The GPL license is emblematic because of the evangelism of its creator, Richard Stallman, for open source, and because Linux adopted it very early on. Yet today, "viral" licenses (like GPL) are no longer typical of open source projects, while permissive licenses (BDS, MIT, Apache) are widespread.

How is the choice of an open source license made? To appeal to programmers, a project must be attractive. Programmers will be warier if a commercial enterprise created the project or has been deeply involved in writing its source code. A GPL license will reassure participants over fragmentation and free riders. Remember also that, for programmers, the visibility of their contributions matter. Their contributions are more visible if the project attracts and is used by many other programmers, rather than simply by end users who never read the source code. The choice of a license is rational, and corresponds to what economic theory would predict. An analysis of forty thousand open source projects in the SourceForge database shows that restrictive licenses are significantly more common when the attraction for open source programmers is weak—i.e., when it is for applications for the public (such as games or desktops), for projects operating in commercial environments or on proprietary operating systems, or for projects whose native language is not English.

There are many other deeply interesting aspects of open source software: What public policies toward it should be adopted? How important for open source software are patents, or insurance against the risk of legal action for patent infringement? Can the open source model be transposed to industries other than software?

Two observations in conclusion: First, it is important that alternative organizational forms are permitted to emerge and are treated equally in terms of policy; it is essential that policies do not tilt choices toward a specific organizational model. Second, there is nothing economically mysterious about the open source phenomenon, even if it might initially appear puzzling in terms of conventional economic reasoning. Economics is everywhere.

AND MANY OTHER DEBATES ...

There are many other fascinating issues concerning intellectual property. For example, there is the question of patent-holding companies, often referred to as "patent trolls" or "patent assertion entities," who do not do R&D themselves, but rather buy portfolios of patents to collect the licensing fees. In 2011, such companies figured in 61 percent of the lawsuits concerning patents in the United States. Do they create an efficient secondary market for patents (small-time innovators lacking the legal capacity and infrastructure required to identify potential infringers and to force users to pay fees)? Or are they a fund-extorting mechanism made possible by the laxity of patent offices in granting patent protection too easily?

How should competition be regulated in a world in which intellectual property is central to the value chain? Should we restrict injunctions, the practice of preventing a company from selling its products if it has not paid license fees, which is a very effective weapon against large companies like Apple or Microsoft? (This threat induced RIM—now Blackberry—to pay $612.5 million to a patent troll.) Should we impose compulsory licenses to the detriment of the intellectual property owner? These are only few of the many questions now being raised everywhere about intellectual property.

SEVENTEEN
Sector Regulation

WHAT'S AT STAKE

In 1982, when I was a young researcher at the École Nationale des Ponts et Chaussées, I had the privilege of working on sector regulation with Jean-Jacques Laffont, the founder of the Toulouse School of Economics. That was how we began our research on procurement and the regulation of network industries. Around the world, there was growing discontent about the poor quality and high cost of public services run by incumbent monopolies regulated by the government. In the United States, President Carter had just deregulated airlines, and other sectors were in the hot seat: telecommunications, electricity, gas, rail, and postal services, which were provided by privately owned, regulated "public utility" monopolies established at the beginning of the twentieth century. In contrast, the European monopolies in these industries were still under public ownership; yet the inefficiency of the American public utilities indicated that privatization would not suffice to solve the problem. It would be necessary to change the incentives of incumbent operators by either making them accountable for their performance or by introducing competition.

Except perhaps to laissez-faire ideologues, the advantages of deregulation and greater competition were not self-evident. There were good reasons for the absence of competition in these sectors. In particular, it would have been very costly for potential entrants to the market to duplicate certain "bottlenecks" (also called "essential infrastructures," to use the terminology of competition law, or "natural monopolies"). It is hard to imagine a railroad operator wanting to enter the market by building a new, duplicate high-speed train line from London to Paris, or new stations in Paris and London. Besides rail tracks and stations, these essential infrastructures included things like electricity grids, postal distribution networks for small letters, gas pipelines, and local loops (the telephone lines between your home or office and the network. Back then, this was a copper line, but today it might be fiber optic or the wireless local loop). Essential infrastructures like these were controlled by an "incumbent operator" (such as France Télécom, British Rail, or Deutsche Bundespost).

Like other researchers working on this subject, Laffont and I faced numerous challenges.[1] We had to construct a coherent conceptual framework for the incentive contracts between the state and regulated businesses, we needed to devise a way to introduce competition in network industries, and we were at pains to establish a set of principles for determining prices for access to essential infrastructures owned by the incumbent operators. In short, we had to work out how to organize regulation in sectors that are essential to the economy and how to define a new vision of the state as regulator.

A FOURFOLD REFORM AND ITS RATIONALE

Reforms in the telecommunications, energy, railroad, or postal sectors since the end of the twentieth century have been a reaction to inefficient management in these sectors. Companies that benefit de jure or de facto from a monopoly position connected with very large economies of scale can demand high prices or impose poor-quality services on captive consumers. Until the 1980s, these sectors were monopolies with weak incentives—in Europe they were public enterprises, and in the United States they were private enterprises that made users bear virtually all the risk and pay for their excessive costs. These enterprises cross-subsidized services in ways that were motivated more by political considerations than by economic logic (a cross-subsidy exists when the low price of one service is financed by a high price being charged for another).

Natural monopoly characteristics explain why, in most countries, the government has long regulated monopolies that serve network industries. Nonetheless, it is not clear how to implement this regulation. Asymmetries of information concerning costs, technological choices, and demand prevent even a well-intentioned and competent regulator from guaranteeing the best services at the lowest prices for citizens. In other words, a regulated business can make strategic use of the information it alone has: it reveals this information when it is advantageous for it to do so, and keeps it to itself when transparency would endanger its revenues.

In the language of economics, the regulators face two types of asymmetries of information: "adverse selection" and "moral hazard." The company[2] has better knowledge of the environment in which it is operating: its technology, its supply costs, the demand for its products, and its services (adverse selection). Its actions also affect cost and demand through the management of human resources, strategic decisions about production capacities, R&D, brand image, quality control, and risk management (moral hazard). It is not surprising that regulatory authorities who overlook the asymmetries of information are not able to regulate efficiently to reduce the cost of the service for the user or the taxpayer. We saw in chapters 8 and 9 two examples of how regulators can sometimes be overconfident in their ability to overcome informational asymmetries that stand in the way of effective regulation. The first is the adoption of a command-and-control approach to environmental regulation; the second is the judicial monitoring of redundancies. Both have proven counterproductive because they end up being too costly for businesses to implement. In the end, their high cost backfired on the intended beneficiaries of the regulations (the environment or the employees, respectively). Ambitions had to be scaled down in the case of the environment; and firms no longer create permanent jobs in countries with judicial monitoring of redundancies. The same principle—that the regulator must adapt policies to the information held by the state—also holds true in the economics of sectoral regulation. Of course, the authorities must try, as in practice they do, to diminish the asymmetry of information. This can be done by collecting data, but also by benchmarking the company's performance against that of similar companies operating in different but analogous markets. It can also be achieved by auctioning monopoly rights, because companies cannot avoid implicitly providing information about the costs in their sector in the course of the auction. Still, experience shows that these practices, though useful, do not eliminate the regulator's informational handicap.

Politics is a second obstacle to reform. The shareholders, managers, and employees of incumbent monopolies are vigilant and often work to prevent or limit reform. Conversely, some lobbies representing users of the services in question can push for liberalization of markets, not in order to promote increased social well-being, but to further their own personal interests.

A FOURFOLD REFORM

Economic theory has helped bring about a fourfold reform over the past thirty years:

- *Improved incentives for efficiency* in natural monopolies through the introduction of mechanisms for sharing efficiency gains between customers and operators. For example, the use of price caps (which set an upper limit for the "average price" of the regulated company's services and let the company keep all its profit so long as this constraint is observed) has become widespread. The caps are usually indexed to inflation, to the price of the inputs (for example, to the price of gas for gas-fired power plants), or less often to comparative indicators ("benchmarked"). The caps are also reduced over time when technological progress is expected.[3]

   In Europe, efficiency gains were also obtained through the privatization of operators. As explained in chapter 6, the state's role has changed, from production to regulation. Under pressure from insiders and with only a weak budget constraint (as taxpayers make good budget shortfalls), companies controlled by the government rarely produce high-quality services at low cost.

- *Rebalancing tariffs* (between individuals and companies, between monthly subscriptions and local and long-distance communications, and so on) by raising prices on market segments with inelastic demand for the purpose of recovering the network's fixed costs. Such rebalancing was desirable because the alternative of covering the fixed costs of networks with big surcharges on the services for which the demand is very elastic led to inefficient underconsumption and slowed the introduction of innovative services.

- *Opening to competition* the activities that do not have natural monopoly characteristics by granting licenses to new entrants and, at the same time, regulating the conditions of their access to the incumbent operator's essential infrastructures. It is hard to overstate the importance of competition to the dynamism of a company, whether it is public or private.
- The *independence of regulatory authorities*. Formerly both judge and judged, the state's engagement now tends to take the form of independent sectoral regulators and competition authorities. The reallocation of regulatory powers toward independent agencies at the expense of ministries reduced the power of lobbies, as explained in chapter 6.

An interesting illustration of the role of incentives and sensible pricing is provided by the 1980 Staggers Act reforms in the United States. In the 1970s, the American railroads (which carry mainly freight) were moribund. Many companies, though protected by monopoly positions, were in great financial difficulties. The share of freight carried by rail had fallen to 35 percent (compared to 75 percent in the 1920s). The infrastructure (the tracks) was dilapidated, and consequently the trains moved slowly. The reforms allowed more freedom both in pricing and in signing contracts with freight companies (while maintaining supervision by a regulator to prevent "abusive" prices). Costs and prices fell, productivity—defined as the number of ton-kilometers per employee—has since increased by a factor of 4.5, quality has improved, and rail freight has regained market share when it might have vanished.

COMPETITION IN THE MARKET AND FOR THE MARKET

The introduction of competition can take place in two ways: *for* the market (ex ante) and *in* the market (ex post).

Competition for the market is competition for the right to serve a given market from a monopoly position. For example, a local authority selects a single operator to manage a service using a "lowest bid" auction, in which best bidder status incorporates both the financial elements (the price for the user, the level of subsidy required) and other variables measuring the quality of service. The quality specifications selected by the authority are either requirements or their choice is left to the bidder, with a "scoring rule" then weighting the various financial and nonfinancial dimensions and aggregating them into a single bid. This competition for the market is one of the mechanisms of public procurement (a general term covering public work contracts, the outsourcing of public services, and public-private partnerships). In the interest of space, I will not discuss the mechanisms of public procurement here, although they are crucially important to the economy.[4] Alternatively, the authorities may decide to allow competition between several operators in the market. For that to be an option, the competing operators need to have open access to essential infrastructures.

In general then, the authorities must choose between the two modes of competition. For example, if the independent authority regulating the railroads in France (Arafer) wanted to create competition in the high-speed train service between Paris and Lyon, it could either create a concession and put it up for auction among different railroad operators (such as SNCF, Deutsche Bahn, Transdev) or allow several operators to compete on the line and divide the timetable. In the European rail sector, some activities, such as freight, are now subject to competition *in* the market; others remain in a monopoly situation, like regional passenger transport, for which European universal service regulations rather envision competition *for* the market in each geographic area. All markets are due to be opened to some form of competition in a couple of years.

INCENTIVE REGULATION

HOLDING COMPANIES ACCOUNTABLE

Economists generally favor strong incentives (holding companies accountable), and they have played a significant role in the recent reforms of the regulation of network industries. Common sense suggests that to have good incentives to reduce costs (to take just one example), the party that controls the level of costs should bear, at least in part, responsibility for them. This implies contracts with strong incentives, in which the regulated company is not responsible for developments which it cannot control, but is held responsible for part or all of the risks that it can control.

In the context of nonmarketed public projects (such as the construction of a bridge that is not subject to a toll), the relevant authority will often offer "fixed price contracts," paying a predetermined sum. The contractor covers all the costs (which therefore do not need to be audited by the regulator). In the context of marketed services, contracts with strong incentives include "price caps" that are not indexed to production costs. In other words (to simplify a little), the regulator authorizes a maximum (average) price, and the company can choose its prices so long as they are below this limit and cover the entirety of its costs.

These examples contrast with contracts with weak incentives, in which the service provider is assured in advance that all or most costs will be covered either by an increase in the subsidy or by an increase in prices paid by the user. Examples include those in which costs are reimbursed in full ("cost-plus" contracts) for nonmarketed services, or contracts indexing the prices paid by users to the actual costs in the previous year ("cost of service" regulation). It is this type of contract that was used, for example, in the regulation of public utilities in the United States until the 1980s.

More generally, the idea underlying the introduction of contracts with strong incentives is to make the company accountable for its performance, thus incentivizing it to serve society better. Take, for example, the high-voltage transmission of electricity. The manager of the network (such as European transmission system operators or America's regional transmission organizations) plays an important role through its investments, maintenance, and dispatch (deciding which power plants need to be generating electricity to meet the end demand at the lowest possible cost given the physical constraints of the network). Dispatch has a direct impact on consumers of electricity. For example, a power plant near the site of consumption, producing electricity at a cost of one hundred dollars per MWh, might be chosen, whereas another, more distant power plant that produces electricity for only twenty-five dollars per MWh, even if available, might not be chosen because of a lack of the capacity on the grid to transmit the electricity from the plant to the consumer, or because the high-voltage power lines may be unstable. The cost of redispatch, which is seventy-five dollars per MWh in this case, is carefully measured, even in complex electricity systems (the French company, EDF, a pioneer in economic analysis in the electricity sector, has done this since the 1950s). This cost results in an economic loss and generates, downstream, a higher price for the electricity consumer. It is desirable for the manager of the transmission network, therefore, to reduce the price of electricity by making investments whose cost is reasonable to relieve congestion. In the 1990s, the British electricity network suffered from congestion. The demand was for transmission from northern England, where production is cheap, to the south, where much of the power is used. The managers of the network, which is independent of the electricity suppliers, were given incentives that would pay them more if congestion (and thus the cost of redispatch from cheap to expensive power plants) were diminished. This incentive led to low-cost investment that reduced congestion, to the benefit of electricity consumers.

The Limits of Accountability

The tension between the absence of profit and incentives. Contracts with stronger incentives must not be introduced naively. The tension between the absence of profits and incentives is an important general issue. The stronger the incentives a network utility faces, the greater its potential profits, unless the regulatory authority has enough detailed information about the costs of production (which is very unlikely) or succeeds in bringing about effective competition in the market.

Can a regulator gauge the level of the company's costs? No. As we have seen, the company has much better information regarding its costs and potential for improvement. What should be done in this situation? There is no "one-size-fits-all" regulation: a company has to be allowed to use its information. In other words, the regulator must take into account this informational asymmetry, and offer the regulated company a "menu" of contracts with different ways of sharing the cost—for example, one cost-plus contract and another offering a fixed price. Cost-plus specifies a low fixed remuneration paid on top of the operator's total cost. Fixed price grants a gross payment: the operator has to cover all the costs, making a net profit equal to the gross total less the actual cost. If the menu of options is well designed, a company that knows that its costs will be low would choose a scheme that offers the strongest incentives (the fixed price option), while a company that thinks its costs will be high would prefer a cost-plus option. Naturally, in the first case the company will try harder to reduce its costs, but the low costs will generate a supranormal profit or "information rent." However, if the menu of options is well designed and coherent, this is the best compromise between good incentives and limiting the company's profit.

This compromise between rents and incentives is often neglected. Consider the frequent recommendation in favor of fixed-price contracts. The argument in favor is (correctly) that they encourage increased efficiency. But people are apt to forget that this might also mean high profits. At first, falling costs resulting from the introduction of incentives make fixed-price contracts popular, but later there is strong political pressure for the regulator to break the "regulatory contract" and confiscate the rents that the contract type has created. But, to use the popular expression, you can't have your cake and eat it too. The gains in efficiency from contracts with powerful incentives will only occur if the company can trust the state to honor its commitments. In the mid-1990s, the British electricity regulator, economist Steven Littlechild, one of the fathers of the fixed price approach, had to give in to political pressure and renege on the contracts he had made with regional electricity companies. Many public-private partnerships around the world encountered problems of this kind. Governments often are inconsistent in their management of incentives and contracts over time.

The need to monitor quality. Strong incentives mean that it costs the company more to provide (necessarily more expensive) high-quality services. The company then has a nonnegligible incentive to reduce the quality of its services, or to find other ways of reducing costs, such as a hospital selecting healthier patients if it has contractual incentives to reduce mortality or to demonstrate better health outcomes. The argument is simple, but regulators often overlook it. The 1984 privatization of the public monopoly British Telecom (BT) involved better incentives for the company to be more efficient. So far, so good. But the regulator had not foreseen that BT would have an incentive to reduce the quality of its service too. Soon the regulator had to introduce quality measures into the contract. Another example, still in Britain but in a different sector, was underinvestment in the maintenance of the railway tracks, resulting in serious accidents, such as the Hatfield crash in 2000, as a result of the incentive structure that had been set up for the management of the railway network. The ideal response to this problem is to monitor the quality of service directly, provided this is feasible. When it is too difficult to monitor quality, weaker incentives, which reduce the advantage to the company of diminishing quality, may be the only solution.

Capture. Regulatory capture, the tendency for regulators to act in the interests of the businesses they are supposed to be regulating, can be encouraged by powerful incentives. When incentives are strong, the scope for profit that can be earned by the company becomes all the more important, and successful lobbying is then associated with large profits. In fact, whatever the motive for the capture (personal or political friendship, a future job in the industry, a conflict of interest connected with a financial contribution, a monetary payment, etc.), the probability of it occurring increases with the stakes for the company—and therefore its performance accountability. If the independence of the regulatory authority cannot be guaranteed, then the risk of capture is cause for choosing contracts with weaker incentives, even though this has harmful consequences for efficiency.

Opportunistic Behaviors by the Regulator and the Regulated

One of the difficulties in managing infrastructure is that contracts are often incomplete, in the sense that they do not clearly specify everything that must be decided, or at least how decision making and payments should be organized in all circumstances. The longer the contract, the greater the uncertainty (as it is usually much easier to make short-term, rather than long-term predictions about technological developments or demand). Incomplete contracts, or anything that allows one of the two parties to behave in an opportunistic way ex post (which includes the example above of the government struggling to honor its commitments) reduces the incentive to invest in a mutual relationship.[5] Putting this in terms of the principal-agent problem, there is a reciprocal danger of expropriation, either of the agent's (company's) investment by the principal (regulator), or of the principal's investment by the agent.

There are multiple ways in which the company's investment can be expropriated during the contract: simple confiscation (for instance, if a company is nationalized without enough compensation for shareholders); unreasonably low caps on prices charged to users (in the case of marketed goods) or nonpayment by the principal (for nonmarketed goods); new technical requirements or environmental constraints that impose extra costs without adequate compensation; inadequate provision of complementary services by the principal (for instance, inadequate access for a new toll road); prohibiting reductions in a workforce that is too big; the unexpected introduction of new competition; and so on. This threat of expropriation is especially a problem when the state's ability to make commitments is weak.

Conversely, the company can become more demanding when the government or regulator has a strong interest in completing the project, or when the smooth functioning of a service is essential. The company might use unavoidable adjustments to the original plan to demand sharp price increases or extra public subsidies, or it can threaten to declare bankruptcy, making others share the burden of the losses, although it alone would have kept all the profits private if circumstances had turned out better.

The first response to the risk of opportunistic behavior would be, of course, to make contracts less incomplete. But there are limits imposed by the costs of drawing up complex contracts (the time spent on this task by managers and lawyers and the time spent negotiating an agreement based on those contracts). If renegotiation of a contract is inevitable, it is a good idea to establish clear procedures for revision at the outset, as well as recourse to arbitration. The reputations that the players (company or public authorities) seek to defend may also act as a restraint on opportunistic behavior.

Ex post competition can also limit the risk of opportunism. For example, a contracting authority can more easily resist a contractor's demand to renegotiate prices for its services if it can (and has the right to) replace, at a low cost, the contractor with a competing company. Here, the ownership of the assets matters. A regional railroad operator is easier to replace if the public authority owns the rolling stock, especially if the trains are not standardized and there is no liquid market for them;[6] in such a case, it is logical to keep the ownership of the rolling stock with the public authority, even if that raises problems both in purchasing (the regional authority probably does not have as much expertise as the contractor) and maintenance (strict monitoring is needed in order to keep the contractor from quietly saving money on maintenance toward the end of the contract). Finally, guarantees[7] discourage behavior like this, and can substitute for a painfully slow legal system to ensure observance of explicit clauses in the contract. They are less useful when it is a question of implementing the spirit of the contract, because the other party can use them as an instrument of blackmail. For instance, a covenant stating that the public authority shall pay a penalty to the company in case of termination of the contract puts it in a weak bargaining position if it asks for a costless and legitimate adjustment that was not specified in the letter of the contract.

PRICES OF REGULATED COMPANIES

Marginal Cost or Average Cost?

Students of economics learn that economic efficiency requires the price of a good or a service to be equal to the marginal cost of producing it. The reasoning behind the principle of pricing according to marginal cost is simple: if something costs ten dollars per unit to produce, as a consumer I will internalize the cost to society of producing the unit I purchased only if it is priced at ten dollars. Say the price is six dollars; then I will buy it even if I am prepared to pay eight dollars—in other words, less than it costs to produce. Conversely, a price of fourteen dollars will dissuade me from buying, even if I am prepared to pay twelve, which is more than the production cost. A price equal to the marginal cost leads to transactions that benefit both consumer and producer, while eliminating transactions that do not.

Because the marginal cost is the cost of producing one additional unit of the product, it does not cover any fixed costs (such as equipment, real estate, management, or R&D) that are invariant to the level of production. Suppose a company prices its product at its marginal cost. The company will not make any profit on its sales, and will make a loss equal to the fixed costs. It will have to cover this loss, either by a government subsidy or by setting a price above marginal cost. The first option—an appeal to the taxpayer—is used in many countries for services like railroads. On the other hand, making the user pay higher prices is often the solution to balancing the budget in the case of telecommunications and electricity. When there is no chance of support from the taxpayer, the company has to make a profit to cover its fixed costs.

WHO SHOULD COVER FIXED COSTS? USER OR TAXPAYER?

Should users pay the cost of the services they use? Or, on the contrary, should this cost be socialized and paid at least in part by third parties, who would then contribute to this service more than they benefit from it? This question can be asked of the enterprise as a whole, or at the level of a particular service it offers.

For rail travel in France and a number of other European countries, users do not pay the full cost of the services they use, and the railroad system reports an operating loss. Hence, the French national rail system has accumulated a debt of approximately forty billion euros. Travelers do not pay the full cost of some journeys, which may be covered either by users of other, more profitable lines, or else by the taxpayer.

Subsidies can keep the price of services to reasonable levels by keeping it close to the marginal cost, i.e., the cost of one more passenger for the journey. But it also makes it impossible to tell whether all these subsidized services should be maintained. For a single service—for example, a little-used rail line—this is not only a question of price, but also whether it is socially desirable to keep or maintain. Since Adam Smith's *The Wealth of Nations* (1776), economists have reflected on the problem of pricing when the social justification for a service is not clear: If service on a rail line is priced only at marginal cost, is there enough consumer surplus[8] to justify the fixed costs of operating it?

One problem is that demand is generally only known locally, around the price that is being charged (in this case, the marginal cost). If the service is partly financed by the taxpayer, or by cross-subsidies from profits derived from other services, then there is not enough information to determine whether we should continue to offer the service—in other words, whether the sum of the consumer surplus and the company's profit exceeds the fixed expenses. In this case, the price needs to go up to test willingness to pay.[9] In contrast, there's no denying the social utility of the service if its pricing covers all its costs (this is what is called average-cost pricing), because the consumer surplus is always positive—consumers cannot lose when this service is maintained, because they are free not to consume it—and the company does not impose expenses on the taxpayer, or on users of other services.

From Abstraction to Practice: Price Caps

Companies operating in natural monopoly, regulated markets (such as electricity or rail or telecoms networks) provide more than one service. If we think the user, not the taxpayer, should be made to pay for the fixed costs, the question is which services should be priced above marginal cost to achieve profit margins. A basic economic approach is the "Ramsey-Boiteux rule." This rule was developed at Electricité de France in 1956 by Marcel Boiteux (an engineer and economist, he later became EDF's CEO and the father of its nuclear power program). The rule has many analogies with rules about optimal taxation put forward in 1926 by mathematician, philosopher, and economist Frank Ramsey, a brilliant student of Keynes who died at the age of twenty-six.

The theory is intuitive. Prices above marginal costs diminish the demand for goods and services produced by the company. It is best to raise prices where this will be least painful, that is, where higher prices do not reduce demand too much. The idea is to cover the fixed costs from profits on services for which demand is the least elastic, and so the economic loss is the smallest. [10]

All this seems rather theoretical: under Ramsey-Boiteux pricing, the markup on a service is a decreasing function of the price elasticity of its demand. But the price structure that results from the Ramsey-Boiteux theory is like that which any private enterprise would choose. In the private sector, business units that sell the company's products always ask how much the market can bear; the implicit basic concept is the elasticity of demand. The major difference between this standard private sector approach and a monopoly regulated according to Ramsey and Boiteux's rule is the price level: prices are higher without regulation, because the purpose of regulation is precisely to limit market power.

How well does reality match economic theory? Until recently, the opposite happened. Prices were set low exactly where higher profit margins would have been painless, i.e., in segments where the elasticity of demand is low; conversely, high prices prevailed in the segments where they hurt. For instance, monthly subscription fees for access to the telecom and electricity networks were kept low, even though higher fees would not have generated disconnections (the few cases in which the users are too destitute to keep paying being dealt with by social tariffs). This was partly political: politically speaking, prices were a relatively painless means of redistribution, as the demand for goods and services such as electricity or telecom connection is inelastic, but an important expenditure for less well-off households. Governments were redistributing to poorer households by creating major economic distortions rather than giving them additional income. To keep prices low on services for which the demand was inelastic, prices on services for which demand was elastic had to rise.

Nor did the redistribution always go in the right direction. Low telephone access rates in rural zones benefited the rich New York City professional who owned a second home in New Jersey or upstate New York as much as they did the poor farmer in Oklahoma. Still, the price of telephone access lines remained low, despite very low elasticity of demand. Had prices been increased in line with the theory, almost all customers would have kept their telephone service; the poorest customers could have been subsidized directly, as sometimes happens with special discounts on electricity bills for the least well-off. Subsidies for services used by well-off households would have ended, and the telephone company would not have had to overprice so many price elastic services (such as long-distance and international calls), which customers consequently used very little. This subdued demand was an economic waste: people had a phone and an access line, but they did not use it as much as they would have if prices had been set in line with theory.

The inefficient pricing structure could be found in most countries, and in different network industries. Boiteux's insight was ignored for forty years. Politics played a role in price setting, but the implementation of a Boiteux price structure was also perceived to be difficult because regulators did not know much about price elasticities and demands. Critics of the economic approach to pricing (and defenders of the status quo) rightly pointed to this information asymmetry.

To return to fundamentals: regulation seeks to ensure that the market power a natural monopoly enjoys does not result in prices that are too high. Yet regulators traditionally did more than regulate the *level* of prices. They also controlled relative prices, that is, the *structure* of prices. In both cases, they were handicapped by a lack of information, but with relative pricing it is less obvious that the regulator should intervene than when it is a question of the general price level. Obviously, a monopoly has an interest in charging high prices on all products, but, a priori, it is less clear that its price structure (i.e., which markups are highest) differs from what is socially desirable.

Regulated prices should ideally follow commercial logic in their structure, but should be lower on the whole than those of an unregulated monopoly. Jean-Jacques Laffont and I have shown that, under certain conditions, the problem of regulation can be broken down like this: 1) the trade-off between limiting the company's profit and encouraging it to reduce its costs must be managed through a rule sharing costs or profit—that is, by a risk-sharing contract that makes the company accountable; and 2) the price structure must follow the Ramsey-Boiteux pricing principle. This has important practical implications. In particular, it makes it possible to make full use of all the information at the company's disposal. A policy of price caps, in which a company is compelled only to charge an *average* price that is lower than a ceiling fixed by public authorities, not only creates powerful incentives by making the company pay attention to its costs, but also leaves it free to choose a price structure on the same principles as pricing in private, unregulated enterprises, on the basis of the detailed information it has regarding its production costs, as well as demand elasticities.

To sum up, the introduction of price caps at the end of the twentieth century was a response, both theoretical and practical, not only to the previous lack of company incentives, but also to inefficient pricing structures. Price cap schemes encourage regulated businesses to use more efficient price structures than before the reforms, when prices were set administratively by regulators and not much related to economic principles. The flexibility allowed a company in its price structure permits it to use all the information at its disposal about what each segment of the market can bear.

REGULATION OF ACCESS TO THE NETWORK

Obstacles to the Introduction of Competition

Incentives encourage a company to improve its performance, and so does competition. Competition does not develop easily, because network industries, by definition, are based on essential infrastructures that create natural monopolies for their operators. High fixed costs make it undesirable to duplicate them, which prevents true competition. On the other hand, there can be competition in complementary sectors. There can be only one high- (or low-) voltage electricity grid, but there can be several electricity suppliers competing with one another to serve industrial consumers and households, provided they have equal access to the transmission (and distribution) networks.

Opening network industries to competition raises delicate questions. For example, in an unregulated market, a firm that controls the essential infrastructure will, in general, want to limit competition downstream in order to avoid eroding its profit. It can do this either by giving priority to its own subsidiary (if it is vertically integrated) or by signing an exclusive contract with or giving privileged access to one of the companies downstream. What could justify exclusivity? It is normal, for instance, for a firm to profit, at least temporarily, from an innovation or an investment with large social value. But, if the monopoly position is the result of luck or a privilege granted by the state (the right to manage an airport or container port, for example), then there is no good reason why the firm should be allowed to obtain monopoly rents by limiting downstream competition (among airlines using the airport, say). These principles inspired the development of competition law in relation to infrastructure such as ports, airports, and computerized reservation systems in the 1980s. This created the need for an analytical framework for the opening of network industries to competition.

The Pricing of Access

Regulation of access—that is, of the prices charged by the incumbent operator to allow access to its infrastructure—is necessary for two reasons. First, because to increase its profits, a company that holds a monopoly on access to essential infrastructure will want to charge access prices that are too high for some competitors serving retail customers (or even price them completely out of the market). This is why regulators fixate on prices for access (and more generally on the conditions for access in terms of quality, capacity, priority, and so on) to essential infrastructure. This regulation must introduce competition while preserving the incentives for the incumbent to maintain and improve the network.

This balance is hard to strike. For example, there have been continuous problems in setting connection prices in telecommunications networks. When this sector was opened to competition in the UK in 1984, there was no model for determining the fees that Mercury (a long-distance communications supplier) ought to pay the incumbent operator, British Telecom, which owned the local "loop" connecting homes to the network (now owned through its Openreach subsidiary). More than thirty years later, the terms on which Openreach gives competitors access to its network are as controversial as ever, with the communications regulator Ofcom introducing new access conditions in 2017.[11] The same question arose concerning the price that competitors of France Telecom/Orange had to pay for access to their networks, and in fact in all the countries whose telephone networks were opened to competition. With my colleagues in Toulouse, Jean-Jacques Laffont and Patrick Rey, I studied the question of how to reconcile the introduction of competition in complementary sectors (long-distance and international telephone service and the Internet, for example) that needed access to key infrastructure (the local loop), and ensuring that there were sufficient incentives for the incumbent operator to invest in the infrastructure itself. Access to the incumbent operator's local loop is "one way," as it is the only operator of the infrastructure. We also studied the new problem proceeding from the existence of multiple local loops requiring mutual access ("two-way access") to develop principles for calculating the costs of mutual interconnection; two-way access interconnection became widespread with the advent of mobile telephony, as well as with the unbundling of the incumbent's copper local loop, allowing entrants to offer full-fledged telephone services.

Generally, the design of price signals (such as access charges) has several objectives, which we can illustrate using the example of railroads.

Promoting allocative efficiency. The first goal is to allocate the scarce available time slots on busy train lines, especially in large cities, with a view to optimal use and distribution among the different activities that need slots, such as long-distance passenger transport, suburban trains, freight, and maintenance. The slots must also be allocated among the different railroad operators. Finally, allocative efficiency involves determining the right level of investment.

Assuring a sufficient level of revenue for the company providing access.
The company that owns the essential infrastructure must have incentives to continue to invest in the infrastructure and maintain it adequately. To analyze this question, we adapted the Ramsey-Boiteux principle (which concerned the price of the final goods and services provided to end users) to account for the presence of intermediate goods. In other words, how could the principles be adapted to the prices that an incumbent operator should charge for providing access to its infrastructure? Laffont and I showed that adapting the Ramsey-Boiteux pricing principles to account for the existence of wholesale offerings (access to the infrastructure) was similar to the question faced by a multi-product monopolist selling only final products. Just as the latter must set prices that cover fixed production costs, so access prices must contribute, along with markups on final goods and services, to the coverage of the infrastructure costs of the monopolist. We therefore proposed an overall price cap encompassing both access and final goods or services. In all cases, the Ramsey-Boiteux formula reflects what the market can bear (in terms of price), taking into account the costs the operator has to cover.

To create the conditions for fair competition downstream, the price charged for access needs to be proportional to use. An access tariff structure whereby the downstream company retailing to final customers pays a fixed charge (let's say, annually) for access to the infrastructure, and then possibly a fee for each use, prevents entrants smaller than the incumbent operator from being able to compete until their size reaches the critical level that justifies paying the fixed charge. The choice of pricing for access and of the industrial structure of the sector are thus connected. To have a competitive market downstream, serving final customers, the price of access must be linear, and its unit price must exceed the marginal cost of giving access in order to participate in the coverage of the infrastructure's fixed costs. On the other hand, in the case in which there is a monopolistic downstream market, two-part pricing consisting of a fixed sum paid to the infrastructure owner (thus contributing to the coverage of the fixed costs) and pricing per access that reflects the marginal cost is appropriate.[12]

Thus, the worst-case scenario is a downstream monopoly with linear pricing. In this case, the access price will be relatively high and will indirectly reduce the number of end users of the infrastructure! There has to be either two-part pricing (a fixed charge plus price per use) or a competitive structure. One cannot simultaneously have a monopoly and regulate the sector as if it were competitive; yet, unfortunately, this is exactly what has been chosen in the French railroad industry over the last twenty years.

To pursue the railroad example, some activities, such as freight, are now subject to competition *in* the market. Others remain monopolies, such as regional passenger transport, in which there is competition *for* the market in different regions. As far as freight is concerned, linear pricing will favor healthy competition. In the case of regional trains run by a single company, it is necessary, on the contrary, to favor two-part pricing, with a lower price for use of the infrastructure. In the end, we must start with this question: Do we want competition *in* or *for* the market for high-speed trains, for example? Once the choice is made, we need to apply the pricing scheme that fits the selected industrial structure, as outlined above.

Access to the Electricity Transmission Network

There has been a lot of research into how access should be given to downstream companies, because the problems vary depending on the sector. When the restructuring of the electricity sector began in the 1990s, regulators and academic researchers focused on the power transmission grid. The electricity sector is organized in three levels: power generation, the high-voltage grid for long-distance transmission, and the low-voltage networks for the local distribution of electricity. The high-voltage network is the physical site of the wholesale market, and there was a wide consensus that access to this network should be open and nondiscriminatory. The liberalizing countries went about this in different ways: most European countries and the United States created network transmission managers independent of the incumbent operators. France and Germany retained their vertically integrated structure, but with an obligation that the transmission operator be neutral about competition between electricity generators, including its affiliated power generation division.

Under what economic conditions should access to the transmission network be sold? That was a new problem when the electricity industry was restructured to introduce competition in generation; as the electricity companies had been vertically integrated and without real competition up to that point, the question had never come up. The first solution, called *physical rights* to transmission, was to consider bilateral exchanges of physical flows of electricity and to define and exchange rights of physical transmission: a sale of electricity by a producer located in A to a consumer (a company or a distributor) located in B then requires the contracting parties to acquire a right of transmission from A to B. For example, a French producer wishing to export to the UK needs to procure the right to use the France-UK interconnect. The aggregate physical transmission rights must conform to the capacities of the lines and the physical laws of networks.[13] Suppose the price of electricity in B is a hundred euros per MWh, whereas producers in A can generate electricity at twenty-five euros per MWh. The line between A and B must have no spare capacity, otherwise prices would even out between the two localities. The market price of a direct physical transmission from B to A will therefore be seventy-five euros per MWh.

Another solution, called *financial rights*, builds on the auction system now used in most electricity markets. Trade is no longer bilateral. Instead, each agent (producer, consumer) indicates willingness to pay through a supply curve or a demand curve in each node of the network. For example, an electricity supplier indicates how much power it is willing to inject into the different nodes of the network to which its generators are connected, as a function of the price prevailing in the node in question: "I am prepared to supply x in A at the price of twenty-five euros per MWh, and an extra y at the price of thirty euros per MWh ..."

The manager of the transmission network, taking into account the physical constraints of the network, then determines the best allocation. For given demands and supplies at the different nodes of the network, and simplifying somewhat, the system minimizes the production cost ("least-cost dispatch") subject to the constraints of the network's reliability. If there is no constraint on the transmission network, least-cost dispatch uses the suppliers who have made the lowest bids; in the event of physical constraints on the transmission network, more expensive suppliers are selected and cheaper ones discarded until the dispatch becomes feasible again. As a vertically integrated operator, EDF, which was a pioneer in economic calculation in this sector, had been doing this internally for sixty years.

The auction approach was new in two ways. First, production costs are revealed by the power generators through their bids in auctions, and not by the company hierarchy. Secondly, producers and consumers can use financial rights to insure themselves against risk. For example, if an aluminum-producing company in an area that imports electricity is worried that congestion on the grid might cause electricity prices in that area to rise, it can acquire financial rights for the quantity it wants. It will lose out by paying at a higher electricity price in the event of congestion, but will recoup this in profit on its financial rights; conversely, in the absence of congestion, the aluminum producer will enjoy lower electricity prices, but its financial rights will be worthless. Overall the producer will have hedged its risk.

To return to our example, even if the cost of production in A is known to be twenty-five euros per MWh, a consumer in B faces the risk of congestion: if the demand in B is weak, there may not be congestion on the line between A and B, and then the purchase price in B will also be twenty-five euros per MWh; but if the demand in B is high, or if the capacity of the high-tension line is reduced by the weather, congestion will cause the price to rise in B to, say, one hundred and seventy-five euros per MWh. A financial right from A to B pays a dividend equal to the difference in price between A and B (0 or one hundred and fifty euros, depending on the case, or seventy-five euros on average if the chances of congestion and no congestion are even). The transmission operator who buys in A at twenty-five euros per MWh and sells in B at one hundred and seventy-five euros per MWh in the event of congestion pockets the price difference between A and B, and redistributes it to the owner of the financial right in the form of a dividend for congestion. The consumer in B can cover himself against electricity price risk by buying a financial right for the same quantity. The financial right is thus no more than insurance cover.

In a key article, Harvard professor William Hogan showed that under perfect competition, a market for financial rights, which pay their holder the difference in price at points of generation and transmission, is equivalent to a market for physical rights. This is no longer so if local markets are not perfectly competitive. With Paul Joskow of MIT, I looked at the situation when markets are imperfect (often the case in practice), and showed, for example, that a producer with a local monopoly power (at a node in the network) or a buyer who is a local monopsony can increase their market power by shrewdly using physical or financial transmission rights. We then set out the principles that should guide competition authorities in this area.[14]

COMPETITION AND UNIVERSAL SERVICE

In network industries, the goal of fairness is traditionally expressed in terms of interventions in pricing matters: social tariffs lead wealthy consumers to subsidize less well-off consumers, who pay lower prices.

Public service obligations force those living in areas that cost little to serve to subsidize those who live in areas that are more costly to serve. Cross-subsidies are then created between consumers located in different regions. They encourage cream skimming in a competitive environment, and are therefore not economically viable. By pricing services above costs in certain areas to compensate for losses in others, an operator with a universal service obligation leaves room for entry by competitors who are equally efficient (or even less efficient), but who do not face the same obligation to offer subsidized prices to the customers who are costly to serve. To counteract cream-skimming strategies, the universal service operator must lower its prices in the areas most exposed to competition (that is, the ones that cost least to serve), which destroys the cross-subsidy.

In most countries where telecommunications, energy, and post have been deregulated, a competitively neutral fund has been set up to compensate companies fulfilling public service obligations. A fee levied on all services, regardless of the provider, subsidizes the services that would otherwise be uneconomical at the prices that the regulator would like to maintain. Thus, an operator serving a less well-off household or a consumer living in a region that is costly to serve receives a subsidy from the fund. This allows competition to operate while maintaining public service policies. Contrary to the commonly held view, there is therefore no conflict between competition and universal service. Even when the introduction of competition rebalances prices, ending cross-subsidies, a universal service obligation protects the less well-off or those in areas that are costly to serve.

Other forms of redistribution could be considered; for instance, through taxes and direct transfers of revenues. In 1976, the economists Anthony Atkinson and Joseph Stiglitz showed that, under certain conditions, any redistribution between individuals should be accomplished through a progressive income tax (and not through public service obligations or other price-distorting policies, such as differentiated VAT rates), so as not to distort consumption choices.

Ultimately, public service obligations affect consumption choices of some categories of people. Atkinson and Stiglitz's idea is that it is better to avoid paternalism, to redistribute revenue through direct taxation, and to let consumers decide what they want to consume, rather than to guide their choices through cross-subsidies. Redistribution through direct taxation makes it possible to increase the incomes of poorer households (by taxing them less or subsidizing them) without altering their choices. In this, Atkinson and Stiglitz are suggesting that a low-income household in a rural area should have more income, but pay more for its telephone, its electricity and its mail service, so that it can make its own choices. Faced with the true prices, the household might prefer to change its consumption pattern, which would increase its well-being.

If some of the Atkinson-Stiglitz theorem's hypotheses are relaxed (notably, when consumers have different tastes—and not just differences in consumption levels stemming from different incomes—or when their incomes are imperfectly observable and therefore taxable, which is often the case in developing countries, making the income tax a very imperfect instrument), then universal service obligations may prove appropriate as an instrument of redistribution. For example, if we do not have all the information necessary to target who should get direct financial aid, subsidizing products or services specifically bought by the group in question can attenuate this information problem. A case in point is the national tariff equalization embodied in universal service obligations, which makes it possible to aid rural households by subsidizing their consumption of postal services. If universal service were replaced by direct financial aid for people who declare that they live in rural areas, urban households might claim a rural address.

Economics has guided reforms encouraging natural monopolies to reduce their costs and to adopt socially efficient prices; it has allowed us to understand how to introduce competition in natural monopoly industries; and it has shown that public service and competition are perfectly compatible. Yet we still have much to learn. Fostering investments in a liberalized market sometimes proves more difficult to achieve than ensuring that allocations are efficient and costs minimized in the short run. Regulated industries are in constant mutation and, like all others, are being transformed by the digital revolution. What used to be an essential infrastructure may no longer be so. New essential bottlenecks emerge from these transformations. New regulations must be invented that reflect the new environment and ensure that markets serve the interests of society.

EPILOGUE

In retrospect, the writing of this book has proved rather timely. All over the world, populists have been having a field day. And while populism comes in many guises, and is triggered by specific causes in each country, it always plays on the electorate's frustrations (unemployment, immigration, the slowdown in economic growth) and fears for the future (rising debt, job-destroying technology, climate change). It exploits these frustrations and fears to foster widespread hostility to immigrants, distrust of free trade, and xenophobia.

There is no doubt that citizens want change, and it is easy to understand why. They feel that policymakers are not doing enough and that they do not have a plan. But change for change's sake is extremely dangerous, particularly when it is based on prejudice and selfishness. Steady, thoughtful change is much less exciting than fast, dramatic change, but it is the only kind of change that can give us hope.

Which brings me to the importance of making economic ideas comprehensible to a general audience. As I have tried to explain in this book, repeatedly blaming politicians for flawed policies won't get us very far. To be certain, some politicians are more courageous or more competent than others. But like us all, they respond to the incentives they face—in their case, the hope of being (re)elected. Very rarely do they go against majoritarian public opinion. So we, the citizens, get the policies we deserve.

Nowadays, people with expert knowledge are often dismissed. Populist politicians and media in particular show complete contempt for elementary economic mechanisms. They skillfully exploit the cognitive biases emphasized throughout this book: our reliance on first impressions, our dependence on heuristics and narratives, our eagerness to believe what we want to believe and to see what we want to see. They promote a vision of an economy free of difficult choices; the bearers of bad news who dare question these fairytales are presented as scaremongers and austerity or climate change ideologues.

Drawing on their scientific knowledge, economists must continue to explain why certain economic policies are at best useless, and at worst downright harmful. Despite the common claim that economics is not a science and that there is no consensus, economists must respond (with all humility) that there are a number of things they do agree upon—instead of always emphasizing the multiplicity of views that naturally arise when complex social science issues are being discussed.

On March 18, 2017, the French daily *Le Monde* published a letter signed by twenty-five Nobel laureates in economics. While the signatories to this letter hold a variety of views on complex issues, such as monetary unions and stimulus spending, and represent a wide spectrum of political opinions, all of them felt, after the *annus horribilis* of 2016 that included Brexit and the result of the American presidential election, that it was their duty to prevent yet another shock, this time in the French presidential election. They felt this all the more strongly because some of the leading candidates (mainly the National Front candidate) had cited Nobel laureates in support of their anti-European economic programs. The letter explained the severe consequences of protectionism, exit from Europe and the Eurozone, and policies inspired by the so-called lump of labor fallacy (the idea that there are a fixed number of jobs in an economy). It noted that migrants, when they are well integrated into the labor force, can constitute an economic opportunity for the host country.

Yes, economics remains an inexact science. Yes, economists' judgment is sometimes impaired by financial conflicts of interest, political friendships, or ambitions for public recognition. But in my view, and contrary to the current mood, economists can play a more important role now than ever. For this to happen, they need to guide their countries through a period of low growth, prepare them for the digital revolution and its many socioeconomic challenges, and design solutions to unemployment, climate change, financial regulation, monopolies, poverty, and inequality. Economists must anticipate change much more than they currently do. Above all, they must explain what they are good at—and what they are bad at too—and, with humility and conviction, harness economics for the common good.

NOTES

Introduction: Whatever Happened to the Common Good?

1. "Cardinal Welfare, Individualistic Ethics and Interpersonal Comparisons of Utility," *Journal of Political Economy* (1955) 63 (4): 309–21.
2. The Soviet "new man" (and woman, although the image was primarily male) was meant by early revolutionaries such as Trotsky and Lenin to bring his exceptional virtues to the service of society, beginning with selflessness but also including physical strength, a determination to work hard (*Stakhanovism*), education, and strict control of impulsive behavior. The belief that the new state would radically transform human nature quickly led to economic failure and the consequent authoritarian desire to apply state control over individuals.
3. This refers to Aristotle's criticism of the notion of the common good as developed by Plato. Plato imagined a community of goods in the ideal society, while Aristotle emphasized that this can raise as many problems as it solves.
4. So long as I do not pollute this air, of course. These goods, for which my use does not compete with yours, are called "public goods" in economics. (The impossibility of excluding certain users is sometimes incorporated into the definition of a "public good." I cannot restrict your access to the air, but it is possible to exclude people from a communal space, an online course, a patented invention, or watching a sports event on television, even though these too can be consumed by many users at the same time.)
5. He described as "dismal" the economists opposed to slavery.

Chapter One: Do You Like Economics?

1. In his article, "Ideology, Motivated Reasoning, and Cognitive Reflection," *Judgment and Decision Making*, 2013, no. 8, pp. 407–424. More precisely, Kahan shows that capacities for calculation and reflective analysis do not improve the quality of the revision of beliefs about the anthropogenic factor. In 2010, only 38 percent of American Republicans accepted the

idea that the planet has grown warmer since the pre-industrial era, and only 18 percent credited an anthropogenic factor in this change.

2. In his book, *The Belief in a Just World: A Fundamental Delusion* (New York: Plenum Press, 1982).

3. Daniel Kahneman, *Thinking, Fast and Slow* (London: Allen Lane, 2011). See also his works with Amos Tversky, in particular a book written with Paul Slovic, *Judgment under Uncertainty: Heuristics and Biases* (New York: Cambridge University Press, 1982). For a different point of view on heuristics, read Gerd Gigenrenzer, *Simple Heuristics That Make Us Smart* (Oxford: Oxford University Press, 1999).

4. Figures given by Charles Kurzman, a sociologist at the University of North Carolina, quoted by Simon Kuper in the November 21, 2015, issue of the *Financial Times*. This figure excludes the September 11 victims, but it gives us an idea of the perception problem. Kurzman added in the *Huffington Post*, December 17, 2015: "So far this year, Americans have been more likely to be killed for being Muslim – than by a Muslim. One in 1 million Muslim Americans died because of hatred for their faith, compared with one in 17 million other Americans who died at the hands of Muslim militants."

5. In their example, half the Harvard students assessed a probability of 95 percent, when the real probability was only 2 percent. See chapter 5 for a description of this experiment.

6. In the United States, students go to medical school not directly following their secondary education, but only after four years of university study in other disciplines.

7. Studied by Michael Kremer and Charles Morcom in "Elephants," *American Economic Review*, 2000, vol. 90, no. 1, pp. 212–234. Similar issues arise in the debate between an outright ban on the trade of ivory or rhino horn powder (the current law in most countries) and regulated trade thereof. Those in favor of regulated trade argue that private breeding of rhinos and elephants does not require killing the animal to extract these items of value, and especially that this would make extinction of these endangered species less likely. On the other hand, strict conservationists are concerned that global demand would be increased by marketing.

8. What counts for the argument is whether the action of reselling goes in the right direction, whatever its level and thus the size of its impact.

9. Historically, our survival has always depended on a strong norm of reciprocity within a limited social group. One of the novelties of recent history ("recent" in the evolutionary sense) is that we have learned to interact peacefully with groups that are foreign to us. See Paul Seabright's book *The Company of Strangers: A Natural History of Economic Life* (Princeton: Princeton University Press, 2010).

10. Paul Slovic, an American psychologist, has shown how the image of a single starving child in Mali can generate an outpouring of generosity much greater than the donations inspired by statistics on famine – for example, data on the millions of children suffering from malnutrition. This reaction clearly doesn't make sense, but it shows how our perceptions and emotions affect our behavior.

11. Part of the "cost" of queuing could be avoided by offering chairs and a heated waiting room, but that would only appear to solve the problem. In this case, potential buyers would come even earlier (the day before, for instance) and wait for longer. The windfall associated with a price lower than the market price would still disappear.

12. There are some caveats to this broad rule, including the need to design auctions so as to preserve competition among the license users, such as wireless network operators. For example, the state must ensure that the auction does not create a monopoly or tight oligopoly. Similarly, actors must have no incentive to withdraw capacity to raise the price – see, for example, the recent concern about the possibility of capacity withdrawal in the so-called reverse auction in the US. Ulrich Doraszelski, Katja Seim, Michael Sinkinson, and Peichun Wang, in "Ownership Concentration and Strategic Supply Reduction" (2016), express concern about the significant purchases of licenses by private equity firms in the run-up to the US government's planned acquisition of broadcast TV licenses to repackage them and resell them to wireless carriers in a forward auction (an estimated forty-five billion dollars in revenue).

13. There are many works on the subject. See for instance two books written by prominent economists who were instrumental in the design of these auctions: Paul Klemperer's *Auctions: Theory and Practice* (Princeton: Princeton University Press, 2004) and Paul Milgrom's *Putting Auction Theory to Work* (Cambridge: Cambridge University Press, 2004).

14. Assuming, of course, that firms are not facing financial constraints, a situation that has been analyzed by researchers to study the way in which auctions should be modified in this case.

15. After a series of negotiations, the United Kingdom contributed very little to the European Union's budget. Similarly, the argument that the rules issued by Brussels are restrictive is questionable (except for the occasional red tape) if only because most of these regulations are entirely desirable, accepted by willing governments, and necessary for international trade. On the other hand, Britain's exit from the EU threatens to lead to stagnant investment because of the uncertainty regarding the country's future, a decrease in direct foreign investment, and the UK's diminished access to the European market. Trade with Europe represents 45 percent of the United Kingdom's exports and 53 percent of its imports. The default agreement in matters of

trade is that of the World Trade Organization. Although the latter has substantially lowered tariff barriers, the chief obstacles to commerce today are not tariffs, but rather non-tariff barriers such as standards, regulations, rules regarding origin, and banking passports (which Switzerland, for instance, does not have). These barriers will probably become important after Brexit, since Europe has little incentive to negotiate a new trade agreement and create a precedent that would encourage other countries to exit the EU – which some populist politicians in other countries support. The econometric estimates of Brexit's cost to the United Kingdom vary greatly, but they all go in the same direction.

16. See for example http://online.wsj.com/public/resources/documents/Econ omistLetter11012016.pdf.

17. On the RTL radio station, March 29, 2014.

18. As Paul Krugman summed it up in the introduction to his *Pop Internationalism*: "Intellectual laziness, even among those who would be seen as wise and deep, will always be a powerful force" ([Cambridge: MIT Press, 1996], p. ix).

Chapter Two: The Moral Limits of the Market

1. *Groundwork of the Metaphysics of Morals*, trans. Mary Gregor and Jens Timmermann (Cambridge: Cambridge University Press, 2012), p. 46.

2. "This much I know," *The Guardian*, April 27, 2013.

3. *World Values Survey*.

4. A merit good is a good (or service) that will be underprovided by the market and is provided to all citizens by the government free or at a low price because it has intrinsic benefits or merit.

5. New York: Farrar, Straus and Giroux, 2012.

6. For a rather similar thesis, see *Spheres of Justice: A Defense of Pluralism and Equality* (New York: Basic Books, 1983) by Michael Walzer, a professor emeritus at Princeton University. For a very different approach to these questions, see *Why Some Things Should Not Be for Sale: The Moral Limits of Markets* (Oxford: Oxford University Press, 2010) by another philosopher, Debra Satz, a professor at Stanford.

7. See chapters 8 and 9.

8. An economic actor (or group) causes an externality when their activity produces, free of charge, a benefit or an advantage (or, on the contrary, a disutility or uncompensated harm) for someone else.

9. On this, see Daniel Golden, *The Price of Admission: How America's Ruling Class Buys Its Way into Elite Colleges – and Who Gets Left Outside the Gates* (New York: Three Rivers Press, 2006).

10. For an in-depth discussion of voting questions, see for example Alessandra Casella, *Storable Votes: Protecting the Minority Voice* (Oxford: Oxford University Press, 2012).

11. For a more detailed discussion of these questions, see James Hammitt, "Positive vs. Normative Justifications for Benefit-Cost Analysis. Implications for Interpretation and Policy," *Review of Environmental Economics and Policy*, 2013, vol. 7, no. 2, pp. 199–218. Many articles have shown the inconsistency of our choices in the matter of protecting life. For example, some policies that cost a few hundred dollars per year of life saved are neglected, whereas others that cost billions of dollars per year of life saved are implemented. (Tammy Tengs, et al., "Five-Hundred Life-Saving Interventions and Their Cost-Effectiveness," *Risk Analysis*, 1995, vol. 15, no. 3, pp. 369–390). Economists have nonetheless attempted to quantify health-related costs to guide decision makers in their policy choices. The disability-adjusted life year (DALY) and quality-adjusted life year (QALY) are among the most popular measurements. The DALY is calculated by adding a measure of the impact of a disease or disability on life expectancy, and an adjustment in the quality of life prior to death. Each specific condition receives a disability weight between 0 and 1. For instance, one DALY is equal to one year of healthy life lost.

12. For a classical utilitarian point of view in moral philosophy, see Peter Singer, *Practical Ethics* (Cambridge: Cambridge University Press, 1993).

13. See Jean-François Bonnefon, Iyad Rahwan, and Azim Shariff, "The Social Dilemma of Autonomous Vehicles," *Science* 352(6293): 1573–1576.

14. Judith Chevalier and Fiona Scott Morton, "State Casket Sales and Restrictions: A Pointless Undertaking?" *Journal of Law and Economics*, 2008, vol. 51, no. 1, pp. 1–23.

15. Roland Bénabou and Jean Tirole, "Over My Dead Body: Bargaining and the Price of Dignity," *American Economic Review, Papers and Proceedings*, 2009, vol. 99, no. 2, pp. 459–465.

16. See chapter 5 for a discussion of the fragility of our morality.

17. Trade in human organs is legal only in Iran, but illegal supply networks exist in several emerging or developing countries.

18. For a theoretical study of the expressive character of law, see my article with Roland Bénabou, "Laws and Norms," unpublished paper, 2013.

19. An alternative foundation for our rejection of "dwarf tossing" is that we do not want to live in a society some of whose members delight in seeing such a show.

20. With Lloyd Shapley, who had, like Roth, studied the allocation mechanisms between both sides of a market.

21. For a description, see for example Alvin Roth's Nobel Prize address, "The Theory and Practice of Market Design," online at the Nobel Foundation website.

22. *The Righteous Mind: Why Good People Are Divided by Politics and Religion* (London: Penguin Books, 2012).

23. Some would add job insecurity. It goes without saying that unemployment is a major contributor to the loss of social cohesion. But as I will show in chapter 9, widespread unemployment results from choices made by society; it is about institutions, not the market itself.

24. Drawing on Marcel Mauss's *The Gift: Forms and Functions of Exchange in Archaic Societies* (London: Routledge, 1922), Bourdieu made this remark in a review of the proceedings of a conference on Mauss's works that was published by Nicolas Olivier in 2008.

25. For further reading on this theme, see Matt Ridley's *The Rational Optimist: How Prosperity Evolves* (Fourth Estate, London, 2011), particularly chapter 3, provocatively titled "The Manufacture of Virtue: Barter, Trust and Rules after 50,000 Years Ago." See also Paul Seabright's *The Company of Strangers* (Princeton: Princeton University Press, 2004).

26. Samuel Bowles, *Microeconomics: Behavior, Institutions, and Evolution* (Princeton: Princeton University Press, 2006). The op-ed piece appeared in the *Wall Street Journal* in 2002.

27. In "The Crisis of 2008: Structural Lessons for and from Economics," Centre for Economic Policy Research, *Policy Insight*, 2009, no. 28.

28. Paul Seabright, *The Company of Strangers* (Princeton: Princeton University Press, 2004). For an analysis of the commercialization of sexuality, see also Seabright's book *The War of the Sexes: How Conflict and Cooperation Have Shaped Men and Women from Prehistory to the Present* (Princeton: Princeton University Press, 2012).

29. A "monopsonistic" employer is one who is the sole buyer (here, of the employee's labor) and is thus able to dictate the terms of the exchange.

30. Although the market, if not corrected by taxation, generates great inequalities, we must also note that other important forms of inequality develop in countries that are less subject to the market economy.

31. Overall inequality is measured by indexes (here, the "Gini coefficient") that take into account the whole revenue curve and not solely the comparison, for example, between the top 1 percent and the rest.

32. *Capital in the Twenty-First Century*, trans. Arthur Goldhammer (Cambridge: Belnap Press, 2014).

33. Facundo Alvaredo, Tony Atkinson, Thomas Piketty, Emmanuel Saez, and Gabriel Zucman, *The World Wealth and Income Database*.

34. For example, inequality increased greatly in the United Kingdom while Tony Blair was prime minister (1997–2007) if we consider the proportion received by the top 1 percent, but the UK became more egalitarian if we consider the relation between the top 10 percent and the "bottom" 10 percent. In short, without necessarily concluding that the United Kingdom became more egalitarian, we should note that it is distribution as a whole

that counts, and not a single aggregated statistic. See John Van Reenen (London School of Economics), *Corbyn and the Political Economy of Nostalgia*, based on the works of Gabriel Zucman and the UK government's Department for Work and Pensions.

35. See David Autor, Larry Katz, and Melissa Kearney, "The Polarization of the U.S. Labor Market" *American Economic Review*, 2006, 96 (2): 189–94, and David Autor and David Dorn, "The Growth of Low-Skill Service Jobs and the Polarization of the U.S. Labor Market" *American Economic Review*, 2013, 103(5), 1553–1597. We find a similar phenomenon in France: see Sylvain Catherine, Augustin Landier, and David Thesmar, *Marché du travail. La grande fracture* (Paris: Institut Montaigne, 2015). I return to this polarization in chapter 15.

36. My account here is both sketchy and incomplete. For example, some observers have pointed the finger at an evolution of institutions that does not serve the workers' interests (decline of unionization, slow growth or decline of the minimum wage). But as David Autor, David Dorn, Lawrence F. Katz, Christina Patterson, and John Van Reenen ("Concentrating on the Fall of the Labor Share", 2017, NBER Working Paper No. 23108) argue, the decline in the labor share affects all countries, regardless of the evolution of institutions.

37. There is a debate among economists as to whether skill-biased technological change is occurring exogenously (just because new tasks are more complex) or endogenously. Daron Acemoglu (in "Directed Technical Change," *Review of Economic Studies*, 2002, 69: 781–809) observes that innovation is directed and that unskill-based innovation occurred in the late eighteenth century and early nineteenth century, when the artisan shop was replaced by the factory. He shows that there are two opposite effects at play: a price effect, as technologies economize on the more expensive factor, and a market size effect, according to which innovations, which benefit from increasing returns to scale, complement the abundant factor of production. The second factor is illustrated by the fact that the wage premium associated with going to college – the "college premium" – has grown swiftly since the 1970s, despite a large increase in college enrolment.

38. Autor et al., op cit.

39. This labor share in GDP used to be stable (although not at the industry level), but has decreased everywhere in the world.

40. Let us recall that the world has undergone a second wave of globalization over the past fifty years, after the very strong wave that ended with the First World War. International trade now represents about one-third of the gross world product.

41. The growth of GDP per capita of 326 percent in India and 823 percent in China in only twenty-five years (from 1991 to 2015) is of course exceptional by any historical standard.

42. Elhanan Helpman, "Globalization and Inequality. Jean-Jacques Laffont Lecture," October, 2015. Among the recent works, see also Anthony Atkinson, *Inequality: What Can Be Done?* (Cambridge: Harvard University Press, 2015), and Joseph Stiglitz, *The Great Divide: Unequal Societies and What We Can Do about Them* (New York: Norton, 2015).

43. "Bonus culture," *Journal of Political Economy*, 2016, 124: 305–370.

44. However, note the work by Cecilia Garcia-Peñalosa and Étienne Wasmer on the brain drain in France ("Préparer la France à la mobilité internationale croissante des talents," Conseil d'analyse économique, note 31). They show that the phenomenon is limited, but concentrated on "talents." They point out that the optimal itinerary for exploitation of the social system is to be trained in France (study is free), go abroad to work, and then return to France when you have to pay for your children's education or need health care. They advocate a series of public policy measures.

45. Linda Van Bouwel and Reinhilde Veugelers show that the best European economics students (as measured by their later careers) return to Europe less often, and that few of them return later if they take their first job in the United States. Other studies corroborate this observation in other scientific domains ("Are Foreign PhD Students More Likely to Stay in the US? Some Evidence from European Economists," in Marcel Gérard and Silke Uebelmesser, eds., *The Mobility of Students and the Highly Skilled* [Cambridge: MIT Press, 2015]). An important question is whether the recent creation of the European Research Council (whose goal is to help keep the best researchers in Europe) will succeed in stemming the flow, or whether, as is more likely, the creation of the council is complementary to reforms of the university system and will chiefly benefit only the countries that make reforms.

46. Finally, the data may be difficult to access or may include omissions (as when an overseas student creates a firm in Palo Alto or in Boston after his or her studies).

47. Some people mention the decline of labor unions, but there seems to be no empirical evidence in favor of this hypothesis.

48. Odran Bonnet, Pierre-Henri Bono, Guillaume Chapelle, and Étienne Wasmer, "Does Housing Capital Contribute to Inequality? A Comment on Thomas Piketty's *Capital in the 21st Century*," unpublished paper, 2015.

49. Philippe Aghion, Ufuk Akcigit, Antonin Bergeaud, Richard Blundell, and David Hemous, "Innovation and Top Income Inequality," unpublished paper, 2015. The authors argue that innovation, although it increases the top 1 percent's share of revenues, promotes social mobility and does not increase overall inequality.

50. For example, a number of benefits may be foregone once one reaches a certain level of income. In some cases, an individual may hardly improve his or her net income, or in extreme cases even lose money when reentering the workforce or increasing gross income.

51. The following borrows from an op-ed piece written with Étienne Wasmer and published in *Libération* on June 8, 2015.

52. World Values Survey. See also Alberto Alesina, Ed Glaeser, and Bruce Sacerdote, "Why Doesn't the United States Have a European-Style Welfare State?" *Brookings Papers on Economic Activity*, 2001, no. 2, pp. 187–278.

53. Mark Granovetter, *Getting a Job: A Study of Contacts and Careers* (Cambridge: Harvard University Press, 1974). For example, Granovetter shows that more than 50 percent of jobs in a city in Massachusetts were obtained using contacts. Granovetter is well known for his theory of the "strength of weak ties," from the title of his article published in 1973 in the *American Journal of Sociology*, vol. 78 (1973), 1360–1380.

54. Roland Bénabou and Jean Tirole, "Belief in a Just World and Redistributive Politics," *Quarterly Journal of Economics*, 2006, vol. 121, no. 2, pp. 699–746.

55. Alberto Alesina, Reza Baqir, and William Easterly, "Public Goods and Ethnic Divisions," *Quarterly Journal of Economics*, 1999, vol. 114, no. 4, pp. 1243–1284.

56. Barry Bosworth, Gary Burtless, and Kan Zhang, "Later Retirement, Inequality in Old Age, and the Growing Gap in Longevity between Rich and Poor" (The Brookings Institution, 2016).

57. In Bosworth, et al. (2016), assuming that the man is still alive at the age of fifty.

CHAPTER THREE: THE ECONOMIST IN CIVIL SOCIETY

1. Burke wrote this in 1793 in reaction to the beheading of Marie Antoinette.

2. In the usual sense of the term: as a manipulator, the sophist tries to persuade his audience by means of arguments that seem coherent but are, in fact, false.

3. The quotation from Burke is ambiguous: Does *calculators* refer here to a group of manipulators acting out of calculation and self-interest, as his accusation of sophism suggests? Or is he blaming mathematicians, whom he no doubt held in similar esteem as economists?

4. There is a famous lawsuit concerning his meager reward for the patented technology in relation to the income it earned for the company.

5. While they are less keen on taking a strong political stance and being involved in a political party, they may be very active in the public debate through blogs, tweets, and op-eds. For example, according to a study by Jean Beuve, Thomas Renault, and Amélie Schurich-Rey ("Les économistes universitaires dans le débat et la décision publics," Conseil d'Analyse Économique Focus paper no. 17), economists located in the United States and the UK are more active than their European counterparts concerning

tweets or contributions to VoxEU, a prominent European policy portal. To be sure, the language factor, the cosmopolitan character of universities in these two countries, and their earlier adoption of new communication tools may of course be part of the explanation, but this strongly suggests that the difference in the patterns of engagement in civil society is not linked to a disinterest in public policy among US and UK intellectuals.

6. For more on this, see *How the French Think: An Affectionate Portrait of an Intellectual People* by Sudhir Hazareesingh (New York: Basic Books, 2015). And especially *The Reckless Mind: Intellectuals in Politics* by Mark Lilla (New York: NYRB Books, 2001), which analyzes the attitudes of eight intellectuals (including Frenchmen Michel Foucault and Jacques Derrida) toward politics.

7. See chapter 6 for an analysis of the state.

8. See chapter 4.

9. *American Economic Review, Econometrica, Journal of Political Economy, Quarterly Journal of Economics, Review of Economic Studies.*

10. John Maynard Keynes, *The General Theory of Employment, Interest, and Money* (Palgrave Macmillan, 1936).

CHAPTER FOUR: THE EVERYDAY LIFE OF A RESEARCHER

1. E.g., John Vickers, Damien Neven, Massimo Motta, Lars-Hendrik Roeller, and Tommaso Valletti in Europe, or Tim Breshnahan, Dennis Carlton, Joe Farrell, Michael Katz, Aviv Nevo, Nancy Rose, Carl Shapiro, and Fiona Scott-Morton to name a few recent chief economists at the US Department of Justice.

2. Partha Dasgupta, "Modern Economics and Its Critics," in Uskali Maki, ed., *Fact and Fiction in Economics: Models, Realism and Social Construction*, (Cambridge: Cambridge University Press, 2002). Partha Dasgupta analyzes 281 articles published between 1991 and 1995; among them, 25 are purely theoretical, 100 apply theory to a particular problem in economic policy, and 156 (thus more than half) are empirical or experimental.

3. Daron Acemoglu (economic institutions, labor economics), Susan Athey and Jon Levin (industrial economics), Raj Chetty and Emmanuel Saez (evaluation of public policies), Esther Duflo (economics of development), Amy Finkelstein (health care economics), Roland Fryer (economics of discrimination), Matthew Gentzkow (the media and economic policy), Steve Levitt (social phenomena and economics, the author of the best-seller *Freakonomics*), to limit myself to the ten researchers who have won the Clark Medal (a prize for the best economist under forty years old who works in the United States) between 2005 and 2015.

4. For example, in the first case, a three-dimensional, homogenous, and isotropic space, and in the second case, the absence of electrostatic interactions.

5. See chapter 8 for more details.

6. See chapter 7.

7. It consists in summing up, in a single figure, financial flows that are, a priori, not directly comparable because they are realized at different times. In order to do this, the interest rate i is used, reflecting the trade-off between 1 dollar today and $1 + i$ dollars a year later (this is a simplification; other factors can come into play, such as risk or the discounting of distant profits. See in particular Christian Gollier's book, *Pricing the Planet's Future? The Economics of Discounting in an Uncertain World* [Princeton: Princeton University Press, 2012]).

8. I cannot cite here the hundreds or thousands of articles devoted to this subject in the literature of economics. For a very limited survey of the references, the reader might consult the works cited in my articles with Roland Bénabou on identity and social norms.

9. Naturally, the sampling has to be truly random. This would not be the case if subjects self-selected into participating in the clinical test; those who choose to participate in a trial usually have characteristics that differ from those of the population as a whole.

10. Another case of random sampling is (or was) the gender of infants born to a couple. For example, it is hard to study how the number of her children affects a woman's career: a mother who benefits from a promotion may decide to have fewer children or to have them later. Then the causal relation is unclear: Does having children cause a mother's career to be compromised or, on the contrary, does being successful in her career cause a mother to have fewer children? However, the fact that a family with two sons or two daughters is more likely to want a third child makes it possible to push forward the analysis of causality (see Josh Angrist and William Evans, "Children and Their Parents' Labor Supply: Evidence from Exogenous Variation in Family Size," *American Economic Review*, 1998, vol. 88, no. 3, pp. 450–477).

11. See in particular Abhijit Banerjee and Esther Duflo, *Poor Economics: A Radical Rethinking of the Way to Fight Global Poverty* (New York: Public Affairs Books, 2011), and more generally the pioneering contributions made by these researchers, who teach at MIT.

12. This is not necessarily true if the contract between sellers and buyers is incomplete; an important condition is that the terms of exchange are clearly specified. Laboratory experiments have been conducted in which there is an excess of "workers" with respect to the number of "jobs." If the effort to be expended on the task is specified in the contract, then Smith's result is verified. If, on the other hand, the effort expended is partly at

the employee's discretion, employers try to appeal to the employee's reciprocity (see chapter 5) and offer higher salaries than the one they need to offer to attract the employee. See for example Ernst Fehr and Armin Falk, "Wage Rigidity in a Competitive Incomplete Contract Market," *Journal of Political Economy*, 1999, no. 107, pp. 106–134.

13. For an overview, see Steven Levitt and John List, "Field Experiments in Economics: The Past, the Present, and the Future," *European Economic Review*, 2009, vol. 53, pp. 1–18.

14. For recent reflections on the scientific status of economics, I recommend Dani Rodrik, *Economics Rules: The Rights and Wrongs of the Dismal Science* (New York: Norton, 2016).

15. Beginning with the discussion of game theory in this chapter. See also chapters 10 and 11.

16. Of course, I could also take examples bearing on microeconomics.

17. This challenge is often called the "rational expectations revolution." Precursors were Columbia's Edmund Phelps and Chicago's Milton Friedman, who argued that well-informed, rational employers and workers would care only about real wages.

18. The conventional wisdom at the time held that economies faced either inflation or unemployment, but not both at the same time.

19. See chapter 11.

20. See in particular the site retraction watch.com. For discussions of the reproducibility of results, see (in psychology, for example) the article in *Science* (*Sciencemag*) on August 28, 2015: "Estimating the Reproducibility of Psychological Science"; in medicine, the article in *PLOS One*, "Does Publication Bias Inflate the Apparent Efficacy of Psychological Treatment for Major Depressive Disorder? A Systematic Review and Meta-Analysis of US National Institutes of Health–Funded Trials," September 30, 2015; in economics, Andrew Chang and Phillip Li's article, "Is Economics Research Replicable? Sixty Published Papers from Thirteen Journals Say 'Usually Not,'" (Federal Reserve Board, 2015).

21. Interview in *Le Monde*, January 3, 2001.

22. The great majority of these students will not become economists, but will instead continue their studies in management, law, or another discipline, or enter professional life.

23. Bruno Frey and Stephan Meier, "Selfish and Indoctrinated Economists?" *European Journal of Law and Economics*, 2005, vol. 19, pp. 165–171.

24. Raymond Fisman, Shachar Kariv, and Daniel Markovits, "Exposure to Ideology and Distributional Preferences," 2009, unpublished paper.

25. For a study of the impact of narratives on behavior, see my article with Armin Falk and Roland Bénabou, "Narratives, Imperatives, and Moral Reasoning," unpublished paper.

26. Recall Adam Smith's famous formula: "It is not from the benevolence of the butcher, the brewer, or the baker, that we expect our dinner, but from regard to their own interest. We address ourselves, not to their humanity but to their self-love." Of course, Smith also wrote a great deal about the necessity of pro-social behaviors and on the necessity of regulation (recommending state intervention to overcome poverty, to prevent usurious lending, and to subsidize education), contrary to the simplistic image of him often given.

27. Isaiah Berlin, *The Hedgehog and the Fox: An Essay on Tolstoy's View of History* (London: Weidenfeld & Nicolson, 1953).

28. As well as writers, who were the subject of Isaiah Berlin's essay. This is just a personal impression, which would have to be confirmed more rigorously by an empirical study similar to Tetlock's, described below.

29. See his books *Expert Political Judgment: How Good Is It? How Can We Know?* (Princeton: Princeton University Press, 2005), and with Dan Gardner, *Superforecasting* (New York: Crown, 2015).

30. Tetlock uses factorial analysis. Some examples of questions might be: "Do you think the most common error in judging situations is to exaggerate the complexity of the world?" or: "Do you think that a classic error in decision making is to abandon a good idea too quickly?" Positive responses to these questions signal a hedgehog cognitive style.

31. Advocates of a minimal state, who see its main role as providing law and order, including court enforcement of contracts and the protection of private property.

32. Nicolas Bourbaki was an imaginary mathematician. A group of talented French mathematicians (including five Fields Medal winners) met from 1934 to 1968 to write treatises (published under the name of Bourbaki) reconstructing mathematics in a more rigorous, abstract, and unified way.

33. Incidentally, I disagree with Milton Friedman's (1953) view that the realism of assumptions is irrelevant and only predictions matter. First, when data are scarce, looking at the realism of assumptions brings extra information. Second, the exact mechanism at work in general needs to be described in order to conduct policy.

34. *Economics Rules: The Rights and Wrongs of the Dismal Science* (New York: Norton, 2016). See also "Why We Use Math in Economics," *Dani Rodrik's Weblog*, September 4, 2007.

35. A good discussion of machine learning viewed from an economist's viewpoint is Susan Athey's "Beyond Prediction: Using Big Data for Policy Problems," *Science* 355, 483–485 (2017). A focus on correlations has several limitations. First, even if the predictions are credible, making predictions at all requires that the environment be stable. However, it

may be unstable because of exogenous or endogenous causes of instability. To grasp the notion of endogenous instability, note that the covariations being analyzed are presumably not just for the sake of pure knowledge; rather, they inform policies. These policies in turn often alter behaviors (although this need not be the case: the fact that my portfolio of book or movie choices is used by Amazon and Netflix for recommendations to others and to myself does not alter these choices). Relatedly, large players must not be able to manipulate the environment. If they are, they will modify their behavior to affect learning and therefore policy. Second, the focus on correlations ignores the issue of causality, which is the bread and butter of the economics profession. Machine learning experts have started working on causality, but it was traditionally absent from their analysis.

36. Goods can be complements at low prices and substitutes at high prices, or the reverse. Similarly, products and their usage change over time; the current pattern of complementarity/substitutability, even well estimated, will not be the same tomorrow. Two drugs covered by two pharmaceutical patents may be combined to cure a disease, but may also be substitutes to combat another disease. A browser can be a complement to an operating system, but with additional code may become a competitor to that operating system.

37. Nash, who won the Nobel Prize in 1994, died with his wife in a car accident in May 2015 after his return from Oslo where he had just received the Abel Prize, the most prestigious prize in mathematics (along with the Fields Medal). His life inspired Ron Howard's 2002 film *A Beautiful Mind*, in which his role was played by Russell Crowe.

38. Ignacio Palacios-Huerta, "Professionals Play Minimax," *Review of Economic Studies*, 2003, no. 70, pp. 395–415.

39. An important clarification: laboratory experiments are usually constructed in such a way as to respect anonymity. Individual choices are made on a computer. For example, if I choose a deviant behavior in the prisoner's dilemma, the person I am playing against will register his loss, but will not know who caused it (and in theory the experimenter doesn't know that, either).

40. A person is risk averse if he prefers a guaranteed income to an income that is equivalent on average but subject to risks (for example, receiving twenty dollars, rather than thirty dollars with a probability of 50 percent or ten dollars with a probability of 50 percent). The more risk averse a person is, the more he will ask that a contract transfer the risk to the principal.

41. Defined by David Kreps and Bob Wilson, researchers at Stanford, and the Nobel Prize winner Reinhardt Selten.

CHAPTER FIVE: ECONOMICS ON THE MOVE

1. But also adopted by many sociologists, such as Max Weber and James Coleman, and in France by Raymond Boudon and Michel Crozier, not to mention other specialists in the social sciences who are not economists, such as the philosopher Karl Popper.

2. More generally, interdisciplinarity (work across several disciplines in a constructive dialogue) is necessary, even if, unfortunately, it is often talked about but seldom practiced, except in a few research centers. The Institute for Advanced Studies in Toulouse (IAST) was founded in 2011 and has as its objective precisely to bring together in one place and around common seminars anthropologists, biologists, economists, legal scholars, historians, political scientists, psychologists, and sociologists.

3. For example, see the literature on "rational inattention" initiated by Christopher Sims (e.g., in "Implications of Rational Inattention," *Journal of Monetary Economics*, 2003, vol. 50, no. 3, pp. 665–690) and the literature on the costs of acquiring information and on incomplete contracts (for instance, my article "Cognition and Incomplete Contracts," *American Economic Review*, 2009, vol. 99, no. 1, pp. 265–294).

4. Needless to say, firms and politicians try to exploit behavioral characteristics such as self-control problems, biased beliefs, and self-deception. George Akerlof and Robert Shiller's *Phishing for Phools* (Princeton: Princeton University Press, 2015) provides many examples in contexts such as finance, politics, advertising, and sin goods. I also highly recommend John Campbell's "Restoring Rational Choice: The Challenge of Consumer Financial Regulation," *American Economic Review*, (2016) 106: 1–30. That article focuses on consumer protection in an environment where financial ignorance is pervasive.

5. Samuel McClure, David Laibson, George Loewenstein, Jonathan Cohen, "Separate Neural Systems Value Immediate and Delayed Monetary Rewards ," *Science*, 2004, no. 306, pp. 503–507.

6. This property is expressed here in an informal way. The probability that the frequency of tails falls between 49 percent and 51 percent, for example, tends toward 1 as the number of draws becomes large; and this concept can be made still more precise.

7. This bias has been observed, for instance, in roulette, where players have a tendency to bet on numbers that have seldom won earlier in the game; that is why this bias is called the "gambler's fallacy."

8. Daniel Chen, Tobias Moskowitz, and Kelly Shue, "Decision-Making under the Gambler's Fallacy: Evidence from Asylum Judges, Loan Officers, and Baseball Umpires," to appear in the *Quarterly Journal of*

Economics. This article argues in favor of an explanation in terms of the "gambler's fallacy" in comparison with alternative explanations.

9. The question was the following: "A disease affects one person out of 1,000. A test diagnosing this illness has a 5 percent rate of false positives, but correctly identifies those who have the disease [i.e., no false negatives]. One person has a positive test result: what is the probability than this person has the disease?" The correct answer is 2 percent (for a representative sample, 5 percent among the 999 healthy subjects, so approximately 50, will be diagnosed; so will the one who actually has the disease; so the probability of having the disease conditionally on being diagnosed is approximately 1/51, or about 2 percent); many of the respondents said 95 percent.

10. Amos Tversky and Daniel Kahneman, "Belief in the Law of Small Numbers," *Psychological Bulletin*, 1971, no. 76, pp. 105–110.

11. The question of identity also plays a role in individuals' choice to vote. Voting is partly expressive, and not simply induced by the quest for self-interest.

12. In most laboratory experiments, the subjects make their choices on a computer. Moreover, a complex "double-blind" procedure ensures that even the experimenter does not know the individual choices made. He or she knows only the statistical distribution of the behavior.

13. This percentage varies a great deal and depends on different factors, including the other participant's socio-professional category (as it is declared by the experimenter), the other's ethnic, religious, or geographical community, or again the Dictator's physical or psychological state. The important thing is that, on average, subjects are prepared to sacrifice a little of their economic interest for others.

14. Patricia Funk, "Social Incentives and Voter Turnout: Evidence from the Swiss Mail Ballot System," *Journal of the European Economic Association*, 2010, vol. 8, no. 5, pp. 1077–1103.

15. Many articles have been written about reciprocal altruism. See for example Ernst Fehr and Urs Fischbacher's synthesis, "The Nature of Human Altruism," *Nature*, 2003, no. 425, pp. 785–791.

16. Joseph Heinrich, Robert Boyd, Samuel Bowles, Colin Camerer, Ernst Fehr, Herbert Gintis, and Richard McElreath, "In Search of Homo Economicus: Behavioral Experiments in 15 Small-Scale Economies," *American Economic Review Papers and Proceedings*, 2001, vol. 91, no. 2, pp. 73–78. The article also reports on behavior in these microsocieties in the Dictator Game and in "public good games." (In public good games, each player chooses how much to contribute. The contributions are then multiplied by a factor, with the resulting payoff being evenly divided

among players. The multiplicative factor is greater than one, so there is a social gain to contributing; but the multiplicative factor is also less than the number of players, so that each player receives less than one to one on the money he contributes).

17. This strategy has also been observed in field experiments seeking to study the behavior of individuals with regard to charitable acts.

18. "Morals and Markets," *Science*, 2013, vol. 340, pp. 707–711. See also Bjorn Bartling, Roberto Weber and Lan Yao, "Do Markets Erode Social Responsibility?" *Quarterly Journal of Economics* (2015), 219–266.

19. Preferring *B* to *A* amounts to attributing a weight of at least one quarter to the well-being of the other in relation to one's own well-being (the sacrifice is 1 and the gain for the other is 4). Similarly, when we compare *B* and *C*, the sacrifice for choice *B* is 5, and the gain for the other is 20, or four times greater.

20. John List, "On the Interpretation of Giving in Dictator Games," *Journal of Political Economy*, 2007, no. 115, pp. 482–493.

21. Richard H. Thaler and Cass R. Sunstein, *Nudge: Improving Decisions About Health, Wealth, and Happiness* (New York: Penguin, 2008). The British government created a "Nudge Unit" in 2010. For an overview of the experiments conducted on default options – that is, options that prevail in the absence of another choice made by the individual – see Cass Sunstein's article "Deciding by Default," *University of Pennsylvania Law Review*, 2013, no. 162, pp. 1–57. A classic article in this domain shows that employees of an American company enrolled in a retirement plan (a savings account subsidized by the United States government) significantly more often when the default option was transformed into a choice between "no enrollment" and "enrollment," the choices offered the employees remaining the same in both cases (Brigitte Madrian and Dennis Shea, "The Power of Suggestion: Inertia in 401(k) Participation and Savings Behavior," *Quarterly Journal of Economics*, 2001, vol. 116, no. 4, pp. 1149–1187).

22. The reader who knows statistics will recognize here the law of large numbers.

23. Nina Mazar, On Amir, and Dan Ariely, "The Dishonesty of Honest People. A Theory of Self-Concept Maintenance," *Journal of Marketing Research*, 2008, vol. 45, pp. 633–644.

24. Benoît Monin et al., "Holier than me? Threatening Social Comparison in the Moral Domain," *International Review of Social Psychology*, 2007, vol. 20, no. 1, pp. 53–68, and, in collaboration with P. J. Sawyer and M. J. Marquez, "The Rejection of Moral Rebels. Resenting Those Who Do the Right Thing," *Journal of Personality and Social Psychology*, 2008, vol. 95, no. 1, pp. 76–93. See also Larissa MacFarquhar's recent book, *Strangers Drowning* (New York: Penguin Press, 2015).

25. "Benchmarking," or rating by comparison, refers to techniques that consist in giving companies or employees models to be followed, and possibly to be used in calculating their remuneration on the basis of the distance separating their performance from that of the model.

26. An article published in 2000 by Juan Carrillo and Thomas Mariotti, ("Strategic Ignorance as a Self-Disciplining Device," *Review of Economic Studies*, 2000, vol. 67, no. 3, pp. 529–544) started this line of research on "behavioral information economics."

27. Roland Bénabou and Jean Tirole, "Self-Confidence and Personal Motivation," *Quarterly Journal of Economics*, 2002, vol. 117, no. 3, pp. 871–915.

28. See for example Roland Bénabou and Jean Tirole, "Willpower and Personal Rules," *Journal of Political Economy*, 2004, no. 112, pp. 848–887; "Belief in a Just World and Redistributive Politics," *Quarterly Journal of Economics*, 2006, vol. 121, no. 2, pp. 699–746; "Identity, Morals and Taboos. Beliefs as Assets," *Quarterly Journal of Economics*, 2011, vol. 126, no. 2, pp. 805–855.

29. For example, the British game show *Golden Balls*. This has been off air for some years, but economists use YouTube clips to illustrate game theory concepts.

30. Michael Kosfeld, Markus Heinrichs, Paul J. Zak, Urs Fischbacher, and Ernst Fehr, "Oxytocin Increases Trust in Humans," *Nature*, 2005, no. 435, pp. 673–676.

31. A neuropeptide. This hormone seems to influence certain behaviors and affect orgasm, social recognition, anxiety, and maternal behaviors.

32. George Akerlof, "Labor Contracts as Partial Gift Exchange," *Quarterly Journal of Economics*, 1982, vol. 97, no. 4, pp. 543–569. For a laboratory test showing this reciprocity, see Ernst Fehr, Simon Gaechter, and Georg Kirschsteiger, "Reciprocity as a Contract Enforcement Device. Experimental Evidence," *Econometrica*, no. 65, pp. 833–860.

33. Rajshri Jayaraman, Debraj Ray, and Francis de Vericourt, "Anatomy of a Contract Change," *American Economic Review*, 2016, vol. 106, no. 2, pp. 316–358.

34. Part of the increase, to be sure, had a legal origin, but part came from the employer.

35. "A Theory of Collective Reputations, with Applications to the Persistence of Corruption and to Firm Quality," *Review of Economic Studies*, 1996, vol. 63, no. 1, pp. 1–22.

36. Hysteresis is the phenomenon in which a system (social, economic, or physical) tends to remain in a particular state after the disappearance of whatever caused that state.

37. Esther Duflo, Rema Hanna, and Stephen Ryan, "Incentives Work: Getting Teachers to Come to School," *American Economic Review*, 2012, vol. 102, no. 4, pp. 1241–1278.

38. The problem of multi-tasking has been analyzed, for example, in the classic article by Bengt Holmström and Paul Milgrom, "Multitask Principal-Agent Analyses: Incentive Contracts, Asset Ownership, and Job Design," *Journal of Law, Economics and Organization*, 1991, no. 7, pp. 24–52.

39. Richard Titmuss, *The Gift Relationship: From Human Blood to Social Policy* (New York: The New Press, 1970).

40. Besides his academic contributions, Dan Ariely is also known by the public for his TED talks and popular books, such as *Predictably Irrational: The Hidden Forces That Shape Our Decisions* (New York: HarperCollins, 2008), *The Upside of Irrationality: The Unexpected Benefits of Defying Logic at Work and at Home* (New York: HarperCollins, 2010), and *The Honest Truth about Dishonesty* (New York: HarperCollins, 2012).

41. Dan Ariely, Anat Bracha, Stefan Meier, "Doing Good or Doing Well? Image Motivation and Monetary Incentives in Behaving Prosocially," *American Economic Review*, 2009, vol. 99, no. 1, pp. 544–555. The subjects' choices were either kept confidential, as in the standard experiments, or revealed to peers.

42. Tim Besley, Anders Jensen, and Torsten Persson, "Norms, Enforcement, and Tax evasion," unpublished paper. The transition in 1990 from a real estate property tax based on the value of the property to a very regressive poll tax greatly increased tax evasion, especially in constituencies with a majority of Labour voters, who opposed Margaret Thatcher's government. It took a long time for tax evasion to fall back to a low level after the poll tax was replaced by a fairer tax in 1993. The article extends the model to a dynamic context to understand this hysteresis, and shows how incentives and predictions regarding the social norm explain reactions in different times and in different districts.

43. Ruixue Jia and Torsten Persson, "Individual vs. Social Motives in Identity Choice: Theory and Evidence from China," unpublished paper. In China, a child born from a marriage between a member of the majority Han ethnic group and a member of an ethnic minority can be declared to be either a Han or a member of the minority group. The extrinsic motivation comes from the advantages from which minorities benefit because of affirmative action programs; the social norm is connected with the reaction of the ethnic community with regard to the choice of ethnic declaration.

44. Daniel Chen, "The Deterrent Effect of the Death Penalty? Evidence from British Commutations during World War I," unpublished paper. In this

case, the extrinsic motivation was the implementation of punishments (including capital punishment). Daniel Chen also identifies the impact of the social norm depending on the period and the provenance of the soldiers (for example, English or Irish soldiers).

45. Roland Bénabou and Jean Tirole, "Intrinsic and Extrinsic Motivation," *Review of Economic Studies*, 2003, vol. 70, no. 3, pp. 489–520.

46. Armin Falk and Michael Kosfeld, "The Hidden Costs of Control," *American Economic Review*, 2006, vol. 96, no. 5, pp. 1611–1630. For example, returning to the game in which Player 1 gives Player 2 a sum between zero and ten dollars, which is tripled upon reception (Player 2 then being able to return as much as he wants), the modified game specifies that Player 1 can also require a minimum return (equal to zero or four dollars, for example). Requiring a minimum of four dollars destroys reciprocity (and moreover, most players do not do it).

47. Robert Cialdini, *Influence: The Psychology of Persuasion* (New York: HarperBusiness, 1984).

48. Roland Bénabou and Jean Tirole, "Laws and Norms," art. cit.

49. For example, see the works of my colleagues in Toulouse, Ingela Alger and Jörgen Weibull ("*Homo Moralis*: Preference Evolution under Incomplete Information and Assortative Matching," *Econometrica*, 2013, vol. 81, pp. 2269–2302), and Paul Seabright (*The Company of Strangers: A Natural History of Economic Life*, Second Edition [Princeton: Princeton University Press, 2010]). On the biological sources of cooperation, see Sam Bowles and Herb Gintis, *A Cooperative Species: Human Reciprocity and its Evolution* (Princeton: Princeton University Press, 2013).

50. Michael Spence, "Job Market Signaling," *Quarterly Journal of Economics,* 1973, vol. 87, no. 3, pp. 355–374.

51. Amotz Zahavi, "Mate Selection – A Selection for a Handicap," *Journal of Theoretical Biology*, 1975, vol. 53, pp. 205–214.

52. For a historical overview, see Laurence Iannaccone, "Introduction to the Economics of Religion," *Journal of Economic Literature*, 1998, vol. 36, no. 3, pp. 1465–1496.

53. "The [clergy] may either depend altogether for their subsistence upon the voluntary contributions of their hearers; or they may derive it from some other fund to which the law of their country may entitle them; such as a landed estate, a tythe or land tax, an established salary or stipend. Their exertion, their zeal and industry, are likely to be much greater in the former situation than in the latter. In this respect the teachers of new religions have always had a considerable advantage in attacking those ancient and established systems of which the clergy, reposing themselves upon their benefices, had neglected to keep up the fervour of faith and devotion in the great body

of the people; and having given themselves up to indolence, were become altogether incapable of making any vigorous exertion in defence even of their own establishment. The clergy of an established and well-endowed religion frequently become men of learning and elegance, who possess all the virtues of gentlemen, or which can recommend them to the esteem of gentlemen; but they are apt gradually to lose the qualities, both good and bad, which gave them authority and influence with the inferior ranks of people, and which had perhaps been the original causes of the success and establishment of their religion." *The Wealth of Nations*, Book V, 1776.

54. Maristella Botticini and Zvi Eckstein, *The Chosen Few: How Education Shaped Jewish History, 70–1492* (Princeton: Princeton University Press, 2012).

55. Mohamed Saleh, "On the Road to Heaven: Self-Selection, Religion, and Socio-Economic Status," unpublished paper, 2016.

56. Eli Berman and Laurence Iannaccone, "Religious Extremism: The Good, the Bad, and the Deadly," *Public Choice*, 2006, vol. 128, no. 1, pp. 109–129. Daniel Chen and Jo Lind, "The Political Economy of Beliefs: Why Fiscal and Social Conservatives and Fiscal and Social Liberals Come Hand-In-Hand," unpublished paper, 2016.

57. See chapter 14.

58. Emmanuelle Auriol, Julie Lassébie, Eva Raiber, Paul Seabright, and Amma Serwaah-Panin, "God Insures the Ones Who Pay? Formal Insurance and Religious Offerings in a Pentecostal Church in Accra, Ghana," unpublished paper.

59. See for example Roland Bénabou, Davide Ticchi, and Andrea Vindigni, "Religion and Innovation," *American Economic Review, Papers and Proceedings*, 2015, vol. 105, no. 5, pp. 346–351, which shows a negative correlation (but not necessarily a causal relation) between religiosity and innovation or openness to science.

CHAPTER SIX: TOWARD A MODERN STATE

1. Published as "Etat et gestion publique" in June 2000.

2. For example, as a young scholar he had declined comfortable positions in the best American universities to build up an economics department from scratch in Toulouse. Later, he contributed to the promotion of economics research and education in several LDCs.

3. See chapter 5.

4. Another inefficiency of inequality is connected with the loss of self-sufficiency. An individual who does not have enough money to eat, use transportation, and pay for housing will find it difficult to get a job.

5. All the buyers prepared to pay more than the price have bought, and all the sellers prepared to sell at the price have sold. Thus the only remaining potential trades are between buyers only prepared to pay less than the price and sellers demanding more than the price. These exchanges thus involve no gain from trade. This has been approximately verified empirically. See chapter 4.

6. Such as subsidies for exports (the list of the beneficiaries of these subsidies was not made public on the grounds that doing so would have destroyed their effectiveness by inciting foreign competitors to go them one better), or the cross subsidies between sectors in unemployment benefits (the lay-off-intensive sectors that draw heavily on these benefits "taxing" the other sectors).

7. A ban on imports from such a country might prove impossible because of international trade agreements (WTO) or other political constraints.

8. By contrast, the judiciary was still subject to political power in France not so long ago.

9. Defining minimal standards for the regulation of banks, including their capital requirements. See chapters 11 and 12.

10. http://www.vie-publique.fr/decouverte-institutions/institutions/adminis tration/organisation/etat/aai/quel-est-role-aai.html.

11. *Democracy in America*, chapter 5.

12. Nonetheless, we must remain vigilant on this issue. For instance, in the European crisis, states have been offloading their problems onto the ECB, which, in addition to its normal role as a supplier of liquid assets, has been drawn despite itself onto political terrain (support of a state). Its power struggle with the Greek government in June and July 2015 was no doubt inevitable, but had Greece abandoned the euro, it could have led to a questioning of the central bank's independence. In the US Senate, in a vote in January 2016, the Republicans (as well as Bernie Sanders on the left) questioned whether the Fed should be independent; fortunately, the Democrats at that stage prevented the Fed from being put under political control.

13. On the other hand, the state can temporarily manage an enterprise or a failing bank if it does not initially find a buyer; then its duty is to resell the enterprise or the bank as soon as conditions are propitious, as the United States did with General Motors in 2013 (saving it from bankruptcy in 2009 ultimately cost the US government about eleven billion dollars net, out of a bailout of fifty billion dollars), and Sweden did when it nationalized banks on the brink of failure in 1992 and resold them later in the same decade.

14. As Gaspard Koenig notes in *Le Révolutionnaire, l'Expert et le Geek* (Paris: Plon, 2015).

15. In France, the idea of a planned economy comes from the Vichy regime and was adopted after the war, as was noted by Marc Bloch, for example. The Vichy regime rejected the revolutionary heritage of banning guilds and terminating the self-regulation of certain professions, and began to regulate culture, expand the civil service, subsidize population growth, and more generally direct the economy. On the development of the role of the state in France since the liberal revolution of 1789, see also Pierre Rosanvallon, *Le Modèle politique français* (Paris: Seuil, 2004).

16. On this subject, see Philippe Aghion and Alexandra Roulet, *Repenser l'État. Pour une nouvelle social-démocratie* (Paris: Seuil, 2011), or the report of the Conseil d'analyse économique, "Économie politique de la LOLF," 2007, no. 65 (Edward Arkwright, Christian de Boissieu, Jean-Hervé Lorenzi, and Julien Samson).

17. The mandatory levies, which include in particular taxes (on income, on businesses, local taxes, etc.), contributions for social welfare programs, and the value-added tax represented only 45.2 percent of the GDP in 2015. The difference between these two figures reflects the nonobligatory levies (revenues from public enterprises and properties, gambling, fines and sanctions, gifts and legacies to the state, etc.) on the one hand, and the public deficit on the other (between 4 and 5 percent in recent years), with the corollary that public debt has increased.

18. Literally "The Glorious Thirty," an expression that refers to the thirty years of growth and prosperity in France between 1945 and 1975. —Trans.

19. To be clear, an elected government definitely has the mandate to extend public services, on the condition that taxes are increased . This is a societal choice concerning which the economist can express an opinion only as a citizen.

20. For instance, France has a large number of players involved in job (re) training programs or in administering social programs, and a multiplicity of retirement systems. Similarly, the juxtaposition of basic state health insurance and private supplementary health insurance plans doubles management costs and leaves no room for maneuver in contracting with doctors and hospitals; there is, therefore, no incentive to improve hospital management. Savings could be made by moving either to comprehensive state health insurance (as in the UK) or to private but regulated health insurance providers (as in Germany, Switzerland, or the Netherlands).

21. France has a plethora of communes (France has 40 percent of Europe's local authorities, but only 13 percent of its population), "départements," and regions, on top of the central government. Parliamentary representation is itself excessive. For example, the US Senate, which is very active, has 100 senators, whereas France, a country with almost one-fifth the

population, has 348 senators (and 577 delegates in the National Assembly); in all, France has almost ten times more legislators per inhabitant than the United States. Personally, I would prefer fewer of them with more active expert advisers.

CHAPTER SEVEN: THE GOVERNANCE AND
SOCIAL RESPONSIBILITY OF BUSINESS

1. See chapter 16.
2. Some of these have, of course, gone public, like Goldman Sachs, which was founded in 1869 and went public in 1999. Some observers think this initial public offering caused the firm to lose sight of the customer's interest and led to short-termism in managerial choices.
3. In France, the "national interprofessional agreement" of 2013 stipulates that employees must have a voice in the deliberations of the boards of directors of large enterprises.
4. See the articles by Gary Gorton and Frank Schmid, "Capital, Labor and the Firm: A Study of German Codetermination," *Journal of the European Economic Association*, 2004, vol. 2, no. 5, pp. 863–905; Stefan Petry, "Workers on the Board and Shareholder Wealth: Evidence from a Natural Experiment," unpublished paper, 2015; and Han Kim, Ernst Maug and Christoph Schneider, "Labor Representation in Governance as an Insurance Mechanism," unpublished paper, 2015.
5. On the other hand, transforming a capitalist enterprise into a self-managed enterprise is more difficult, because employees generally do not have the means to compensate the investors who own the firm—except when the investors' shares have lost their value, in which case employees can easily take over the firm. Another case is that of "leveraged buyouts" or LBOs, in which the employees (maybe only the managers) put the firm deeply in debt in order to raise the money to buy the shares.
6. Enron was one of the biggest American corporations specializing in natural gas and energy brokering. Having speculated on the electricity markets, it suffered losses that were concealed as profits via accounting manipulations and no less than three thousand offshore corporations. Enron declared bankruptcy in 2001; the result was twenty thousand redundancies, and many employees lost part of the retirement funds that they had invested in Enron shares. This financial scandal and another scandal at WorldCom led to the Sarbanes-Oxley Act of 2002, which dealt with accounting reform for companies whose shares are traded on the stock market and with the protection of their investors. Arthur Andersen, one of the largest auditing firms in the world, which certified Enron's accounts, also disappeared as a result of its bankruptcy.

7. Cambridge: Harvard University Press, 1996.

8. In the case of card payment platforms such as Visa and MasterCard, there may be misalignment between the interests of small issuers—who cannot develop new services, security features, and brand labeling of their own and therefore want the platform to provide extensive services—and those of large issuers—who may want to self-provide a subset of services to differentiate themselves and thereby gain a competitive advantage. Another possible conflict arises when members differ in their relative focus on cardholders (the issuing function) and on merchants (the acquiring function).

9. Of course, board members can request access to this information, but nonselective, undigested information is not of much use.

10. See my article written with Philippe Aghion, "Formal and Real Authority in Organizations," *Journal of Political Economy*, 1997, vol. 105, no. 1, pp. 1–29.

11. Or hand over much more information than is relevant, so as to make it impossible for board directors to develop a clear analysis in a (necessarily) limited amount of time.

12. See chapter 16.

13. A stock option is an option to buy shares granted to managers or employees of the company. These options authorize their holder to buy a certain number of shares in the company at a date and a price set in advance—for example, to buy one hundred shares at the price of ten dollars in four years. If the share is worth fifteen dollars in four years, the value of the options will then be five hundred dollars. If it is worth less than ten dollars, the options will be valueless.

14. A clawback covenant specifies that any reward that has been given out be returned in special circumstances or events that are specified in the contract.

15. Among the classic empirical studies showing the possibility of this kind of connivance are those of Marianne Bertrand and Sendhil Mullainathan, "Are CEOs Rewarded for Luck? The Ones without Principals Are," *Quarterly Journal of Economics*, 2001, vol. 116, no. 3, pp. 901–932, and of Lucian Bebchuk and Jesse Fried, *Pay without Performance: The Unfulfilled Promise of Executive Compensation* (Cambridge MA: Harvard University Press, 2004).

16. These subjects in themselves deserve one or several chapters. See for example my book *The Theory of Corporate Finance* (Princeton: Princeton University Press, 2006).

17. See chapter 8.

18. See chapter 9.

19. In its 2001 green paper, *Promoting a European Framework for Corporate Social Responsibility.*

20. The following discussion is based on my article written with Roland Bénabou, "Individual and Corporate Social Responsibility," *Economica*, 2010, no. 77, pp. 1–19.

21. See Augustin Landier and Vinay Nair, *Investing for Change: Profit for Responsible Investing* (Oxford: Oxford University Press, 2008).

22. A first-tier supplier is one that supplies the company directly; a second-tier supplier is a subcontractor of the first-tier subcontractor, etc.

23. The task of extrafinancial rating agencies is difficult. These agencies rely on scanty and conflicting data.

24. The example of Starbucks has been commented upon at length in the press. A study conducted on American data suggests that companies that engage the most in socially responsible action are also those that most aggressively avoid paying ("optimizing") taxes; there is no proven causal relationship, but it is an interesting correlation (Angela Davis, David Guenther, Linda Krull, and Brian M. Williams, "Do Socially Responsible Firms Pay More Taxes?" *The Accounting Review*, 2016, vol. 91, no. 1, pp. 47–68).

25. I refer the reader to chapter 1 for a discussion of inadequate understanding of certain policies.

CHAPTER EIGHT: THE CLIMATE CHALLENGE

1. In practice, the different gases are lumped together under the term "carbon equivalents." This chapter will sometimes conflate CO_2 and GHG.

2. The COP (Conference of the Parties) takes place every year. For example, COP 23 in 2017 took place in Bonn. The fifteenth and twenty-first COPs were the major meetings in Copenhagen and Paris.

3. Figures 8.2 and 8.3 describe both total emissions and those (usually positive) due to agricultural policy and deforestation and/or reforestation. In general, the two figures yield similar images, with the exception of two countries. The non-energy part of the emissions is substantial in the case of Brazil and even more in that of Indonesia, countries that have engaged in extensive deforestation.

4. http://www.oecd.org/about/secretary-general/oecd-inventory-of-sup port-measures-for-fossil-fuels-2015.htm.

5. This chapter borrows from an article written with Christian Gollier and published in 2015 by *Economics of Energy & Environmental Policy*: "Negotiating Effective Institutions against Climate Change," vol. 4, no. 2, pp. 5–27. This article deals with many subjects that we will not take up

here, such as the uncertainty and volatility of carbon taxes or the price on the market for tradable emissions permits, long-term commitment to environmental policies, and compensation formulas. It also contains a detailed study comparing different economic approaches. In addition, I refer the reader to my 2009 report to the French Conseil d'analyse économique (CAE) pointing out the lack of ambition in the coming Copenhagen negotiations.

6. Jared Diamond, *Collapse: How Societies Choose to Fail or Succeed* (New York: Penguin Books, 2005).

7. Elinor Ostrom, *Governing the Commons: The Evolution of Institutions for Collective Action* (Cambridge: Cambridge University Press, 1990).

8. Moreover, this mechanism may encourage the emerging countries concerned not to adopt environmental legislation and to refuse to sign restrictive international accords. Adopting environmental legislation would in fact discourage projects to reduce emissions: it would exclude them from access to CDM credits by depriving them of their "additional" character!

9. See Christian Almer and Ralph Winkler, "Analysing the Effectiveness of International Environmental Policies: The Case of the Kyoto Protocol," in *Bath Economics Research Papers* 39 (2015), University of Bath and University of Bern.

10. The Clean Air Act Amendment.

11. In practice, all emissions are not subject to the requirement of holding emissions permits: for example, less than half of European emissions are now part of a market for permits to emit CO_2.

12. The prices mentioned in this chapter will be by ton of CO_2. Even if I speak informally of the "carbon tax," it must be remembered that a ton of carbon corresponds to 3.67 tons of CO_2. Thus the price of carbon is 3.67 times the price of CO_2.

13. On top of the obligation of obtaining permits for those industries subject to the European tradable emissions permits program. The carbon tax was increased to twenty-two euros per ton of CO_2 in 2016. As always, it provided for many exceptions: trucking companies, taxis, farmers, fishermen, and so on.

14. And a couple of other small countries' carbon taxes.

15. The Quinet report, whose methodology was adopted by the Rocard Commission on the carbon tax. Alain Quinet, *La Valeur tutélaire du carbone* (Paris: La Documentation française, "Rapports et documents," 2009).

16. In 2013, the United States Interagency Working Group offered three different estimates depending on three possible discount rates (2.5 percent, 3 percent, and 5 percent). Taking a real discount rate of 3 percent, the group estimated that carbon's social cost was thirty-two dollars in

2010, reaching fifty-two dollars in 2030, and seventy-one dollars in 2050. These values obviously tend to be revised upward, because the international community's inaction reduces our room to maneuver and further increases the cost of emissions.

17. The expression is that of Harvard economist Robert Stavins.

18. According to some estimates, purchasing the carbon credits necessary to meet its Kyoto commitments would have cost Canada about fourteen billion dollars.

19. In 2006–2007, prices had already fallen following an overallocation of permits (pressure exerted by industrialists had led to an inflation of permits) and a defective conception of the European system in phase I (2005–2008): permit holders could not save their permits beyond the end of 2007, which meant that even a very slight excess of permits brought the price down to zero. We are concerned here with the second collapse, the one that occurred after the crisis and that was not due to technical causes.

20. An additional problem proceeds from the fact that the EU ETS schema covered only a fraction of the European Union's emissions. Many emitters, for example in the transportation and construction sectors, benefited de facto from a price of carbon that was equal to zero.

21. This lack of information implies that any accord that results from an INDC process will lead to an inefficient allocation of the efforts agreed upon, because some economic agents will undertake expensive efforts to attenuate emissions while other agents will continue to emit GHGs whose elimination would be much less expensive; I shall return to this point.

22. Joseph E. Stiglitz, "Overcoming the Copenhagen Failure with Flexible Commitments," *Economics of Energy and Environmental Policy*, vol. 4, no. 2 (2015).

23. Tellingly as well, a composite low-carbon world equity portfolio underperformed relative to a straight world equity index in the year following the accord, when it should have overperformed if the announcement had been good news about the fight against climate change (private communication from Christian Gollier).

24. Although an economic instrument can be used to encourage the use of thermal insulation in houses by including the price of carbon in the price of home heating, the resulting economic calculus is complex for consumers, who do not always have the necessary information and may engage in short-term thinking (investments in insulation are amortized over decades). A well-conceived standard is therefore fully justified. My reservation is that standards are often established without a clear analysis of the implicit price of carbon involved, the objectives of the policy, and the alternative policies that would make it possible to achieve them. In

addition, standards are often coelaborated by established firms and sometimes allow those firms to fend off potential entrants to their market.

25. Denny Ellerman, David Harrison, and Paul Joskow, *Emissions Trading in the US: Experience, Lessons and Considerations for Greenhouse Gases* (Pew Center on Global Climate Change, 2003); Thomas Tietenberg, *Emissions Trading: Principles and Practice*, 2nd ed. (London: Routledge, 2006); Robert Stavins, "Lessons from the American Experiment with Market-Based Environmental Policies," in John Donahue and Joseph Nye, eds., *Market-Based Governance: Supply Side, Demand Side, Upside, and Downside* (Washington, DC: The Brookings Institution, 2002), pp. 173–200.

26. It may seem surprising that some profitable investments do not move forward. In certain cases, the agent concerned may not have the information; in other cases, he may not have enough available money to make the investment (a modest household's shortage of cash that prevents it from investing in insulation, for instance).

27. See Claude Crampes and Thomas-Olivier Leautier, "Le côté lumineux des subventions aux renouvelable," *La Tribune*, November 2, 2015.

28. For example, the US Climate Plan (http://www.usclimateplan.org/at-a-glance) and Sandbag (https://sandbag.org.uk/carbonpricing/). For French-speaking readers, the Nicolas Hulot Foundation has produced a very instructive video on carbon pricing: http://www.fondation-nicolas-hulot.org/magazine/pourquoi-et-comment-donner-un-prix-au-carbone.

29. An encouraging sign in France is the law on energy transition passed on July 22, 2015. The parliament endorsed the objective of quadrupling the price of carbon between 2016 and 2030.

30. https://www.project-syndicate.org/commentary/carbon-pricing-fiscal-policy-by-christine-lagarde-and-jim-yong-kim-2015-10.

31. Of course, this means setting a single total carbon price: adding a uniform carbon price to an already existing national carbon price would be on the one hand ineffective and on the other hand unfair to a country like Sweden, which had been virtuous even before the international accord, and for which the effect would be to make the past surplus contribution permanent.

32. Proposed by Peter Cramton, Axel Ockenfels, and Steve Stoft, "An International Carbon-Price Commitment Promotes Cooperation," *Economics of Energy & Environmental Policy*, 2015, no. 4, pp. 51–64.

33. In recent years, despite the existence of a binding program and the involvement of the troika representing the creditors, Greece has made little progress in its battle against tax evasion. This shows how difficult it is for third countries to force the collection of a tax if the national government is not much inclined to apply it. In the context of climate change, there is no troika in each country to monitor what is going on.

34. Let us recall that in France, in 2014, the carbon tax on fossil fuels was compensated (for one year only) by an equivalent decrease in the internal tax on the consumption of energy products, and thus had no effect on the prices of gasoline and heating oil.

35. A construction standard that further insulates a house leads to fewer emissions. To properly measure the effort made, we need to estimate the savings in emissions achieved on the houses to which the norm is applied, as well as the estimated additional cost of the standards for construction. These operations are complex to carry out.

36. Albedo is the relation of the solar energy reflected by a surface to the incident solar energy; reflection of the sun's rays cools the planet, and thus diminishes GHG emissions. Trees on snow-covered land can limit the reflection.

37. The price on the market is now low, for several reasons. First, the recession that raged in the United States until recently slowed emissions. Second, the discovery of shale gas and the threat (which has still not material-ized) of nonnegligible taxes on GHGs discouraged investment and the consumption of coal. This low price thus also corresponds to lesser local environmental damage.

38. See chapter 11.

39. See Jean-Jacques Laffont and Jean Tirole, "Pollution Permits and Com-pliance Strategies," *Journal of Public Economics*, 1996, no. 62, pp. 85–125.

40. Some negotiable emissions permit systems specify a short time limit for using the permits granted, thus generating high volatility: at the end of the set period, let's say a year, the price is either zero if there is an excess of permits, or very high (equal to the penalty for a lack of permits) if there is excess demand. Consequently, every development that takes place before the end of the year has substantial effects on the market price. However, in general the possibility of "banking" permits, which exists in many countries, reduces volatility.

41. The NASA Orbiting Carbon Observatory-2, or OCO-2, is already in orbit around the earth. The ESA's CarbonSat project is also promising.

42. According to the Green Climate Fund, the firm commitments made by thirty-eight countries amounted, on November 20, 2015, to 5.9 billion dollars, plus 4.3 billion dollars in promises that had not yet been signed.

43. http://www.oecd.org/env/cc/Climate-Finance-in-2013-14-and-the-USD -billion-goal.pdf.

44. The small part of the financing going to emerging and developing countries that are targeted for adaptation—16 percent in 2013–2014 as opposed to 77 percent devoted to attenuation—remains a sensitive subject. Emerg-ing and developing countries are asking for more adaptation, whereas the developed countries benefit essentially from mitigation policies.

45. The question of transparency is one of the reasons why many programs for fighting pollution throughout the world have adopted a cap and trade scheme and have dealt with the question of financial transfers through the allocation of tradable quotas (often a system of grandfathering), which are less sensitive politically. In the United States, the major transfers to Midwestern states that were generated by the Clean Air Act Amendment of 1990 have never really made newspaper headlines. To be sure, the transfers made in the context of national cap and trade programs differ in nature from the international payments in the framework of an international cap and trade system. However, in the framework of the European Union's Emission Trading Scheme, billions of euros could potentially have been transferred to countries in eastern Europe and the former Soviet Union (that was the spirit of the program known as "hot air," by way of the allocation of quotas to convince them to sign the Kyoto Protocol).

46. Some of these principles are set forth in the previously cited article that I coauthored with Christian Gollier, which does not, however, go into detail about what a good formula would be. A more precise study is provided by the ETH Climate Calculator http://ccalc.ethz.ch/ (Zurich).

47. It remains to be seen whether a permit to emit in one system is equivalent to the same permit in another system. The more virtuous countries, having issued fewer permits, might then feel that they have lost out.

CHAPTER NINE: LABOR MARKET CHALLENGES

1. See chapter 15. On the changing nature of jobs, see in particular David Autor, "Why Are There Still So Many Jobs? The History and Future of Workplace Automation," *Journal of Economic Perspectives*, 2015, vol. 29, no. 3, pp. 3–30.

2. In France, this statistic is provided by the National Institute of Statistics and Economic Studies, or INSEE.

3. Individuals are counted as unemployed in the ILO's sense if they meet three criteria: 1) they have not worked during the week in question; 2) they are available to work within the next two weeks; 3) they have actively sought employment within the past month (or found a job that begins in less than three months).

4. Or, more precisely, the *Direction de l'animation de la recherche, des études et des statistiques* (DARES).

5. Category B: jobseekers expected to have made active efforts to find employment and who have worked in a short reduced-time job (i.e., seventy-eight hours or less in the course of a month)—716,400 in November

2015. Category C: jobseekers expected to have made positive efforts to find employment and who have worked in a long reduced-time job (i.e., more than seventy-eight hours in the course of a month)—1,151,300 in November 2015. Category D: jobseekers not expected to have made positive efforts to find a job (because they were doing an internship, participating in a training program, were ill, etc.)—280,900 in November 2015. Category E: jobseekers not expected to have made positive efforts to find a job who are employed (benefiting from subsidized contracts, for example)—420,000 in November 2015.

6. On average, French people from sixteen to seventy-five years of age worked much less than Americans or Britons in 2008, in proportions of 28 percent and 13 percent respectively, whereas they worked just as much as the latter in 1968 (see Richard Blundell, Antoine Bozio, and Guy Laroque, "Labor Supply and the Extensive Margin," *American Economic Review, Papers & Proceedings*, 2011, vol. 101, no. 3, pp. 482–486). The disparity has thus grown. Half of it can be attributed to the decrease in the work week and the other half to the stagnation of the employment rate in France, whereas employment rates in the United States and Britain have greatly increased. It is true that middle-aged and elderly French women work more, but this development has been more than counterbalanced by a major decrease in the employment of young people of both sexes, and of men no matter what their age.

7. And this is not because they are in training: 17 percent of those between fifteen and twenty-four are unemployed and are not participating in a training program. Nine hundred thousand have given up any effort to find work and are not counted as unemployed.

8. See Jean-Benoît Eyméoud and Étienne Wasmer, "Emploi des jeunes et logement. Un effet Tanguy?" IEP Paris, unpublished, 2015.

9. It is hard to determine whether reduced social security contributions should be attributed to employment policy, because obviously what counts is the net amount (contributions less reductions in these contributions). Moreover, the reductions have more effect when they affect low salaries, those close to the minimum wage (see Pierre Cahuc and Stéphane Carcillo, *Améliorer l'assurance chômage* [Chaire sécurisation des parcours professionnels, 2014]).

10. OECD, Public Expenditure and Participant Stocks on LMP.

11. Expenditures to benefit employment and the labor market, whether targeted or general, are estimated by DARES to have been 85.7 billion euros in 2012, or 4.1 percent of the GNP (DARES analysis 019, March, 2015).

12. According to a 2011 report of the French General Accounting Office (*Cour des Comptes*), "concerning the impact of subsidized jobs on return to employment, econometric models show a positive effect for subsidized

contracts in the commercial sector and no effect for subsidized jobs in the noncommercial sector." The noncommercial sector includes entities that provide services free of charge or at very low prices: public agencies, local governments, works councils, NGOs, etc.

13. Social security is further financed through various taxes, such as the *contribution sociale généralisée* (CSG), the *taxe sur les salaires* or the *taxes sur le tabac et les alcools*. Social security contributions amounted to 16.9 percent of GDP in 2015, while the European average was 12.3 percent.

14. See Corinne Prost and Pierre Cahuc, *Améliorer l'assurance chômage pour limiter l'instabilité de l'emploi*, (Conseil d'analyse économique, 2015), note 24.

15. Despite strong fiscal incentives not to use fixed-term contracts (additional unemployment insurance contributions) and to transform fixed-term positions into permanent positions (at termination of a fixed-term contract, the employer must pay a severance package equal to at least 10 percent of the total gross remuneration paid during the contract; also, the employer receives tax exemptions during three to four months if people under twenty-five are hired under a permanent contract).

16. See OCDE, "*Perspectives de l'emploi 2014*," p. 182.

17. In France, those employees who negotiate with businesses and with the state, and who can cause trouble for the existing government, are not much affected by unemployment (these are mainly public sector employees and permanent employees of large companies). It is not surprising that their positions do not necessarily reflect the interests of the unemployed or workers with fixed-term contracts.

18. Resignations in theory do not allow the worker to receive unemployment benefits. In practice, employer and employee often collude to disguise a quit and transform it into a redundancy, so as to allow an access to unemployment benefits. In France, such deals are actually now legal under the heading of "*ruptures conventionnelles.*"

19. Bureau of Labor Statistics, Current Population Survey (Annual Social and Economic Supplement): CEA calculations.

20. See Thomas Philippon, *Le Capitalisme d'héritiers*, which presents the international rankings in quality of work relationships (Paris: Seuil/ La République des idées, 2007). Yann Algan, Pierre Cahuc, and André Zylberberg, in *La Fabrique de la défiance et comment en sortir*, analyze the sources and mechanisms of mistrust in France ([Paris: Albin Michel, 2012], p. 120).

21. Nicolas Lepage-Saucier and Étienne Wasmer, "Does Employment Protection Raise Stress? A Cross-Country and Cross-Province Analysis," 2011, report prepared for the Economic Policy Panel, 2012.

22. On the feeling of security, see also Andrew Clark and Fabien Postel-Vinay, "Job Security and Job Protection," *Oxford Economic Papers*, 2005, vol. 61, pp. 207–239; and Fabien Postel-Vinay and Anne Saint-Martin, "Comment les salariés perçoivent-ils la protection de l'emploi?" *Économie et statistique*, 2005, no. 372, pp. 41–59.

23. Largely indirect in the case of France, as its banks were much less affected by exposures to subprimes and real estate than many of their counterparts abroad.

24. In recent years, the French budget deficit has been around 4 or 5 percent.

25. The following reflections are inspired by studies carried out in collaboration with Olivier Blanchard (a professor at MIT and chief economist of the IMF from 2007 to 2015). See in particular *Licenciements et institutions du marché du travail*, a report for the Conseil d'analyse économique, La Documentation française, 2003, pp. 7–50; and "The Optimal Design of Unemployment Insurance and Employment Protection: A First Pass," *Journal of the European Economic Association*, 2008, vol. 6, no. 1, pp. 45–77. See also Pierre Cahuc and André Zylberberg, *Le Chômage. Fatalité ou nécessité?* (Paris: Flammarion, 2004).

26. See chapter 8.

27. For a description of American institutions, see Julia Fath and Clemens Fuest, "Experience Rating of Unemployment Insurance in the US: A Model for Europe?" *CESifo DICE Report*, 2005, vol. 2.

28. For more details, see Olivier Blanchard and Jean Tirole "The Joint Design of Unemployment Insurance and Employment Protection: A First Pass," *Journal of the European Economic Association*, 2008, vol. 6, no. 1, pp. 45–77. For the aspects more specific to the financing of enterprises and the notion of making good on liabilities within groups or more informal commercial relations, see this article and also my article, "From Pigou to Extended Liability: On the Optimal Taxation of Externalities under Imperfect Capital Markets," *Review of Economic Studies*, 2010, vol. 77, no. 2, pp. 697–729. Facing financial constraints, companies may seek to mutualize part of the risk associated with the cost of dismissals insofar as companies are exposed to economic shocks that are at least partly independent of each other (or course, macroeconomic impacts cannot be mutualized, and stabilizing bottom lines then requires government intervention).

29. Severance pay, which corresponds to a private cost of dismissal for the company, cannot be less than one-fifth of the employee's monthly salary per annum of seniority, to which must be added two-fifteenths of a month per annum beyond ten years of seniority. The indemnity provided for by the collective agreement or the labor contract may be more advantageous for the employee than the legal indemnity.

30. Here, the analysis of legal procedures is very schematic, even simplistic. I refer the reader to the work of Jean-Emmanuel Ray, *Droit du travail. Droit vivant*, 22nd ed. (Éditions Liaisons, 2013) for a detailed analysis of the legal aspects.

31. Since the law on job security passed in 2013. More generally, the limitation period before a labor court varies depending on the object of the demand—six months for the shortest period (denunciation of a settlement: *dénonciation d'un reçu pour solde de tout compte*) and as much as ten years for the longest (in the case of bodily damage caused by work).

32. Unless the employees concerned are reclassified (provided with another job) in house, which requires that there be room in another activity, for which the employees to be transferred must, moreover, be competent. The obligation to reclassify as part of a restructuring plan, for example, may prove to be both extremely complex, in particular for an international group (how to prove to the judge that everything has been tried?) and not very effective, especially since in the case of dismissal on economic grounds the employer has to respect criteria (seniority, age, family obligations, etc.) that are connected neither with the vocational abilities of the employees concerned nor with the demand that the company has experienced for its products. Furthermore, an administrative body (the *Direction régionale des entreprises, de la concurrence, de la consommation, du travail et de l'emploi* [DIRECCTE]) has to approve the conformity of the reclassification plans.

33. In dual labor markets like France's, outsiders (excluded workers having no permanent job) are usually distinguished from insiders (socially integrated workers having a permanent job).

34. See for example Jean-Emmanuel Ray, "Une mue salutaire, pour que la France épouse son temps," *Droit social*, December 2013, no. 9, pp. 664–672.

35. Pierre Cahuc and André Zylberberg, *Les Réformes ratées du président Sarkozy* (Paris: Flammarion, 2009).

36. See Franck Seuret, "Licenciements. La grande triche," *Alternatives économiques*, December 2006, no. 253, under the rubric "Tendances."

37. In their report, "De la précarité à la mobilité: vers une sécurité sociale professionnelle," (La Documentation Française, 2005).

38. Note 7 of the *Conseil d'analyse* économique (Guillaume Plantin, David Thesmar, and Jean Tirole, "Les enjeux économiques du droit des faillites," 2013) advocates a transfer of control to the creditors of enterprises in difficulty.

39. The effect of a reform of job protection is complicated to measure empirically, because numerous other variables change at the same time, either because of the reform itself (for example, the Italian reform of 2014 was

accompanied by subsidies for hiring), or because of changes in the macroeconomic environment. Economists' goal is to isolate the effect of the change in protection (and thus to identify the causality). In fact, many econometric studies show that granting more flexibility produces a net positive effect on employment, sometimes a large effect, but also sometimes a very small one (the positive impact of granting more flexibility bears more on young people and women, it appears). A classic study is that of David Autor, John Donohue, and Stewart Schwab, "The Costs of Wrongful Discharge Laws," *Review of Economics and Statistics*, 2006, vol. 88, no. 2, pp. 211–231. For a review of the methodology, see Tito Boeri, Pierre Cahuc, and André Zylberberg, "The Costs of Flexibility-Enhancing Structural Reforms: A Literature Review," OECD Working paper, October 2015. The long-term effects described below are undoubtedly more important.

40. See chapter 8. The losers (the biggest polluters) have generally been compensated by granting them tradable emission rights free of charge; this does not mean, of course, that the reforms are pointless—quite the contrary. The number of permits is limited (half the earlier annual pollution in the case of sulfur dioxide in the United States in 1990). The big polluters have an incentive to diminish their pollution, because they can resell their excess permits (or have to buy new permits if they do not sufficiently diminish their pollution).

41. The Italian reform created fiscal incentives promoting conciliation (recourse to the courts has much diminished) as well as the signature of new contracts. And it has also eliminated the possibility of reinstating the employee. One difference between France and Italy is that the latter did not sign the ILO's convention 158, which requires a valid reason for each dismissal. This article gives the employee a systematic right of recourse before the judge. The question of course is how to determine what constitutes a valid reason. Since article 4 of this convention connects the valid reason with "the worker's aptitude or behavior" or "the necessities for the functioning of the enterprise, the institutions, or the service," it can be interpreted in multiple ways. Spain, which signed convention 158, reformed its labor market in 2012 by limiting severance agreements and clarifying the conditions for a dismissal on economic grounds.

42. See Roland Bénabou and Jean Tirole, "Laws and Norms," unpublished; and chapter 1 for a discussion of the reasons why the public finds it hard to assimilate the economic message.

43. See for example George Loewenstein, Deborah Small, and Jeff Strand, "Statistical, Identifiable, and Iconic Victims," in Edward J. McCaffery and Joel Slemrod, eds., *Behavioral Public Finance* (New York: Russell Sage Foundation, 2006), pp. 32–35.

44. Economists cast a critical eye on the French tradition of co-determination (by bosses and employees unions) of vocational training and apprenticeship. Training often does not respond to the needs of companies and of employees; it is often not properly aimed at those workers who need it most, those for whom the return on vocational training is the highest (for example, more than a quarter of "apprentices" are university students!). And the evaluation and system of certification, which is intended to provide employees with training programs that would be truly useful to them, leave much to be desired.

   For an analysis of the aspects of the French vocational training system that run counter to the goals of redistribution and making the parties accountable, as well as of the inefficiency of the layers of bureaucracy, see for example Pierre Cahuc, Marc Ferracci, and André Zylberberg, *Formation professionnelle. Pour en finir avec les réformes inabouties* (Institut Montaigne, 2011); Pierre Cahuc and Marc Ferracci, *L'Apprentissage. Donner la priorité aux moins qualifiés* (Paris: Presses de Sciences Po, 2015); and Pierre Cahuc, Marc Ferracci, Jean Tirole, and Étienne Wasmer, *L'Apprentissage au service de l'emploi* (Conseil d'analyse économique, 2014), note 19.

45. According to the Institut Montaigne, 5.2 percent of French people between the ages of fifteen and twenty-four were in apprenticeships in France in 2013, as opposed to 16 percent in Germany.

46. Paul Samuelson, one of the greatest economists of the twentieth century, rebelled against this concept in his famous textbook. See also, for example, Paul Krugman's editorial in the *New York Times*, "Lumps of Labor," October 7, 2003.

47. David Card, "The Impact of the Mariel Boatlift on the Miami Labor Market," *Industrial and Labor Relations Review*, 1990, vol. 43, pp. 245–257.

48. For example, the 2000 law that mandated the thirty-five-hour week introduced the ability to count work time in days rather than hours (*forfait jour*). Managers (with the exception of the top management) are theoretically subject to the same working time limits as the other employees. However, measuring their work time is complex, as it is more generally for employees with substantial work autonomy, such as traveling salespeople. For this reason, the limit in terms of hours for such employees became a limit on the number of yearly working days, with more extensive paid leave.

49. These methods are analogous to the techniques of comparing control groups and treatment groups in scientific experiments. They make use of what is called in the language of economics the method of difference-in-difference.

50. A summary of these contributions is found in Pierre Cahuc and André Zylberberg, *Le négationnisme économique* (Paris: Flammarion, 2016).

See also Tito Boeri and Jan van Ours, *The Economics of Imperfect Labor Markets* (Princeton: Princeton University Press, 2013); Pierre Cahuc, Stéphane Carcillo, and André Zylberberg, *Labour Economics* (Cambridge: MIT Press, 2014); and the classic article by David Autor, John Donohue, and Stewart Schwab, "The Costs of Wrongful Discharge Laws," *Review of Economics and Statistics*, 2006, pp. 211–231.

51. See for example Frédéric Docquier, Çağlar Ozden, and Giovanni Peri, "The Labour Market Effects of Immigration and Emigration in OECD Countries," *Economic Journal*, 2014, vol. 124, no. 579, pp. 1106–1145. The effects on the salaries of employees in the host country are not negative, even on the lowest salaries. Also, they usually contribute more in taxes than they cost the country. Of course, dysfunctional labor market institutions like those in France weaken the argument, because they offer less flexibility for the creation of jobs and thus for integrating these workers.

52. See George Borjas, "The Economics of Immigration," *Journal of Economic Literature* 32, pp. 1667–1717; or the 1991 book edited by John Abowd and Richard Freeman, *Immigration, Trade and the Labor Market* (Chicago: University of Chicago Press, 1991). More recent evidence can be found in the *Journal of Economic Perspectives*' fall 2016 symposium on immigration and labor markets.

53. See David Autor, David Dorn, Gordon Hanson, and Jae Song, "Trade Adjustment: Worker-Level Evidence," *Quarterly Journal of Economics*, 2014, vol. 129, no. 4, pp. 1799–1860.

54. In Germany, Wolfgang Dauth, Sebastian Findeisen, and Jens Südekum ("Adjusting to Globalization: Evidence from Worker-Establishment Matches in Germany," 2016, CEPR Discussion Paper 1145; see also their 2017 *American Economic Review, Papers & Proceedings* article) show that those who lose their jobs in industries subject to competition from imports do not find new jobs in industrial exporting companies, but have to take service jobs instead.

55. See the empirical references in Pierre Cahuc's paper presented in the seminar on employment policies at Bercy on November 20, 2015 (synthesis of the speeches and discussions).

56. Pierre Cahuc, paper cited in preceding note. Decentralization has been greater in Germany since 2004: see Christian Dustmann, Bernd Fitzenberger, Uta Schönberg, and Alexandra Spitz-Oener, "From Sick Man of Europe to Economic Superstar: Germany's Resurgent Economy," *Journal of Economic Perspectives*, 2014, vol. 28, no. 1, pp. 167–188. This does not mean that German enterprises do not use sector agreements. But their doing so is usually a choice (extensions are state decisions and are rare; the sectors do not have the legal capacity for extension, otherwise one could

imagine that they would force firms to apply the sector agreement), but one that is part of a package, because the employers' organization also provides other services. The fact that the adoption of sector agreements is voluntary greatly changes things, because sector agreements then have to be attractive for companies, since they cannot be constrained, and institutions are more in phase with competition law.

57. In practice, the labor code remains directive in some of its dimensions and leaves negotiation no room to maneuver. This is what the Combrexelle report (2015) calls the "conventional public order," from which management and labor cannot deviate (minimum wage, overtime beginning at thirty-five hours, priority of permanent contracts). This report advocates an extension of negotiation between management and labor in France.

58. See chapter 8.

59. See chapters 14 and 15.

Chapter Ten: Europe at the Crossroads

1. Barry Eichengreen, "Is Europe an Optimal Currency Area?" National Bureau of Economic Research, 1991, Working Paper no. 3579.

2. More generally, intra-European trade is considerable: intraregional trade makes up almost 70 percent of total exports in the larger European Union (EU-28). For more detail, see https://www.ecb.europa.eu/pub/pdf/other/art2_mb201301en_pp59-74en.pdf.

3. See Luigi Guiso, Paola Sapienza, and Luigi Zingales, "Monnet's Error," *Economic Policy*, (2016) 31 (86): 247–297.

4. The euro was introduced in 1999 for financial transactions. Households started using the legal tender in the form of bills and coins on January 1, 2002.

5. Christian Thimann, "The Microeconomic Dimensions of the Eurozone Crisis and Why European Politics Cannot Solve Them," *Journal of Economic Perspectives*, 2015, no. 3, pp. 141–164.

6. See chapter 9 for the case of France.

7. Here I am not taking into account the adjustments made by southern Europe. If we consider only intra-European trade, we can, of course, conceive of a rise in prices and salaries in Germany as a substitute for a decrease of prices and salaries in southern Europe.

8. One variant of which was the proposal in France for a "TVA sociale."

9. Jeremy Bulow and Ken Rogoff note that Greece's GDP per capita moved from 41 percent of Germany's in 1995 to 71 percent in 2009, and then fell back to 47 percent in 2014 ("The Modern Greek," *Vox EU*, June 10, 2015).

10. Olivier Blanchard and Francesco Giavazzi, "Current Account Deficits In the Euro Area: The End of the Feldstein-Horioka Puzzle?" *Brookings Papers on Economic Activity*, 2002, vol. 2, pp. 147–209.

11. The endogenous nature of public policy in reaction to the ownership of financial assets is a classical theme of economic theory (it is, for example, the argument often given in favor of fully funded retirement schemes that are based on capitalization and make the population—and not only its most affluent members—the owners of enterprises through their shares in pension funds, thus creating popular support for policies favorable to investment). In the case of international finance, and regarding the benefits of investors' home bias (to the detriment of the international diversification of domestic savings), see for example my article "Inefficient Foreign Borrowing: A Dual- and Common-Agency Perspective," *American Economic Review*, 2003, vol. 93, no. 5, pp. 1678–1702.

12. Despite the "no bailouts" clause of the 1992 Maastricht Treaty specifying that member states should not be liable for, nor assume, the commitments or debts of another member state.

13. Carmen Reinhart, Kenneth Rogoff, *This Time is Different: Eight Centuries of Financial Folly* (Princeton: Princeton University Press, 2009).

14. On this subject, see the IMF's report, "Global Financial Stability Report," IMF, June, 2012.

15. An additional problem: they then raised capital, issued preferred stocks (a form of debt in which the distribution of coupons can be interrupted so long as no dividends are paid to shareholders, thus providing a certain flexibility for the borrower in comparison to ordinary debt), and subordinated debts to new entities, which were themselves financed by Spanish investors, who were often also depositors. This made participation by the private sector in future bailouts politically difficult.

16. This strengthened the rules in several ways: a deficit cap at 0.50 percent (for the structural deficit, that is, adjusted to the economic cycle); automatic sanctions, cancelled only in the event of a majority vote; implementation of decisions by the European Court of Justice.

17. In addition to the evidence cited below, Europe was not prepared and had no firewall; but the situation has changed somewhat.

18. Domestic banks today find themselves holding a lot of government bonds, which incidentally raises concerns about possible "doom loops."

19. In November 2015, despite debt at 240 percent of GDP, the interest rate on thirty-year government bonds was only 1.36 percent!

20. For an interesting comparison of the role of reputation with that of sanctions, see Jeremy Bulow and Ken Rogoff, "Why Sovereigns Repay Debts to External Contributors and Why it Matters," *Vox EU*, June 10, 2015.

21. In 2012, Judge Thomas Griesa of the United States Southern District Court of New York ruled in favor of "vulture funds," which had refused to settle with Argentina. This ruling not only specified favorable financial terms for the vulture funds; crucially, it also prohibited Argentina from making any payments to creditors who had settled before the vulture funds had been repaid in full.

22. See Guillermo Calvo, "Servicing the Public Debt: The Role of Expectations," *American Economic Review*, 1988, vol. 78, no. 4, pp. 647–661.

23. Citi Global Perspectives & Solutions, "The Coming Pensions Crisis," 2016.

24. In Europe, attempts have recently been made to extend the part of the debt that cannot be bailed out by going beyond shares: large deposits (in theory, not insured) in Cyprus, and subordinated debt and hybrid securities in the case of the SNS Reaal bank.

25. Unlike Europe, the United States is a federation. I will return to this point at the end of the chapter.

26. Private lenders are by definition willing to grant a country a loan at the market interest rate if they are sure that this loan will be repaid. Unless the IMF takes a risk of nonrepayment, the specificity of its loan with respect to those of the market lies elsewhere.

27. Michael Bordo, Lars Jonung, and Agnieszka Markiewicz, "A Fiscal Union for the Euro: Some Lessons from History," *CESifo Econ Stud*, 2013, vol. 59 no. 3, 449–488.

28. Thomas Philippon, "The State of the Monetary Union," *Vox EU*, August 31, 2015.

29. The troika is composed of the IMF, the ECB, and the European Commission. It was formed in 2010 to set up plans for coming to the rescue of Greece, and later Ireland, Portugal, and Cyprus.

30. From 25 percent at the beginning of 2014, according to a European Commission report.

31. See Jeremy Bulow and Ken Rogoff, "The Modern Greek Tragedy," *Vox EU*, June 10, 2015. To be sure, the first bailout partly benefited the French and German banks, which held a lot of Greek debt; but the money that went to those banks was a substitute for the payments that were supposed to have been made by Greece.

32. "Greece: Past Critiques and the Path Forward," *imf-Direct* (blog), July 9, 2015.

33. In the late 1980s, bank lenders in deeply indebted Latin American countries received negotiable instruments with a large discount in relation to their initial debt. The liquidity of these bonds allowed them to make a fresh start and to remove the debt from their balance sheets by selling the instruments.

34. "PIIGS": Portugal, Ireland, Italy, Greece, and Spain.

35. The *acquis communautaire* refers to the whole set of laws that apply more generally to the countries of the European Union. It is generally accepted that the *acquis communautaire* has made it possible to protect governments against powerful national lobbies, and that it has thus been beneficial for countries that have joined the EU (in contrast with other countries: compare, for example, the very different paths taken by Poland and Ukraine, even before the tragedy that has recently overwhelmed the latter).

36. Private creditors holding Greek government debt were asked to extend the maturity of their debt, to decrease the interest rates, and to reduce the nominal value of the debt by more than 50 percent. This private sector involvement (PSI) operation led to a decrease in debt of over one hundred billion euros through a haircut on privately held debt.

37. Which centralizes the prudential regulation of banks through the "Single Supervisory Mechanism" and is broader than the Eurozone (it includes twenty-six EU member states).

38. This is a shortcut. The treaty is well known for leading to the creation of the euro, on which we focus, but had other provisions as well.

39. Jean Tirole, "Country Solidarity in Sovereign Crises," *American Economic Review*, 2015, vol. 105, no. 8, pp. 2333–2363.

40. The nominations are validated by the European Union. The councils report to the latter and to the European Court of Justice. The members of these councils are supposed to be competent and experienced.

41. In France, the *Haut Conseil des finances publiques* consists of four magistrates from the *Cour des comptes* and four other experts (with expertise in macroeconomic forecasts, public finance, etc.) appointed to five-year terms. Its missions are 1) to validate growth forecasts, 2) to give an opinion on the proposed finance law and the way back to a balanced budget, and 3) to possibly ask for corrective actions in the course of the year.

42. On the other hand, Europe would not be a federation like others, because the segmentation of the financial market in periods of crisis limits the risk sharing by the financial market.

43. Alberto Alesina and Ed Glaeser, *Fighting Poverty in the US and Europe: A World of Difference* (Oxford: Oxford University Press, 2004).

CHAPTER ELEVEN: WHAT USE IS FINANCE?

1. A "swap" is a contract exchanging financial flows between two parties. For example, Airbus and its financial counterparty (such as a bank) can agree on a future transfer of one dollar by Airbus in exchange for x euros by the counterparty. Thus Airbus would be less badly affected by a fall in the

dollar. (Of course, it will be unfavorable to Airbus if the dollar rises, but in that case its revenues would increase as well; this is like any insurance contract.)

2. For example, in 2012, the departments of Rhone and Seine-Saint-Denis had, respectively 418 and 345 million euros in toxic loans; the commune of Argenteuil had 118 million.

3. Public-private partnerships, which can provide advantageous solutions for financing public infrastructure by combining public goals with the efficiency of the private sector, have historically been adopted for bad reasons: the private partner took responsibility for the initial expenditure, while the public authority committed itself to making considerable but distant payments (or else gave up its rights to future revenues connected with the investment). Public accounting systems have tried to penalize such strategies of delaying payment.

4. The IMF in particular regularly publishes studies on the functioning of fiscal rules. For example, "Expenditure Rules: Effective Tools for Sound Fiscal Policy?" February 2015, working paper.

5. It might be useful to add other supervisory controls over public sector borrowing—for example, by requiring that for each public program there is some specified means in the subsequent years of financing associated expenditures (except perhaps in the case of very long-term investments that need a longer horizon).

6. A currency that seemed to involve no risk, but was in reality very risky: the Swiss central bank was artificially keeping the Swiss franc undervalued at 1.2 Swiss francs to the euro—until January 2015, when it let the Swiss franc rise by about 20 percent against the euro.

7. Boris Vallee and Christophe Perignon, "The Political Economy of Financial Innovation: Evidence from Local Governments," *Review of Financial Studies* (forthcoming). These authors show that the large local authorities (which, a priori, had a more highly qualified finance department and access to external expertise) had more recourse to structured loans; the same goes for mayors with extensive training—for example, those with backgrounds as high-ranking civil servants.

8. An over-the-counter transaction is one in which the transaction is made bilaterally, between the buyer and the seller, with a contract that is usually not very standardized. On the other hand, exchange trading involves an organized market in which numerous buyers and sellers exchange relatively standardized securities.

9. Warren Buffet, one of the wealthiest people on the planet, is considered one of the smartest investors. For more than forty years, his Berkshire Fund has outperformed the S&P 500 and the Dow Jones stock indexes, which is exceptional.

10. For a discussion of the incentive effects and dangers of securitization, see (among many other sources, because this point has been extensively discussed in the economic literature) Mathias Dewatripont and Jean Tirole, *The Prudential Regulation of Banks* (Cambridge: MIT Press, 1994).

11. Benjamin Keys, Tanmoy Mukherjee, Amit Seru, Vikrant Vig, "Did Securitization Lead to Lax Screening? Evidence from Subprime Loans," *Quarterly Journal of Economics*, 2010, vol. 125, no. 1, pp. 307–362.

12. I will not go into the complexity of the process of securitization here. The issuers handed over their loan portfolios to "conduits" ("structured investment vehicles") that then sold more or less risky "tranches" of these loans to provide products suited to the risk appetites of different investors (many investors want high-grade securities to enable them to manage their risks better, or for regulatory reasons). For example, the prudential rules for commercial banks required 8 percent of the bank's own equity to back assets weighted by their risk. For AAA tranches (the highest grade), the risk is estimated at only 20 percent, so requiring 1.6 cents of the bank's own funds per dollar of such securities. The credit lines granted by banks to the conduits that they had created did not have strong requirements either. I refer the reader to my 2010 monograph with Mathias Dewatripont and Jean-Charles Rochet, *Balancing the Banks* (Princeton: Princeton University Press, 2010) and to the many articles devoted to this subject.

13. The rating agencies (Standard and Poor's, Moody's, Fitch) have scales ranging from AAA to D (which means "in default"): AAA, AA+, AA, AA–, A+, etc... . Investments below BB+ are called *speculative*, even though such a line of demarcation is, of course, to some extent arbitrary.

14. The reader may disapprove of an investor receiving coupons from a company that makes money at the expense of its customers' health. Some socially responsible investment funds (see chapter 7) avoid investing in this kind of company, and it is also up to the state to assume its responsibilities. The point is that since profits are being made, in this case it is better that they go to savers rather than being reinvested in the company.

15. That is, good quality bonds. Junk bonds can be just as risky as stock shares.

16. A security of this kind is called a *consol*. If r is the interest rate (here, 0.10), the fundamental value of the console is $[1/ (1+r)] + [1/ (1+r)^2] + [1/ (1+r)^3] + \ldots = 1/r = 10$.

17. This argument does not consider the "aura" discussed by Walter Benjamin (see *The Work of Art in the Age of Mechanical Reproduction*, 1936). For Benjamin, the term "aura" refers to the quasi-mystical relationship we have with the original work of art produced by its creator. This magical aspect disappeared with the invention of reproduction (the printing press, photography, and film in Benjamin's time); authenticity cannot be reproduced. On the other hand, a reproduction can make us aware of the

original's aura. From the point of view of economics, it suffices to note that the absence of reproduction is crucial for the existence of both a bubble and an aura.

18. Princeton: Princeton University Press, 2009.

19. For instance, Olivier Blanchard (a professor at MIT, then the IMF's chief economist for eight years) and I separately published several papers on this subject in the early 1980s.

20. Jean Tirole, "Asset Bubbles and Overlapping Generations," *Econometrica*, 1985, pp. 1499–1528. The condition involving comparison of the interest rate and the growth rate has a long academic tradition going back to the works of Maurice Allais (1947) and Paul Samuelson (1958) on fiat currency.

    It is difficult to tell whether this condition has been met or not, because it implements long-term predictions regarding these two variables. François Geerolf (in an article entitled "Reassessing Dynamic Efficiency," UCLA, 2014) shows that the condition seems to be met by most of the countries in the OECD.

21. First, note the qualifier "on average": the risk that the bubble might burst requires a yield higher than the interest rate (so long as it has not burst) to compensate for the risk of bursting. Next, the rule of average growth at the interest rate is only approximately true. Agents' aversion to risk and the fact that the bursting of a bubble will be reflected in falling interest rates imply some corrections to this rule.

22. For example, it has been shown that hedge funds sometimes contribute to a bubble's growth, and often get out before it bursts (Markus Brunnermeier and Stefan Nagel, "Hedge Funds and the Technology Bubble," *Journal of Finance*, 2004, vol. 59, pp. 2013–2040).

23. Emmanuel Farhi and Jean Tirole, "Bubbly Liquidity," *Review of Economic Studies*, 2012, vol. 79, no. 2, pp. 678–706.

24. See for example his book *Irrational Exuberance*, 3rd ed., revised and expanded (Princeton: Princeton University Press, 2015).

25. The relevance of another ratio, the relationship between the mortgage payment on the loan and the borrower's income, stems from a household's debt capability: the ability to borrow depends on the ability to pay back the loan, and therefore the borrower's income. In turn, the ability to borrow determines whether new borrowers or those who are moving to improve the quality of their accommodation can pay the price asked by the sellers. If the banks anticipate a rise in real estate prices, the borrower will be able to borrow more against a given income, because the bank, which will foreclose on the property if the borrower can no longer make the loan payments, is taking less risk.

26. The definition of an investment bank (also called a merchant bank) may vary. In this chapter, we distinguish between a retail bank (also called a commercial bank), which receives deposits from small depositors and generally simultaneously makes loans to small and medium-sized enterprises, and an investment bank, which has no small depositors (and until recently was practically unregulated). The investment bank deals with initial public offerings on the stock market, bond issues, and mergers and acquisitions for large corporations, bond issues for governments, and the design of derivatives; it fulfills the function of a deal maker (market making) in organized markets and as a counterparty in over-the-counter (OTC) markets.

27. At the outset, the game is a zero-sum game, the profits made by some being compensated by the losses of others; but it becomes a negative- sum game when we take into account the costs of investment in software, fiber optics, and colocation.

28. Thomas Philippon and Ariell Reshef, "Wages and Human Capital in the US Finance Industry: 1909–2006," *Quarterly Journal of Economics*, 2012, vol. 127, no. 4, pp. 1551–1609.

29. Thomas Philippon, "Has the US Finance Industry Become Less Efficient?" *American Economic Review*, 2015, vol. 105, no. 4, pp. 1408–1438.

30. On bank runs, the pioneering article is Douglas Diamond and Philip Dybvig, "Bank Runs, Deposit Insurance, and Liquidity," *Journal of Political Economy*, 1983, vol. 91, no. 3, pp. 401–419; on sovereign debt panics, the pioneering article is Guillermo Calvo, "Servicing the Public Debt: The Role of Expectations," *American Economic Review*, 1988, vol. 78, no. 4, pp. 647–661.

31. Mary Poppins is a nanny employed by a bank employee. One day he takes his children to his workplace. The branch manager advises the son to invest his money in the bank; the son asks that his money be returned, and the depositors present in the bank, hearing this request, think they are confronted by a bank run and the rumor spreads. These depositors also demand the return of their money, creating a real bank run.

32. That is, for example, the case for loans to small and medium-sized enterprises, which reflect a great deal of information about the bank that is not known to other financial intermediaries.

33. See also chapter 5.

34. For instance, markets can react excessively to very salient trends (say, something an analyst can pick out in Google Trends) and generate a temporary change in the valuation of an asset.

35. Roland Bénabou, "Groupthink: Collective Delusions in Organizations and Markets," *Review of Economics Studies*, 2013, vol. 80, no. 2, pp. 429–446.

36. A classical application of these ideas concerns the domain of health. Human beings tend to repress thoughts connected with illness and death, whether regarding themselves or those close to them. This attitude is partly functional: it allows us to enjoy a more serene, carefree life because most of the time it allows us to escape anxiety-producing thoughts. However, it also involves dysfunctional aspects: not having regular checkups, leading a not very healthful way of life, etc.

37. Bénabou shows that the denial of reality tends to be contagious when it creates negative externalities (other people's errors make the situation worse).

38. In the context of an auction, this is called "the winner's curse": the person who makes the winning bid should take into account the information contained in the fact that he has won the bidding, that is, that other buyers are not prepared to pay as high a price for the object on sale.

39. The state can then "resuscitate" these markets, but at a financial cost: see Thomas Philippon and Vasiliki Skreta, "Optimal Interventions in Markets with Adverse Selection," and my article "Overcoming Adverse Selection: How Public Intervention Can Restore Market Functioning," *American Economic Review*, 2012, vol. 102, no. 1, pp. 1–28 and 29–59, respectively.

40. The limits to arbitrage can have even greater consequences: in particular, some institutional investors face constraints that produce predictable liquidity shocks. For example, insurers have to get rid of downgraded bonds, or investment funds experience massive withdrawals. In anticipation of these shocks, hedge funds sell short the securities that have to be sold by these institutions, further destabilizing the market. See Markus Brunnermeier and Lasse Pedersen, "Predatory Trading," *Journal of Finance*, 2005, vol. 60, pp. 1825–1863.

41. Ultimately, US taxpayers profited overall from the bank bailouts, but this could not have been known in advance, and in other countries taxpayers have lost money on financial sector rescues.

42. I refer the reader to my book with Mathias Dewatripont, *The Prudential Regulation of Banks*, (Cambridge: MIT Press, 1994) for a discussion of the "representation hypothesis" and the reasons why things are different in the stock market.

43. This weight was later reduced to 0.35 to reflect a decrease in the perception of risk connected with real estate, ironic in light of later events.

44. This possibility of "regulatory arbitrage" has been studied, for example, by George Pennacchi and Giuliano Iannotta in "Bank Regulation, C Ratings and Systematic Risk," unpublished paper; and by Matthias Er in "Arbitraging the Basel Securitization Framework: Evidence from G man ABS Investment," unpublished paper (the latter also discusses othe ways of arbitraging the Basel regulation).

45. Pension funds sponsored by states, broker-dealers, and mutual funds themselves were already compelled or encouraged to invest in assets that were sufficiently highly rated.

46. Following this logic, we have to reduce reliance on ratings if the rating agencies do not show greater integrity in their process than they did before the 2008 crisis. For example, following Basel II, 7.5 times more equity was required to pass from a security rated AAA or AA to a security rated BB+ to BB–; such an impact on the profitability of banks requires considerable confidence in the process of rating, without which sensitivity of requirements to ratings must be reduced.

Chapter Twelve: The Financial Crisis of 2008

1. During a visit to the London School of Economics on November 5, 2008.

2. On the other hand, the banking problems in Italy, Portugal, and Greece are due more to the poor performance of their economies (see chapter 10).

3. For example, Ben Bernanke, *The Courage to Act: A Memoir of a Crisis and Its Aftermath* (New York: W. W. Norton & Company, 2015); Gary Gorton, *Slapped by the Invisible Hand: The Panic of 2007* (Oxford: Oxford University Press, 2010); Randall Kroszner and Robert Shiller, *Reforming US Financial Markets* (MIT Press, 2011); Paul Krugman, *The Return of Depression Economics and the Crisis of 2008* (New York: Norton, 2009); Atif Mian and Amir Sufi, *House of Debt: How They (and You) Caused the Great Recession, and How We Can Prevent It from Happening Again* (Chicago: University of Chicago Press, 2015); Robert Shiller, *The Subprime Solution: How Today's Global Financial Crisis Happened, and What to Do about It* (Princeton: Princeton University Press, 2008); the symposiums in the *Journal of Economic Perspectives* on the tightening of credit (Fall 2009), macroeconomics after the crisis (Fall 2010), the financial "plumbing" (Winter 2010), financial regulation after the crisis (Winter 2011), and the bailouts connected with the crisis (Spring 2015). Several books published by economists at New York University: Viral Acharya and Matthew Richardson, eds., *Restoring Financial Stability: How to Repair a Failed System* (New York: John Wiley & Sons, 2009); Viral V. Acharya, Thomas Cooley, Matthew Richardson, and Ingo Walter, eds., *Regulating Wall Street: The Dodd-Frank Act and the New Architecture of Global Finance* (New York: John Wiley & Sons, 2010). See also my monograph *Balancing the Banks: Global Lessons from the Financial Crisis*, written in collaboration with Mathias Dewatripont and Jean-Charles Rochet (Princeton: Princeton University Press, 2010).

4. Fortunately, that was not the case in Europe, where the ECB pursued a tighter policy. Naturally, loose monetary policy is only one facilitating

factor, as is shown by the experiences of Britain and Australia, two countries in which a real estate boom developed despite more normal interest rates.

5. France was largely spared by this phenomenon. French banks have traditionally lent to solvent households, this practice being confirmed by jurisprudence (the Court of Cassation having ruled that a credit institution that grants a borrower a loan disproportionate to his present or future ability to repay it had failed to do its disclosure duty). Loans at variable interest rates, which have long been very popular in the United States, always remained very much in the minority in France (24 percent of outstanding loans in 2007), and always with a small proportion (less than 10 percent) at variable rates without a ceiling limiting the rates or the amount of monthly payments.

6. This group of borrowers was given the nickname "NINJA": no income, no job, and no assets.

7. These sales at rock-bottom prices increased the cost for banks beyond the transaction cost through administrative fees, the nonoccupation and deterioration of the property, unpaid taxes and insurance policy premiums, and the commissions of real estate agencies.

8. The ratings market is very concentrated. There are only three major agencies, and two of them (Moody's and Standard and Poor's) hold about 80 percent of the market. Since two ratings are often required, these agencies are frequently in a quasi-monopoly situation.

9. In other words, they kept the risk of the products off the balance sheets, and this risk now required little in capital. They also resorted to monoline insurers who were themselves overrated. And they staked their reputations without hoarding any capital in return (thus, Bear Stearns went far beyond its legal obligations to bail out the conduits it had created).

10. This rescue of an unregulated actor was not the first of its kind. In 1998, the Fed had already organized a rescue plan and had lowered its interest rates several times in order to avoid the collapse of a speculative fund, Long Term Capital Management (LTCM).

11. Another sore point is that AIG had also distributed a very large dividend to its shareholders only two weeks before it was bailed out by the US government.

12. These "Government Sponsored Enterprises" (GSEs) bought real estate loans from the issuers. Their 5,300 billion dollars in assets was broken down into a portfolio of 1,600 billion dollars and a securitization (including its part in the securitized portfolio) of 3,700 billion dollars.

13. But they nonetheless repaid, in the form of dividends, the public aid (nearly two hundred billion dollars) received in 2008.

14. They were regulated by a special agency rather than by the banking supervisor. Their regulator, the Department of Housing and Urban Development (HUD) did not really have expertise in matters of prudential supervision, and moreover it had incentives to support the real estate market.

15. See John Cochane's blog (*The Grumpy Economist*, May 9, 2017); and a working paper by Greg Buchak, Gregor Matvos, Tomasz Piskorski, and Amit Seru "Fintech, Regulatory Arbitrage, and the Rise of Shadow Banks." Quoting John Cochrane: "the market share of shadow banks in the mortgage market has nearly tripled from 14% to 38% from 2007–2015. In the Federal Housing Administration (FHA) mortgage market, which serves less creditworthy borrowers, the market share of shadow banks increased … from 20% to 75% of the market. In the mortgage market, 'fintech' lenders, have increased their market share from about 5% to 15% in conforming mortgages and to 20% in FHA mortgages during the same period."

16. For example, in the case of Crédit Foncier (a bank that specializes in financing real estate transactions in France, part of the BPCE group).

17. A model, on the basis of the theory of credit rationing, of the idea that the state has one ability that markets do not have—providing liquidity in difficult situations—is developed in my works written with Bengt Holmström ("Private and Public Supply of Liquidity," *Journal of Political Economy*, 1998, vol. 106, no. 1, pp. 1–40; and *Inside and Outside Liquidity* (Cambridge: MIT Press, 2011); and with Emmanuel Farhi ("Collective Moral Hazard, Maturity Mismatch, and Systemic Bailouts," *American Economic Review*, 2012, vol. 102, no. 1, pp. 60–93). The latter article also shows that a loosening of monetary policy should be used to save the banks even if the state can also bail out the banks through personalized transfers.

18. Strictly speaking, the central bank does not go into debt when it issues liquidity—for example, by accepting poor quality collateral under a repurchase agreement (repo) when making a loan to a bank. However, if the central bank suffers losses on these loans, it will have no choice but to create money or else receive it indirectly from the taxpayer. If it creates money, holding money will be "taxed" by inflation.

19. The chairman of a London hedge fund, Marshall Wace, wrote a commentary in the *Financial Times* in September 2015 with the provocative title "Central Banks Have Made the Rich Richer."

20. Of course, in theory, sellers of life assurance should ensure that their assets have the same duration as their liabilities. Then, if rates fall, this will increase the price of the assets "dedicated" to the payments due to customers. In practice, however, policyholders have the option of extending

their contracts, which they will logically do when rates fall and alternative saving instruments become less attractive; the result is an imbalance of maturities between assets and liabilities. It probably is better to deal with the incentive to take risks directly, through prudential supervision, rather than abandoning low interest rates if they are useful to the economy. We must nonetheless be aware of the risk posed by this level of interest rates.

21. To be sure, there are transaction costs in holding cash, and thus it is possible to have slightly negative nominal rates, which some central banks have today (for example, at the date of this writing, the European Central Bank is paying a minus 0.4 percent interest rate on excess reserves; central banks of other European countries, such as Sweden, Switzerland, and Denmark, also have negative interest rate policies); but interest rates cannot be very negative.

22. The creation of inflationary expectations, forward guidance (announcing low interest rates not only for the present but also for the future), quantitative easing (the central bank's acceptance of risky assets as collateral—for example, risky bonds or commercial paper issued by businesses, mortgage securities, or even bonds issued by countries in financial difficulties), or fiscal stimulus (the latter not being in the domain of the central bank, of course).

23. The notion of secular stagnation is very old, but it was made fashionable again in 2013 by Lawrence Summers, a professor at Harvard and formerly Bill Clinton's secretary of the treasury. For an overview of the debates on this subject, see Coen Teulings and Richard Baldwin, eds., *Secular Stagnation: Facts, Causes and Cures* (CEPR Press/VoxEU.org Book, 2014).

24. Ricardo Caballero and Emmanuel Farhi, "The Safety Trap," forthcoming in *Review of Economic Studies*.

25. Other causes have been suggested. For example, the slowing of innovation that is supposed to make the demand for investment diminish, about which I personally have doubts, but regarding which it is hard to find decisive evidence. Others have proposed the hypothesis that technological progress in the sector of investment goods has the same effect of diminishing investment.

26. Jean Tirole, *Leçons d'une crise*, Toulouse School of Economics, TSE Notes, no. 1 (English translation by Keith Tribe in *Balancing the Banks: Global Lessons from the Financial Crisis*, written in collaboration with Mathias Dewatripont and Jean-Charles Rochet [Princeton: Princeton University Press, 2010]).

27. However, some of these contracts (like foreign exchange swaps) are still traded over the counter.

28. The default in 2006 of Amaranth, a big hedge fund that traded especially in natural gas futures contracts on centralized platforms, had practically no systemic effect; the hedge fund did not need to be bailed out.

29. For an evaluation of this approach, see for example my article "The Contours of Banking and the Future of Its Regulation," in George Akerlof, Olivier Blanchard, David Romer and Joseph Stiglitz, eds., *What Have We Learned?* (Cambridge, MIT Press, 2014), pp. 143–153.

30. These two arguments are developed in Holmström-Tirole, "Financial Intermediation, Loanable Funds, and the Real Sector," *Quarterly Journal of Economics*, 1997, vol. 112, pp. 663–692; and "Private and Public Supply of Liquidity," *Journal of Political Economy*, 1998, vol. 106, no. 1, pp. 1–40. My book written with Mathias Dewatripont, *The Prudential Regulation of Banks* (Cambridge: MIT Press, 1994), suggested reducing the procyclical character of regulation by introducing insurance premiums that were themselves procyclical.

31. See the preceding chapter.

32. Some economists demand a much higher level, in particular Anat Admati and Martin Hellwig, *The Bankers' New Clothes* (Princeton: Princeton University Press, 2013).

33. If here I take the example of CEOs, we must not forget that these principles of remuneration do not apply solely to the management team. Bonuses distributed farther down the hierarchy are often substantial in the world of finance.

34. An indemnity the enterprise pays a manager after his dismissal.

35. See my article written with Roland Bénabou, "Bonus Culture,", *Journal of Political Economy*, 124(2): 305–370.

36. Of course, we are well aware of this argument's limits. Long-term remuneration plans (in particular stock option plans with very deferred effects) are systematically renegotiated if the incentives they create have become nonexistent or perverse after the arrival of bad news.

37. See my article with Bengt Holmström, "Market Liquidity and Performance Monitoring," *Journal of Political Economy*, 1993, vol. 101, no. 4, pp. 678–709.

38. Xavier Gabaix and Augustin Landier ("Why Has CEO Pay Increased So Much?" *Quarterly Journal of Economics*, 2008, vol. 123, no. 1, pp. 49–100) connect the distribution of remuneration with the size of the company (considered as an indicator of the importance of managerial talent) and show a strong link between the growth in the size of companies and that of CEO remuneration between 1980 and 2003 (this study is not specific to banking).

39. For an account of the role of hubris in finance, see for example William Cohan's *House of Cards: A Tale of Hubris and Wretched Excess on Wall Street* (New York: Doubleday, 2009).

40. Since 2010, a "renationalization" of financial markets has resulted in a situation in which government bonds held on banks' balance sheets are essentially domestic; the banks are consequently very exposed to the risk of their sovereign's default; conversely, states are exposed to the risk of having to bail out their banks. This interdependence between banks and states gives rise to the possibility of a vicious circle (called in this case a "doom loop" or "deadly embrace") in which the markets' concerns about a country's solvency devalues the bonds it has issued and destabilizes domestic banks that hold these bonds, which then forces the state to bail out the banks, thus reinforcing the markets' worries about the state's solvency, making the price of sovereign obligations fall still further, etc.

41. There is a strong temptation for governments to live comfortably when prices of raw materials are high, instead of setting up (as Norway and Chile did, for example) a sovereign wealth fund to smooth out activity and protect themselves against periods when raw materials prices are low. Thus, since 2001 Chile has applied a budgetary rule that makes public expenditures conditional not on revenue (which is heavily dependent on the price of copper), but rather on revenue adjusted to the copper cycle. This kind of rule enables states to avoid spending heavily when raw materials prices rise and then finding themselves in budgetary difficulties when they fall. A contrario, Venezuela—a country with the largest known oil reserves in the world, which was profligate when oil prices were high and today is in a desperate economic and humanitarian situation—demonstrates the importance of smoothing country income through budgetary rules and sovereign wealth funds.

42. The excessively systematic resort to bailouts using public funds has logically been replaced by an attempt to apply a consistent policy of making imprudent investors pay—"bail ins"—although no clear doctrine concerning its scope has emerged.

43. Of course, little credit should be granted those who predicted the crisis without describing its mechanisms, insofar as (to paraphrase Paul Samuelson) they had a tendency to predict nine of the last five crises (mocking economists' inability to predict, Samuelson had declared: "Wall Street indexes predicted nine out of the last five recessions"). Among the well-known economists who provided substantiated warnings against the dangers of the situation, we can mention Raghuram Rajan (University of Chicago; former governor of India's central bank) and Nouriel Roubini (New York University). Robert Schiller (Yale) had also expressed strong concerns about the real estate bubble.

44. I refer the reader to chapter 4 for a discussion of prediction in the scientific domain in general.

45. See the preceding chapter.

46. John Maynard Keynes, "Great Britain's Foreign Investments," in *Collected Writings*, vol. 15 (London: Macmillan, 1971), p. 46.

Chapter Thirteen: Competition Policy and Industrial Policy

1. France has only recently been converted to idea of competition and to the need to monitor it. A 1986 order put an end to the administered economy and to price control by the state, and it established the Competition Council. The Germans were converted much earlier, and with bipartisan agreement. In the United States, the Sherman Antitrust Act (the basis of antitrust law) dates from 1890. There are, of course, antecedents, such as the antimonopoly decisions in England in the early seventeenth century.

2. More precisely, until the 2008 Modernization of the Economy Act.

3. According to McKinsey, labor productivity (the value of output per hour of labor) in the French automobile sector grew at a rate of almost 8 percent from 1992 to 1999 (and 15 percent from 1996 to 1999), thanks to better purchasing policy, administrative reorganization, and the simplification of production. Still, the value added per employee in the automobile industry remains below the European Union average.

4. See for example Nicholas Bloom, Mirko Draca, and John Van Reenen, "Trade Induced Technical Change? The Impact of Chinese Imports on Innovation, IT and Productivity," unpublished paper.

5. "(Not) made in France," *Lettre du Cepii*, June 2013.

6. For the United States, see Lucia Foster, John Haltiwanger, and C. J. Krizan, "Aggregate Productivity Growth: Lessons from Microeconomic Evidence," *New Developments in Productivity Analysis*, National Bureau of Economic Research, 2001, pp. 303–372. For France, see Bruno Crépon and Richard Duhautois, "Ralentissement de la productivité et réallocations d'emplois: deux régimes de croissance," *Économie et statistique*, 2003, no. 367, pp. 69–82.

7. Some argue that local consumption reduces carbon emissions. This is correct, provided that local production is not more carbon intensive than nonlocal production. However, the solution is not to distort markets, but rather to make firms accountable for the emissions associated with the transportation of their goods. As we have seen in chapter 9, this is best achieved through carbon pricing.

8. Introduced by Edward Chamberlin and Joan Robinson in 1933, this approach says market structure affects firms' behavior ("conduct") and that this in turn affects their performance, with feedback loops occurring between these.

9. See chapter 9.

10. Examined in chapter 8.

11. Here, of course, I remove Mao's formula in his famous "Hundred Flowers" speech (February, 1957) from its context.

12. For a study focused on China, see Philippe Aghion, Jing Cai, Mathias Dewatripont, Luosha Du, Ann Harrison, and Patrick Legros, "Industrial Policy and Competition," *American Economic Journal: Macroeconomics,* 2015, 7(4): 1–32.

13. I exclude the sectors in which the state is necessarily a buyer (education, health care, armaments, infrastructure, etc.) and is therefore compelled to intervene.

14. I refer the reader to the famous study by AnnaLee Saxenian, *Regional Advantage: Culture and Competition in Silicon Valley and Route 128* (Cambridge: Harvard University Press, 1994), which suggests that the culture of informal exchanges in Silicon Valley gave it an advantage over the hi-tech center in Boston, which was located along Route 128.

15. See the study by Gilles Duranton, Philippe Martin, Thierry Mayer, and Florian Mayneris, which notes that "in fact, there are very few examples of successful policies of support for clusters" (*Les pôles de compétitivité. que peut-on en attendre?* [Paris: Cepremap, 2008]). In 2007, there were seventy-one competitiveness clusters (*pôles de compétitivité*) in France.

16. For example, out of 105 submissions for becoming a competitiveness cluster in France in 2005, 67 were accepted.

17. Damien Neven and Paul Seabright, "European Industrial Policy: the Airbus Case," *Economic Policy*, 22, September 1995.

18. Postwar Japan was constructed essentially around private groups, with a state that planned (the famous MITI) but was less interventionist.

19. Philippe Aghion, Mathias Dewatripont, Caroline Hoxby, Andreu Mas-Colell, and André Sapir, "Universities," *Economic Policy*, June 2010. This article emphasizes the complementary relation between the autonomy of universities and competition (intuitively, competition can play an important role only if universities are free to adopt their own strategies). It also shows the impact on patents of the type of financing provided by the NSF and NIH.

20. In their book *État moderne, État efficace. Évaluer les dépenses publiques pour sauvegarder le modèle français* (Paris: Odile Jacob, 2012), Marc Ferracci and Étienne Wasmer propose to invert the burden of proof: according

to them, it should be incumbent upon the defenders of the policy concerned to prove, after x years, that it has been effective, and thus that it should be continued; if this proof is not forthcoming, the policy should be abandoned.

21. The reader may object that if the private sector is willing to finance the project, then there is no market failure and no need for government intervention. Perhaps a better interpretation of the call for private financing is that private financiers may receive a rate of return above that of the public sector (requiring differentiated claims), as long as the return differential is not too large. This approach may put a boundary on the amount of money that the government might lose in the process. The return differential may be larger for those projects that create large spillovers.

22. For an excellent analysis of this country, see Bruce Greenwald and Joseph Stiglitz, *Creating a Learning Society* (New York: Columbia University Press, 2014). On the other hand, I have doubts about the argument that without an industrial policy South Korea would necessarily have remained a rice producer, which was its comparative advantage in 1945. First of all, comparative advantage is a dynamic notion. Starting from the moment that the country invested in education and infrastructure and made access to credit easier, there was no reason why the economy could not turn toward industrial jobs. Then, pushing the country to specialize in rice would have been a perfect example of industrial policy!

23. Élie Cohen and Jean-Hervé Lorenzi, "Des politiques industrielles aux politiques de compétitivité en Europe," in *Politiques industrielles pour l'Europe* (Paris: La Documentation française, 2000).

24. See for example Mark J. Perry (University of Michigan Flint) "Charts of the day: Creative destruction in the S&P500 index," American Enterprise Institute, January 26, 2014.

25. Gauging threshold effects is complex. See for example Nila Ceci-Renaud and Paul-Antoine Chevalier, "L'impact des seuils de 10, 20 et 50 salariés sur la taille des entreprises françaises," *Économie et statistique*, 2010, vol. 437, pp. 29–45. It is not only the French state that is responsible for threshold effects. The European Parliament has opted for a reduction in the equity capital required of banks when they make loans to SMEs.

26. Luis Garicano, Claire Lelarge, and John Van Reenen, "Firm Size Distortions and the Productivity Distribution: Evidence from France," *American Economic Review*, 2016, 106(11): 3439–3479. These authors estimate the cost at about 5 percent, which is in large part due to the rigid labor market in France (they estimate that in a country like the United States, the cost of such a regulation would be at most 1 percent). This cost may, of course, differ depending on the country and the time, but it does not seem to be negligible.

27. See for example my note written with Guillaume Plantin and David Thesmar, "Les enjeux économiques du droit des faillites," Conseil d'analyse économique, 2013, note 7, on proposals for reform. An order issued in March 2014 on bankruptcy law moved in this direction by authorizing creditors to convert their debts into capital and to propose a recovery plan concurrent with the CEO's.

28. The report of the Conseil d'analyse économique, "Faire prospérer les PME" (October 2015) notes that the rate of (forced) conventional coverage by sector agreements is abnormally high in France in comparison with the rest of the world (93 percent in 2008, as compared with an average of 56 percent for the OECD). See chapter 9.

29. See Yves Jacquin Depeyre, *La Réconciliation fiscale* (Paris: Odile Jacob, 2016).

CHAPTER FOURTEEN: HOW DIGITIZATION IS CHANGING EVERYTHING

1. Machine learning is statistical and uses an algorithm that allows a robot or computer to gradually learn to recognize a face, to walk, or to complete any other kind of complex learning.

2. Or multisided markets: for instance, Microsoft Windows has to attract users (you and me), computer manufacturers, and application developers.

3. Glenn and Sara Ellison, "Match Quality, Search, and the Internet Market for Used Books," unpublished paper.

4. It is not known whether this economic model can be indefinitely replicated. Even though advertising is more effective when the target (that is, ourselves) receives the advertisement repeatedly, in the end there are decreasing yields from exposing the target to a given advertisement; moreover, a weariness and increased inattention to advertisements in general may ensue. Finally, more and more software programs make it possible to escape commercial advertisements (like TiVo for television).

5. The manufacturers of printers sell a printer at a loss, or without much profit, when they also sell their own exclusive ink cartridges, on which they then make their profits. Purchasers of printers should anticipate that they will have to pay high prices for their cartridges. However, the situation is different from that of videogames. In the case of the printer, there is only one side to the market; the same consumers buy the printer and the cartridges. The manufacturers of the printer have to find ways of reassuring the consumer: either they set a very low price on the printer to attract the consumer, or they promise to adopt an open architecture that will allow other cartridge manufacturers to supply the buyer of the printer, thus lowering the price of cartridges through competition; the printer

manufacturer can then sell the printer at a high price, and make its profit on it rather than on the cartridges.

6. David Evans and Richard Schmalensee, *Matchmakers: The New Economics of Platform Businesses* (Cambridge: Harvard Business School Press, 2016). See also the same authors' book, *Catalyst Code* (Cambridge: Harvard Business School Press, 2007); and the one written in collaboration with Andrei Hagiu, *Invisible Platforms: How Software Platforms Drive Innovations and Transform Industries* (Cambridge: MIT Press, 2006). I also recommend reading the book by Marshall Van Alstyne, Geoff Parker, and Saugeet Paul Choudary, *Platform Revolution* (New York: Norton, 2016).

7. Apple has fewer customers, but they spend more money than Android's customers, and are therefore more attractive to developers of applications.

8. See Tim Bresnahan, Joe Orsini, and Pai-Ling Yin, "Demand Heterogeneity, Inframarginal Multihoming and Platform Market Stability: Mobile Apps," unpublished paper.

9. For an account of Apple's demise in the 1980s, see Jay Yarow's "How Apple Really Lost its Lead in the '80s," *Business Insider*, December 9, 2012.

10. Even if it was accused of not having given sufficient access to its code and of favoring its browser, on the whole Microsoft has always been a very open system.

11. In the case of Apple, a successful version—Apple II—had been released in 1977, so the brand was well established in the 1980s.

12. This opening to the outside is done by publishing Application Programming Interfaces (API). Of course, things don't go entirely smoothly: platforms and the external services designed for these platforms are sometimes in conflict before arbitrating competition authorities on questions of "tie-in sales," i.e., the presumption that the platform favors internal applications. See below.

13. New regulations, such as the Macron Law in France, have limited these requirements in some countries. The Macron Law stipulates that hotel owners are completely free to set their prices.

14. See for example Renato Gomes and Jean Tirole, "Missed Sales and the Pricing of Ancillary Goods," unpublished paper. See also the literature on "hold-ups" and attributes hidden from consumers. Focusing on card payments, Hélène Bourguignon, Renato Gomes, and Jean Tirole in "Shrouded Transaction Costs," unpublished paper, argue that the new regulations limiting the amounts of surcharges for paying by card in the United States, the United Kingdom, and Australia are too lenient.

15. In 2015, Booking.com made commitments to the French competition authority. Hotels will have more freedom of action. In particular, they

will be able to charge prices lower than those offered on Booking.com, not only on other platforms, but also through their own offline channels (reservations by telephone or by email) or, in the framework of loyalty programs, online on their own websites. In theory, Booking.com is supposed to extend these commitments to the rest of Europe.

16. See Jean-Charles Rochet and Jean Tirole, "Cooperation among Competitors: Some Economics of Payment Card Associations," *The Rand Journal of Economics*, 2002, vol. 33, no. 4, pp. 549–570; and Ben Edelman and Julian Wright, "Price Coherence and Adverse Intermediation," *Quarterly Journal of Economics*, 2015, vol. 130, no. 3, pp. 1283–1328.

17. For example, chapter 8, on the environment.

18. This principle is called "the avoided cost test" or the "tourist test" (would the merchant prefer that the customer pay by card rather than in cash, knowing that the customer is in the store, that both payment methods are available, and that the customer will no longer be a customer in the future—for example, he or she is a tourist?). The theory corresponding to the European Commission's guidelines was developed in my article with Jean-Charles Rochet, "Must Take Cards: Merchant Discounts and Avoided Costs," *Journal of the European Economic Association*, 2011, vol. 9, no. 3, pp. 462–49.

19. We include in this category the metasearch sites, which (contrary to the reservation agencies) do not process the reservations themselves.

20. See the following chapter.

21. For a more complete discussion of the question of competition law and tie-in sales, see my article "The Analysis of Tying Cases: A Primer," *Competition Policy International*, 2005, vol. 1, no. 1, pp. 1–25.

Chapter Fifteen: Digital Economies

1. Cookies are small files stored on our computers. Through them, sites collect personal information that can be used later, for example to send us targeted commercial offers or, for search engines, to help us find what we are looking for more easily or return to a site that we have already visited.

2. And the transaction has to be repeated: what we learn about the person to whom we have entrusted our savings or about the surgeon is not of much use to us if we have lost our savings or our health. Besides, it is difficult to gauge the effectiveness of certain goods, such as vitamins, even after we have consumed them.

3. With its famous slogan, "Life is short. Have an affair."

4. However, the Federal Trade Commission and state courts intervened to limit the extent of the data transfer.

5. There are, of course, other considerations to be taken into account regarding the gap between the United States and Europe, such as the distance that still separates Europe from a single market.

6. Which is the case under European law. Granting competing platforms free access to data is an alternative, but it raises questions of confidentiality.

7. Blue Button is an app that allows patients to download their personal health records or to view them online.

8. What role will the physician play in this new environment? I am not competent to make that prediction. At one extreme of the medical fiction spectrum, the doctor of tomorrow will just be a safeguard—making a commonsense judgment when the computer system might have been hacked—and will further offer the patient a human contact. Whatever the future of this profession, it will (at the least) rely on a provisional, but exhaustive, diagnosis made by software on the basis of analyses.

9. Since 2008, this has been a legal way to break open-ended contracts in France. To terminate an employee by mutual consent, the employer now pays an indemnity of at least the amount of the legal termination payment. Termination by mutual consent is not a resignation, and the employee therefore receives unemployment benefits.

10. Similarly, when local authorities are aware of flood risks but nonetheless grant a building permit in such a zone, they should be held responsible.

11. Hypochondria itself is on the borderline between adverse selection (a real problem of anxiety) and moral hazard (a lack of control over one's behavior). The pathology is clearly involved when individuals constantly seek medical advice on the Internet, though moral hazard cannot be blamed, because they are not imposing any cost on the health insurance system.

12. Starting at one euro per biological analysis, examination by a doctor, or instance of medical imaging; eighteen euros per treatments whose cost exceeds one hundred and twenty euros; fifty cents per box of medication and per paramedical treatment; two euros per transportation by ambulance, with an annual ceiling of fifty euros; and eighteen euros per day of hospitalization.

13. Economists call this phenomenon "the Hirshleifer effect" after an article by Jack Hirshleifer, "The Private and Social Value of Information and the Reward to Inventive Activity," *American Economic Review*, 1971, vol. 61, no. 4, pp. 561–574.

14. The Swiss system is analyzed in Brigitte Dormont, Pierre-Yves Geoffard, and Karine Lamiraud in "The Influence of Supplementary Health Insurance on Switching Behavior: Evidence from Swiss Data," *Health Economics*, 2009, vol. 18, pp. 1339–1356.

15. By making employees' contributions deductible from income taxes and granting an exemption for social security contributions made by the employer. The income tax deduction was eliminated in 2014, but supplementary group insurance policies were extended to all employees in private enterprises.

16. See my note, "Refonder l'assurance-maladie," cowritten with Brigitte Dormont and Pierre-Yves Geoffard, *Conseil d'analyse économique*, note 12.

17. Robert Reich's blog, February 2, 2015 (robertreich.org/post/10989409 5095).

18. One might ask why the employer doesn't simply deduct the extra cost of expenses (like taking a taxi) from the employee's paycheck. The answer is simple: the use of a taxi, like expensive air tickets (with flexible dates, business class, etc.), is a form of disguised remuneration that, unlike salary, is not subject to social security charges and income tax. For managers who don't want to post high salaries, it also makes it possible to underestimate the cost of the perks given employees.

19. We here focus on economics-related debates. There are also current debates concerning rampant sexism, the possible theft of autonomous-car technology, and the use of software to evade transport regulators.

20. For a theoretical analysis of collective and individual reputations, see my article "A Theory of Collective Reputations, with Applications to the Persistence of Corruption and to Firm Quality," *Review of Economic Studies*, no. 63, pp. 1–22.

21. George Baker and Thomas Hubbard, "Contractibility and Asset Ownership: On-Board Computers and Governance in US Trucking," *Quarterly Journal of Economics*, 2004, vol. 119, no. 4, pp. 1443–1479; and "Make Versus Buy in Trucking: Asset Ownership, Job Design, and Information," *American Economic Review*, 2003, vol. 93, no. 3, pp. 551–572.

22. Diane Coyle, "Precarious and Productive Work in the Digital Economy," *National Institute Economic Review*, May 10, 2017.

23. Except Part VI of the labor law, bearing (essentially) on independent labor.

24. See Diane Coyle, "Precarious and Productive Work in the Digital Economy," *National Institute Economic Review*, May 10, 2017.

25. Anthony Atkinson, Thomas Piketty, and Emmanuel Saez, "World Income Database," *wid.world*.

26. Erik Brynjolfsson and Andrew McAfee, *The Second Machine Age* (New York: Norton, 2014).

27. $1,884 per resident in 2014.

28. David Autor, "Why Are There Still So Many Jobs? The History and Future of Workplace Automation," *Journal of Economic Perspectives*, 2015, vol. 29, no. 3, pp. 3–30.

29. See James Bessen, *Learning by Doing: The Real Connection Between Innovation, Wages, and Wealth* (New Haven: Yale University Press, 2015).

30. Except in countries like those of southern Europe, whose labor markets, as I explained in chapter 10, present certain specific challenges.

31. In "Economic Possibilities for Our Grandchildren," where he suggested that this change would require only two generations.

32. "Will Humans Go the Way of Horses?" *Foreign Affairs*, July–August 2015.

33. "Ireland considers the company to be tax-resident in Bermuda, while the US considers it to be tax-resident in Ireland. The result is that when royalty payments are sent to the company, they go untaxed—unless or until the money is eventually sent home to the US parent company." Vanessa Houlder, *Financial Times*, October 9, 2014 (www.ft.com/content/f7a2b958 -4fc8-11e4-908e-00144feab7de). A further refinement is the "double Irish with a Dutch sandwich," which routes profits through one Irish subsidiary, then a Dutch one, then another Irish one headquartered in a tax haven.

34. As they did in the past to eliminate double taxation.

Chapter Sixteen: Innovation and Intellectual Property

1. Economic institutions are another decisive factor, as shown by many economists, notably Daron Acemoglu and James Robinson in *Why Nations Fail: The Origins of Power, Prosperity, and Poverty* (New York: Crown Business, 2012).

2. Here I use Philippe Aghion and Peter Howitt's terminology.

3. Edmund Phelps (Nobel Prize, 2006), "What's Wrong with the West's Economies," *New York Review of Books*, August 13, 2015.

4. Stimulated by the works of Michael Kremer, professor of economics at Harvard. See "Making Markets for Vaccines: Ideas to Action, Center for Global Development," 2005. A major actor is GAVI (Global Alliance for Vaccines and Immunization), a public-private consortium formed by several countries and the Bill and Melinda Gates Foundation.

5. For points of view that are both very critical of institutions but draw divergent conclusions, see Adam Jaffe and Josh Lerner, *Innovation and Its Discontents: How Our Broken Patent System Is Endangering Innovation and Progress, and What to Do about It* (Princeton: Princeton University Press, 2004); and Michelle Boldrin and David Levine, *Against Intellectual Monopoly* (Cambridge: Cambridge University Press, 2008).

6. US 5960411 (1999).

7. Many patents were granted for practices that had existed before the Internet, sometimes for centuries; for example, the online use of the Dutch

auction model, in which the auctioneer begins with a high asking price and lowers it until a bidder accepts it.

8. Carl Shapiro, "Navigating the Patent Thicket: Cross Licenses, Patent Pools, and Standard Setting," in Adam Jaffe, Joshua Lerner, and Scott Stern, eds., *Innovation Policy and the Economy*, vol. 1 (Cambridge: MIT Press, 2000), pp. 119–150.

9. There were thirteen tolls between Mainz and Köln alone. The situation was similar to that on the Elbe or on the French rivers (the Rhône, the Seine, the Garonne, and the Loire): see Robert Spaulding, "Revolutionary France and the Transformation of the Rhine," *Central European History*, 2011, vol. 44, no. 2, pp. 203–226.

10. See Garrett Hardin, "The Tragedy of the Commons," *Science*, vol. 162 (1968), 1243–1248.

11. In fact, all the tolls on the Rhine were simply eliminated.

12. To tell the truth, I didn't know what the term "patent pool" meant when I began working on industrial economics while writing my doctoral dissertation.

13. Another problem is that patents can be both complements when license fees are low (the users will make use of the whole set at low prices, and an increase in the price of a given license reduces the demand for the general technology) and substitutes when licensing fees are high (an increase in the price of the license for a patent can lead to a shift of demand toward licenses for other patents).

14. Josh Lerner and Jean Tirole, "Efficient Patent Pools," *American Economic Review*, 2004, 94(3): 691–711.

15. Assuming a zero cost of marketing licenses, the monopoly price is the price maximizing the product, $PD(P)$, of the price of the license P and of the demand $D(P)$ for the use of the technology, a decreasing function of P.

16. Unequal sharing of the dividend would imply that the patent holder with the smaller share would have an even greater incentive to reduce the price; the argument for undercutting the pool price would be even stronger.

17. For a bad pool, the competitive equilibrium in individual licenses still restores the level of competition before the pool when there are more than two patents and/or when patents are imperfect substitutes. With more than two patents, problems of coordination may result in several equilibria: owners of two complementary patents may fail to coordinate in their individual license fees to undercut the pool. Aleksandra Boutin ("Screening for Good Patent Pools through Price Caps on Individual Licenses," *American Economic Journal Microeconomics*, 2016, 8: 64–94) shows that adding the requirement of unbundling (described later in the text) privileges the equilibrium that reestablishes competition.

18. "Tacit" because firms do not need to sign a cartel agreement (which would in any case be illegal almost everywhere in the world), or even meet to discuss coordination of a "peaceful" mode of behavior.

19. See my article written with Patrick Rey, "Price Caps as Welfare-Enhancing Coopetition," Toulouse School of Economics, unpublished paper.

20. In practice, an obstacle to the formation of pools concerns the distribution of dividends, members having clearly divergent interests in this area. Sharing these dividends in proportion to the number of patents held, independent of the value of their contribution to the technology, can incite the owners of particularly important patents to remain outside the pool. Agreements of mutual moderation ("I agree to reduce my royalties by so much if you agree to set a ceiling on yours at such a level …") like the one described here implicitly determine this sharing.

21. The goal of requiring commitments regarding the price of licenses is to avoid the licenses for standard-essential patents from becoming too expensive. This does not necessarily please owners of intellectual property, but the standard-setting organization needs these patent holders to identify the patents and construct the standard. Moreover, the patent holders often have a choice among several standard-setting organizations and may turn to one that is more accommodating if the standard-setting organization in question demands price commitments. See my articles with Josh Lerner, "Standard-Essential Patents," *Journal of Political Economy*, 2015, vol. 123, no. 3, pp. 547–586; and "A Better Route to Tech Standards," *Science*, 2014, vol. 343, pp. 972–973.

22. Frederik Neumeyer, *The Employed Inventor in the United States: R&D policies, Law and Practice* (Cambridge: MIT Press, 1971).

23. Later, after a legal suit, he received about nine million dollars.

24. In "What's Wrong with the West's Economies," *New York Review of Books*, August 13, 2015.

25. See Gaspard Koenig, *Le Révolutionnaire, l'Expert et le Geek* (Paris: Plon, 2015), p. 89.

26. Technically, Linux is only a kernel of an operating system (OS). Android, which is a complete OS, is based on a Linux kernel. Complete operating systems refer to "GNU/Linux." They are then packaged in a convenient form in what are called "Linux distributions" (Ubuntu is probably the one best known to the general public; Red Hat Enterprise Linux is the best known of the companies).

27. The following discussion is inspired by our articles "Some Simple Economics of Open Source," *Journal of Industrial Economics*, 2002, vol. 50, no. 2, pp. 197–234; and "The Scope of Open Source Licensing," *Journal of Law, Economics and Organization*, 2005, no. 21, pp. 20–56.

28. Free programs such as LyX have tried to emulate Scientific Workplace's ease of use.

29. See N. Taylor Thompson, "When 'Scratch Your Own Itch' Is Dangerous Advice for Entrepreneurs," *Harvard Business Review*, May 19, 2014. hbr.org/2014/05/when-scratch-your-own-itch-is-dangerous-advice -for-entrepreneurs.

30. Apache 2.0.

31. Late 2007. The iPhone had been launched in early 2007.

32. The LGPL (*Lesser General Public License*) is a version modified to be less restrictive regarding its use in conjunction with proprietary software.

Chapter Seventeen: Sector Regulation

1. My work with Jean-Jacques Laffont on incentive regulation (but not our work on opening up to competition, part of which came later) is synthesized in *A Theory of Incentives in Regulation and Procurement* (Cambridge: MIT Press, 1993).

2. The company is the agent in this context, thinking of this in terms of a principal-agent problem. An *agent* performs a task for a *principal* who defines the task and pays the agent for services on the basis of performance.

3. A common form of price cap regulation, "RPI minus X," lets the price cap automatically adjust for the previous year's retail price inflation (RPI) and for expected efficiency improvements (X) during the time period the price adjustment formula is in place.

4. Consider, for example, public markets for supplies and services to local authorities, hospitals, universities; mass transportation, water, and sanitation; construction projects (schools, highways, bridges); and athletic and cultural equipment. The reader may consult, for example, my note written with Stéphane Saussier, "Renforcer l'efficacité de la commande publique" (Conseil d'analyse économique, note 22); and Stéphane Saussier's book, *Économie des partenariats public-privé* (Brussels: De Boeck, 2015).

5. The so-called "hold-up problem" associated with contract incompleteness was emphasized by Oliver Hart (2016 Nobel laureate) and Oliver Williamson (2009 Nobel laureate).

6. The alternative is to create a leasing market for rolling stock, as in Britain with the ROSCOs (rolling stock operating companies).

7. The goal of these guarantees is to ensure that the creditor is paid, and to deal with the debtor's insolvency. The guarantees can take the form of caution money or collateralized assets.

8. Consumer surplus is the net benefit from consuming this good; as the French engineer-economist Jules Dupuit showed in 1844, it can be calculated on the basis of the demand function. To understand how it is calculated, let's take the following example: Suppose a good is sold at the price of ten dollars, and that there are ten consumers prepared to pay more than ten dollars for a single unit each. The consumer who wants to buy it most will buy as long as the price does not exceed twenty dollars, the second is prepared to buy as long as the price does not exceed nineteen, etc., down to the last, who is prepared to pay eleven dollars. The consumer surplus is their total surplus: $(20 - 10) + (19 - 10) + (18 - 10) + \ldots + (11 - 10) = 55$. Thus, the service is justified as long as the fixed expenses do not exceed fifty-five dollars.

9. See my article with Glen Weyl, "Market Power Screens Willingness-to-Pay," *Quarterly Journal of Economics*, 2012, vol. 127, no. 4, pp. 1971–2003.

10. In technical terms, the relative margin (the markup above the marginal cost expressed relative to the product's sale price) must be inversely proportional to the elasticity of demand, where the elasticity of demand is equal to the percentage demand loss for a 1 percent increase in the price.

11. www.ofcom.org.uk/about-ofcom/latest/media/media-releases/2017/duct-pole-access

12. Applying the Ramsey-Boiteux formula, the price for access in this case might even be less than the costs, because it makes sense to compensate partly for the monopoly's distortion.

13. Particularly the Kirchhoff laws.

14. Paul Joskow and Jean Tirole, "Transmission Rights and Market Power on Electric Power Networks," *Rand Journal of Economics*, Autumn 2000, 31(3): 450–501.

INDEX

academic researchers: distrusted by citizen-taxpayers, 67–68; funding for, 76, 370, 372; influencing economic policy, 69–70, 78–79; media involvement of, 72–73; motivations of, 66–67; paid for external activities, 70–71; personal ethics of, 76; political involvement of, 73–75; working with organizations outside the university, 68–69, 76–78. *See also* economic research; economists

accountability: of businesses to stakeholders, 185–86; in classical liberalism, 161–62; of employers, 243, 244, 247, 249; of regulated utilities, 462–64; of unelected decision makers, 163, 168

acquis communautaire, 265, 286, 294, 356, 526n35

adverse selection, 117, 120; insurance and, 409–10; regulation of network industries and, 457. *See also* asymmetries of information

Affordable Care Act, 165, 411, 412

agency problems, 312–15, 320

AIG (American International Group), 321, 327, 334, 340, 533n11

Airbus, 297, 370

Allais, Maurice, 95

allocation: constructing better methods of, 45; of funds by finance, 297; of resources, 24–27, 33, 101, 161

altruism, 100–101, 128–35, 146, 188. *See also* moral wiggle room; pro-social behavior

Amazon, 391, 394, 414–15, 435

Android, 388, 448, 451, 452

Apple, 388–89

arbitrage, limits to, 318, 319–20, 531n40

Aristotle, 485n3

Arrow, Kenneth, 105, 107, 115

artificial intelligence (AI), 232, 409, 423. *See also* machine learning

assumptions, 106, 497n33

asymmetries of information, 12; agency problems and, 314; bank loans and, 183; buying admission to university and, 37; on costs and benefits of policies, 162–63, 506n6; derivatives as source of, 301; financial crisis of 2008 and, 327; formal vs. real authority and, 181; games involving, 119; incorporated in economic models, 103; liquidity in financial markets and, 319; market failures due to, 327; in real estate lending, 329–30; regulation of network industries and, 456–57, 462–63, 470

attention, economics of, 379–82

auctions: of bandwidth, 27–28, 87–88, 487nn12–14; laboratory tests of strategies for, 90

authority, formal vs. real, 181

average-cost pricing, 468

avoided cost test, 543n18

bailouts of banks: in Europe, 271, 272–73, 278, 524n15; excessive risk based on expectation of, 187, 312–13, 314–15; financial crisis of 2008 and, 326–27, 334; replaced by "bail ins," 537n42; risk of sovereign default and, 537n40; US taxpayers profiting from, 334, 531n41

bailouts of governments, 281–82; of Greece, 279, 287, 525n31; Maastricht Treaty and, 274–75, 278, 279, 290, 524n12; US history and, 279–80, 281–82, 292